CONSTITUTING DEMOCRACY
Law, Globalism and South Africa's Political Reconstruction

Against the backdrop of South Africa's transition from apartheid, this provocative book explores the role of late twentieth century constitutionalism in facilitating political change. Using South Africa as a case study, Klug's larger project is to investigate why there has been renewed faith in justiciable constitutions and democratic constitutionalism despite the widespread recognition that courts are institutionally weak, lack adequate resources and are largely inaccessible to most citizens. He places this question in a broader context, evaluating the appeal of different constitutional models and illustrating how globalized institutions can be adapted to serve local domestic needs. Incorporating constitutional law, politics and legal history, this examination of South Africa's constitution-making process provides important insights into the role of law in the transition to democracy.

HEINZ KLUG is Assistant Professor in the Law School at the University of Wisconsin, Madison and Honorary Research Associate, School of Law, University of the Witwatersrand. Growing up in Durban, South Africa, he participated in the anti-apartheid struggle as a journalist and ANC activist. After eleven years in exile, he returned to South Africa in 1990, teaching law at the University of the Witwatersrand. He has worked with various ANC commissions and government ministries on a range of issues including constitutional questions, land affairs and water policy. He has published widely in such journals as the *South African Journal on Human Rights*, the *Review of Constitutional Studies*, *Journal of Legal Pluralism*, *Verfassung und Recht in Übersee*, *Contemporary Sociology*, *American Journal of International Law* and the *South African Law Journal*. This is his first book.

CAMBRIDGE STUDIES IN LAW AND SOCIETY

Series editors:
Chris Arup, Martin Chanock, Pat O'Malley
School of Law and Legal Studies, La Trobe University
Sally Engle Merry, Susan Silbey
Departments of Anthropology and Sociology, Wellesley College

Editorial board:
Richard Abel, Harry Arthurs, Sandra Burman, Peter Fitzpatrick, Marc Galanter, Yash Ghai, Nicola Lacey, Bonaventura da Sousa Santos, Sol Picciotto, Jonathan Simon, Frank Snyder

The broad area of law and society has become a remarkably rich and dynamic field of study. At the same time, the social sciences have increasingly engaged with questions of law. In this process, the borders between legal scholarship and the social, political and cultural sciences have been transcended, and the result is a time of fundamental re-thinking both within and about law. In this vital period, Cambridge Studies in Law and Society provides a significant new book series with an international focus and a concern with the global transformation of the legal arena. The series aims to publish the best scholarly work on legal discourse and practice in social context, combining theoretical insights and empirical research.

CONSTITUTING DEMOCRACY

Law, Globalism and South Africa's
Political Reconstruction

Heinz Klug
University of Wisconsin, Madison

CAMBRIDGE
UNIVERSITY PRESS

PUBLISHED BY THE PRESS SYNDICATE OF THE UNIVERSITY OF CAMBRIDGE
The Pitt Building, Trumpington Street, Cambridge, United Kingdom

CAMBRIDGE UNIVERSITY PRESS
The Edinburgh Building, Cambridge CB2 2RU, UK
40 West 20th Street, New York, NY 10011–4211, USA
10 Stamford Road, Oakleigh, VIC 3166, Australia
Ruiz de Alarcón 13, 28014 Madrid, Spain
Dock House, The Waterfront, Cape Town 8001, South Africa

http://www.cambridge.org

First published 2000

Printed in China by Everbest Printing Co. Ltd

Typeface New Baskerville (*Adobe*) 10/12 pt.   *System* QuarkXPress®   [PK]

A catalogue record for this book is available from the British Library

National Library of Australia Cataloguing in Publication data
Klug, Heinz, 1957–
Constituting democracy: law, globalism and South Africa's
political reconstruction
Bibliography.
Includes index.
ISBN 0 521 78113 2.
ISBN 0 521 78643 6 (pbk.).
1. Constitutional history – South Africa. 2. Constitutional law – South Africa.
3. South Africa – Politics and government. I. Title.
342.6802

ISBN 0 521 78113 2 hardback
ISBN 0 521 78643 6 paperback

CONTENTS

ACKNOWLEDGEMENTS

As with most intellectual projects this one owes a great debt to my inter-actions with colleagues, comrades and friends. This project has its origins in my experiences in exile, working with the ANC in Southern Africa and in the United States and, after 1990, back in South Africa. From 1991 when I began teaching at the University of the Witwatersrand Law School, I benefited from interaction with colleagues and students as well as from continuing to participate actively in ANC discussions about the negotia-tions and new constitution. From 1993 I began to put the South African case in a more global context as a result of discussions with colleagues and fellow graduate students at the University of Wisconsin. This project has also benefited greatly from my continuing engagement with col-leagues: at the University of Witwatersrand Law School, where I spent the first half of 1999 as an Honorary Research Associate; in the Law and Soci-ety Association; and at the University of Wisconsin Law School where I have taught since August 1996.

My gratitude goes first to Joseph Thome who patiently commented on each draft of my S.J.D. thesis and to Linda Greene and David Trubek who served on my committee. I am also deeply indebted to a number of col-leagues who made extensive comments on the manuscript as I began rewriting, especially Rick Lempert who gave me the extraordinary bene-fit of a line by line engagement. I also received extremely valuable com-ments on earlier drafts from Neil Komesar, Christina Murray, Erik Olin Wright, as well as readers for Cambridge University Press, including Hugh Corder and Jonathan Klaaren, and also from the Law and Society series editors, Chris Arup and Martin Chanock. I am also grateful to many others who generously shared their time and insights with me at different points of this project, including: Rick Abel, Kader Asmal, John Brigham, Geoff Budlender, Firoz Cachalia, Arthur Chaskalson, Matthew Chaskalson, Aninka Claasens, Brun-Otto Bryde, John Dugard, Yash Ghai, Derek Hanekom, Nicholas Haysom, Christina Harrington, Dirk Hartog, Pius Langa, Mac Maharaj, Neva Seidman Makgetla, Zeph Makgetla, Etienne Mureinik, Sol Picciotto, Lauren and Pete Richer, Albie Sachs, Boaventura de Sousa Santos, Ann and Robert Seidman, Judy Seidman, Zola Skweyiya, Bill Whitford and Stu Woolman.

I received valuable support for my research from both the University of Wisconsin Law School, through the Smongeski Research Professorship which allowed me to spend a semester back in South Africa from January to July 1999, as well as from the University of the Witwatersrand Law School which gave me office space and generously provided me with faculty privileges during 1999. I also wish to thank librarians Jacqueline Bokeer, Thembi Monyane and Aysha Patel at the Oliver Schreiner Law Library, University of the Witwatersrand, Patricia Booysens at the John Dugard Resource Centre, Centre for Applied Legal Studies, University of the Witwatersrand, and Michael Morgalla at the University of Wisconsin Law School Library.

Finally, and most importantly I wish to thank my parents, Murial and Erwin Klug, and brother, Neil Klug, who have always stood by me, and especially Gay Seidman and our two boys, Benjamin and Matthew – the three who make it all worthwhile.

ABBREVIATIONS

ACLA	Advisory Commission on Land Allocation
ANC	African National Congress
Azasm	Azanian Students Movement
Azapo	Azanian People's Organization
CA	Constitutional Assembly
CALS	Centre for Applied Legal Studies
CDF	Conference for a Democratic Future
Codesa	Convention for a Democratic South Africa
Consag	Concerned South Africans Group
CPs	Constitutional Principles
CPSU	Communist Party of the Soviet Union
CSCE	Conference on Security and Co-operation in Europe
GATT	General Agreement on Tariffs and Trade
IFP	Inkatha Freedom Party
KZN	KwaZulu-Natal
LAPC	Land and Agriculture Policy Centre
LGTA	Local Government Transition Act
MDM	Mass Democratic Movement
MPNP	Multi-Party Negotiating Process
Nadel	National Association of Democratic Lawyers
NAFTA	North American Free Trade Area
NCOP	National Council of Provinces
NEC	National Executive Committee (ANC)
NP	National Party
NT	New Text
OAU	Organization of African Unity
RRP	Rural Restructuring Program (World Bank)
SADF	South African Defence Force
SCC	Special Cabinet Committee (NP Government)
TCCI	Technical Committee on Constitutional Issues (MPNP)
TRC	Truth and Reconciliation Commission
UF	Urban Foundation
UN	United Nations
USSR	Union of Soviet Socialist Republics
WTO	World Trade Organization

INTRODUCTION

South Africa's dramatic political transition was accompanied by an equally dramatic legal revolution.[1] This legal revolution witnessed the demise of a tradition of parliamentary sovereignty and its replacement with a supreme Constitution, a Constitutional Court and broad political support for democratic constitutionalism. While South Africa's system of apartheid, or legally-constituted racism, may have been unique in the last quarter of the twentieth century, the decision to embrace democratic constitutionalism as the basic legal element of the country's political reconstruction was much less unusual. Instead, South Africa's political reconstruction and its embrace of democratic constitutionalism were part of a massive international process of political reconstruction culminating in the collapse of state socialism in 1989.[2] One hallmark of this process of 'democratization' was the formal adoption of bills of rights as the essential marker of constitutional change in the emergence of each new democratic regime.

While the adoption of a bill of rights may seem to be an obvious response to the gross violations of human rights that were the hallmark of the apartheid regime,[3] it does not explain the degree of faith in the judiciary implicit in both the 'interim' 1993 Constitution[4] and the 'final' 1996 Constitution.[5] Faith in the judicial branch of government is also reflected globally in widely-spread judicial training programmes, legislative programmes and an emphasis on the 'rule of law' as being an essential component of post-socialist and post-authoritarian state reconstruction. However, this faith is simply extraordinary when placed in the context of an equally widespread recognition that courts are institutionally weak, lack adequate resources and are largely inaccessible to the majority of the world's citizens. Why, then, this renewed faith in justiciable constitutions and democratic constitutionalism as the building blocks of democratic governance?

In order to throw light on this broader puzzle, I will investigate the role of constitutionalism and the question of faith in the judiciary by exploring the emergence and early impact of constitutionalism in South Africa's democratic transition and the implications this may have for the construction of post-apartheid South Africa. I argue that understanding

1

the construction of democratic constitutional orders – as examples of legal transplants – at the end of the twentieth century involves recognizing the interaction of three elements: (1) the transmission and globalization of political traditions; (2) the emergence and development of an international imperative of rights, epitomized by the international human rights movement, containing both hegemonic and counter-hegemonic aspects; and (3) the particular national context, including both the pre-existing institutions and legal culture as well as the political struggles or circumstances leading to the creation and implementation of a new constitutional order.

LAW, GLOBALISM AND POLITICAL RECONSTRUCTION

In the first half of the 1990s well over a billion dollars was spent on rule of law projects in every conceivable corner of the globe. A host of different institutions, from private foundations, non-government organizations and state agencies, through to the United Nations Development Programme, are engaged in this new 'rule of law' movement. For example, in announcing a major economic law reform project to assist the People's Republic of China in the reform of its legal framework, the World Bank argued that the 'key to any market system is the reliance on a fair and credible legal framework: legal norms and procedures are needed to substitute for government control of economic decisions and to demarcate government's regulatory role in many areas of economic activity'.[6] While legal reform is not restricted to the dramatic developments in public law accompanying the enormous political reconstructions of the post–cold war era, the adoption of new, justiciable constitutions, has been a major product of this movement.

The response of many scholars has been to herald a new age. David Beatty, a Canadian scholar of comparative constitutionalism, describes ours as 'an age of constitutionalism',[7] while Bruce Ackerman has recently published an essay entitled 'The Rise of World Constitutionalism'.[8] For these scholars the significance of this new age is the adoption, by nations creating justiciable constitutions, of the universal principle – central to understandings of modern constitutionalism – of a 'commitment to limitations on ordinary political power'.[9]

That a 'globalizing constitutionalism' should take this form right now is rather unremarkable in an age where the state is in retreat and where constitutionalism provides a means to attain the goals of both those struggling for human rights and those who argue that the market most efficiently mediates the demands of autonomous individual needs. While this confluence of anti-state interests explains the popularity of this latest constitutionalist wave, it does not give us any reason to believe that this latest commitment to the rule of law should fare any better than the multitude of past law and development or judicial reform programmes. Even if we accept the empirical evidence that more and more nations have adopted written constitutions with bills of rights and have empowered their courts to uphold these new charters as the supreme law of the land, it is not self-evident that the outcome, or even the meaning of these new institutions, is the same in all these societies. While we may recognize a globalizing constitutionalism, the challenge is to understand the specifics of its incorporation into particular national legal systems as well as to understand the potentially multiple roles that constitutionalism is playing in the reconstruction of different polities.

Even critical law and development scholarship has traditionally looked at this process in terms of a cultural diffusion model, at the motives behind and consequences of transplanting law into new contexts.[10] In earlier debates over the transfer and imposition of law, scholars raised troubling concerns about the goals, consequences and effects of these processes. On the one hand, it was argued that local legal cultures 'proved remarkably resilient in the face of American legal models' with the effect that 'legal-transfer mechanisms' attributed to the law and development movement were seen as largely ineffective.[11] On the other hand, stinging critiques were mounted, condemning the movement as 'an exercise in "cultural imperialism", one more manifestation of a desire to extend United States cultural and economic "domination" through foreign aid and development assistance programs that reinforced American influence by strengthening the role of cooperating local elites, in this case local legal elites'.[12] Questioning their own motives and roles in the law and development movement, some scholars withdrew from active participation and through their critiques played an active role in the movement's demise.[13] Recent contributions to this debate have, however, looked beyond the particular experience of the law and development movement in the United States. Accepting that efforts to export law have at times been the product of misguided '"missionary" notions of sharing with the Third World the legal modernity and "know-how" thought to have been realized in the United States',[14] these new participants have called for continuing engagement 'in concrete work in developing countries', as a way to get beyond the persistent crisis in law and development theory.[15]

While these criticisms and re-evaluations may reveal some of the underlying motivations and problems of the law and development movement, they fail to acknowledge that 'legal transfer' or the exchange of legal forms has been a hallmark of the creation and practice of law since at least the twelfth century, with the 'revival' of the study of Roman law at European universities – particularly Bologna.[16] Indeed, the incorporation of new legal doctrines, in particular within the Anglo-American system, is a basic form of the common law method.[17] Within the civil law system, the transfer or adoption of legal codes, beginning with the Napoleonic Code itself, has also been unremarkable.[18] The widespread adoption of justiciable constitutions and bills of rights in the 1990s merely reflects, from this perspective, a continuation of legal exchange or the adoption by particular states or local élites of legal forms most applicable to their present goals and circumstances. What is different, however, is a sense of universality and the will of at least some section of these local élites to become part of some wider, transnational, sensibility. This 'internalization' of, or colonization by,[19] 'the global' is epitomized in the reasoning of Indian Supreme Court Justice B. L. Hansaria, who, after traversing the cultural, philosophical, legal and religious spectrum, strikes down the criminalization of attempted suicide, concluding:

> May it be said that the view taken by us would advance not only the cause of humanisation, which is a need of the day, but of globalisation also, as by effacing Section 309, we would be attuning this part of our criminal law to the global wave length.[20]

While critics of the law and development movement recognized that local élites in the host countries were deeply implicated in the transfer of legal forms, there has been little attempt to explore the role of local actors in shaping the reception of particular legal doctrines, or the manner in which these doctrines were deployed locally to achieve particular aims or to gain advantage in particular local contests over power and resources.[21] Thus, instead of focusing on the imposition of law and the competing interests of those engaged in the export of the 'rule of law', I wish to explore the specific contours of legal incorporation and exchange from an opposite, 'internal' perspective, in order to understand the extent to which participants in post-colonial settings at least draw on and reinterpret legal forms (rules, doctrines, standards and codes) from a variety of jurisdictions to suit their own locally-defined ends. This will involve both an exploration of how different interests are furthered and shaped by the deployment of different incorporated rules and practices, as well as how the sources and local articulation of these different rules and practices lend specific weight to their successful incorporation and hybridization.

While this focus may be compared to an earlier literature, which focused on the reception of law and legal institutions,[22] I believe that there is a clear distinction between the earlier phases of reception and the process of incorporation inherent in this latest 'global' wave of political reconstruction. Both the colonial reception of imperial law and the post-colonial imposition of bills of rights in independence constitutions adopted at Westminster may be clearly contrasted with most of the recent democratic transitions, which have been driven by social and political movements demanding the incorporation of human rights that have gained international recognition in the period since the Second World War.[23] The embrace of constitutionalism in the context of these democratic transitions is a complex form of reception, where local competitors draw on available international resources in order to pursue their own local and ultimately transnational agendas. The mechanisms of this process are best analogized to what Paul DiMaggio and Walter Powell describe as 'institutional isomorphism', in which organizations seek legitimacy by adopting what they understand to be the successful practices of other organizations, and therefore come to resemble each other over time.[24] Most significantly in this context they identify mimetic, coercive and normative isomorphism as different processes through which this transfer of ideas, practices and understandings takes place. While direct coercion is not a significant aspect of the South African processes of negotiation and constitutional reconstruction, processes of mimicry and normative pressure are central mechanisms in the shaping and reshaping of viable constitutional alternatives.

In developing this argument I will argue that the adoption locally of a globally bounded notion of democratic constitutionalism both enables political reconstruction or democratic transition to proceed and tests the institutional capacity of the incorporated framework to address the conflicts arising from often irreconcilable political demands. The realm of bounded possibilities created by the introduction of constitutionalism is constantly infused with the incompatible constitutional imaginations of local contestants. In order to demonstrate this process of incorporation and to explore the way in which it circumscribes the bounds of legitimate alternatives, I will focus on South Africa's constitution-making process and on the jurisprudence of the new Constitutional Court. I will argue that these processes and institutions provided a means, in effect, to civilize the bitter political conflicts which until now have tended to degenerate into violent confrontation.

THE ROLE OF LAW IN DEMOCRATIC TRANSITIONS

Most analyses of political transition do not recognize the role of law in the reconstitution of the state.[25] Instead the focus has been on the political negotiations and constraints – seen as élite-pacting or in terms of a balance of power between different political interests – that have produced radical political change in so many countries since the collapse of state socialism. Where attention has been paid to the explosion of constitution-making in the context of the post–cold war transitions, the emphasis has been on the way in which this process represents a new beginning, a foundational act of the new state,[26] or on the nature of the rights these constitutions should protect in order to facilitate their political and economic transition to democratic capitalism.[27] Bruce Ackerman argues, for example, that in South Africa the collapse of communism undermined the appeal of the Bolshevik model within the ANC, allowing Nelson Mandela 'to make the negotiation of a constitution, not the consolidation of ANC rule, the fundamental act of a new beginning in South African political identity'.[28] Where there has been some consideration of the role of law in political transitions, it has been tied to the reintroduction of the rule of law and related to the prosecution of officials of the *ancien régime* who violated human rights. Justice in this context has, however, continued to be assumed to be a 'function of political power'.[29]

Exceptions to this trend have focused on the role of courts and their exercise of expanded powers of judicial review of legislation, or constitutional review, in the breakdown of authoritarian rule,[30] and on the ways in which new regimes use law to deal with the legacies of authoritarian rule – including gross violations of human rights on the one hand and the restitution of property on the other. This study of the role of law and questions of justice in relation to past injustice has, however, fostered an analysis of the constitutive role of law in the process of political reconstruction. Ruti Teitel argues that both the realist–idealist antinomy and critical legal theorizing on the relationship between law and politics fail to account well for the role of law in periods of political change,[31] and instead presents a view of 'transitional justice' in which law plays a paradoxical role by both providing order and stability while simultaneously enabling transformation.[32] In Teitel's view, neither the realist view, that constitutions merely reflect the prevailing balance of political power,[33] nor the idealist notion of constitutional foundationalism, in which constitution-making 'functions as the very basis of the new democratic political order',[34] come to terms with the 'relationship between reconstitution and political change'.[35] Instead, Teitel argues, it is the 'legal responses [within political transitions that] play an extraordinary constituting role'.[36]

Teitel's notion of transitional constitutionalism, based on the concept of 'transitional jurisprudence', in which law plays a 'paradigmatic [role] … in the normative construction of the new political regime',[37] is a valuable contribution to our understanding of the role of law in political transitions, yet its focus on the internal dynamics of the law and changing conceptions of justice fails to address the nature and sources of this constitutive capacity. While this analysis takes us a step beyond the notion that the introduction of bills of rights and constitutional courts may be understood simply as a response to past injustice, the focus on justice blinds us from seeing the external, institutional and cultural dimensions, which, I will argue, play a constitutive role in framing the constitutional choices that different political actors may deploy in the process of political change. Among these external elements are the range of existing 'legitimate' constitutional models, the advice of a plethora of constitutional carpet-baggers – both individuals and government agencies – as well as the symbolic capital gained by 'western' law through the interaction of corporate lawyers and human rights advocates in the transnational realm.[38]

Teitel suggests that 'transitional justice' – which defines a period in which law both ensures stability by appealing to the notion of legal continuity and enables transformation by embracing a normative shift in understandings of justice – is the consequence of legal responses to political change generating 'a sui generis paradigm of transformative law'.[39] However, the constitutions that have been enacted since 1989, which are the product of this constitutive process, reflect common trends that belie their diverse national origins and political histories. Despite these common features, I will not argue that the constitutional and political outcomes are anything but sui generis. Rather, I wish to argue that it is the occurrence of these common elements – including bills of rights, constitutional courts and a host of other provisions – that requires explanation.

Exploring the source and persistence of constitutional commonalities provides a view of the role of law in the context of political change that recognizes the emergence and impact of global dynamics. Central to these, I will argue, is the emergence of a thin, yet significant, international political culture, which is shaping the outer parameters of feasible modes of governance. Although we may debate the effectiveness of law as a mechanism for social change and even wonder whether changes in the law merely reflect new social patterns, it is generally acknowledged that rules, whether established through statute or as administrative regulations within the powers granted by legislation, are the primary means available to a democratic state to intervene in society. While constitutional amendment is in one sense merely a more complex form of legislation – in the requirement of increased majorities or special procedures – processes of state reconstruction, in which the fundamental structures of power are reorganized, are moments of fluidity and uncertainty quite distinct from normal politics or lawmaking.

While the indeterminacy inherent in the creation and application of law[40] always plays a constitutive role in the juridification and thus rationalization of political competition and conflict, I argue that constitutional indeterminacy[41] plays a pivotal role in integrating competing forces in the post–cold war process of state reconstruction. It is law's very indeterminacy, along with its contradictory yet corresponding capacity to set boundaries on the range of viable political options or responses, that characterizes the relationship between law and politics. Constitution-making and the law it produces provide in this sense a paradigmatic example of law's constitutive role. At the same time, I will argue, the politics of constitution-making also reaffirms the role of political struggles, histories and culture in shaping and defining the feasibility and content of the available legal models that might be brought to bear in the process of state reconstruction.

POLITICAL RECONSTRUCTION AND CONSTITUTIONAL CHANGE

Ever since Aristotle's *Politics* the classic political science view of constitutional change is as the product of fundamental political change. In fact, with the emergence and spread of written constitutions – of the 197 single-document constitutions in effect in 1991, only about twenty predate 1950[42] – the consolidation of fundamental political change and constitutional amendment or renewal has become synonymous. While it cannot be denied that countries such as the United Kingdom, New Zealand and Saudi Arabia, for example,[43] have equally vibrant constitutional systems, it is in the amendment and redesign of single-document written constitutions that the conscious reconstruction of states is most clearly visible. In this sense a constitution is a primary symbol of modernism, embodying the Enlightenment's aspiration of rational design. In an opposing sense, however, the very nature of constitutions – their emphasis on general principles and the indeterminacy implicit in their interpretation and implementation – provides a vortex into which contending aspirations may be poured and at least temporarily accommodated. It is in this latter sense that constitutionalism came to dominate processes of political reconstruction at the end of the twentieth century.

Although it is generally assumed that constitutional change reflects a nation's or country's internal development – reflecting both a people's shared ideals and its weaknesses[44] – Said Arjomand argues that internal factors are less important to the outcome of efforts at political reconstruction than the availability of constitutional models.[45] In support of his argument, concerning the flow of political ideas and the creation of an international political culture, he traces the historical emergence of the core principles of the international constitutionalist tradition. He begins by identifying a number of key ideas and steps in the march to where we are today, including: (1) the 'idea of the impersonal rule of man-made law', which survived the Roman empire; (2) the gradual conversion within the Christian tradition of the power of finding the law into the power to legislate assumed by the Popes by the thirteenth century; (3) the medieval fragmentation of authority which led to the separation of the definition of right from the administrative order; (4) Montesquieu's idea of the separation of powers and his assertion of popular sovereignty in the argument that a prerequisite of individual freedom is that the people as a body must have legislative power; and (5) the emergence of specific procedures for constitution-making by a collective representative body and through ratification of draft constitutions by popular vote in Virginia and Massachusetts respectively.[46] To this list I would add a twentieth-century contribution, what Robert Dahl terms the Strong Principle of Equality – the idea 'that all the members of the association are adequately qualified to participate on an equal footing with the others in the process of governing the association', thus producing a logic of political equality.[47] Lawrence Beer adds to this analysis, arguing that three phenomena have attended a global trend towards written constitutions:

> (1) a convergence in the world towards relatively few living traditions of modern law … ; (2) the achievement of at least formal global political consensus on the centrality – once national independence and stability are achieved – of human rights to sound and moral government … ; and (3) … interactions among profoundly different cultures, all reciprocally accepted for the first time as authentically human by educated international elites.[48]

Despite introducing a valuable global perspective to constitutionalism, these authors do not provide an understanding of the relationship between these global dynamics and national processes of state reconstruction.

They do, however, make it clear that the defining feature of the wave of political reconstruction and constitution-making that has characterized the end of the cold war is its historical timing. Not only has the alternative of state socialism and many of its associated forms been at least temporarily discredited, but there has also emerged a hegemonic notion of electoral democracy and economic freedom that is rooted in the history of twentieth-century struggles for democracy and individual freedom. From the suffragettes to the civil rights and feminist movements; from early European labour struggles to the struggle for self-determination and decolonization; from the struggle for democratization in Latin America, against apartheid in South Africa, and against a bureaucratized state socialism in Eastern Europe – the sum and combination of social movements and struggles that have characterized the twentieth century have shaped international political culture. It is this legacy that has eclipsed the state-centred notions of politics that were the product of the massive interstate conflicts of the nineteenth and early twentieth centuries.

Apart from these extremely broad traditions that may be distilled from the course of history, it is also possible to define certain trends that may be particularly salient in the context of each episode or wave of state reconstruction. Particular institutions, such as constitutional courts, have, for example, reappeared at different times as significant elements of the constitutional structure adopted in the reconstruction of states, yet been completely absent as a viable option at other times. Likewise, each new wave of state reconstruction seems to produce new variations in the division of power, between centre and periphery and between different organs of government, as well as new conceptions of the relationship between different branches of government. The latest wave has seen the mass adoption of bills of rights and constitutional courts, as well as the creation of a range of new independent institutions designed both to protect democracy on the one hand and simultaneously to circumscribe the powers of legislative majorities and democratically elected governments on the other.

While it may be possible to define particular features of an international political culture that has shaped the most recent wave of political reconstruction, it may also be possible to identify different periods of state reconstruction during the course of the twentieth century that have reflected, in part, the fluctuations inherent in the shaping and reshaping of a transnational political culture. Four distinct periods of political reconstruction may be broadly identified over the course of the twentieth century. First, in the post–First World War period, with the disintegration of the Ottoman and Russian empires, there was a period of state construction and constitutional innovation that was framed in part by the Russian Revolution and the claim for national self-determination supported by the United States. A significant development in this period was the emergence of a particular constitutionalist innovation – a centralized constitutional court – introduced by Hans Kelsen in the Austrian Constitution of 1920 and replicated in a weak form in the Weimar Constitution.[49] The end of the Second World War witnessed another wave of state reconstruction, which exhibited more explicitly the contradictory impulses generated by a tension between a purely state-centred political culture and the emergence of human rights as both a reaction to the horrors of the holocaust and the product of domestic social and political struggles. On the one hand, the United Nations system, which emerged in this period, reasserted a state-centred approach in its recognition and respect for the sovereignty of member states, while simultaneously, on the other hand, adopting a paradigm of individual human rights that provided an international stage for emergent social movements and struggles. This period also saw the resurgence of Kelsen's constitutionalist model, as well as the division of the world along cold war lines which would, in the years that followed, create a climate in which international political culture was temporarily fractured – producing a plethora of undemocratic state forms relying for their sustenance on the support or acquiescence of the dominant cold war contestants. The third process or period of twentieth-century state reconstruction came out of the process of decolonization. Apart from seeing an extension of the principle of self-determination to the peoples of colour around the world, this period was shaped in large part by the competition of the cold war. While at its inception, with the independence of India, it seemed to provide space for an innovative period of alternative constitutional arrangements shaped by the difficulties of underdevelopment and cultural diversity, in time this process became increasingly dominated by the prerogatives of imperial paternalism and cold war competition – with states being either 'given' a constitution, often written by colonial officials and experts, as was the case in many African states – or adopting forms of political authority that arose out of the ideology and circumstances of their own often violent struggles for self-determination, as in Vietnam, Angola and Mozambique. The fourth and latest period of state reconstruction, following the collapse of state socialism, but prefigured by struggles for democracy in Latin America, Iberia and many post-colonial states, has seen the emergence and reassertion of an international political culture reflective of an increasingly globalized world that seems to have achieved at least ideological hegemony at the end of the century.

While there are clearly counter-hegemonic examples and trends – particularly in the adoption of explicitly Islamic constitutions in a number of states – local or national events still determine the particular nature and even timing of political reconstruction in different states in this latest wave. Yet, it is the existence of a particular hegemonic form of international political culture, itself the product of struggles for human rights and democracy, as well as the triumph of the market in the economic realm, that provides the broad framework within which local political forces confront and accommodate their own histories and divisions.

STATE RECONSTRUCTION IN THE LATE TWENTIETH CENTURY

If this latest period of political reconstruction has been dominated by an international political culture fashioned out of the political hegemony gained by the collapse of state socialism at the end of the cold war, this does no more than set the outside parameters to the politics of constitution-making. Furthermore, this does not mean that there are no exceptions, nor that the new hegemony does not contain within itself a degree of conflict and indeterminacy that allows for a range of alternative responses by those engaged in the constitutional politics of state reconstruction within different national contexts. In fact, even those states consciously attempting to define themselves as part of the 'new world order' exhibit a range of responses that reflect not only their own particular historical contexts, but also their historical experiences of the social and political struggles that have shaped the now dominant international political culture that these different processes of reconstruction are addressing.

While reflecting many of the broad trends identified by Arjomand and Beer, international political culture is characterized in this period by a contradictory set of alternatives. On the one hand there is the emphasis on human rights as the core contribution of twentieth-century constitutionalism, while on the other hand there are a set of institutional arrangements and claims for institutional and economic autonomy that demonstrate the power of the Bretton Woods institutions and transnational capital in this latest wave of state reconstruction. Thus, although bills of rights and constitutional courts empowered to review the constitutionality of legislative enactments are a common feature of post–cold war constitutions, these constitutions are also marked by broad guarantees for the creation and protection of market economies, independence of national banks controlling the value of a state's currency, independent oversight of state expenditures, and an emphasis on the new state's recognition and incorporation of international or global norms, rather than the nationalist assertion of local identity so common in the rhetoric of state formation.

Although the magnitude of this final twentieth-century wave of state reconstruction is extraordinary – with over fifty-six per cent of the 188 member states of the United Nations Organization making major amendments to their constitutions in the decade between 1989 and 1999, the most remarkable aspect is that of these states, at least seventy per cent adopted completely new constitutions.[50] While the fate of each state's process of reconstruction may never be predetermined, the common features which characterize a good proportion of the resulting constitutions provide adequate testimony to the hegemonic normative trends in this post–cold war period. At least one quarter of all of the member states of the UNO introduced bills of rights and some form of constitutional review into their constitutional orders during this period. As a result, at least ninety-two countries, or approximately fifty per cent of member states, have incorporated bills of rights, fundamental rights, or some form of individual and/or collective rights into their constitutional orders. While the content of these rights varies dramatically in form as well as application, it may nevertheless be argued that the notion of enforceable rights, whether individual or collective, has become a central aspect of constitutionalism in the late twentieth century.

The legalization of political conflict inherent in this turn to the courts marks a central shift in the structure of constitutionalism around the globe. Prior to 1989, approximately ten countries had effective systems of constitutional review in which a constitutional court or the courts in general *regularly* struck down proposed or validly enacted legislation as contrary to the state's constitution. This is an extremely important quali-fication, because, although many constitutions have incorporated some form of constitutional review, the application of this power by the judi-ciary has been so limited in many jurisdictions that it is extremely difficult to argue that an effective system of constitutional review exists despite its formal constitutional status. So, for example, while the Malaysian Consti-tution of 1957 explicitly provided for judicial review, during the first thirty years the Constitution was in force 'no single legislative enactment ... has been held to be void for being unconstitutional'.[51] Now, only ten years since the beginning of this latest constitutional wave, at least seventy states, or approximately thirty-eight per cent of all member states of the UNO, have adopted some form of constitutional review. A much larger percentage have legislative guarantees of individual rights, bills of rights or chapters of fundamental rights in their constitutions, but limit their enforcement to the reversal of particular acts of government in individual cases with limited or no impact on the validity of the implicated legislation.

Lest I be misunderstood, the adoption of constitutional review guar-antees neither its survival nor its effective implementation in any of these states; however, it does indicate at least the normative power, at the end of the century, of the notion of governance under law. Also, it is important to note that there are three alternative models of enforcement which coexist within this process. First, there is the notion of diffuse judicial review characteristic of the American form of constitutional review, which, despite claims of the Americanization of the world, has been adopted in very few instances. Second, there is a very weak yet developing form of prior-review characteristic of the French system and adopted by many former French colonies and some of the states of the Middle East. Finally, Kelsen's centralized Constitutional Court model has dominated the recent wave of constitutionalism, with approximately thirty-six states, or nearly twenty per cent of member states of the UNO, creating new constitutional courts at the pinnacle of their legal systems since 1989.

The emergence of these different processes of constitutional review was part of a larger process of judicialization,[52] which played a central part in the process of state reconstruction at the end of the twentieth cen-tury. Although judicial reform was designed to address a range of rule of law issues, it was the creation of constitutional courts in particular that heralded the global expansion of judicial power or – as some character-ized it – the legalization of political disputes.[53] Thus, despite the institu-tional weakness of courts, in comparison to the other branches of government and in their capacity to hear and adjudicate on no more than a handful of conflicts which might fall within their jurisdiction, there developed a general sense that the rule of law and the judicial system may be ideal 'instruments of a depoliticized conception of social transformation'.[54] Contrary to this notion of the courts as depoliticized instruments of social change, the experience of the South African Constitutional Court demonstrates how constitutional courts in particular may play a highly political role by providing a space in which often irreconcilable conflicts may be temporarily if not permanently mediated, allowing the political contestants to embrace democratic procedures and outcomes while continuing to imagine their own particular, even if conflicting, visions of the future.

Constitutional courts in this perspective may in some situations function as key institutions in consolidating the democratic transition, maintaining social peace and stability while addressing, or at least 'judicializing', often severe problems of political and economic dislocation. Thrust into this role, the more successful of these new courts have relied upon the traditional features of a court's mode of operation: limiting the scope of a decision to its narrowest point; refusing to decide the many related issues on the grounds that they are not directly presented by the case; and using the growing power of transnational legal principles to frame and justify the court's own interpretation or choice of rules. The new South African Constitutional Court provides a prime example of this development. Not only has the Court established itself as a central institution in the new post-apartheid order, but already it has served to diffuse some of the most difficult problems left unresolved by the constitution-making process. These have included not only such unresolved issues as the death penalty, but also claims of greater regional powers, the preservation of cultural identity, and disputes over which level of government should pay traditional leaders. Furthermore, even those parties who walked out of the negotiations and refused to participate in the Constitutional Assembly, such as the Inkatha Freedom Party, have accepted the Court's interpretation of their claims. The result, in South Africa and in many other jurisdictions, has been a shift in power to the courts, coupled with a refusal by courts simply to preclude alternative understandings of the role or meaning of the rules they are required to interpret – particularly when these have been the fundamental rules of the political game.

While this embrace of rights and constitutionalization of politics has been heralded by some as the rise of world constitutionalism,[55] the jury is still out when it comes to judging either the meaningful implementation or the effectiveness of these new institutions. In some cases, the decisions of constitutional courts have already been explicitly rejected by executive authorities or the courts themselves disbanded. In other cases, despite the explicit inclusion of a power of constitutional review in the constitution, the judiciary has declined or very rarely exercised this power to strike down a legislative act. In more extreme cases, the constitutional developments so heralded in the first half of the 1990s have already been swept aside by military coups or have been ignored in the face of protracted civil wars. However, for those states where there is an attempt to consolidate the process of political reconstruction which swept through so dramatically in the early 1990s, the balance between adherence to a globally defined constitutionalism and the imperatives of local political dynamics remains a central legacy of this latest wave of state reconstruction.

OVERVIEW

In broad outline I will argue that the adoption locally of a globally-bounded notion of democratic constitutionalism both enables political reconstruction and the democratic transition to proceed and has profound implications for the choices open to constitution-makers. Furthermore, the introduction of a supreme constitution has significant institutional implications; however, the successful implementation of constitutional review increases the capacity of governance to address the conflicts arising from often irreconcilable political demands. In developing this argument, I will focus on the introduction of democratic constitutionalism in the context of South Africa's democratic transition. In order to understand these developments, however, I first trace the history of conflict over governance in South Africa, focusing on both the particular interactions between property and equality within that history and on the global context within which these struggles are played out.

Before turning to the South African story, however, Chapter 1 briefly considers the possibility that democratic constitutionalism may not only be viewed as the product of particular choices in constitution-making and political reconstruction, but may in fact play an essential role in both enabling democratic transitions and in providing an institutional mechanism for the management of conflict within the democratic system. Understanding that democratic constitutionalism may play different roles provides an opportunity to explore a dynamic understanding of constitutionalism and its role in mediating struggles over social and economic resources. Placed in the context of a globalized world, this approach provides a way to understand the relationship between the imperatives of 'universal' principles and both the source of these principles in local struggles as well as the impact of local histories and context on the reshaping of this 'globalized constitutionalism'.

Discussion of the South African story begins in Chapter 2, by questioning whether the embrace of human rights, commonly seen as a reaction to past abuse, implies placing a new faith in the judiciary as the guarantors of democracy. Considering different aspects of South Africa's inherited constitutional tradition, as well as the legal legacy of apartheid, this chapter ends by rejecting any notion that the embrace of constitutionalism in post-apartheid South Africa is explained by either a shared faith in the judiciary or prior constitutional choices. Rejecting any strong claim of path determinacy, it is argued that the source of South Africa's embrace of constitutional supremacy must be sought in the democratic transition itself.

Chapter 3 shifts the focus back to the global arena and seeks to explore both globalism's implications for governance, and hence political reconstruction, as well as ways in which local and transnational developments shape the very nature of the dynamics that give rise to global imperatives. The chapter reviews the global context within which constitutionalism is being constructed and transmitted as a central element of international political culture, paying special attention to the role of apartheid, as an antithesis of the post–Second World War human rights consensus, and the transnational anti-apartheid movement it spawned, in the reconfiguration of notions of sovereignty and the emergence of a globalized notion of legitimate governance. This chapter argues that the process of constitution-making evolved in the late twentieth century into an act of imposed self-binding in which an increasingly homogenized international political culture interacts with the internal dynamics and struggles of territorially centred political reconstructions.

Chapter 4 explores South Africa's dramatic shift to democratic constitutionalism through an examination of the ways in which the major parties came to embrace the notion of constitutional supremacy. The chapter then turns to discuss the positions of the major political players at the beginning of the democratic transition in order to understand both the impact of globally-bounded imperatives and the limits placed on these alternatives by the historic claims and perspectives of the different parties. Chapter 5 develops this further by seeking to understand how these globalized perspectives are locally incorporated. By focusing on the democratic transition and on the constitution-making process in particular, this chapter looks at how this commitment to a justiciable constitution at once informs and shapes the goals of the parties. Here the local imperatives of the transition, including political mobilization and degrees of participation, shape the contours of incorporation.

Chapter 6 explores the outcome of the constitution-making process in order to understand, first, the impact of global imperatives on the process of state reconstruction in South Africa and, second, the ways in which the incorporation of 'universal' principles in a specific local context in fact transforms or hybridizes them and provides a new source of alternatives for the global arena. This is done primarily by focusing on the struggle to formulate a property clause in first the 1993 Constitution and then again in the 'final' 1996 Constitution. Here it is possible, by focusing on the specifics of a particular conflict, to demonstrate how different understandings of what was possible and necessary could be transformed through local and transnational engagements. At the same time, the very specific result provides both an example of a hybridized 'universal' principle as well as a resource for future constitution-makers and legislators in other local contexts.

After discussing the formulation of the post-apartheid constitutional order, the argument shifts in Chapter 7 to explore the institutional implications of South Africa's embrace of constitutional supremacy. Together with Chapter 8, this part of the argument considers the role of the new Constitutional Court and its task of constitutional interpretation in resolving or at least managing conflicts which cannot be resolved through political compromise and agreement. It is argued that in order to do this the Constitutional Court has to both establish its role within the new constitutional order as well as hold out the possibility of justice to all the contending parties. This is explored in Chapter 8 through consideration of a series of specific conflicts contextualizing ongoing struggles and debates over social resources and authority in South Africa. These examples are used to demonstrate the role of the Constitutional Court in enabling political change and managing political and social conflict. This role is facilitated by the Court's ability to draw on both global and local sources in accepting or denying particular claims to constitutional rights and powers. While the Court is aided in this by the traditions of judicial decision-making, it is also contended that the particular nature of constitutional review, combined with the status of 'universal' principles and their interpretation though the marshalling of international and comparative legal authorities, provides a unique opportunity to perpetuate the processes of political integration generated by the democratic transition. Constitutionalism in this view provides a link between a globalizing political tradition and local circumstances which will define how the ideals of democratic constitutionalism will be incorporated locally.

Finally, in a brief Conclusion, I stress the significance that the embrace of constitutional supremacy represents for both South Africa and state reconstruction on the eve of the twenty-first century. Whether the promise of this development will be achieved will depend not only on the quality of judges and lawyers but also on the quality of democratic politics and the productive interchange of ideas and experiences which is implied in at least some examples and experiences of globalism.

CHAPTER 1

POST–TWENTIETH-CENTURY CONSTITUTIONALISM?

While the introduction of a justiciable constitution may, at one level, be presented as an indication of faith in the law and the judiciary and a response to past oppression, this view does not take into consideration the role played by the introduction of constitutionalism in enabling a democratic transition. Once this perspective is placed at the centre of the analysis, it is possible to see how democratic constitutionalism provides an opportunity for compromise, by postponing decisions on sensitive and potentially unresolvable questions.

On the one hand, this may be simply understood as a successful constitution-making strategy. On the other hand, it is also inherent in the nature of a justiciable constitution, in that the judicial resolution of constitutional questions rarely, if ever, forecloses on the possibility of an alternative outcome in the future. By creating a political order in which opposing parties can find their contending faiths in the constitution, and retain a belief that their understanding may in time be vindicated, the introduction of democratic constitutionalism may make possible the civilization of unnegotiable and seemingly unresolvable political conflicts.

CONSTITUTIONALISM: SELF-BINDING, REPRESENTATION AND THE LIMITS OF PARTICIPATION

Constitutionalism is commonly understood as a 'commitment to limitations on ordinary political power',[1] and therefore as an essentially anti-democratic strategy or, as Robert Dahl terms it, quasi guardianship.[2] In fact, most discussions of judicial review begin by considering the role of courts in constitutional interpretation and inevitably gravitate towards what is termed the 'countermajoritarian dilemma'.[3] Recognizing that the exercise of judicial review to strike down acts of a democratically elected legislature 'thwarts the will [of the] ... people',[4] scholars have produced a range of justifications either discounting the difficulty or justifying the role of judicial review in upholding democracy and individual rights against temporary majorities.[5]

Even among those constitutional theorists who have focused in their work on the democratic function of constitutionalism and, along with John Hart Ely, argue that 'constitutions can be democracy-reinforcing',[6] there is an implicit assumption of the continued salience of the concern about a tension between the judicial power of constitutional review and majoritarian democracy. The anti-majoritarian implications of judicial review lead, furthermore, to concerns that politics will be increasingly juridified, thus removing more and more questions from public deliberation and into the courts.[7] Applied in a context of vast inequalities, where economic dislocation and social marginalization have an uneven racial impact – which still defines the fate of the majority of South Africans – such a notion of a restricted democracy is inherently delegitimizing.

An alternative understanding of constitutionalism argues that democracy 'is never simply the rule of the people but always the rule of the people within certain predetermined channels, according to certain pre-arranged procedures'[8] – for example, representative democracy is always bounded by franchise rules and the division of electoral districts. From this perspective, the precommitments inherent in constitutionalism make democracy stronger, not weaker,[9] and the 'idea of "possibility-generating restraints" helps explain the contribution of constitutionalism to democracy'.[10] Applying this understanding of constitutionalism as precommitment to the South African case, Tribe and Landry present constitution-making as an opportunity to structure the future. Out of crisis and compromise, they argue, comes the opportunity to design institutions, to lay the framework for building a new nation and 'to compose the atmosphere in which the politics of the future will be conducted'.[11]

While precommitment and design may indeed capture the essence of constitution-making in the tradition of democratic constitutionalism, they ignore the issue of participation. If earlier constitutions were 'presented as an exchange of promises between separate parties',[12] who entered into a compact in order to secure social stability, 'modern constitutions are typically styled as frameworks which "we the people" give ourselves'.[13] As such, the precommitments entered into in the constitution-making process are presented as a form of self-binding, implying democratic participation in the constitution-making process. Questions of participation and representation in the constitution-making process are not addressed solely to the issue of future generations[14] but also provide the motivation for incorporating all the eligible members of the present generation. It is this logic that calls for a democratically-elected and representative constitution-making body, which, when created on the basis of proportional representation, provides the greatest opportunity of including the voices of all those willing to enter into a compact of future self-restraint.

Recent contributions in political philosophy have considered constitutionalism and its implicit countermajoritarian practice from the perspective of democratic theory and constitutional design – self-binding strategies,[15] gag rules,[16] precommitment[17] and preference formation[18] – however, I see constitution-making and the role of constitutionalism as two distinct phenomena.[19] The South African experience shows, I believe, how constitutionalism is linked to 'drawing and sustaining boundaries'[20] between two key sets of constitutional issues: those associated with property rights and individual autonomy, and those associated with equality and governance or participation in social decision-making, control and the exercise of social power. The first set concerns the duality inherent in property rights; they have historically provided a basis for individual autonomy but at the same time they have undergirded corporate and individual power over socially important resources. This has in effect, if not in form, undermined the autonomy of resource poor individuals and communities. The second set involves the nexus between equality and governance. It includes a range of constitutional principles and mechanisms, which span the relationship between formal equality and group-regarding policies designed to address structurally embedded group inequalities and the continuing allocation of power and resources between distinct social groups or solidarities.

While the dominant constitutionalist discourse presents property rights as the basis of individual autonomy and liberty, this perspective fails to recognize that the distribution of property rights is also, and has always been, intimately bound together with access to and the exercise of public power. This relationship between property and power is deeply contested and has always been historically mediated by struggles for recognition and equality. Formal equality among property holders and potential property holders with respect to certain forms of personal property provides a necessary boundary between the state and civil society in struggles over the most appropriate location and source of authority for the exercise of governance over resources and persons. However, given the way control over property facilitates the exercise of power, a more substantive notion of equality is needed to balance the material inequalities which inevitably sustain and reproduce severe and dysfunctional differentials in the exercise of public power.

The significance of the nexus of property and equality lies in its historical and substantive character as a 'focus' of constitutional justification and theory. First, the protection or possession of property has been key to constitutional justification, legitimacy and the acknowledgment of individual autonomy.[21] Second, the principle of formal equality and its historical extension into a universal right to participate in governance have together formed a construct within which issues of identity, difference and participation interact with structural and procedural mechanisms both to frustrate and to facilitate the process of democratization. The relationships between property and autonomy from social domination and oppression, and property and equality in social and political participation can, depending on how they are resolved, give rise to or support both hegemonic and counter-hegemonic pressures. Defining property to support both autonomy and democratic participation while striking a sustainable and appropriate balance between hegemonic and counter-hegemonic forces is a major challenge of democratic constitutionalism.

This challenge underscores the importance of questions about the choice of any particular understanding of constitutionalism and the impact any related institutional mechanisms may have on a society's future trajectory. Participants in the many symposia on South African constitution-making held in the early 1990s assumed, for example, that by adopting an internationally recognized form of constitutionalism – a justiciable constitution with a bill of rights – constitutional politics and jurisprudence in South Africa would merely incorporate the core principles of a limited constitutional democracy. Moreover, it was also assumed that South Africa would become similar if not identical to other jurisdictions – such as Canada and Germany – which have adopted some form of constitutional review modelled on the form of review originally formulated and introduced through the United States Supreme Court's decision in *Marbury v Madison*.[22]

This shared assumption, however, masked two fundamentally different understandings of the nature and role of constitutionalism in liberal democracies. These differences were clearly illustrated, for example, in papers presented at the symposium on 'Constitutional Federalism: The United States Experience – Implications for South Africa', at the American University Law School in Washington, DC, in 1992. Morton Halperin, Director of the Washington Office of the American Civil Liberties Union, argued that the core principles of a limited constitutional democracy include free elections, legitimacy of political opposition, limits on arbitrary arrest, detention and punishment, and the protection of minority rights.[23] This view treats constitutionalism as protecting free political activity; or, by extension, as facilitating formal equality as the basis for participation in the democratic process. On the other side, Roger Pilon, Director of the Center for Constitutional Studies at the Cato Institute, took direct issue with this approach, presenting an understanding of constitutionalism as securing a private realm within which liberty flourishes.[24] This conception assumes a natural right of individual freedom based on property, which is viewed as the foundation of all legal rights. In this interpretation, the business of government is to secure the world of rights and obligations created in the sphere of private relationships. These different emphases within liberal democratic constitutionalism represent a tension between claims for equal participation in the political process and claims for the privileging of property and contractual rights in the name of individual freedom.

Although constitutionalism ensures both the protection of fundamental rights and the structural differentiation of political power, most analyses of societies based on liberal democratic constitutionalism privilege civil rights – including freedom of speech, association, assembly and petition – and attribute the enjoyment of these rights to the existence of a healthy civil society. The enjoyment of civil rights is, however, simultaneously and circuitously credited as the source for the creation and preservation of a public sphere within constitutional systems.[25] A focus on the internal dynamics of constitutionalism provides an alternative perspective in which the vitality of the public sphere or different public spaces[26] may be better understood as a consequence of a continuous process of democratization – moulded by the interaction of property and participation – which pervades liberal democratic constitutionalism. This internal interaction between participation and property is thus the key to understanding the dynamic of constitutionalism as a 'mode of regulation' linking 'complex mechanisms of social ordering and their interaction'[27] to the constitution of social power through particular constitutional arrangements.

This relationship between participation and autonomy, or, more specifically, between democratic participation and fundamental rights, is presented in liberal constitutionalism as a contradictory tension – a tension that John Hart Ely suggests may reinforce democracy, by allowing a wider range of competing substantive visions room for contestation.[28] Jürgen Habermas takes this further in developing an understanding of the connection between private and public autonomy and the role of the constitutional state in converting the discursive sources of democracy into the formal institutions necessary for the 'rule of law'.[29] A less philosophical approach may be to understand this relationship in the context of struggles inspired by notions of rights, and to investigate the ambiguous relationship between the awareness of rights, or rights consciousness,[30] and its institutionalization.[31]

South Africa's legal and social history illustrates these perspectives, providing a rich source for the examination of struggles for rights, and in defence of rights. By tracing this relationship between struggles over property and participation in South Africa, I will argue that these histories provide a source for giving locally-grounded content to South Africa's newly adopted constitutionalism. The South African case study shows that, paradoxically, it is the tension within constitutionalism – arising from the interaction of social struggles over property and participation – which moulds the character of any particular process of democratization, and which is the 'universal' element received into national constitutional systems through the global diffusion of liberal democratic constitutionalism.

This perspective may contribute, too, towards a reconceptualization of a democratic version of the rule of law. As Otto Kirchheimer argued, any progressive and sustainable vision of the rule of law needs to locate the generality or universality of law primarily in its democratic participatory origins.[32] The future of South Africa's new found constitutionalism is likewise dependent: first, on its location within the global circumstances shaping the context in which it was introduced; and second, on shaping its specific content to correspond with the contours of social struggles etched into the political landscape of South Africa.

REGULATING POLITICAL CONFLICT AT THE END OF HISTORY

If constitutionalism is historically the struggle to regulate political competition, then we should not be surprised to discover that different constitutional elements or options in fact reflect continuing ideological and political alternatives. The politics of constitution-making[33] is thus festooned with the claims of competing political tendencies which project their ideological perspectives and political goals into constitutionalist forms. While the post–Second World War response to the violation of human rights produced a movement that could insist on the recognition and promotion of human rights through both international and domestic fora, the re-emergence of a nineteenth-century liberalism in the guise of a nineteen-eighties' neo-liberalism had profound implications for the politics of constitution-making in the post–cold war era. In this context, Friedrich von Hayek's argument that politics is a threat to a complex, but delicate, liberal economic and cultural order[34] provided a central argument for those who desired a shrinking of the state, yet understood the necessity to redesign the very structure of the state during the democratic transition that gained momentum with the collapse of state socialism. Although radical democrats, constitutional scholars and democratic theorists, such as Robert Dahl, have long been concerned about 'guardianship' and the anti-democratic implications of constitutional review, neo-liberal concerns emphasized not only the rule of law – requiring an independent judiciary with powers of judicial review – but demanded a constitutionalization of many other institutions and areas of governance as a means to limit the destabilizing impact of politics.

Despite the seeming victory of a conservative or neo-liberal vision – often referred to as the Washington Consensus – at the end of the cold war, the politics of constitution-making remains eclectic. Although the vast majority of states undergoing reconstruction through processes of constitutional change in this period seemed to accept the liberal paradigm of individual human rights and multiparty democracy, this did not preclude the simultaneous inclusion of a range of alternative constitutional elements, including socio-economic and cultural rights, which reflect alternative traditions. Significantly, the dominant liberal democratic tradition itself contains different trends, sometimes complementary, sometimes contradictory, advanced by different social forces and reflecting a plurality of interests. Of these, the two trends having the most direct impact on processes of post–cold war state reconstruction are those emphasizing liberty and equality. While there is a significant overlap in liberalism's ideological commitment to liberty and equality, emphasis on one or the other provides a range of alternatives within the liberal democratic tradition. These extend from classic 'nineteenth-century' liberalism, with its emphasis on individual freedom and property rights, to the claims of the democratic collectivity inherent in the social democratic liberalism of the post–Second World War era. While both aspects of this tradition emphasize electoral democracy and the protection of individual rights, they also contain contradictions with important consequences for the shape and role of the state.

While the struggle for equality, whether aimed at economic or racial inequalities, elicited the power of the state to address entrenched private power, the struggle for individual freedom has eschewed the state, often characterizing governmental power as the very source of oppression. These different responses to the state have obvious consequences for the structure of government, the most dramatic being the emphasis on the need to downsize or limit the role and capacity of the state. Combined with a reaction against the commanding role held by the state in socialist societies and strengthened by the fiscal crisis of the state in western democracies, this tendency achieved a significant degree of influence in shaping the international political culture that framed the post–cold war process of state reconstruction. By contrast, the classic elements of a social democratic state, including the state's social welfare orientation and regulatory role in the relationship between capital and labour, including the creation of corporatist institutions which gave organized labour an important voice in social organization, fell into political and ideological disrepute and began to be dismantled.

It is in this context that we must rethink longstanding assumptions about traditional constitutional values, in order to understand their role in the construction and maintenance of different constitutional orders. In my view there are three sets of values which frame traditional notions of constitutionalism: (1) federalism, or the spatial division of power; (2) the separation of powers between different branches of government; and

(3) the notion of constitutional rights. Each of these sets of values addresses different aspects of the 'problem' of power – its allocation, application and restriction – within the nation-state. While these constitutional values with their diverse historical origins have become increasingly 'universalized', their application in increasingly varied historical, cultural, and political contexts has produced a diversity of approaches and understandings, which provide a diverse 'global text' for political actors, constitution-makers, constitutional interpreters and litigants.

So, for example, the classic understandings of the allocation of legislative power between a federal government and states or provinces has been transformed from a list of designated subject-matter competencies and theories of pre-emption, via notions of concurrent powers, into an idea of co-operative governance in which the regions participate in the creation of central legislation and the designation of authority may be constantly rearranged according to a set of designated constitutional principles. In South Africa's new Constitution, the notion of 'co-operative government' is based, according to Nicholas (Fink) Haysom, legal advisor to President Mandela and a former member of the African National Congress (ANC) Constitutional Committee, on a break with the nineteenth-century approach to federalism, which allocated 'areas of responsibility to one particular area of government only'.[35] What the new South African approach does, argues Haysom, is to

> give the different areas of government the right to legislate on the same topic or area but only in respect of their appropriate responsibilities. Responsibility, in turn, is decided relative to appropriate interest, capacity and effective delivery but the apportionment of it is more complex than merely isolating an area of social life and parceling it out to a single sphere of government.[36]

While this new understanding of the division of powers does not preclude continuing jurisdictional conflict and constitutional adjudication, it does provide an opportunity for achieving constitutionalism's promise – the taming and reshaping of irreconcilable political goals. Here the indeterminate nature of constitutional formulations and subsequent shaping of constitutional imaginations through constitutional discourse provides the key to overcoming or managing potentially destructive social forces.

Similarly, with respect to the separation of powers between different branches of government and in the content and application of bills of rights, there have been significant shifts. While the separation of powers between executive, legislature and judiciary has been premised on the unity of lawful jurisdiction within the nation-state, its strict construction, as in the United States, has given way on the one hand to the realities of the administrative state, while on the other hand, a globalized world has brought forth both a dispersal of jurisdictional authority beyond the state, as well as a fragmentation of power within the state. Whole realms of authority have migrated from exercises of strictly national sovereignty: through the resurgence of a privatized legal pluralism, such as the *lex mercatoria*;[37] through treaties and developing transnational regimes; to international and transnational authorities such as the regionally authoritative European Courts[38] and the decision-making panels under NAFTA or at the World Trade Organization (WTO). At the same time, new national constitutional dispensations are replete with a fragmentation of authority through the creation of constitutionally independent institutions: to conduct democratic elections; uphold human rights; promote gender equality; protect cultural, language and religious minorities; or simply to ensure clean government.

In the realm of constitutional rights, the classic focus on political and civil rights, while in many respects still dominant, has been infiltrated by claims for socio-economic and other even more aspirational rights. Likewise, the understanding of the purpose of constitutional rights – to protect the individual or distinct minorities against state or majoritarian power – has also been broadened through attempts to expand the application of rights into arenas of power beyond the state. While earlier recognition of socio-economic rights was implicit in the constitutional definition of the state as a social state,[39] more explicit recognition occurred in the constitutionalization of policy goals in the form of directives of social or state policy.[40] Unlike the effervescence of the declaratory statement of socio-economic rights which characterized the state socialist constitutions, these directives of state policy have developed into interpretive guides,[41] giving socio-economic rights a jurisprudential reality that provided a basis for their inclusion in more recent bills of rights as enforceable constitutional rights.[42] Significantly, there has been a similar trend in the expanded application of rights. From the interpretive expansion of the state action requirement to include privately formulated, racially discriminatory contracts by the United States Supreme Court, to the notion of *Drittwirkung* in the jurisprudence of the German Constitutional Court, there has been a constant struggle over the impact of constitutional rights on the private exercise of power. While the requirement of state action has remained largely constrictive in the United States, the German Constitutional Court has long recognized the radiating effect constitutional rights have on private actions impugning the rights of other private parties. Although this horizontal application of the Bill of Rights was at first rejected by the South African Constitutional Court in its interpretation of the 1993 Constitution, the reaction of the Constitutional Assembly was to rewrite the application clause in the 'final' 1996 Constitution to apply the Bill of Rights explicitly to relevant private action.

INTERNATIONAL POLITICAL CULTURE AND 'LEGITIMATE' GOVERNMENT

Given the diversity of multiple processes of globalization and the often contradictory responses they evoke, leading simultaneously to an increased cosmopolitanism and heightened particularism – seen, for example, in the increasing claims of nationalism and ethnicity – it is important to remain alert to the complexities of any particular factor's impact in a globalized context, whether economic, technological or cultural in form.[43] Furthermore, the disjunctures inherent in cross-boundary cultural flows will mean that the interaction of local and global processes must be context-dependent.[44] This context-driven variation both undermines the logic of homogenization propagated by the neoliberal advocates of economic globalization and offers an approach to understanding the process of cultural hybridization, in which 'at least as rapidly as forces from various metropolises are brought into new societies they tend to become indigenized in one or another way'.[45]

Two kinds of cultural flows are of particular interest to the process of a globalizing constitutionalism. First, there is the flow of political-legal ideas contained in the historically available models of constitutional experiences which help shape (and no doubt limit) the imaginations[46] of the individual and institutional participants in subsequent efforts at political reconstruction. Second, there are the interconnected flows of ideas, information and resources which are implicit in the interactions of a potentially global civil society. Thus, while internal factors are arguably less important to the outcome of efforts at political reconstruction than the availability of constitutional models, it is also true that the defining feature of the wave of political reconstruction and constitution-making that has characterized the end of the cold war is its historical timing. Said Arjomand agrees, arguing that, despite the influence of a society's preconstitutional institutional structure and the increasing 'syncretism' of later constitutions, the impact of the prevalent international political culture on constitution-making means that the timing of constitution-making is more 'consequential than the institutional structures of different countries'.[47] The significance of this point is evident in the consolidation of international political culture since the collapse of state socialism. The ideologically inspired diversity of constitutional alternatives – one-party states, military dictatorships, liberal democracies, people's democracies, etc. – characteristic of the cold war period and reflected in the increasing 'syncretism' of post-colonial constitutions gave way to an increasing hegemonization. By the early 1990s liberal constitutional principles were hegemonic, at least at the ideological level, with constitutional review by an independent judiciary[48] increasingly becoming a prerequisite for international constitutional respectability.[49]

CHAPTER 2

LEGAL LEGACIES AND
CONSTITUTIONAL PATHS

A standard explanation for the shift to democratic constitutionalism, and the empowerment of courts it implies, in states emerging from dictatorships and social conflict is that the shift is a reaction to that society's particular past. While the rejection of tyranny and the embracing of rights may seem a logical consequence of their prior denial, this explanation does not explain why this should include a turn towards the judiciary as the ultimate protectors of such rights. This is particularly so when the judiciary and the law in general were intimately associated with the construction and maintenance of the prior oppressive regime.

As the history of English constitutionalism and until recently the legislatively enacted Bill of Rights in pre-1982 Canada demonstrate, there is no inherent link between the recognition and protection of rights and the empowerment of a judiciary to strike down laws passed by a democratically elected legislative majority. In the South African context judicial review of legislative authority had historically been explicitly rejected, and in the more recent past the major parties were committed to notions of democracy which assumed parliamentary sovereignty. This makes the turn in South Africa to a constitutionalism with a privileged judiciary not just seemingly unnecessary to goals of democratization, but downright puzzling.

The struggle against apartheid in South Africa was always understood as a struggle against racial oppression and minority rule, and conversely, as a struggle for democratic rights and majoritarian democracy.[1] While participants in the struggle tried to defend themselves in the courts against the abuses of the state,[2] it was only in later years that they began actively to engage the judiciary in an attempt to challenge apartheid laws and to create legal spaces for contesting the policies and actions of the apartheid state.[3] Although these local developments may be understood as indicating some faith in the judiciary, there was little evidence, in the midst of the States of Emergency which dominated the late 1980s, to suggest that the different parties and social groupings locked in battle for control over the state would, within ten years, reach consensus on a constitutional framework in which legislative authority is circumscribed by a constitution as interpreted and upheld by the judicial branch of government.

This chapter maps a South African legal history[4] which demonstrates that the adoption of democratic constitutionalism marks a dramatic shift, providing the basis for understanding the limits of path dependency[5] and local context in the shaping of future possibilities. The chapter also traces the evolution of the relationship between legal struggles over equality and property, highlighting the primacy and interconnectedness of these rights in the denial and construction of citizenship within the local context. Finally, the chapter addresses the debate over the role of law under apartheid and questions claims that it was the relative legitimacy of the courts that explains the new faith in the law which characterizes post-apartheid South Africa. Instead I argue that local context is not determinative, but rather provides the stage, cluttered with historical props and limited resources, upon which alternative possibilities are introduced and successively exhausted.

REJECTING JUDICIAL REVIEW

With the adoption of the 1996 'final' Constitution, the history of constitutionalism in South Africa may be summarized as the rise and fall of parliamentary sovereignty. Despite its short-lived hegemony, compared to pre-colonial and colonial forms of governance based on participation by status-defined subjects or imperial command, it was the rise and dominance of parliamentary sovereignty that shaped South Africa's modern constitutional history. Given this history,[6] consensus on the adoption of a justiciable constitution as one of the defining features of post-apartheid South Africa is an extraordinary outcome.

Union and the Construction of a Bifurcated State
Formally, the *South Africa Act* of 1909[7] brought together four settler colonies into a single Union of South Africa,[8] but, in effect, it created a bifurcated state.[9] On the one hand, the Union Constitution granted the white minority parliamentary democracy, while on the other it subjugated the majority of black South Africans to autocratic administrative rule. Excluded from the 'National Convention', black leaders protested against the refusal to extend the Cape Franchise to the former Boer Republics, but were rebuffed as not representative of African society.[10]

Instead, African society was presented as essentially 'traditional', to be governed separately by chiefs in a system of feudal hierarchy with the Governor-General in Council at its apex.

The immediate origins of bifurcation are to be found in the process of unification, which gained momentum after the establishment of the South African Native Affairs Commission (Lagden Commission) and a pan-South African Customs Union in 1903.[11] Although the recognition of African territories and land holdings came out of the interaction of independent African communities and expanding colonialism,[12] the Inter-Colonial Customs Conference of 1903 elevated this recognition into a principle of governance, arguing that 'the reservation by the State of land for the sole use and benefit of natives involves special obligations on their part towards the State'.[13]

Appointed to explore the 'possibility of a unified Native and labour policy',[14] the Lagden Commission adopted in its Report the principle of 'special obligations' and developed a vision of a future South African federation[15] based on the territorial segregation of black and white 'as a permanent mandatory feature of public life'.[16] While the Commission's endorsement of territorial separation merely coincided with the 'establishment of segregated "locations" for urban Africans' by the governments of all four colonies, it also gave approval to established Shepstonian policy and practice of creating 'native reserves' or 'locations' as a basis for administrative rule. As 'Diplomatic Agent to the Native tribes' in Natal from 1845 to 1853 and 'Secretary for Native Affairs' from 1853 to 1875, Theophilus Shepstone improvised an administrative hierarchy for colonial rule based on the African system of Chieftainship. Shepstone 'recognized traditional chiefs and headmen where discernible and created new chiefs and headmen where necessary; he attached every location African to a chief; and he made the chiefs and headmen responsible for law and order, in theory under the Governor, who was proclaimed supreme chief'.[17]

The Lagden Commission found in this reservation of land and the 'special obligations' arising out of it a principled basis for political segregation. The Commission's argument first identifies 'Natives' as having 'distinct rights' to the reserved lands as the 'ancestral lands held by their forefathers'. These tenure rights are then characterized as amounting to a form of group ownership under which the 'Tribal Chief' administers the land in 'trust' for the people. Finally, the Chiefs are said to have transferred their sovereign rights, including their powers of administration over communal lands, to the Crown through a process of 'peaceful annexation'. Having received all the rights and obligations previously possessed by the Chief as sovereign, the Crown then had the duty to administer 'natives' according to traditional forms of governance 'tribalism'.

The Commission's description of this 'tribal system,' as one where, as the 'father exercises authority within his family ... so the Chief rules the tribe and guides its Destinies', leaves no doubt as to the degree of paternal autocracy envisaged by the Commission. Instead of merely acknowledging a plurality of systems of governance, the Commission clearly places authority in the hands of the white administration, which, according to the Commission must govern the 'Natives' 'as a nation in its nonage'.[18]

This creation of 'differential spheres of citizenship for "European" and "Native" populations within one territory'[19] was reflected in s 147 of the *South Africa Act* of 1909. While the bulk of the *South Africa Act* dealt with the powers of a government, to be essentially representative of 'European male adults',[20] s 147 states that: 'The control and administration of native affairs ... throughout the Union shall vest in the Governor-General in Council.' The connection between the exercise of authority over 'natives' and land is made explicit by s 147, which states that the executive (the Governor-General in Council) 'shall exercise all special powers in regard to native administration hitherto vested in the Governors of the Colonies or exercised by them as Supreme chiefs, and any lands vested in the Governor ... for the purposes of reserves for native locations shall vest in the Governor-General in Council, who shall exercise all special powers in relation to such reserves as may hitherto have been exercisable by any such Governor'.

From Compromise to the Union Constitution
Although the all-white 'National Convention' agreed on the basic issues – the forging of white political unity in the face of African anti-colonial resistance[21] and for economic advantage[22] – the convention was divided by both the Natal-delegation's demand for a federal structure for the new state[23] and the question of the Cape Franchise. Despite Judge J. G. Kotze's public plea before a meeting of the Convention for a rigid constitution with a bill of rights,[24] based on the original Orange Free State's adoption of an American-style constitution, s 152 of the *South Africa Act* empowered Parliament to 'repeal or alter any of the provisions of this Act' by a simple majority in both Houses. However, there were exceptions to this principle in the form of entrenched clauses. These represented compromises reached by the Convention to: Natal's demands for rigidity; the Cape's demand to retain the Cape Franchise; the general concern to guarantee language equality among whites; and the sop of overrepresentation in Parliament granted to the two smaller provinces. Thus, while Natal lost its demand for a federal constitution and agreement was achieved on equal status for the English and Dutch (later Afrikaans) languages, the controversy over the extension of the Cape Franchise was resolved, with reference to the Imperial capitulation in the Treaty of

Vereeniging, by the retention of the existing colonial franchise arrangements. In the end, the only significant compromise was the introduction of procedures designed to prevent the easy repeal of either the equal language clauses or the existing Cape Franchise.[25]

Parliamentary Sovereignty Supreme

While white settlers in the Cape Colony only received self-government in the mid-nineteenth century, the notion of parliamentary sovereignty was introduced with British colonization and the imposition of British public law on the former Dutch colony. By 1806, when the British occupied the Cape, the principle that Parliament could 'do everything that is not naturally impossible',[26] had come to dominate English law. Although the notion that judicial review over Parliament's legislative authority 'mandated by some fundamental law of reason and justice' was not unknown in English jurisprudence,[27] by the time self-government was granted to the Cape and Natal, legislative supremacy was the defining feature of British parliamentarianism.[28]

Despite the dominance of English constitutionalism in the Cape and Natal, the Boer Republics established in the mid-nineteenth century sought alternative sources of constitutionalism. Drafters of the Orange Free State Constitution of 1854, for example, turned amongst others to the Constitution of the United States of America and adopted rigid rules of amendment and guaranteed rights of peaceful assembly, petition, property and equality before the law.[29] Although the 1854 Constitution did not explicitly provide for judicial review or a Supreme Court, a court was established by legislation in 1876 and its power of judicial review was 'accepted as an inherent feature of the Constitution'.[30] Despite this formal recognition of constitutional review in the Orange Free State, judicial review of legislation was applied in only one case. In this case, *Cassim and Solomon v The State*,[31] the High Court of the Orange Free State reviewed a law of 1890 which prohibited 'Asians' from settling in the state without the permission of the President.[32] Challenged on the grounds that it violated the constitutional guarantee of equality before the law, the legislation was upheld by the Court, which argued that the constitutional guarantee had to be 'read in accordance with the *mores* of the Voortrekkers'.[33] Thus, even this early experiment with constitutionalism was tainted with the distinctions of racial citizenship which came to dominate later constitutional law and practice.

The attempt by Chief Justice J. G. Kotze in the High Court of the South African Republic (another Boer republic) to assert the right of judicial review was, however, even less successful. With repeated references to United States Chief Justice Marshall's reasoning in *Marbury v Madison*, Kotze argued that, as sovereignty was vested in the people of the Republic and not the *Volksraad*, it was the court's duty to strike down legislation incompatible with the fundamental law of the *Grondwet*.[34] Although grounded in the Constitution's formulation of legislative power being granted by the people,[35] this attempt to exercise the power of judicial review in *Brown v Leyds NO* threw the state into crisis. President Kruger first secured an emergency resolution of the legislature declaring that 'the judges had not and never had had the testing right'.[36] Then, as the crisis deepened, Kruger dismissed the Chief Justice and at the swearing-in ceremony of the new Chief Justice warned the judges not to follow the devil's way as 'the testing right is a principle of the devil', which the devil had introduced into paradise in order to test God's word.[37] While Kotze was supported by judges on the Orange Free State Bench, important members of the Cape Bench and the Johannesburg bar, influenced by English legal doctrine – including Sir Henry De Villiers and Jan Christian Smuts – supported President Kruger's assertion of legislative supremacy.[38]

Although the Union Constitution of 1909 followed the English tradition in adopting parliamentary sovereignty, the legislature was not completely free from external restraints. Until passage of the Statute of Westminster by the British Parliament in 1931, the *Colonial Laws Validity Act* of 1865[39] continued in theory to restrict the sovereignty of the Union Parliament. Even after the Dominion Parliaments received their independence from Britain, the South African Parliament remained bound, at least procedurally, by the entrenched clauses of the Union Constitution.

While the significance of entrenchment was weakened by the removal of African voters from the common voters' roll in 1936,[40] it was the constitutional struggle over the removal of coloured voters that secured the dominance of Parliament over the Constitution. The survival of the entrenched language clause, guaranteeing the equality of English and Afrikaans, was more a symbolic restraint than an effective constitutional entrenchment of equal language rights, and relied more on a political consensus among whites. In effect, the growing *de facto* dominance of Afrikaans within the civil service under National Party rule after 1948 belied the official equality respected in the translation and reproduction of official government publications and legislation.

The rise of parliamentary sovereignty over even the limited entrenchment of the Cape Franchise was finally secured with the adoption of the 1961 Republican Constitution.[41] From the passage of the *South Africa Act Amendment Act* in 1956, which provided that '[n]o court of law shall be competent to enquire into or to pronounce upon the validity of any law passed by parliament'[42] other than those effecting the surviving language clause, government was determined to secure the primacy of parliamentary sovereignty. Prime Minister Verwoerd rejected calls for the adoption of an entrenched bill of rights by the

Natal Provincial Council, stating that it would be unthinkable, as 'no suggestion was made as to how rights could be effectively guaranteed without sacrificing the sovereignty of Parliament'.[43]

The passage of the 1961 Republican Constitution secured the dominance of parliamentary sovereignty. Section 59 specifically incorporated the language of the *South Africa Act Amendment Act,* thus constitutionalizing the exclusion of the courts from substantive review and explicitly limiting any judicial review over substantive legislative enactments to those effecting the language clause guaranteeing the equality of English and Afrikaans. As if to emphasize this ascendancy, s 59(1) stated that: 'Parliament shall be the sovereign legislative authority in and over the Republic, and shall have full power to make laws for the peace, order and good government of the Republic.'

Despite these obviously substantive criteria for the passage of legitimate laws and the courts' initial resistance, the courts soon recognized that the will of a racially-exclusive Parliament was to be paramount. The crude logic of this unrestrained conception of parliamentary sovereignty is summed up in an earlier decision of the Appellate Division in *Sachs v Minister of Justice; Diamond v Minister of Justice,* in which Stratford ACJ stated that 'arguments are sometimes advanced which do seem to me to ignore the plain principle that Parliament may make any encroachment it chooses upon the life, liberty or property of any individual subject to its sway, and that it is the function of courts of law to enforce its will'.[44] This doctrine's impact on human rights and its 'debasement of the South African Legal System' are now part of the history of apartheid.[45]

FAITH IN THE LAW

For Africans in South Africa, the impact of official law in the colonial and apartheid eras usually resulted in the denial and removal of rights. Given this experience, the demise of apartheid alone could not have induced the majority of South Africans to place their faith in the legal system and the judiciary as guardians of the new democracy. Yet, despite the close relationship between law and the construction of apartheid, there seems to be a high degree of political support for South Africa's turn to constitutionalism.

While recent studies have highlighted the ways in which the law was used by communities and opponents of apartheid to resist the denial of rights and state repression in the closing years of apartheid,[46] it is important to keep in mind the reasons why it is highly unlikely that the adoption of judicial review in fact represents a pre-existing deep faith in the law. For the majority of Africans in South Africa, their original loss of rights in property coincided in the first instance with the denial and reshaping of indigenous political relationships. Representing a pivotal moment in the construction and recognition of property rights in 'colonial' society, *Hermansberg Mission Society v Commissioner of Native Affairs and Darius Mogale*[47] hinges on an African chief's refusal to recognize an alleged land-sale contract concluded between his father and the plaintiff missionary society. The chief argued that a chief may not alienate tribal land without the direct consent of the community. Rejecting his argument, the Court held that an African chief, as trustee of the community's land, may alienate land with the consent of the chief's council and without the direct participation of the community. While a seemingly subtle distinction, the shifting of chiefly accountability for the control and distribution of community resources from the *Pitso* – a body made up of all married males, the recognized political participants in this community – to the chief's council, had profound consequences for the future recognition of community and ultimately individual property rights in African polities.[48] The case reveals a story of colonial interaction spanning a period during which African communities were transformed from autonomous political entities into subject groups not only whose territory was incorporated into the colonial state but also whose land rights were formally transferred 'in trust' into the hands of the colonial administration.

While the Court denied the right of the *Pitso* to control the chief's authority over the alienation of community land, the Lagden Commission[49] discovered the 'tribal system' of 'government perfectly understood by the Natives, [which] carried with it mutual responsibilities and suretyship, and required implicit obedience to authority. It possessed a ready means of communication and control extending from the Paramount Chief to the individual Native in his Kraal.'[50] This failure to recognize the chief's accountability to political institutions internal to African society coincided with the colonial reconstruction of African political relationships so as to deny the existence of any rights or accountability below the level of the chief and his councillors.

This denial of the chief's accountability to the community, which was legally recognized in *Hermansberg Mission Society*, culminated in the adoption of the *Bantu Authorities Act* of 1951[51] 'which broke the dependence of the chiefs on their councils and turned them, in effect, into paid agents of government policy'.[52] Drawing out the political consequences of these developments Adam Ashforth argues that, by elaborating 'an account of the political relationship between the division of territory and citizenship'[53] (i.e., 'an account of relations between people and place [you may say property]'), 'a state could be devised which instituted differential spheres of citizenship for "Europeans" and "native" populations within the one territory'.[54] Thus, through a complex interaction of struggles over land and political participation – driven by colonial imperatives and African resistance – African societies were officially reconceived in the image of European feudalism. This process effectively expunged those political and property relations internal to African societies in the context of conceiving and imposing a system of colonial governance on the African majority.[55]

This interaction, between property and equality, dispossession and inequality, can be historically traced at a number of levels; however, it is the constitutional implications of this relationship that are of particular significance in the present context. In order to draw these out, I will trace two processes of convoluted interaction between property rights and principles of equality: first, the history of the franchise, in which property and equality are simultaneously connected and disconnected; and second, the interaction of the common law principle of equality and the construction of apartheid, particularly the destruction of black property rights under policies of forced relocation and removal.

Participation and Denial: The History of the Franchise
The story of the franchise and the fragmentation of voting rights provides a means of viewing the interaction between property rights and access to political participation as it unfolded and shaped the construction of citizenship in South Africa. While immigration law encouraged the expansion of a 'European' community, it was the constant manipulation of voting rights that determined the character of South African citizenship and the apartheid constitutional order.

While each of the territories that came together in the Union had its own franchise system, their notions of citizenship were fundamentally at odds. At opposite ends, the Cape, with its qualified, non-racial franchise, recognized equal rights for 'all civilized men',[56] while the Transvaal, with its racial but otherwise unqualified franchise, specifically declared that no equality shall be permitted between 'coloured people and the white inhabitants, either in Church or State'.[57] Although the Cape franchise reflected a notion of citizenship not unlike contemporary British norms, in which adult males who met certain cultural or property standards had a right to participate in governance, the Transvaal maintained a clearly racist distinction and even attempted further to restrict franchise rights in 'presidential and *Volksraad* elections to those who, besides being naturalized citizens, had lived in the Republic for fourteen years'.[58] Even in the Cape, however, the *Glen Grey Act* of 1894 had begun to undermine the link between property rights and the franchise when the allocation of individual plots to African families in terms of the Act was specifically divorced from the property requirements for obtaining the franchise. This was achieved by analogizing the property defined under the *Glen Grey Act* to communal forms of tenure which had already been excluded as a source of property rights for determining franchise rights. Although Natal formally adopted a 'civilized' standard, the colony was able, through 'a number of ingenious conditions attached to the franchise'[59] to ensure that by 1907 over ninety-nine per cent of registered voters were 'European'[60] and only six Africans had managed to register as voters.[61] Natal Law No. 11 of 1865 disenfranchised 'native voters other than those specially given the vote by the Lieutenant-Governor, in his free discretion, on the grounds of twelve years residence, exemption from native law for seven years, recommendation by three European voters and possession of the ordinary property qualifications'.[62] Citizenship in the Cape and Natal was thus formally tied to a process of assimilation to colonial standards of education and property, while in the Transvaal and the Orange Free State citizenship and political participation had an expressly racial construction.

African communities expected the Cape's non-racial franchise to be extended as a result of the 'considerable political and military support' they rendered the British during the South African War of 1899–1902.[63] Instead, Article 8 of the Treaty of Vereeniging 'made the enfranchisement of non-white people in the new colonies dependent on the consent of the white' people.[64] As a result of this agreement, the Transvaal and Orange River Colony retained their racially exclusive constructions of citizenship when they received self-government in 1907. With the formation of the Union of South Africa in 1910, the effective pre-Union denial of African political rights in all parts of the Union except the Cape was constitutionalized. After some initial conflict over whether the Cape Franchise should be extended to the rest of the Union, the all-white National Convention came to a compromise, providing that '[a]ll laws dealing with the franchise and qualifications of electors at the date of the Union in any Colony shall remain in force until repealed or altered by the Parliament of South Africa',[65] except that on the insistence of the Cape delegates, the Cape Franchise was constitutionally entrenched.[66]

While black voting rights remained frozen by the Union compromise, the South African Parliament soon began extending the voting rights of whites. White women were given universal suffrage in 1930[67] and the following year this was extended to white males in Natal and the Cape who were still subject to the pre-Union income or property qualification.[68] Full Union citizenship was now extended to all white adults but, in order to close the door on any future advance in black electoral power, and in accordance with the Union Constitution's logic of a racially divided citizenship, the white Parliament began to move against the Cape Franchise – as originally recommended by the South African Native Affairs Commission (Lagden Commission) in 1905.[69]

The formation of the coalition or 'Pact' government in 1924 triggered government efforts to remove African voters from the common voters' roll. The first step was passage of the *Native Administration Act,*[70] which implemented the system of bureaucratic governance over African communities implicit in the Union Constitution. However, this was challenged by a registered African voter as an illegal attack on the Cape Franchise. The case, *Rex v Ndobe*,[71] arose in 1929 after the Department of Native Affairs established a process to standardize titles among African land owners. The appellant's fears were aroused by a draft proclamation, which, if implemented, would have substituted his title deeds with forms of title 'deemed to be … communal tenure',[72] thus excluding his land from the calculation of the value of property held by a potential African voter under the Cape Franchise. Although the Court rejected the appellant's argument on the grounds that those proposals directly attacking the Cape Franchise had not been promulgated, and that those property rights interfered with 'cannot be construed as an alteration of the qualifications of voters',[73] the Court did affirm that the powers of the Union Parliament to prescribe the qualifications of voters were strictly limited by the provisions of s 35.[74]

When African voters were removed from the common voters' roll by the *Representation of Natives Act*[75] in 1936, the Act was passed in accordance with the entrenched procedures of s 35. Challenging the validity of the Act, the appellant in *Ndlwana v Hofmeyr NO and Others*[76] counterintuitively argued that, as a consequence of the passage of the Statute of Westminster in 1931, the Union Parliament was no longer bound by the entrenched clauses and therefore use of the entrenched procedure was invalid. Rejecting this argument, the Court (per Stratford ACJ) held that an Act of Parliament cannot be questioned, as 'Parliament, composed of its three constituent elements, can adopt any procedure it thinks fit; the procedure express or implied in the South Africa Act is so far as Courts of Law are concerned at the mercy of Parliament like everything else'.[77] Even indirect representation of Africans in Parliament was abolished on 30 June 1960 as a consequence of apartheid policy and the *Promotion of Bantu Self-Government Act* 46 of 1959.[78]

The final exclusion of Africans in the Cape from the franchise was followed by attacks on the rights – to property and participation – of the Indian and Coloured communities. In 1945 there were only two 'Asiatics' on the voters' roll in Natal when Smuts' government introduced the *Asiatic Land Tenure and Indian Representation Act*.[79] Designed to provide for the representation of Indians in Natal and the Transvaal by three members of Parliament, the Act was boycotted by the Indian community and was abandoned with the introduction of apartheid policies three years later.[80]

In the case of the Coloured community, the struggle over the denial of voting rights was to reach unprecedented levels, culminating in a constitutional crisis as the apartheid government sought ways to discipline a rebellious Supreme Court. Despite the Court's refusal to accept jurisdiction in the case of *Ndlwana v Hofmeyr*,[81] the judiciary did an about face in *Harris v Minister of the Interior*.[82] In *Harris* the Appellate Division of the Supreme Court rejected the *Separate Representation of Voters Act* 46 of 1951, declaring that removing Coloured voters from the common roll by a simple majority of both Houses violated the constitutionally entrenched procedures.

The government responded with the *High Court of Parliament Act*,[83] which provided that any judgment of the Appellate Division which invalidated an Act of Parliament would be reviewed by the Parliament itself, sitting as the High Court of Parliament. However, this Act too was struck down by the courts.[84] Despite increased support at the polls, the government was unable to muster the two-thirds majority of both Houses of Parliament required by the Constitution to remove an entrenched clause. The government then embarked on a process which included packing both the Senate and the Court.[85] The *Appellate Division Quorum Act*[86] and *Senate Act*[87] allowed the government to appoint judges and senators sympathetic to its proposed constitutional changes, thus facilitating the passage of the *South Africa Act Amendment Act* of 1956.[88] This Act both excluded the jurisdiction of the courts and reinstated the 1951 *Separate Representation of Voters Act.*

Responding to the process of decolonization that was sweeping through Africa in the late 1950s, the apartheid government produced a scheme which extended franchise rights to the African majority but only within geographically bound and fragmented entities. The logic of this scheme was the eventual denationalization of the majority of black South Africans and their reconstitution as foreign citizens exercising full political rights outside of the South African constitutional framework. The *Promotion of Bantu Self-Government Act* of 1959[89] thus took the logic of land reservation a step further by setting aside those same reserved lands which the Union Constitution cast as islands of 'tribal' governance as the areas in which Africans would in future exercise their political aspirations. This scheme, referred to by the apartheid regime as the policy of 'separate development',[90] led to the creation of four 'independent' bantustans and aimed to engineer a permanent balkanization of the country.[91] Implementation of the 1959 Act began through the *Transkei Constitution Act* of 1963,[92] and was extended in terms of the *Black States Constitution Act* of 1971.[93] The *Transkei Constitution Act* and the 'independence' of the Transkei bantustan in 1976 served as the prototype of what government spokesmen considered a process that is 'in form and timing comparable to African decolonization'.[94] Rejected by the majority of South Africans and the international community as a violation of black South Africans' right to self-determination,[95] 'separate development' became a process of denationalization in which the citizenship of black

South Africans was recreated as foreign citizenship regardless of the individual's place of birth or preference.

Denying Equality and Violating Property: The Construction of Apartheid

Between 1960 and 1983, approximately 3 548 900 people were forcibly removed under apartheid relocation policies, including farm evictions, group areas removals, black spot removals, bantustan consolidation and urban relocation.[96] This massive invasion and destruction of black property rights added to the 1913 prohibition on Africans acquiring further land rights outside the 'reserves' – which would after 1936 amount to a mere thirteen per cent of the land area of South Africa – is the source of apartheid's deepest legacies of poverty and inequality. While addressing this legacy remains central to the creation of a legitimate property regime in South Africa, it also provides a rich source for understanding the nature and impact of the apartheid legal system.

After the final collapse of sovereign African societies in the closing years of the nineteenth century, African communities actively entered the land market, raising capital collectively and competing effectively with whites. In fact the Beaumont Commission of 1916 found evidence of active land purchases by African syndicates who 'paid good prices for land which the white owners were forced to sell to meet debts incurred during the Anglo-Boer War'.[97] In response white settlers – both propertied and unpropertied in the Transvaal and Orange Free State – used their access to political power through the vote to demand and win the exclusion of Africans from the land market.

While it would seem that the well-established Roman-Dutch and common law principles of equality before the law should have aroused judicial concern about the partial and unequal impact of legislation – such as the 1913 Land Act[98] – as between different classes, legislative and executive distinctions between black and white seemed to have raised few questions. Even in the 'liberal' Cape, the combination of an extremely broad judicial interpretation of parliamentary sovereignty – to include the presumed intentions of the legislature – and segregated social practice based on a presumption of racial superiority, led to an easy acceptance of formal racial segregation. In *Moller v Keimoes School Committee*,[99] Lord De Villiers, the first Chief Justice of South Africa, was required to define the meaning of 'European', in the context of an application for a court order to compel the admittance of children into a school established in terms of the *Cape School Board Act* of 1905 for children of 'European parentage or extraction'. In rejecting the argument that the children, whose father was white and whose mother was coloured, were of European extraction, Lord De Villiers argued that 'the vast majority of Europeans have always condemned such unions, and have regarded the offspring of such unions as being in the same racial condition as their black parents'.[100] The effect of this 'racial condition,' he explained, is 'a matter of public history [in which] we know that the first civilized legislators in South Africa came from Holland and regarded the aboriginal natives of this country as belonging to an inferior race, whom the Dutch, as Europeans, were entitled to rule over, and whom they refused to admit to social or political equality'.[101] The consequence of this 'racial condition' – exclusion – is justified in terms of white racism, as Lord De Villiers argued: 'We may not from a philosophical or humanitarian point of view be able to approve ... but we cannot, as judges, who are called upon to construe an Act of Parliament, ignore the reasons which must have induced the legislature to adopt the policy of separate education for European and non-European children.'[102] This bracketing of the common law principle of equality before the law with respect to race was stated even more starkly in the 1934 case of the *Minister of Posts and Telegraphs v Rasool*,[103] where Beyers JA 'remarked that the principle that all are equal in the eyes of the law is doubtless subject to qualifications and that, as far as the Transvaal was concerned, it was clear that Europeans and non-Europeans were never in important respects equal in the eyes of the law'.[104]

Refusing to accept the majority's argument that the mere fact of racial segregation of a post office did not amount to inequality of treatment, Gardiner AJA dissented. Arguing that equality before the law is a fundamental principle of the common law, which it must be assumed the legislature intends to respect, he stated:

> In view of the prevalent feeling as to colour, in view of the numerous statutes treating non-Europeans as belonging to an inferior order of civilisation, any fresh classification on colour lines can, to my mind, be interpreted only as a fresh instance of relegation of Asiatics and natives to a lower order, and this I consider humiliating treatment. Such treatment is an impairment of the *dignitas* of the person affected, and it is the Legislature only that can cause that impairment.[105]

Gardner AJA's dissent was vindicated in 1950, when the Appellate Division limited the scope of *Rasool* by defining the majority position as accepting differentiation on the grounds of race as valid so long as it is not coupled with 'substantial inequality'. Striking down the reservation of railway coaches for different races[106] because there were no first-class coaches set aside for blacks, the Court in *R v Abdurahman*[107] reasserted the principle of reasonableness formulated in *Kruse v Johnson*[108] to evaluate the legality of official action, arguing that it was the 'duty of the Courts to hold the scales evenly between different classes of the community and to declare invalid any practice which, in the absence of the authority of an Act of Parliament, results in partial and unequal treatment to a substantial degree between different sections of the community'.[109] Responding to the Court's assertion of equality as a fundamental principle of the common law, the apartheid legislature enacted the *Reservation of Separate Amenities Act* in 1953,[110] expressly providing that racial division may result in substantially unequal treatment.

This concerted attack on the principle of formal equality – which, while seemingly compatible with racial segregation, was resistant to blatant acts of discrimination – coincided with the increasing disregard and destruction of black property rights formally recognized under Roman-Dutch property law. Although the *Group Areas Act* was initially passed in 1950, the pace of forced removals accelerated during the 1960s 'following the suppression of popular black organisation and resistance through widespread bannings and trials'.[111] Within urban areas alone, approximately 860 400 people were subject to Group Areas removals in the twenty years between 1965 and 1985.[112] It was within this context – of the massive destruction of black property rights – that common law principles of fairness or 'natural justice' and equality continued to be undermined.

The *Group Areas Act*[113] enabled the apartheid state to establish 'controlled areas', introducing racial controls on ownership and occupation – the racial classification of the owner controlling who could legally occupy the property.[114] Once a group area was declared for a particular racial group within the controlled area, then any persons, including juristic persons, who were not of the defined racial group were deemed 'disqualified persons' in terms of the Act and were prohibited from holding property rights in the defined area.[115] Establishment of a 'group area' was initiated by Group Areas Boards submitting reports to the relevant cabinet minister, who would make a recommendation to the executive, which was empowered to proclaim the area a group area. It was a criminal offence for a member of one racial group to occupy or own land in an area set aside for another state-defined racial category.

Seeking to contest the information and proposals contained in the reports of the Eastern Cape Committee of the Group Areas Board, the applicants in *Cassem v Oos-Kaapse Kommittee van die Groepsgebiederaad*[116] sought a court order compelling the committee to allow them – under the principle of a right to a fair hearing – to examine its reports on the grounds that the proclamation of a group area would 'gravely affect their rights, interests and property'.[117] In making the application they were encouraged by the decision in *Ramjee v Eastern Cape Committee, Group Areas Board*,[118] in which the Eastern Cape Provincial Division had granted a similar application arguing that the 'right to a fair hearing is the most important of the principles of natural justice', and that 'a body vested with authority to make a decision calculated to affect the rights of, or involving legal consequences to, a person had to observe the principles', particularly when the 'consequences for people who were uprooted from their homes, were a "drastic interference with civil rights" '.[119] Reversing *Ramjee* and upholding the lower court's denial of their application, the Appellate Division in *Cassem* argued that granting a right to access to reports 'could assume dimensions which would be barely manageable and which would impede the implementation of the Act in such a way that it can hardly be supposed that the legislator implicitly wished to ordain such quasi-procedural limitations of the Board's freedom of action'.[120] As David Dyzenhaus points out, Chief Justice Steyn's reasoning is that 'there is an implicit legislative wish that the board not be hampered by being subjected to requirements of fairness',[121] a legislative intention deduced from the assumption that 'the executive should determine policy unconstrained by common law constraints'.[122] Such disregard of the rights of apartheid's black victims by the Chief Justice provides a dramatic illustration of the decomposition of common law rights within the legal system from a time when a former Chief Justice, in upholding a scheme designed to enable black land ownership, argued: 'It is a wholesome rule of our law which requires a strict construction to be placed upon statutory provisions which interfere with elementary rights.'[123]

The principle of equality, invoked once more in the context of the *Group Areas Act* to challenge the validity of a proclamation dividing the city of Durban into group areas,[124] was decided and finally rejected by the decision that, while the power to discriminate unreasonably had to be given expressly or by necessary implication, the very nature of the apartheid project meant that it was 'clearly implied'.[125] Rejecting the appellants' argument that the proclamation was invalid in that all the best areas had been given to whites and suitable accommodation was unavailable to Indians in the areas assigned to them, the Court argued:

> The Group Areas Act represents a colossal social experiment and a long term policy. It necessarily involves the movement out of Group Areas of numbers of people throughout the country. Parliament must have envisaged that compulsory population shifts of persons occupying certain areas would inevitably cause disruption and, within the foreseeable future, substantial inequalities.[126]

And so in the construction of apartheid, the embrace of inequality and the disregard of human dignity went hand in hand with the destruction of property rights.

LEGITIMACY OF THE COURTS

Despite this legacy, it has been argued that black South Africans retained a significant degree of confidence in the legal system, and the courts in particular.[127] This confidence it is argued lent a 'measure of legitimacy to the legal system', which, when coupled with the history of anti-apartheid lawyering, 'might have encouraged South Africans to see virtue in the ideals of fearless advocacy, independent judging, and the rule of law', offering the 'promise that these same ideals would be honored in a post-apartheid South Africa'.[128] While these conclusions seem strained, given the contrary evidence and nature of the opinion polls that Ellmann him-self notes, they do suggest that the turn to the judiciary may indeed be rooted in a confidence in the courts that survived the apartheid era. The difficulty with this proposition is twofold. First, as Ellmann indicates, a 1993 poll indicates a dramatic decline in this perceived legitimacy, the source of which cannot be adequately explained.[129] Second, it is metho-dologically confounding to measure the legitimacy of the legal system on the basis of distinctions in attitudes between the apartheid courts, parliament and police, and then to verify its existence based on the turn to legalism in the democratic transition. While the empirical nature of poll results is extremely attractive, both the qualitative data offered by Ellmann in his own reported interviews and an understanding of the role of the courts – particularly the lower courts, where the vast majority of South Africans experienced the legal system – raise serious qualms as to the possible link between the standing of the courts in the apartheid period and the decision to adopt constitutional review as a central ele-ment of the post-apartheid political order.

Although the victories in the Supreme Court against the State of Emergency, such as requiring the police to account for their actions,[130] were significant, it is important to distinguish the Supreme Court from the lower courts. Even apart from the reversal suffered by anti-apartheid lawyers in the mid-1980s, when their early court victories against the worst restrictions of the State of Emergency gave way to successive judg-ments by the Appellate Division which held that the state had virtually unlimited power under Emergency provisions,[131] the role of the courts in both highly publicized inquest hearings and in what came to be described as a system of 'punishment by process' provides a completely different perspective. While more than seventy political detainees are known to have died in security police detention between 1963 and 1990, the courts repeatedly exonerated their torturers 'either because the con-spiracy of silence and outright lying by police officers made it impossible to reach the truth or because the courts too readily believed the fairytales proffered as fact ... [and] in the face of glaring evidence to the contrary, they resolutely declared that no one was to blame'.[132]

Furthermore, it may be argued that the magistrates' courts in fact acted 'as part of the state's disciplinary machinery'.[133] This was most evident in the stream of 'public violence' cases that flowed through the magistrates' courts after 1985, in what came to be described as 'punishment by process'.[134] Mass arrests, including 'substitute arrests – brother for brother, father for son, neighbour for neighbour', assaults and torture, followed by detention while awaiting trial, and protracted court proceedings often ended in dismissals for lack of evidence.[135] Nine months of monitoring by the Black Sash (a human rights organization made up predominantly of white women) revealed 'that 42% of those accused were juveniles, and that only 13% of adults and 17% of juveniles were found guilty'.[136] The Black Sash concluded that

> very large numbers of innocent people are arrested in random fashion and charged on flimsy evidence that cannot stand up to examination in court. They are thus made to endure a protracted period of punishment by process with little hope of redress … When the accused are acquitted or discharged, the family is too weary and disturbed to want to face any suit for wrongful arrest or further court proceedings: it is sufficient to be free.[137]

Even the superior courts came under direct criticism, particularly by external bodies such as the International Commission of Jurists, whose observer at the treason trial of Helene Passtoors in 1986 concluded that there is 'justification to the viewpoint of black people and concerned whites that most South African courts in their uncritical and "positivist" approach to apartheid legislation merely serve as instruments of repression'.[138]

Apartheid's Legal Legacy

The submissions to the Truth and Reconciliation Commission's (TRC) 'institutional hearing' on the role of the legal community reflected the fundamental division within the South African legal community over the role of law under apartheid. On the one side there was the 'argument of the establishment bodies', who, like former Chief Justice Michael Corbett, continued to argue:

> Prior to the coming into effect of the interim Constitution on 27 April 1994, Parliament was supreme. For practical purposes it could pass any law it liked; and it did so. The courts had no power to question the validity of the laws Parliament made. Still less could they declare them invalid. The courts had no option but to apply the law as they found it, however unjust it might appear to be.[139]

On the other side, there was the 'counter argument' made by the traditionally anti-apartheid sections of the legal community, including the Black Lawyers Association, Lawyers for Human Rights, the Legal Resources Centre and the National Association of Democratic Lawyers. These bodies argued that 'lawyers and the courts under apartheid, with very few and notable exceptions, had co-operated in servicing and enforcing a diabolically unjust political order'.[140] They went on to reject parliamentary sovereignty as an adequate defence or explanation, arguing that the 'validity of such a defence depended on at least a substantial degree of democracy in the political order, as well as a basic respect for the rule of law as a direct or necessary adjunct to legislative omnicompetence. Neither prerequisite was present to any significant degree in South Africa.'[141] Finally, it was argued that: 'Judicial independence was a myth that had been exploded in the daily experience [of the] courts.'[142] Although there were numerous submissions that adopted less polarized versions of these analyses,[143] the Commission's conclusions in its final report emphasized that one of the reasons for the 'longevity of apartheid was the superficial adherence to "rule by law" by the National Party whose leaders craved the aura of legitimacy that "the law" bestowed on their harsh injustice',[144] and that this was exacerbated by the subconscious or unwitting connivance of the courts and the legal profession in the legislative and executive pursuit of injustice.[145]

Despite this condemnation of the law and legal profession under apartheid, the Commission acknowledged the existence of both a space for resistance and active defiance by a few lawyers, including judges, teachers and students, who 'used every opportunity to speak out publicly and within the profession against the adoption and execution of rules of law that sanctioned arbitrary official conduct and injustice'.[146] Although the Commission found that participation in the system afforded credibility to the claim of an independent legal system, it concluded that the 'alleviation of suffering achieved by such lawyers substantially outweighed' any harm done.[147]

Thus, while it may be reasonable to believe that the victims of apartheid would support the introduction of a bill of rights in response to the massive denial of rights under apartheid, there is less reason to believe that there should be an equivalent faith in the judiciary as the upholders of such rights. Even the experience of the 1980s, where the courts were used as a site of struggle against the imposition of unjust laws and to defend the rights of those engaged in resistance against apartheid, is unlikely to have overcome the legacy of injustice meted out under apartheid laws. Rather, communities and individuals learned that the law and the judiciary were not necessarily at the whim of the executive but instead there was always the possibility, but only the possibility, of justice before the courts. Given the degree to which law and the judicial system were implicated in the construction and daily functioning of the apartheid system, the key to understanding the 'new faith' in the judiciary must be sought in the particular dynamics of the democratic transition.

CHAPTER 3

CONSTITUTIONALISM IN GLOBAL PERSPECTIVE

South African history is important, but it is a mistake to limit the explanation of South Africa's dramatic constitutionalist turn to the dynamics of local developments. The limits of path dependency dictate that the adoption of democratic constitutionalism in South Africa must also be viewed in the light of a globalizing constitutionalism; that is, the need for South Africa to reintegrate itself into the international community and economy by conforming to the dominant international political culture of the moment. Constitutionalism, in this analysis, becomes both a natural way for élites to think[1] and a passport to international acceptability.[2]

South Africa's constitutional transition is best understood as the product of a dialectical interaction between a global 'text' constituted by the histories, practices and normative prescriptions of nation-states, international bodies and organizations – such as the United Nations and World Bank – and, increasingly, transnational corporate and non-governmental organizations, and the 'local' struggles and processes through which the new constitutional regime was created and implemented. At the same time, the creation and emergence of a post-apartheid constitutional order in South Africa provides a context in which the global 'text' is being constantly reformulated. Not only are the elements of 'universal principles' hybridized through their particular application in the specific context of local struggles and histories, but the new forms become the building blocks for a transformed understanding of available alternatives. I will term this continuing process a 'globalizing constitutionalism', which is characterized by the coexistence of two seemingly contradictory yet indispensable elements. On the one hand it is marked by a significant degree of indeterminacy, while on the other it carries a normative power that defines the outer limits of constitutional legitimacy and thus shapes the imaginations of those seeking alternative forms of governance in the context of their own very specific struggles for political and constitutional change.

In order to set the stage for understanding the impact of global forces and developments on the possible outcomes of local struggles, this chapter places the adoption of South Africa's new Constitution in a global context. While highlighting the link between South Africa's new Constitution and non-domestic legal standards, both international and foreign, the chapter also traces the role of local or domestic struggles in the emergence of a global system. Discussion of this relationship focuses on South African examples in order to emphasize how the local, domestic struggles over political participation and social resources have worked to shape the form of the global. This leads to a perspective which asserts that global currents and forces are not autonomous from local struggles and histories – in fact it may be argued that in one sense the global is merely the sum and interaction of all locals. Exploring this interaction reveals the interdependence of these often juxtaposed sites and demonstrates that any understanding of the shift to constitutionalism in South Africa must include an analysis of the interaction between the local and the global in the process of political reconstruction. South Africa's twentieth-century drama allows us to examine, in the context of a specific country's history: the formulation and transmission of an international political tradition; its impact on the continuing process of political reconstruction; and the contesting ideas and social forces that shaped this impact. This process of political reconstruction in a global context reflects, I argue, neither crude imperialism nor wishful harmonization, but rather a continuing process of hybridization,[3] a fierce contest between the construction of social legitimacy and struggles over who wins or loses political, economic, social and cultural imperatives or rights.

GLOBALIZATION AND ITS IMPLICATIONS FOR SYSTEMS OF GOVERNANCE

While the term 'globalization' has entered academic and popular discourse,[4] any attempt to specify its exact meaning is undermined by the range of ways the term is used to characterize and propagate recent dramatic changes in the international political economy.[5] But, despite this diversity, the discourse on globalization rests on two essential ideas. The first is the qualitative transformations of global economic and cultural interactions[6] that have occurred in recent years, so that today we may speak of a global economy involving the transnational co-ordination of production, markets and finances, and increasingly of emerging global norms reflected most clearly in the emergence of transnational social movements in the arenas of human rights and the environment.[7] Second is the recognition that because of 'the intensification of worldwide social relations' distinct localities are linked 'in such a way that local happenings are shaped by events occurring many miles away and vice versa'.[8]

Recognition of the processes of globalization has led to a wide ranging debate over the future of the nation-state and the impact of globalization on governance. Most participants in the debate acknowledge that the role of the nation-state as a focus of governance is dramatically affected by globalization, indeed among some it has become fashionable to assert that the nation-state is *passé*.[9] Globalists of both the right and left assert that a globalized capitalist economy has become ungovernable.[10] For the right, not only is the global economy effectively ungovernable, but any attempt to create an institutional framework is unnecessary, given that the market is for them the most efficient mechanism of co-ordination. Left globalists agree that national control of economic life is no longer possible, but they also see the emergence of supranational institutions such as the General Agreement on Tariffs and Trade (GATT), North American Free Trade Association (NAFTA) and the European Union, as well as 'private-government collaborations that constitute various "working groups" within them' as promoting a regressive 'one world' vision of international harmonization which will, in effect, result in the internationalization of human subordination.[11] A more textured view of these questions begins by recognizing the paradox represented by the fact that, while democratization is sweeping the world, increasingly greater areas of human endeavour are being organized on a global level, thus compromising the viability of the independent nation-state and challenging the 'efficacy of democracy as a national form of political organization'.[12] From within this trend the understanding has developed that: 'Politics is becoming more polycentric, with states as merely one level in a complex system of overlapping and often competing agencies of governance.'[13]

In this context, while the world financial markets may have acquired a kind of 'structural power' over democratically-elected governments,[14] it is still possible to view the nation-state as having an important role in 'suturing' the different levels and functions of governance. This process of suturing, defined as the 'policies and practices of states in distributing power upwards to the international level and downwards to sub-national agencies',[15] helps narrow or close gaps in governance and elaborates a division of labour in regulation – between local, national and international institutions – without which vital capacities for control would be lost.[16] According to this vision: 'Authority may now be plural within and between states rather than nationally centralised, but to be effective it must be structured by an element of design into a relatively coherent architecture of institutions.'[17]

A vision of politics as polycentric – in which authority is spatially dis-
tributed and functionally disaggregated – provides the basis for a reformulation of the question of governance. While such an approach would
recognize the continued vitality and centrality of the modern territorially-
defined state 'at the intersection of the distribution of political power',[18]
it stimulates a reconceptualization of the notion of governance as well as
a reconsideration of our understandings of sovereignty and democracy
and their interaction within the international political economy.

The adoption of particular forms of social regulation is in this understanding the repeated outcome of a continuing global–local interaction.
Within this context, adopted forms of regulation are deeply embedded in
local practices and histories, yet are simultaneously shaped by international or global forms. Global alternatives establish a bounded framework within which local regulation or governance is constantly being
reshaped – where local agency and social competitors position themselves
for local advantage and in relation to global opportunities and constraints.

BEYOND THE NATION-STATE

Globalization involves increased awareness of the interconnectedness of
local events and international trends, but it is also impelled by a declin-
ing confidence in the capacity of public authority to regulate or exercise
political control over key aspects of the national polity and economy.
From the Peace of Westphalia (1648) to the emergence of the United
Nations Charter model (1945),[19] the concept of sovereignty has provided
the linchpin of a state-centred model of international politics. The Peace
of Westphalia endorsed and created the opportunity for the establishment of 'a singular and stable relationship between political authority
and territory'.[20] This provided states with the requisite autonomy to
'impose' political authority, in the name of internal sovereignty, on their
societies. At the international level the notion of sovereignty has evolved
into the United Nations model – 'a sovereignty of management',[21] in
which rights are disaggregated, 'pragmatically bundled, rearranged and
balanced'. A similar transformation, from an absolute notion of sovereignty to popular sovereignty and on to an understanding of state power
as a mediated interaction of alternative jurisdictions of governance, has
occurred in understandings of national or internal sovereignty.[22]

State sovereignty has, however, never been as mono-dimensional or
exclusive as the Westphalian model claims. Rather, since the emergence
of nation-states as powerful ideological constructs or imagined communities,[23] the exercise of state power has always involved both multiple
geographic contacts, through transborder social and economic activities, as well as an assertion of transnational power based on bonds of
allegiance between the state and its nationals abroad.[24] Although the

modern territorially-defined state remains at the intersection of the distribution of political power, and sovereignty 'functions as a particular way of legitimating the distribution of political power', a focus on the functional content of state sovereignty – state jurisdiction – makes it possible to understand how highly flexible and fragmented sovereignty is in character and content.[25] Each state's jurisdiction – understood as the 'scope within which the power of public or state authorities can *effectively* and *acceptably* be exercised'[26] – must thus be understood as 'flexible, overlapping and negotiable'.[27]

This understanding of the content of state sovereignty makes it possible to understand the tension within international law between the continued assertions of state sovereignty – emphasizing territorial integrity or non-intervention in the domestic affairs of states – and the emergence and development of international obligations focused on the right to self-determination, respect for human rights, and even recognition of a right to democracy. While these twentieth-century doctrines all seem to challenge and undermine traditional notions of sovereignty, their development and trajectory may be best understood in the context of the process of globalization, which is subjecting the territorial state to at least three sets of pressures.[28] First, the very nature, scope and capacity of the sovereign state is being changed from above by processes of economic, political, legal and military interconnectedness. Second, the nation-state is being challenged from below by local groups, movements and nationalisms questioning its status as a representative and accountable power system; and third, the nature and dynamics of national political systems are being reshaped by the 'chains of interlocking political decisions and outcomes among states and their citizens', created by global interconnectedness.[29]

Human Rights and the Changing Subjects of International Law

South Africa's assertion of domestic jurisdiction as a defence to United Nations concern over the development of apartheid[30] provides a means of exploring these interactions[31] and their impact on notions of state sovereignty, democracy and self-determination. When the issue of racial discrimination in South Africa was first raised in the United Nations General Assembly in 1946 – in the context of a local passive resistance campaign[32] and a complaint by the Indian Government against the South African government's increasingly discriminatory policies towards South African nationals of Indian descent – Field-Marshal Smuts of South Africa objected, arguing that 'within the domain of its domestic affairs a State is not subject to control or interference, and its actions could not be called into question by any other State'.[33] Asserting that Article 2(7) of the United Nations Charter 'embodied an over-riding principle qualifying ... all the other provisions of the Charter', Smuts warned that, if it was decided that a recommendation by the General Assembly on such an issue was not an intervention in the domestic affairs of a member state under Article 2(7), then 'every domestic matter could be taken through every stage in the procedure of the Assembly'.[34]

While the General Assembly rejected South Africa's argument, the assertion of its authority to make general declarations on human rights issues and to apply the Charter to concrete situations, despite objections based on a claim of domestic jurisdiction,[35] was made in terms of the existence of special bilateral agreements between South Africa and India.[36] It also relied on the advisory opinion of the Permanent Court of International Justice in the *Nationality Decrees Issues in Tunis and Morocco*[37] case, in which the Court held that 'the question whether a certain matter is or is not solely within the jurisdiction of a State is an essentially relative question; it depends upon the development of international relations'.[38] This enabled the General Assembly both to reassert a commitment to the notion of a 'reserved domain' of domestic jurisdiction and to argue that 'the right of a State to use its discretion may nevertheless be 'restricted by obligations which it may have undertaken towards other States', in which case, 'jurisdiction which, in principle, belongs solely to the State, is limited by rules of international law'.[39]

While the General Assembly was initially able to argue that the agreements between South Africa and India provided an exceptional basis for the Assembly's jurisdiction, the continuation of the conflict over the discriminatory treatment of 'Indians and "other non-Europeans" ' in South Africa led the Assembly to broaden the basis of its jurisdiction by arguing that the situation in South Africa was 'a humanitarian question of international importance', and that under Article 14 of the Charter, the Assembly 'had the necessary competence to recommend measures to ensure the peaceful adjustment of a situation which had, in the Assembly's opinion, led to the impairment of friendly relations'.[40] Although the Canadian delegation emphasized the 'necessity of making a distinction between the right of the Assembly to discuss the problem under the terms of the Charter and its competence to intervene', which they argued would depend on 'the kind of action the Assembly might be invited to take',[41] the Assembly proceeded to strengthen the legal basis of its jurisdiction by, on the one hand, suggesting the weakest form of intervention by merely inviting the parties – India, South Africa and Pakistan – 'to enter into discussion', while, on the other hand, extending the grounds upon which concern could be raised, by stating that the discussion should take into consideration the 'purposes and principles of the Charter of the United Nations and the Declaration of Human Rights'.[42] Despite South Africa's continued assertion of domestic jurisdiction and a failed attempt to have the words 'and the Declaration of Human Rights' deleted from the resolution, the General Assembly continued to expand its jurisdiction over the South African problem by starting to discuss the parallel issue of 'the policies of apartheid' in 1952 and then by merging the two issues in 1962.[43]

In September 1952, thirteen Asian and African countries requested that the issue of apartheid be placed on the General Assembly's agenda, on the grounds that these policies created a 'dangerous and explosive situation, which constitutes both a threat to international peace and a flagrant violation of the basic principles of human rights and fundamental freedoms which are enshrined in the Charter of the United Nations'.[44] Rejecting as 'completely unfounded and quite preposterous' the notion that apartheid constituted a threat to international peace, South Africa argued that the only exception to the prohibition against interference in the domestic affairs of a member state was when the Security Council is authorized to intervene under Chapter VII of the Charter and only in situations specified in Article 39. Furthermore, South Africa argued, the General Assembly is not authorized to intervene in any manner – including by resolutions, recommendations or even by discussion – as the Charter provides no other exceptions outside Article 39, and certainly contains no 'additional exception with respect to questions of human rights'.[45] It is interesting to note that National Party leader and former State President F. W. de Klerk still maintains this position. In his submissions and appearances before the Truth and Reconciliation Commission in 1997, de Klerk continued to reject the description of apartheid as a crime against humanity,[46] arguing that the international convention declaring apartheid a crime against humanity was invalid as it was merely a General Assembly resolution and not a resolution of the United Nations Security Council.[47]

Proceeding to address the issue of apartheid, the General Assembly adopted two resolutions in 1952 in which the Assembly affirmed that governmental policies of Member States which are not directed towards the goal of 'ensuring equality before the law of all persons regardless of race, creed or colour', but which, instead, 'are designed to perpetuate or increase discrimination, are inconsistent with the pledges of Members under Article 56 of the Charter'.[48] The South African government subsequently refused to co-operate with the commission[49] established by the General Assembly to study and report on the racial situation in South Africa. In response, the commission reviewed South Africa's objections to the exercise of jurisdiction by the General Assembly and argued that the General Assembly was authorized by the Charter 'to undertake any studies and make any recommendations to Member States which it may deem necessary in connection with the application and implementation of the principles to which the Member States have subscribed by signing the Charter'.[50] Furthermore, the commission concluded that this 'universal right of study and recommendation is absolutely incontestable with regard to general problems of human rights and particularly of those protecting against discrimination for reasons of race, sex, language or religion'.[51]

The outcome of this process was to favour the international or global over the local. Over the next forty years the international community, driven by struggles in South Africa and the emergence of an international anti-apartheid movement, continued to extend its jurisdiction over the issue of apartheid: moving from recommendation to condemnation;[52] from encouraging discussion of racial discrimination to the rejection of the apartheid government's credentials to represent South Africa in the General Assembly;[53] from support for the victims of apartheid[54] to the imposition of mandatory sanctions in the form of an arms embargo;[55] from the rejection and condemnation of the 1983 Constitution[56] to the establishment of a set of principles for an internationally acceptable democratic transition and constitutional framework.[57] While many of the participants may have thought that apartheid in South Africa presented an exceptional case, these developments were important markers in the negotiation of state sovereignty and the exercise of supranational jurisdiction over fundamental political choices and decisions. It was this initial assertion of General Assembly jurisdiction 'to study and recommend' in the field of human rights that provided the stepping stones over which activists and states would manœuvre in the building of an international human rights movement, which only came to prominence through the struggles of national and international social movements, from the civil rights movement in the USA to the mothers of the Plaza de Mayo in Argentina, and on to the international anti-apartheid movement itself. Despite the old formal doctrine that states are the sole or primary subjects of international law, by the end of the twentieth century the fact of the constant renegotiation of state sovereignty was well established, providing a smorgasbord of subjects – international organizations, non-government organizations, transnational corporations and movements, as well as individuals – and a fragmentation of jurisdiction in which the nation-state provides the locus for constant renegotiation, realignment and reassignment of jurisdictional powers.

Legitimacy of Governance and the Emergence of a Normative Claim to Democratic Governance

A central aspect of the fragmentation and assignment of jurisdictional power in contests over governance is the issue of legitimacy. This is evoked, for example, in the manner in which the concept of sovereignty has 'functioned as a particular way of legitimating the distribution of political power'.[58] This quest for legitimacy, as a basis for claiming just authority or jurisdiction over subjects, spaces and events, leads at times to appeals to 'established', historically laden concepts, such as sovereignty. At other times the same quest leads to the assertion of new bases of legitimacy, such as expertise, professional standards, or normative claims of respect for human rights or democratic procedures or practices. Significantly, the motivation behind this quest for legitimacy in contests over jurisdictional authority is suggested by the assertion that the legitimacy bestowed by the subjection of the political process to democratic rules 'gives back far more power to those who govern than they surrendered'.[59]

While at one level it may be the case that 'the fiction of unlimited internal sovereignty is complemented and sustained by its corollary, the sovereign equality of states',[60] as Sol Picciotto notes, the 'key prop in this legitimation is a particular form of legality, based on abstract and universalist principles, which claims to underpin and guarantee the formal equality and freedom of legal subjects',[61] whether internally among 'citizens' or externally among 'sovereign states'. Even in transnational space, for example, in the construction of an international legal field (a new field of symbolic power in the competition for jurisdiction between professionals), legitimacy and authority have been sought in the championing of the 'return of law,' which draws on, among other sources, the human rights activities of lawyers.[62]

This search for legitimacy in contests over the distribution of jurisdiction or decision-making powers is always open to challenge. This vulnerability to challenge is inherent in legitimacy's normative nature, since norms have no indisputable logical source or empirical content. When it comes to issues of jurisdiction, the basis of legitimacy is founded upon highly abstract and general principles. Hence, the room for challenge is especially great. It is precisely this vulnerability which is being exploited in the arguments for different notions of sovereignty[63] and the development of an emerging right to democratic governance in international law.[64] According to Thomas Franck, democracy is on its way to becoming a global entitlement based on the recognition of governments 'that their legitimacy depends on meeting a normative expectation of the community of states', who increasingly expect 'that those who seek the validation of their empowerment patently govern with the consent of the governed'.[65]

Tracing the development of notions of democracy within international law,[66] Franck identifies three building blocks in the construction of an emerging international right to democracy: the right to self-determination; the right of free political expression; and the emerging normative requirement of a participatory electoral process. While the right to self-determination entered international law in arguments for the protection of minorities at the Versailles Peace Conference following the First World War and became the driving force behind the United Nations–crafted process of decolonization, its post-colonial reincarnation has been towards the evolution of a 'more general notion of internationally validated political consultation'.[67] Through its enunciation in the 1970 United Nations Declaration on Friendly Relations and its application – in the context of the International Covenant on Civil and Political Rights – to the rights of ethnic, religious and linguistic minorities, the right of self-determination has evolved from 'being a principle of exclusion (secession) and become one of inclusion: the right to participate' – the right of 'peoples in all states to free, fair and open participation in the democratic process of governance freely chosen by each state'.[68] Demonstrating a right to free political expression requires even greater reliance on the assertion of a normative order – by pointing to the Universal Declaration of Human Rights, the International Covenant on Civil and Political Rights,[69] and to the development of regional human rights regimes such as the European Convention for the Protection of Human Rights and Fundamental Freedoms. However, it is through an examination of the practice of states and international organizations, particularly in processes of decolonization and democratization, that Franck is able to show how the combined impact of the normative assertions of self-determination and the right to free political expression have given rise to practices of election monitoring in particular that have contributed towards the emergence of a right to democratic participation.

The emergence of a normative right to democratic participation is internationally linked to at least three processes which culminated in and flowed from the dramatic transformation of world politics in the late 1980s: the process of *perestroika* in the former Soviet Union;[70] the dynamic evolution of the Helsinki process;[71] and the collapse of the authoritarian–paternalistic model of development in sub-Saharan Africa. While the United Nations General Assembly responded to these developments by adopting resolutions expressing the conviction that 'periodic and genuine elections are a necessary and indispensable element of sustained efforts to protect the rights and interests of the governed',[72] and that such elections are a 'crucial factor in the effective enjoyment ... of a wide range of other human rights',[73] it was within the evolution of the Conference on Security and Co-operation (CSCE) in Europe that the concept of democratic entitlement gained its greatest specificity. At the Conference on the Human Dimension of the CSCE held in Copenhagen in June 1990,[74] the member states declared that 'the will of the people, freely and fairly expressed through periodic and genuine elections, is the basis of the authority and legitimacy of all government', and that the participating states 'recognize their responsibility to defend and protect ... the democratic order freely established through the will of the people'.[75]

57

These commitments were given institutional form five months later with the adoption of the Paris Charter which included the establishment of the Office of Fair Elections.[76]

While it may be debated whether or at what point a right to democratic governance comes into existence in international law, it is clear that issues of democratic governance have become part of international legal discourse. Within this context, questions of a state's commitment to democratic governance – in the form of a 'regard for the rule of law, democracy and human rights'[77] – have begun to play a central role in international legal discourse over the recognition of states.[78]

GLOBALIZATION AND INTERNATIONAL POLITICAL CULTURE

The discourse on globalization generally stresses economic and technological factors as the driving forces of this process, while relatively little attention has been paid to other, non-economic, processes. Thus, it came as quite a surprise when, in the 1990s, the 'rule of law' became a central tenet of the international discourse on legitimate systems of governance, and the adoption of new, justiciable constitutions – with bills of rights as their centre-pieces – became a major product of this movement. In order to understand this development, it is important to look to the precursors of the rule of law movement, such as the emergence and impact of a transnational human rights movement in the post–Second World War period. Grounded in national or local social struggles – for equality, political recognition and economic sustenance – the appeal to rights in the transnational context was at its inception based directly on the normative framework of the Universal Declaration of Human Rights[79] adopted by states in response to the horrors of the holocaust. This interstate initiative was formally institutionalized in regional human rights conventions, beginning with the European Convention for the Protection of Human Rights and Fundamental Freedoms[80] and later including the American Convention on Human Rights[81] and the African Charter on Human and Peoples' Rights.[82]

Non-government normative and activist movements began to achieve a transnational life in reaction to the torture, detention and disappearance of opponents of military regimes in Latin America, and through the development, beginning in the 1960s, of an international anti-apartheid movement. Although overshadowed in some instances by the ideological conflicts of the cold war, the deployment of a human rights paradigm, both within the context of the cold war and increasingly as a mechanism for challenging the domestic policies and practices of states, infused international political culture with new standards for evaluating and regarding the internal political structures and practices of States in the international community.

Initially the '*realpolitik*' of states' responses was to assert their state sovereignty and the United Nations Charter's prohibition against interference in the internal affairs of member states.[83] However, the normative power of the rights discourse, combined with political activism, gradually pressed governing élites to engage these movements and international institutions on the issue of human rights standards. Official commitment to the normative frameworks promoted by the human rights movement, in its various transnational and local guises, provided those struggling to advance 'domestic' human rights with rhetorical ammunition. Working within an emerging global 'civil society', dominated by human rights and environmental NGOs, activists deploy the legitimacy of these normative standards to embarrass and isolate offending governments through the documentation and exposure of systematic and gross violations of human rights. This process is dramatically enhanced by the interaction of two factors: the technological innovations (including email, the World Wide Web and satellite television), which allow information and ideas to carry across state boundaries; and United States cold war policy, which led to a rhetoric of human rights talk, but reality of support for anticommunist dictators in quasi-client states. The demise of the cold war left the human rights talk of states and the claims of activists standing with no counterbalancing *realpolitik* claims on the other side, thus intensifying their legitimacy and divorcing human rights claims from the United States and West European mould, to which they had largely been confined. Even before the collapse of state socialism and the Soviet Union as a superpower, events in, for example, Iran and the Philippines showed that human rights claims could break free of *realpolitik* restraints and were a force even when not triumphant. Add to this the developments in communications and economic interdependence – including trade and investment – and the force of these claims has become tremendous.[84] A new restraint has, however, appeared, in the guise of economic and trade imperatives, where the importance of markets is used, much as anti-communism once was, to justify a softening or blunting of human rights claims – witness United States relations with China.

Non-State Actors and the Creation of a Globalized Normative Order

Pivotal to struggles over the creation and establishment of a globalized normative order or international political culture – in the context of the interactions and interconnections generated in an emerging, denationalized, global civil society – is the emergence and development of what Kathryn Sikkink and Margaret Keck term Principle Issue Networks. This development of 'an international movement of private actors'[85] was most dramatically demonstrated by the unprecedented influence exercised by more than 1500 NGOs, from all regions of the world, over the agenda of the World Conference on Human Rights in Vienna in 1993.[86]

These networks consist of formal and informal links between a host of agents – including individuals, non-government organizations, parts of international organizations and even state agencies. Participants in a network focus on particular goals organized around a particular issue of principle, whether in support of human rights, against abortion, or in opposition to environmental degradation.[87] The significance of these networks for an understanding of the forces driving processes of globalization is twofold. First, they demonstrate how the exchange and strategic mobilization of information – which is the currency used by these networks – may be deployed to gain 'leverage over much more powerful organizations and governments'.[88] Second, by transforming the understandings and practices which comprise and reinforce the 'shared set of understandings and expectations about the authority of the state',[89] they not only work towards but to a degree also succeed in reconstituting the very notion of sovereignty upon which state authority is constructed. While in the first instance these networks provide the grounding for claims about the emergence of an incipient global civil society,[90] in the second instance they provide examples of globalized political processes that help to shape both the normative content of international political culture and the practice of governance in different arenas. These range from the reform of local practices violating human rights norms to a reconceptualization of the relative autonomy of states in a transnational context.

The international anti-apartheid movement provides an interesting example of the creation and practice of a transnational social movement or issue network. Constructed around the shared principles of anti-racism and anti-colonialism, the anti-apartheid movement included a vast range of organizations – from international bodies to local cultural groupings – which shared information and campaigned to reshape international understanding and practice towards the internal policies and sovereignty of a member state of the United Nations, namely South Africa. Activities of the movement ranged from providing material support to victims of apartheid, including the South African national liberation movements, to the mobilization of alumni votes at Harvard University for the election of a slate of anti-apartheid activists to the Harvard Board of Overseers – in order to challenge the University's refusal to divest from United States and transnational corporations with investments in South Africa. Participation in the movement included such diverse behaviour as individually boycotting South African products, establishing bodies to monitor investment and divestment patterns, promoting and monitoring the international arms embargo, and campaigning for anti-apartheid legislation within nation-states: for example, the campaign for the United States Congress to impose sanctions on South Africa.

A remarkable feature of the anti-apartheid movement's impact in the United States – as a consequence of the manner in which issues and concerns over race-consciousness and racism in the United States resonated with the movement's principal issue – was its ability to persuade ordinary people that their own town or city's economic links, through contracts or even pension fund investments, with companies active in South Africa created a moral link with apartheid which required and enabled them to act locally to challenge racism and apartheid as a global phenomenon. To this end individuals and groups engaged in boycotts and advertising, educational and electoral campaigns, as well as providing material support, establishing cultural exchanges and initiating people-to-people diplomacy through sister-city projects and other innovative activities. In this sense, then, the anti-apartheid network managed not only to mobilize a particular understanding of and practice towards apartheid as a violation of human rights in the international community, but also to 'globalize' apartheid by making it an issue for millions of individuals and organizations around the world who adopted new understandings and activities based on their perceived linkages, however tenuous, with the abhorred practices of the apartheid regime.

The international anti-apartheid movement as a transnational social movement was in scope and form an early example of what has been called 'globalization-from-below'. It was part of an array of transnational social forces animated by diverse concerns that continue to challenge the 'homogenizing tendencies of globalization-from-above'.[91] In other words, at the same time as the forces of global capitalism were replacing the anti-communist crusade as an instrument for integrating South Africa into the international global order, a world-wide social movement with a non-economic logic of organization was challenging the global integration of South Africa which the transnational capitalist economic logic seemed to demand. In this sense the experience of the international anti-apartheid movement demonstrates the diversity of interconnected forces generating the multiple processes of globalization.

GLOBALIZING CONSTITUTIONALISM

As democratic transitions swept the world following the collapse of military dictatorships in Latin America in the 1980s and the unravelling of state socialism in the Soviet Union and Eastern Europe after 1989, interest in questions of constitutionalism was revitalized. These developments 'paved the way for the completion of the worldwide thrust towards constitutionalism that began shortly after the end of World War II'.[92] Although the international human rights movement grew steadily from the end of the Second World War, the recent hegemony of fundamental rights as a basis for constitutional reconstruction is quite dramatic when compared to the situation in the mid-1970s, when it was possible to argue that constitutional bills of rights were increasingly being abandoned.[93] Indeed, after an extensive survey of the role of the judiciary under the constitutions of African Commonwealth countries, Professor B. O. Nwabueze was able to conclude, in 1977, that, despite the existence of fundamental rights in their constitutions, not a single statute had been declared unconstitutional by the courts of Zambia, Kenya, Tanzania or Botswana.[94] Although that study pointed to a heritage of legal positivism, the statutory exclusion of the courts' jurisdiction, expatriate judges and English legal education as causes of the judiciary's failure creatively to protect fundamental rights, it did not consider the impact of the international environment in which the imperatives of cold war alliances were more significant to a country's international standing than its internal human rights record.

Specific 'local' events – the end of an era of colonization, the unravelling of military dictatorships and the collapse of state socialism – coincided with and precipitated an increasing assertion of democratic principles in the international political arena. This development was closely associated with the growth of an international human rights movement and the increasing legitimation of bills of rights at both the regional and national level.[95] Tied to this was the emergence of constitutional review as the essential element in the institutionalization of individual human rights and the constitutionalization of bills of rights.[96] The development of these trends within international political culture is reflected in a number of different processes which together have produced what Karen Knop identifies as a new 'rights' strain in international legal discourse.[97] Five processes served to link this new 'rights' strain to the globalization of constitutionalism: (1) the domestic 'rights revolution' within post-war western democracies; (2) the transnationalization of constitutionalism in the emergence of regional human rights systems; (3) the international community's adoption of 'constitutional principles' in guiding particular processes of democratization; (4) the elevation of a respect for human rights as a precondition to regional security; and (5) the elevation of the need for good governance based on the rule of law as a precondition for effective economic development.

Governance, Democratic Transitions and Constitutional Principles
First, there was the resurgence of domestic constitutionalism – or rights revolution – in the post–Second World War period. This encompassed both the adoption of written constitutions incorporating bills of rights and constitutional review by independent judiciaries in a number of European states, as well as the resurgence of constitutional adjudication in the United States.[98] This domestic process was driven by a series of

social movements within western democracies, including the organized labour movement throughout Western Europe and the civil rights, free speech, anti-Vietnam war and feminist movements in the United States alone. Of these, the equal rights movement in the United States, as a consequence of a rising United States ideological and cultural hegemony, become a global model of individually defined rights. In many ways the left- and right-wing libertarian revolt against government interference in the 1990s may also be traced to shifts in international political culture related to the discrediting of state socialism. This development produced a greater emphasis on property rights, and particularly private property rights, in both the international and national discourse on fundamental rights. In part a response to and a consequence of international revulsion at the Holocaust and other Nazi atrocities, the heightened awareness of human rights within domestic politics after the Second World War coincided with and was stimulated by the development of an international human rights movement inspired by the adoption of the Universal Declaration of Human Rights by the United Nations General Assembly in 1948.[99]

Second, there was the initial transnationalization of constitutionalism. Rooted in this same historical period, this process finds its inception in the development of a regional system of human rights protection launched by the Council of Europe in 1950 with the adoption of the European Convention on Human Rights. Unlike the aspirational Universal Declaration on Human Rights and even subsequent regional systems, the European Convention established specific institutions for its enforcement, including the European Commission on Human Rights and the European Court of Human Rights. While the jurisdiction of the European human rights machinery in Strasbourg was significantly enhanced by the adoption of the 'optional clause' of Article 25 of the Convention, which enabled parties to the Convention to accept the Commission's and Courts' jurisdiction over individual complaints brought against those states by their own citizens, it has been through the jurisprudence of the European Court of Justice that the European Convention on Human Rights has been truly transnationalized.

With jurisdiction to review national legislation rooted in the pre-eminence of Community Law in terms of the Treaty of Rome,[100] which established the European Economic Community (now European Union), the European Court of Justice has recognized that Community Law is bound to respect a higher unwritten community law 'based on the constitutional traditions of (not *one*, but *all*) the member states, as well as on such international treaties as the European Convention on Human Rights to which all the members of the Community have adhered'.[101] Although the notion that community law could override domestic constitutional rights was initially resisted – for example, when the German Constitutional Court struck down Community Law as inconsistent with the fundamental rights provisions of the German Constitution[102] – the assertion of a higher unwritten community 'bill of rights' by the European Court of Justice was formally confirmed by the European Community's political branches with the adoption by the European Parliament, the Council of Ministers and the Commission of a Joint Declaration on Fundamental Rights. The parties to the Declaration noted the 'prime importance they attach to the protection of fundamental rights, as derived in particular from the constitutions of the Member States and the European Convention for the Protection of Human Rights and Fundamental Freedoms', and stressed their commitment to respect these rights 'in the exercise of their powers and in pursuance of the aims of the European Communities'.[103]

A third development was the adoption of a set of 'constitutional principles' by the Western Contact Group on Namibia,[104] establishing a minimum framework as a precondition for an internationally acceptable resolution of the Namibian conflict. This was the international community's first application of substantive principles, beyond a simple exercise of self-determination through a national plebiscite, in the context of decolonization. While the notion of an internationally acceptable constitutional framework guiding the work of constitution-making bodies may be traced back to the relationship between the Allied powers and the constitution-making bodies of Germany,[105] Italy and Japan[106] after the Second World War, there was no attempt in these cases explicitly to codify specific constitutional principles. A similar and more explicit process of constitutional guarantees was developed in the context of international involvement in creating new constitutional orders in Cyprus in 1960 and Bosnia in 1995.[107] Although tied to foreign occupations and/or guarantees following international interventions, these experiences provided the genesis of the notion of internationally recognized constitutional principles as a means to support and frame the negotiation of local conflicts.

Later incorporated into the United Nations Security Council's peace plan for Namibia, the 1982 Constitutional Principles included both a process for constitution-making through a democratic election and the establishment of a Constituent Assembly, as well as a set of principles to guide the Constituent Assembly in its formulation of the constitution. These principles included: the supremacy of the constitution; an electoral democracy; a declaration of fundamental rights including rights to equality and the protection of property; and a right to judicial enforcement of these rights. While the newly elected Constituent Assembly unanimously resolved, at its first meeting, to adopt these principles as a 'framework to draw up a constitution for South West Africa/Namibia', it has been widely argued that 'as part and parcel of Security Council Resolution 435' the 1982 Constitutional Principles had become 'binding on all members of the United Nations, as well as on the internal political parties'.[108] The argument that the Constitutional Principles incorporated in the UN peace plan for Namibia through Security Council Resolution 632 of 1989[109] continues to bind the Namibian legislature as they form the 'conditions of Namibian statehood'[110] seems incorrect as a principle of international law, since it would clash with the principle of self-determination. The importance of this argument, however, lies in its understanding of the role of this mechanism as an attempt to shape the progress of constitutional transformations in the post-colonial context. It was this understanding of the role of constitutional principles that allowed the National Party government to relinquish the constitution-making power to an elected body in which it would be in the minority, while believing that the interests of its constituents would be protected. Francois Venter, who served as a National Party adviser and as a member of the Technical Committee on Constitutional Issues to the Multi-Party Negotiating Council, argued that the Constitutional Principles appended to South Africa's 1993 Interim Constitution provided the basis for an analysis from which 'an almost complete picture, though not the exact wording, of the new constitutional text emerges'.[111] While this characterization of the constitution-making role of the Constitutional Assembly did not prove strictly true – and despite the contested nature of the claim that the constitutional principles should have some limiting effect on future constitutional change[112] – it is important to note the significance of this mechanism in enabling democratically-elected constitution-making bodies to be formed in both Namibia and South Africa.

Fourth was the development of the CSCE's human rights system, particularly through the follow-up process of intergovernmental conferences provided for in the Helsinki Final Act.[113] Most significant of these was the Vienna Follow-up Meeting, which lasted from 1986 to 1989. Taking place in the context of transformation within the Soviet Union under Gorbachev, the Vienna Meeting saw a dramatic breakthrough on issues of human rights, with agreement on the holding of conferences to address the 'human dimension of the CSCE' and the establishment of the Human Dimension Mechanism to deal directly with allegations of failure by a party to uphold its human dimension commitments.[114] Moving beyond a traditional human rights framework, the Copenhagen Meeting of the Conference on the Human Dimension agreed that 'pluralistic democracy and the rule of law are essential for ensuring respect for all human rights and fundamental freedoms'.[115]

Finally, a fifth and significant development in the African context was the World Bank's 1989 conclusion following a three-year study of Africa's economic malaise, that no economic strategy would reverse Africa's economic decline unless political conditions in the continent improved. This conclusion, placing the blame for economic decline on the lack of public accountability and disrespect for individual rights, pointed directly to a new focus on the rule of law as an essential component of good governance.[116] By the late 1990s, approximately seventy-eight per cent of all conditionalities imposed by the international financial institutions in loan agreements and structural adjustment programmes were aimed at legal reform and the propagation of 'the rule of law'.

GLOBALISM, CONSTITUTIONALISM AND THE 'RULE OF LAW'

Advocacy of the rule of law and the promotion of constitutionalism emerged as a major part of international development assistance and programmes in the 1990s. Well over a billion dollars is being spent in 'exporting what is called "the rule of law"'[117] by a host of different institutions from non-government organizations through to the United Nations. Programmes range: from that of the Ford Foundation, which has historically supported social movements struggling for democratic rights; through the United States Agency for International Development's programmes 'designed to support the creation of legal and political environments that will promote processes of democratization and market-based reform',[118] in the former Soviet Union; to the World Bank's Economic Law Reform Project launched in October 1994 to assist China in the reform of its legal framework.[119]

For participants in this rule of law advocacy community, there seem to be few questions about the substantive content and consequences of adopting the rule of law. The First Global Rule of Law Conference, held in July 1994 in Washington, DC, was told that 'not only is there international legal agreement on what the rule of law means, but international legal agreement on the obligations of states to protect those rights for its citizens'.[120] Addressing the audience as people 'who have been on the ground in country after country carrying out the "Rule of Law" programs which are changing the lives of millions around the world', the Hon. Mark L. Schneider said: 'I know that you share my conviction that movement toward the rule of law is one of the most important factors in determining a country's progress ... The extent of access to justice to protect one's rights is a good indicator of the achievement of real democracy.'[121] For critics 'this is the 1960s "law and development" movement all over again, only now operating on a global scale, with immense resources',[122] but with all the same assumptions about modernization, progress and the nature of democracy.

While the imperial march of the 'rule of law' assumes a notion of democracy based on a ' "symmetrical" and "congruent" relationship between political decision-makers and the recipients of political decisions',[123] the exact parameters of this newly hegemonic principle within international political culture remain deeply contested. While Louis Henkin deems it possible to define seven principal demands of constitutionalism: (1) popular sovereignty; (2) constitution as supreme law; (3) political democracy and representative government; (4) limited government based on the separation of powers and an independent judiciary; (5) respect for and guarantees of individual rights; (6) institutions to monitor and ensure respect for the constitutional blueprint; and (7) respect for self-determination,[124] there are vast differences in how these principles may be framed or what effects they may have on the distribution of power in society.

Local Constitutions and a Globalized Constitutionalism
Despite widely differing notions of the role to be played by law and constitutionalism in political reconstruction, and even the tendency in comparative discussions of constitutions and constitution-making to emphasize the historical uniqueness of individual national constitutions and the futility of the imposition of 'foreign' constitutional formulations,[125] it may be argued that the vast majority of the world's constitutions reflect the appropriation of a heterogeneous range of constitutional principles from the 'prevalent international political culture'.[126] Some analysts dismiss the significance of the normative impact of this constitutionalist tradition, arguing that in many cases constitutions – particularly in the Third World, especially Africa – are merely symbolic and bear no relation to reality within the particular polity;[127] but Said Arjomand argues that constitutions are important social realities and, even when suspended or breached in practice, 'they delegitimize governments and constitute normative assets for the opposition'.[128]

The international revival of constitutionalism in the last decade of the twentieth century provides the grounding for Arjomand's argument, yet it remains necessary to trace both the general parameters of this new formulation of international political culture and to examine its engagement within the specific contours of South Africa's constitution-making process. The end of the cold war, the extension of human rights at both the regional and international level, and the recognition by international agencies such as the World Bank that a country's economic success may be in part related to the state of governance[129] provide important markers in the changing international environment. Indeed, this new international situation may not only have made the democratic transition possible, as F. W. de Klerk argued in 1990,[130] but the timing also reinforced particular political options, shaping the options of the participants in the constitution-making process.

It is within this general context then that the African National Congress's constitutional principles were first developed and in which the African National Congress sought the adoption of an internationally recognized framework for negotiations in South Africa. Likewise, the apartheid regime saw the opportunity of gaining international recognition of even a modified version of its racially-based 1983 Constitution collapse with the adoption of the Harare Declaration[131] and its subsequent incorporation into the UN Declaration on Apartheid in 1989.[132] While the various parties to the South African conflict would continue to clash over the nature and content of the political transition away from apartheid, in wider perspective the broad outlines of this transition were framed by the international context and the specific crystallization of the interaction between local and international processes.

Whether we understand this crystallization of possibilities as a product of foreign imperialism, the harmonization of local and international understandings, or alternatively as a hybridity between international consensus and local conflicts will depend to a large degree on our perspective on and understanding of local outcomes. If we view these outcomes solely in terms of the distance the major parties moved from their respective visions of apartheid and people's democracy to the embracing of constitutional democracy, then we may be tempted to view the outcome as dominated by an imperial framework in which the world is being progressively Americanized. If, however, we view these outcomes from the perspective of the debates and negotiations which dominated their formulation, then we may be tempted to argue that indeed there has been a progressive harmonization of views in which constitutionalism is adopted internationally and locally as an option most conducive to resolving conflicts of governance.

Finally, however, it may be more productive to view these outcomes as the product of a continuing hybridization both internationally and locally. While the processes of globalization are driving people and places into increasingly deeper interaction, in which conflicts are conducted within an increasingly common vocabulary of strategies and tactics, persistent differences – in resources, perspectives, understandings, desires and imaginations – require and allow a myriad of applications of similar and different, compatible and incompatible forms of governance – all bundled and presented as meeting the demands and standards of a globalized constitutionalism.

CHAPTER 4

CONSTITUTIONAL STRATEGIES

If apartheid, and the transnational social movement formed in opposition to it, helped shape the international political culture of the late twentieth century, how did South Africans come to embrace this culture of constitutionalism as a means to transcend their own bitter conflicts? Although law was central to the creation and maintenance of apartheid, reliance on law and the judiciary to overcome apartheid and its legacy was by no means a logical outcome of the struggle against apartheid. The dismantling of discriminatory laws and extension of democratic rights to the majority of South Africans had become a central demand of the international community from the mid-1970s, but the notion of a justiciable constitution as a necessary part of an internationally acceptable post-apartheid order would only come much later.

Despite the obvious internationalization of the question of apartheid and the struggle against it, the dominant view of South Africa's political transition is that it was a local 'miracle'.[1] Accounts of participants in the negotiations[2] and even the semi-official history of the constitution-making process now assert that there was no external role in this process.[3] Of course this is formally correct. Unlike other processes of decolonization in Africa, there was no formal role for external parties, whether foreign states or international organizations; rather, the negotiations and constitution-making process were conducted as purely South African affairs. The problem with this 'correct' version of history is that it fails to acknowledge or understand that, in the post-imperial, post-colonial age, the modes of international interaction have changed.[4] Indeed, the formal exclusion of foreign participation included, in the case of the South African Constitutional Assembly which produced the final 1996 Constitution, a specific prohibition on foreign advisers, as compared to the earlier negotiated process in which foreign advisers at times played significant parts – such as that played by Inkatha Freedom Party (IFP) adviser Mario Ambrosini.[5] As Christina Murray, one of the constitutional advisers to the Constitutional Assembly observed, the effect of this ban was that foreigners got real 'hearings' programmed into the Constitutional Assembly's program, while local 'experts' remained silenced unless they worked for a political party.[6] Thus, instead of direct participation, in which foreign or colonial states act as mediators or official observers – let alone as the conveyors of completed constitutions and formal political status – the new globalism involves processes of interactive exchange and the marking of boundaries, processes both more subtle and possibly more pervasive than the earlier forms of direct engagement.

Instead of envisioning international political culture as determinative, this chapter considers the historical legacies and the responses of the major political players in South Africa's democratic transition in order to understand how domestic, or local, actors initiate the processes of incorporation – political and ideological – so central to a successful constitutional transformation. Before embarking on this exercise, however, it is necessary to address a number of obvious alternative explanations. First, it may be argued that the embrace of judicial review is the product of South Africa's own particular constitutional history. But, as I have argued, this explanation must confront a history in which judicial review was explicitly rejected.[7] Second, the anti-apartheid movement's appeal to human rights and the old regime's commitment to protect property and minority rights may be seen as the basis of an 'élite pact', of which the judiciary, empowered with constitutional review, could be seen as the guarantor. This explanation faces two difficulties. On the one hand, the history of the transition demonstrates that the process of negotiations was accompanied by unprecedented levels of violence and political mobilization, belying a notion of simple consensus. Rather it indicates a constant struggle for political advantage and the fragmentation of power which required political accommodation under the threat of mutual destruction. On the other hand, the struggles over the scope, content and meaning of constitutional guarantees, as well as the structure and appointment of the judicial organs, indicate the limits of any actual mutual trust in, or even 'imagined' reliance on, the judiciary. Third, the turn to constitutionalism could be understood as reflecting a fundamental faith in law and the judiciary rooted in the law's impartiality, a joint faith shared by the majority of South Africans – oppressed and oppressor alike. As I have argued, such faith would be a surprising product of a system in which law and the courts were used as the basic building blocks and enforcers of apartheid's discriminatory and oppressive policies.[8] Furthermore, such a belief would have to accommodate the fact that as late as 1985, neither of the two major players in the negotiated transition – the African National Congress and the National Party – was even close to accepting the notion of constitutional supremacy. Even Kader Asmal, who argues that the African National Congress (ANC) was able to draw on a 'much richer vein of historical support for its adoption' of the notion of constitutional supremacy, acknowledges that both the major parties only came to this position in the run up to negotiations.[9] Thus, the constitutional history of South Africa and the history of apartheid and even the struggle against apartheid make it clear that neither early path determination nor faith in the law is an adequate explanation for the constitutionalist shift that occurred in the late 1980s and early 1990s. Instead, this chapter will consider the historical, political and international sources which may explain this shift.

Explanations for South Africa's dramatic shift to democratic constitutionalism are now being constructed in order both to understand and to justify the juridification of South Africa's democratic transition. Central to these efforts is the theme of negotiations: from the first meetings between the apartheid government and their prisoner – Nelson Mandela;[10] to contacts with the exiled ANC leadership;[11] and then on to the series of minutes,[12] accords,[13] understandings[14] and ultimately constitutions[15] that are today the history of South Africa's democratic transition. While the story of the negotiations is both extremely important in its own right and essential to the creation of post-apartheid South Africa's founding myth of mutual discovery and national reconciliation, it fails to explain the turn to constitutionalism which so marks the outcome of this 'negotiated revolution'.[16] The stories of negotiation explain in part why South Africa embarked on a process of democratic transition when it did, and even show how the different parties managed to sustain the transition through the bleakest of moments. Perhaps even more significantly, they demonstrate how much the success of the democratic transition was based upon the vast experience of negotiating developed from the early 1970s, with the emergence of the independent trade union movement, in struggles over community boycotts and forced removals.[17] This process is personified in the character of Cyril Ramaphosa, a lawyer who gained his negotiating experience as Secretary-General of the National Union of Mineworkers and became the ANC's chief negotiator and finally Chairman of the Constitutional Assembly. What is left to be explained is how the notion of constitutional supremacy enters and becomes central in enabling and shaping the democratic transition.

TURNING TO CONSTITUTIONALISM

The simplest explanation is to argue that the political players realized that neither party could achieve its aims without some form of settlement, and thus there emerged the political will necessary for the acceptance of democratic constitutionalism as the guiding motif of a new South Africa.

However, if we look to mid-1985, less than ten years before the adoption of the 1993 Constitution, we see that both major political players in the South African context held positions that were inimical to even the notion of a bill of rights and judicial review. Furthermore, this suggestion must be squared with the reality that, only a few years before the adoption of the 1993 Constitution, such a turn to the judiciary seemed unthinkable. In fact, the ANC continued to question the legitimacy of the South African judiciary, accusing them in official policy statements, as late as 1989, of being 'accomplices of murder, abduction and torture' and suggesting that the death sentence was being meted out 'so as to quench the judicial thirst for the blood of the Blacks'.[18] On the one hand, then, the African National Congress, holding its second National Consultative Conference, or 'council-of-war',[19] in mid-June 1985, committed itself to stepping up the 'all-round political and military offensive … directed at making apartheid unworkable and the country ungovernable'[20] in order to pursue the 'aim of seizure of power by the people through a combination of mass political action and armed struggle'.[21] On the other hand, the National Party Government responded to the popular uprisings which had began in late 1984 by declaring a limited state of emergency from mid-1985 and engaging in large scale repression and military occupation of the black townships – which despite the massive violation of human rights failed to end the insurrection.[22] Instead, 'by May 1986 South Africa was mired in an unstable and very violent impasse'.[23]

The unlikelihood of democratic constitutionalism as the basic conception of democratic governance in a future South Africa was reflected also, in mid-1985, in the basic goals and understandings of the opposing parties. On the one hand, the ANC's policy statements demonstrated a commitment to and particular understanding of people's power. Furthermore, most activists in the movement in this period understood the call for people's power in terms of notions of democratic centralism,[24] which provided the justification for state socialism and one-party states, which at that time were the prevalent state form of many of the ANC's closest allies. Nevertheless, others within the movement retained a conception of people's power consistent with parliamentary and majoritarian democracy,[25] which also accorded with the post-colonial experience of other African countries. Common to and implicit in all these conceptions, however, was the unrestrained authority of a 'democratic and sovereign parliament'.[26]

On the other hand, for over a decade the National Party government had claimed, in response to international pressure, to be moving away from apartheid, yet remained committed to retaining at least a group-based veto-power over political developments. After a series of visits to South Africa in the first half of 1986, the Commonwealth Eminent

Persons Group concluded that 'while the Government claims to be ready to negotiate, it is in truth not yet prepared to negotiate fundamental change, nor to countenance the creation of genuine democratic structures, nor to face the prospect of the end of white domination and white power in the foreseeable future'.[27] Instead, the National Party government's commitment to the 1983 Constitution's[28] construction of group rights as the fundamental principle of governance – implemented through a vague distinction between 'own' and 'general' affairs – would be retained well beyond F. W. de Klerk's 2 February 1990 public call for a justiciable bill of rights.[29] Dan O'Meara argues that, for at least two years following the beginning of the political opening in 1990, 'NP [i.e., National party] insiders saw the process of negotiations essentially as a simple extension and widening of the old "consociational" approach',[30] and that in fact group rights and consensus decision-making remained de Klerk's bottom line. It was this bottom line that was reflected in the 1983 Constitution and the extension of the franchise to 'Indians' and 'Coloureds' in a tricameral legislature. However, while purporting to be a move away from white minority control, the 1983 Constitution had retained specific mechanisms ensuring that power remained safely in the hands of the dominant white party. First, the running of government was effectively centralized under an executive State President with extraordinary powers in both the executive and legislative arenas. Second, all significant decisions within the legislature – such as the election of the President – were to be automatically resolved by the 4:2:1 ratio of White, Coloured and Indian representatives, which ensured that even if the 'Indian' and 'Coloured' houses of Parliament voted in unison, the will of the 'White' house would prevail. The exclusion of the African majority from this scheme and resistance from within the two target communities – Indian and Coloured – meant that the 1983 Constitution was practically stillborn. The escalation of resistance and rebellion which began in late 1984 and led to the imposition of repeated States of Emergency from mid-1985 sealed its fate.[31] It was in this context that the issue of protecting rights arose. Thus before addressing the central question – how the parties came to embrace constitutional supremacy – it is important to review South Africa's own, 'indigenous', rights tradition.

South Africa's Rights Tradition

The views of both the ANC and the National Party government must not be understood as rejecting claims of rights, but rather as a common understanding of representative democracy and parliamentary sovereignty shared by South Africans from all sides of the political spectrum. While both political groupings made claims of right as part of their respective political positions, neither assumed that these claims implied the right of the courts to challenge a duly passed Act of Parliament. This interpretation is evident in their common rejection of the position of the neo-liberal Democratic Party, which, drawing on the tradition of the Progressive Party and its Molteno Commission of Inquiry,[32] called for a justiciable constitution and a bill of rights to protect individual freedom and property rights in a federal system of government, even if it failed to give unconditional support to the democratic rights of the majority of South Africans.

If shared notions of legislative sovereignty did not preclude claims for rights, how do we understand the relationship between South African rights talk and its meanings before 1990, and the constitutionalist shift that took place then? Historically, the advocacy of human rights and demands for political and social rights kept the notion of inalienable rights alive within the anti-apartheid movement and within social movements inside South Africa. Two documents stand out as the products of these claims. First is the ANC's *African Claims in South Africa*, which reformulated the Atlantic Charter's principles of freedom and democracy from the perspective of Africans in South Africa.[33] Adopted by the ANC on 16 December 1945, this 'Bill of Rights ... made the revolutionary claim of one man one vote; of equal justice in the courts, freedom of land ownership, of residence and of movement ... claimed freedom of the press, and demanded equal opportunity in training and in work'.[34]

The Freedom Charter, adopted on 26 June 1955 by the Congress of the People at Kliptown, is the second expression of the aspiration of the majority of South Africans for a charter of rights.[35] The Congress of the People was launched by the Congress Alliance in 1954. It was not a single event but a series of discussions culminating in the adoption of the Freedom Charter. Professor Z. K. Mathews, who proposed the Congress of the People, called for 'a gathering to which ordinary people will come, sent there by the people. Their task will be to draw up a blueprint for the free South Africa of the future'.[36] While the Freedom Charter, with its guarantee of individual and collective rights, was to remain the blueprint of the ANC's vision for a post-apartheid South Africa, it in no way contradicted the organization's understanding of legislative supremacy. The assertion of both political and socio-economic rights in the Freedom Charter represented the claims of the people against the apartheid government and the promises of a future ANC government, not the justiciable rights of individuals or even collectivities.

While formulated in the language of rights, it must be recognized that the substance of these claims was for equal treatment and did not include a claim for the constitutional protection of rights, nor for the constitutional empowerment of the judiciary as the guardian of rights. Instead, it was assumed that these rights would be upheld by the courts as the legal rights of citizens once the legislature removed all discriminatory laws – such as the 1913 Land Acts and franchise restrictions – which prevented the exercise of self-evident common law rights. It must, however, also be recognized that, as human rights claimants, the authors of both the *African Claims* document and the Freedom Charter did not apply themselves to the problem of how these rights would be enforced; rather they focused on demanding the recognition of rights they were denied. Neither the *African Claims* document nor the Freedom Charter mentions the enforcement or even entrenchment of the rights claimed; rather it is assumed that a sovereign and democratic government would both recognize and uphold the people's rights.

The first claim for a justiciable bill of rights in the contemporary period comes surprisingly enough from within the 'bantustan' system. Speaking at the Progressive Party Conference in September 1973 – in the wake of the largest workers' strikes of the era – Chief Executive Councillor of KwaZulu, Chief Gatsha Buthelezi, proposed that the 'bantustan' constitutions 'should have human rights constitutionally safeguarded and placed beyond the reach of fleeting majorities'.[37] He also suggested that 'such judicial control of power would eliminate many fears from many a breast among our minority groups ... [and] if the homelands ended up in a federation, we would welcome the establishment by all States of a common constitutional court to interpret, enforce and expand these civil rights'.[38] In fact, it was to be the adoption of bills of rights in the Ciskei and Bophuthatswana 'bantustans' in the 1980s that provided the first hesitant and often confusing experiments with constitutional review of a bill of rights by South African courts in the modern era.[39] While the courts began to demonstrate a greater willingness to implement these documents after 1990, some of the early decisions provide an extremely incoherent account of the standards to be applied in constitutional interpretation.[40] Significantly, the acceptance of justiciable bills of rights in these apartheid-created entities did not include an adoption of constitutional supremacy; rather, these bills of rights were entrenched statutes subject to amendment by supreme legislatures.

Although this brief foray into South Africa's rights tradition does not adequately recognize the common law sense of legal rights which remained a central part of South Africa's legal tradition, it does indicate that 'rights talk' was framed in the language of claims of right. It was not linked to the broader notion of constitutional supremacy, which emerged in the late 1980s and 1990s as a central component of the international political culture of democracy and human rights. What, then, is the significance of South Africa's rights tradition? First, it provides a legitimate historical basis for building an indigenous culture of rights in which a 'rights consciousness'[41] may be built and supported by acknowledging the claims of right which characterized the struggle against apartheid. Second, this history has already been repeatedly used to justify the constitutional shift to a bill of rights and constitutional supremacy itself. Even the history of 'bantustan' bills of rights and the original acceptance of constitutional supremacy by the Orange Free State Republic were presented as sources for the acceptance of human rights by the old order.[42]

Changed Circumstances, Changing Imperatives

According to Jeremy Sarkin, a prolific writer on the South African constitutional transition, the 'new constitutional order ... must be seen to be the result of several factors: the strength of the old order during the negotiating process, the old order's suspicion of the new environment, the adherence of the ANC to the notion of fundamental rights, and the strong belief ... that ethnicity and division, ought not be part of a post-apartheid South Africa'.[43] Implicit in this argument is the mutual discovery of a justiciable constitution as a means to resolve two concerns or goals – the old order's fear of the new environment and the ANC's commitment to fundamental rights. This comports with the description given by Albie Sachs, who argues that the notion of a bill of rights in South Africa had, until around 1987, 'usually been projected ... as serving as a mechanism to ensure that if one day, majority rule was indeed established in South Africa, the property, privileges, power and positions of the white minority would not be disturbed in any way'.[44] In fact, at a conference organized under the auspices of the Society of University Teachers of Law at Pretoria University in 1986, even John Dugard, a long-standing supporter of a bill of rights for South Africa, expressed concern that those 'who have suffered long outside the protection of the law are now unwilling to see their oppressors brought within the protection of the law',[45] and thus advocated the immediate adoption of a limited bill of rights as a strategic means to protect human rights through what he saw as an inevitable shift in political power. Others at this meeting advocated different roles for a bill of rights: from being a simple limitation on government power; to an aspirational standard against which government action could be measured; to the creation of a 'socially activist document, in which the very real inequalities in our society were recognized, confronted and sought to be overcome'.[46] Even here, constitutional supremacy was not assumed.

Furthermore, the notion that the ANC was committed to fundamental rights protected in a bill of rights is, according to Sachs, the product of an internal ANC discussion that began at a meeting of exiled members, organized by the Constitutional Committee of the ANC in Zambia in 1987. Even then, Sachs speaks of the trepidation he felt in arguing at that meeting for a bill of rights based on the principled reason that a future government could not always be trusted, rather than on merely tactical and strategic grounds.[47] In fact, even after this meeting the ANC continued to refer to the acceptance of an entrenched bill of rights in purely strategic terms – as a means to assure those who would fear the violation of human rights under majority or democratic rule. It is also clear that the ANC embraced the notion of individual rights in this period as a strategic means to argue against the notions of group and minority rights which were the basis of the apartheid regime's proposals. Although strategic reasons for entrenching rights – including the recognition that the white minority would refuse to negotiate a transition without some guarantees of the outcome[48] – may explain the constitutionalist shift that takes place over this period, a broader understanding of the turn to constitutionalism, which goes beyond the protection of rights and embraces constitutional supremacy over the very distribution and allocation of power within the state and among the different branches and levels of government, comes from placing the decisions of the parties in the changing international political context of the late 1980s.

Despite the tradition of rights and the ANC's calls for the creation of a non-racial and democratic South Africa, the ANC's 'council-of-war' conference at Kabwe, Zambia, in June 1985, placed negotiations low on its list of priorities: resolving that 'we cannot even consider the issue of a negotiated settlement of the South African question while our leaders are in prison'.[49] Yet it must also be recognized that it was at Kabwe that the leadership obtained two significant mandates from the membership which set the conditions for the transformation of the ANC's position. First, in response to the bloody mutiny at the ANC's Quatro Camp in Angola and complaints of brutality by ANC security personnel, there was a call for the creation of an internal code of conduct establishing standards of treatment as well as procedural guarantees for those accused of spying for the apartheid regime or of having committed criminal violations within the exiled ANC community. According to Albie Sachs, it was this concern and the effort to create an internal code of conduct based on acceptable international principles that directly introduced the concept of legality into ANC debates.[50] As a consequence, Zola Skweyiya, who had received a doctorate in law in the German Democratic Republic, was recalled from his posting as the ANC's diplomatic representative in Ethiopia and given the task of establishing a Legal Department.[51] Second, the issue of negotiations with the apartheid regime was formally raised and, although the conference clearly rejected the notion of unconditional talks, it provided a framework within which the possibility of talks could be explored. Following these developments, the decision was also made to establish a Constitutional Committee in the President's office. Created in January 1986, the Constitutional Committee was initially chaired by Jack Simons and drew on members of the Legal Department

77

– including Zola Skweyiya, Penwell Maduna, Teddy Pakane and later Bridget Mabandla – as well as two internationally recognized ANC legal academics – Kader Asmal and Albie Sachs.[52] With these internal developments, the ANC found itself well placed to respond to the dramatic changes taking place around it.

The launching of the Commonwealth mission to 'facilitate a process of dialogue for change'[53] in South Africa, placed negotiations on the international agenda and linked them to the further isolation of the apartheid regime through the debate over the imposition of economic sanctions. The ANC also came under increasing pressure – as contacts increased with Western governments which had not previously recognized the ANC and with various groupings from within South Africa – to declare its position on negotiations and to begin to formulate a vision of South Africa's future system of governance. Having observed the negotiations at Lancaster House which led to the independence of Zimbabwe in 1980, and also aware of the constitutional principles produced by the 'western contact group' on Namibia in 1982, the ANC was concerned not to have a future constitutional dispensation thrust upon it. Furthermore, the ANC was acutely aware of its own vulnerability in a changing world. Having experienced virtual exclusion from Africa with the closure of ANC military camps in Tanzania in 1969,[54] as well as the impact on its activities as a result of the March 1984 Nkomati Accord between Mozambique and South Africa,[55] the ANC was concerned at the danger of being excluded by either international or domestic developments.

By November 1986, when Oliver Tambo met with Mikhail Gorbachev in Moscow, it was becoming clear that internal developments in the USSR[56] would have an impact on the amount and form of future military support the ANC could expect from that quarter. This was confirmed after the third Reagan–Gorbachev meeting in December 1987, when the Communist Party of the Soviet Union (CPSU) Central Committee sent a confidential letter assuring the ANC that discussions with the Americans over the peaceful resolution of regional conflicts should not be construed as an indication of a withdrawal of 'solidarity with the liberation struggle of peoples'.[57] The beginning of talks linking the withdrawal of Cuban troops in Angola to the withdrawal of South Africa from Namibia clarified these concerns. It was immediately obvious that an Angolan–Namibian settlement would require the ANC to remove its military camps from Angola – further weakening the organization's capacity to support or lead a sustained armed insurrection inside South Africa. This made negotiations inevitable; the only question was when and under what conditions.

Responding to these developments already in early 1987, the National Executive Committee reiterated the ANC's 'commitment to seize any opportunity that may arise to participate in a negotiated resolution of the conflict',[58] and began to outline the ANC's vision of the future political order. Although the statement made a clear commitment to multiparty democracy – barring those parties organized to propagate 'ideas of fascism, racism and ethnicity' – it carefully linked the guarantee of individual rights to equal treatment and substantive equality, arguing that the 'transfer of power to the people must ... be accompanied by the democratisation of the control and direction of the economy so that indeed the people share in the wealth of our country'.[59] While the statement explicitly noted that the 'revolution will guarantee the individual and equal rights of all South Africans ... and include such freedoms as those of speech, assembly, association, language, religion, the press, the inviolability of family life and freedom from arbitrary arrest and detention without trial', it implied that these rights would be achieved by ensuring 'thorough-going democratic practice'.[60] In October 1987, the ANC released a 'Statement on Negotiations', in which the organization outlined its preconditions for negotiation.[61] Significantly, the statement also declared for the first time that, in order to guarantee the equality of South African citizens 'without regard to race, colour or ethnicity', the 'ANC accepts that a new constitution for South Africa could include an entrenched Bill of Rights to safeguard the rights of the individual'.[62] Rejecting the apartheid regime's call for a National Council[63] in which negotiations would be held based on the recognition of 'group' interests, and following its own statement on negotiations, the ANC was compelled, according to Zola Skweyiya, 'to explain and expand on its thinking on a post-apartheid blueprint for South Africa and a constitutional model occupied a central place in this post-apartheid strategy'.[64]

Another initiative would be a massive diplomatic effort aimed at framing the process of future negotiations. Given the framework established by the international 'Contact Group' on Namibia, the ANC recognized the importance of providing an internationally acceptable framework, and the advantage of having it adopted by the international community. This would be particularly important as a means to preclude an 'internal' settlement aimed at excluding the ANC. The apartheid government had in fact appointed a Special Cabinet Committee (SCC) in 1983 to investigate the constitutional position of Africans. The expansion of the SCC into a larger informal negotiating forum in mid-1985 was clear evidence of the regime's efforts to seek an 'internal' solution. The SCC would, in the words of State President P. W. Botha, 'enter into negotiations with black leaders who reject violence as a political solution',[65] an explicit exclusion of the banned political organizations including the ANC.[66] Again, the experience of the Smith regime's efforts to promote an internal settlement, including the creation of Zimbabwe-Rhodesia, with the hope of achieving international acceptability while continuing to exclude particular groups or parties from participation, was well understood by the ANC. While the ANC was aware that the Zimbabwean liberation movements were able to defeat the internal settlement with military power, the prospect of simultaneous changes on the international and national fronts seemed to preclude this option for South Africa and required that the ANC take the initiative.

The first product of this initiative was the ANC's publication in 1988 of a set of constitutional principles,[67] which, according to the 8 January 1989 National Executive Committee (NEC) Statement, were 'tabled for consideration by all the people of our country'.[68] Denying that they amounted to an ANC blueprint for a future constitution, Zola Skweyiya told a conference of Afrikaans lawyers and legal academics in Harare, Zimbabwe, in early 1989, that the 'ANC is of the opinion that the drafting of a constitution for a democratic nonracial South Africa can only be the task of elected representatives of all the people of our country in a constituent assembly'.[69] The second product was the Harare Declaration,[70] a set of principles produced by the ANC and adopted by the Organization of African Unity's (OAU) Ad Hoc Committee on Southern Africa in August 1989.[71] This document both outlined the minimum principles of a post-apartheid constitution acceptable to the international community and specified the procedural requirements of an acceptable negotiation process. The ANC, mainly in the persons of Oliver Tambo and Thabo Mbeki, waged an international campaign, having the Harare Declaration or its substantive equivalent adopted by the Non-Aligned Movement, the Commonwealth and the United Nations General Assembly.[72] The success of this strategy, however, had important and possibly unintended consequences for the ANC. On the one hand, the key benefit of linking ANC strategy to the recognition of an explicitly democratic and internationally recognizable framework was that it undermined both the possibility of a unilateral and 'limited democratization' process and presented, in its embrace of individual rights, a strategic counterweight to the apartheid regime's insistence on group rights. On the other hand, linking the ANC's vision of a future system of governance to the emerging international consensus on democratic and constitutional norms meant that the Harare Declaration and the Constitutional Guidelines were out of step with the understanding among activists of the ANC's rhetoric of a 'people's war', 'people's power' and 'ungovernability', which dominated the struggle in South Africa in the late 1980s.[73]

While this had important implications for the ANC's own vision of the future, the significance of this disjuncture for the organization's revolutionary programme should not be exaggerated. Ever since the adoption of the Green Book[74] in 1979, the ANC's strategic perspective was based on the primacy of political mobilization and the dynamics of the struggle articulated in terms of four distinct pillars of struggle: united mass action; underground organization; armed struggle; and the international isolation of the apartheid regime.[75] Articulating the preparation for and advent of negotiations as merely a particular terrain of struggle for which the recognized pillars of the struggle needed only to be reconfigured provided the key to convincing at least the organization's activists of the relationship between the different perspectives if not their mutual consistency. This is evident from the way in which the internal mass movement and ANC underground responded to these developments. In late 1989, despite 'extreme hostility among organizations and activists on the ground to the idea of negotiations',[76] the Mass Democratic Movement (MDM) – a stand-in for the restricted United Democratic Front – organized the Conference for a Democratic Future (CDF). Conceived as a 'way to bring organizations towards the idea of negotiations',[77] the CDF brought together a wide cross-section of anti-apartheid groupings, including the trade unions, churches and various political organizations, including: the black consciousness–aligned Azanian People's Organization (Azapo), the Pan African Congress–aligned Azanian Students Movement (Azasm) and the ANC-aligned MDM. The Democratic Party was invited, but attended as observers only. The organizers received a clear message from the ANC in Lusaka, through the underground, that the 'Harare Declaration was not to be presented as an ANC document but rather as an OAU document to be adopted by all'.[78] Yet, despite the fact that the meeting took place after the UN General Assembly's adoption of the Declaration on Apartheid, the nearly 5000 delegates at the CDF in Johannesburg 'still adopted the Harare Declaration because they understood it to be the ANC's version'.[79]

Publication of the 'Constitutional Guidelines for a Democratic South Africa' in mid-1988 thus marked an initial shift away from unrestrained legislative authority in the perspective of the South African liberation movement. By publicly committing itself to the adoption of a bill of rights enforceable through the courts, the ANC assured fellow South Africans and the world of its commitment to the introduction of judicial review.[80] Yet, despite this seeming acceptance of a constitutionally-entrenched bill of rights and the assumptions which may be drawn from this for the role of the judiciary, it is clear from the elaboration of these signals that at this time the ANC was still moving towards a full embrace of the notion of constitutional supremacy. In the paper – 'Towards a Bill of Rights in a Democratic South Africa' – which Albie Sachs delivered to the ANC In-House Seminar on Constitutional Guidelines held in Lusaka in early March 1988, he challenged the 'assumption in most current writing on a Bill of Rights … that its final watchdog should be a body of highly trained and elderly judges, applying traditional legal wisdom in what is considered a neutral and unbudgeable manner'.[81] Instead he argued, if the 'dog is to watch the interests of the formerly oppressed, it would have to have a totally different pedigree and training'.[82] While this could be interpreted as warning against placing a new bill of rights in the hands of the old-order judges, the paper makes it clear that Sachs was thinking of what he terms 'the important and delicate question of the relationship of a Bill of Rights to the legislative power of Parliament'.[83] Noting that the 'objective of a Bill of Rights should be to reinforce rather than restrict democracy', he argued that 'it is unthinkable that the power to control the process of affirmative action should be left to those who are basically hostile to it'.[84] Instead he conceded: 'In later years, when the foundations of a stable new nation will have been laid and when its institutions will have gained habitual acceptance, it might be possible to conceive of a new-phase Bill of Rights interpreted and applied by a "mountain-top" judiciary.'[85] According to this view, the Bill of Rights would be implemented by being 'entrusted to institutions that are democratic in their composition, functioning, and perspective, and that operate in a manifestly fair way under the overall supervision of the people's representatives in Parliament'.[86] Likewise, in January 1989 Zola Skweyiya described the Bill of Rights included in the Constitutional Guidelines as not only guaranteeing the fundamental rights of the citizen, but also 'the centrality of socio-economic liberties in the post-apartheid reconstruction policy'.[87] Furthermore, he linked the enjoyment of human rights in the post-apartheid era to social development, arguing that the 'transition from one stage of ... development to another, we hope will bring about broader rights and freedoms and stronger guarantees for their implementation and effective protection'.[88] Clearly, then, the architects of the ANC Constitutional Guidelines did not see the entrenchment of a bill of rights as altering the fundamental power of the democratically-elected legislature. However, given the participation of someone like Kader Asmal, who as a teacher of law at Trinity College in Dublin was well acquainted with the Irish Constitution and its functioning, it is clear that the notion of constitutional supremacy was not alien to the members of the ANC's Constitutional Committee, who must have understood the implications of their work. Yet, the focus was on a bill of rights, not the wider project of constitutionalism.

During the late 1980s, a number of academic and legal conferences were held, focusing on the specific contours of a post-apartheid order. Some of these conferences focused directly on the question of a bill of rights and served to bring together both progressive lawyers from inside South Africa and members of the ANC's Constitutional Committee, thus engaging the committee with longstanding debates within the South

African legal fraternity.[89] Two of these conferences stand out as fora in which the exposure to different positions began to mediate the ANC's perspective. First, at a conference organized by Louis Henkin and Jack Greenberg at Columbia University, several members of the ANC Constitutional Committee presented papers on aspects of the Bill of Rights. In ensuing discussions, these participants both explained the ANC's view and began to mediate their own understandings of these issues. This meeting also saw the participation of Pius Langa, President of the National Association of Democratic Lawyers, who would later co-ordinate meetings between the ANC and lawyers inside the country before himself joining the ANC Constitutional Committee.[90] Second, there was the now-famous Oxford conference organized by Ronald Dworkin, which for the first time brought South African judges together with some ANC lawyers.[91] In this case the then National Party Minister of Justice became aware that ANC lawyers might attend and demanded that the judges immediately return to South Africa. Significantly, the judges present caucused and refused to obey the Minister, staying on to meet ANC lawyers (Albie Sachs and Oliver Tambo were precluded because they were considered ANC politicians[92]) and progressive lawyers from inside South Africa, such as Pius Langa and Hugh Corder, with whom they might not have engaged in frank and open discussion in South Africa. At the same time, the ANC Constitutional Committee was expanding its own membership by incorporating a number of lawyers from inside South Africa who had long histories of representing opponents of apartheid in political trials or in the litigation that increasingly challenged apartheid laws – such as the pass laws – in the 1980s. After the unbanning of the ANC in early 1990, Pius Langa organized a number of lawyers, including both George Bizos and Arthur Chaskalson, to go to Lusaka to meet the ANC Constitutional Committee.[93] Chaskalson and Bizos were then incorporated into the committee. Chaskalson notes that he and George Bizos only joined the committee on the condition that they would not become members of the ANC and would remain 'independently minded'.[94] The first task given this newly-reconstituted committee, now chaired by Zola Skweyiya, was to draw up a proposed bill of rights and a new constitution for the ANC itself.[95]

The publication of two documents by the Constitutional Committee inside South Africa in 1990 introduced the ANC's constitutional ideas to the public as well as to the ANC's new legally-constituted membership. Significantly, the two documents demonstrated a dramatic recasting of the ANC's position. While claiming merely to implement the Constitutional Guidelines and the Freedom Charter – which is presented as the source for the Bill of Rights – these documents now clearly adopted constitutional supremacy as the premise of a new constitutionalism.

The document entitled 'What is a Constitution?' explicitly noted that the 'Constitution is the most important law of a country ... Parliament itself functions within the Constitution. The laws are made within the framework of the Constitution.'[96] Furthermore, the document introducing a proposed 'Bill of Rights for A New South Africa' now addressed the issue of implementation providing that 'the fundamental rights and freedoms contained in this Bill of Rights shall be guaranteed by the courts',[97] and that '[p]rovision shall be made for the establishment of a constitutional court'.[98] Significantly, in its introduction the document explicitly ties the ANC's proposals to the international human rights documents – from the Universal Declaration of Human Rights, through the International Covenants to the European Convention, African Charter and to foreign constitutions including explicitly the Indian, German, United States and Namibian Constitutions.[99] Thus the ANC made the journey from strategic engagement with international political culture in the last throes of the cold war to advocates of democratic constitutionalism. Whether it was the unintended consequence of linkage or the imperatives of a strategy which effectively prevented the ANC's exclusion as the 'new world order' dawned, the outcome was a commitment to constitutional supremacy that now had to be won both inside the ANC and outside.

From the apartheid regime's side, the need to give greater protection to human rights was only conceded as the country went into a spiral of economic decline and violent confrontation in the mid-1980s. The Minister of Justice, H. J. Coetzee, announced in April 1986 that he had requested the South African Law Commission 'to investigate and make recommendations regarding the definition and protection of group rights ... and the possible extension of the existing protection of individual rights'.[100] Despite recognizing the need to protect individual rights, this initiative remained within the apartheid paradigm of group rights, understood at this time as racial or ethnic group rights. Nor did it foresee the possibility of reducing the sovereign status of Parliament or adopting a supreme constitution. Significantly, after an extensive study of international law and human rights regimes – including specific reference to the protection of national minorities under the Helsinki Accords, which emerged from the Conference on Security and Co-operation in Europe[101] – the Law Commission concluded that it would be 'juridically unsound to adopt the standpoint that there are statutorily definable groups with statutorily definable "rights" in this country'.[102] Thus, between the time of its appointment in 1986 and the issuing of its first working paper in March 1989,[103] political developments internally and exposure to international frameworks had refocused the enquiry away from group rights and towards the adoption of an entrenched bill of rights, which could be applied by the courts to declare any laws or acts in conflict with the bill of rights invalid.[104] This development within the Commission also refocused the National Party government, which in 1991 issued its Manifesto for the New South Africa,[105] adopting the idea of 'a constitutionally guaranteed and justiciable bill of rights', protecting both 'the rights of all individuals and minorities defined on a non-racial basis'.[106]

While the major parties had thus come to embrace constitutional supremacy, it would only be jointly acknowledged with the adoption of the Declaration of Intent at the first meeting of the Convention for a Democratic South Africa (Codesa) on 21 December 1991. Here all the significant parties – except for Inkatha and the Bophuthatswana 'government', who refused to sign, and the Pan Africanist Congress, who had walked out of Codesa – adopted a set of principles which essentially conformed to the requirements of the Harare Declaration and the UN Declaration on Apartheid. Yet, they also included, separate from the reference to a bill of rights, the provision that 'the Constitution will be the supreme law and that it will be guarded over by an independent, non-racial and impartial judiciary'.[107]

CONSTITUTIONAL RESPONSES TO APARTHEID'S LEGACY

Apartheid was by definition premised on inequality. In contrast, the struggle against apartheid was premised on the promise of a future South Africa in which all people would enjoy equal rights and opportunities. Despite these high aspirations, the builders of a new South Africa face a formidable legacy of inequality, social dislocation and destitution.[108] From the beginning they understood that only if this legacy was confronted directly would the promise of equality in South Africa be realized. Moreover, the extreme forms of inequality apartheid embodied were not only the product of colonial dispossession and economic exploitation, but were entrenched by a system of racially-constituted barriers, which prevented black economic advancement and stripped many black communities and families of economic resources. Significantly, this process of destructive social engineering and dispossession was achieved not through extra-legal mechanisms but through the creation and implementation of apartheid laws by a racially-exclusive white parliament and state. It therefore seemed natural that a democratically-constituted and elected legislature would seek legislative means to deploy the power of the state to confront these past wrongs. This was the context in which the ANC thought about the responsibility of governance and framed its constitutional options.

Recognizing this potentially fundamental shift in the role of the state, the leaders of South Africa's white minority came, as they saw their hegemony collapse, to embrace notions of federalism, power-sharing, and the protection of rights as means to reduce and restrict the state's role in society.[109] Given a history of state lawlessness, the leaders of South Africa's democratic movement also recognized that a new democratic legislature and executive must be subject to the rights of the people. This principle motivated those within the ANC who became committed to the adoption of a bill of rights promised in the ANC Constitutional Guidelines.[110] However, the ANC's Guidelines stressed the need for a new constitutional order to empower an affirmative state to address the vast inequalities and deprivations which were to be inherited from the apartheid state. This tension – between the need for state intervention to remedy the inequalities created by the apartheid state and the need for protection against the abuse of state power – was manifest in the alternative approaches to constitutionalism and in the bills of rights originally proposed by the African National Congress[111] and the South African Law Commission.[112]

These two documents represent the most substantial exposition of the constitutional starting points of the opposing sides in 1990 and therefore formed the initial parameters of constitutional discussion in the South African transition. It is from the perspective of these starting points, that the contents of South Africa's 'interim' and 'final' Bills of Rights and consequently the parameters of a constitutional programme to address apartheid's legacy may best be considered. To understand the interaction between global and local contexts in the shaping of constitutional possibilities it is necessary to have a general comprehension of the respective strategies proposed in the two drafts.

Alternative Strategies to Confront Historical Injustice

The South African Law Commission's draft weighed strongly in favour of the protection of existing rights against future state action. This emphasis was evident in the focus of the first article of the draft, which asserted that all the

> rights set forth in this Bill are fundamental rights to which every individual and, where applicable, also every juristic person in South Africa is entitled in relation to legislative and government bodies, and save as otherwise provided in this Bill those rights shall not be circumscribed, limited, suspended or infringed by any legislative or executive or administrative act of any nature.[113]

Leaving aside the difficulties of constitutional interpretation that may arise from the description of all rights as fundamental and the reality of often-conflicting rights,[114] the Commission's primary emphasis on limiting the scope of state action had profound implications for programmes designed to address the vast inequalities a democratic government would inherit from apartheid. For example, the Law Commission's draft made no attempt to reach beyond the strictly formal notion of 'equality before the law'. The draft framed the right to equality before the law as a negative restriction on the activities of the state rather than as a positive right of each citizen to equal treatment or equal protection of the law. Although this negative interpretation was not cited as the exclusive meaning of the article,[115] nothing in the draft stressed the need to address the historic exclusion of the black majority by working towards equal participation in the society or even the lesser standard of equal opportunity.

The narrowness of the Commission's approach to equal opportunity was confirmed in its handling of the problem of private discrimination. Tackling this issue, the Commission simply asserted that

> no legislation or executive or administrative act shall directly or indirectly make available to an individual who or a group which merely on the ground of race or colour refuses to associate with any other individual group, any public or state funds to foster the creation or maintenance of such discrimination or exclusion.[116]

Under this formulation the state could not fund discriminatory action; however, at the same time the Commission proceeded to assert that the state could not 'compel individuals or groups to associate with other individuals or groups'.[117] This approach elevated, to constitutional status, a negative interpretation of the right to association – a right to dissociation – over the right to equality. Thus, while the state would be prohibited from funding discriminatory organizations and activities, the state would also be prohibited from outlawing or restraining private organizations that sought to limit their membership to certain groups, even if these limits were on grounds that were widely viewed as unacceptable, such as race and gender. The Law Commission assumed that a bill of rights should apply only to the relationship between the state and its citizens. However, given South Africa's history of racist exclusion and economic inequalities, a constitutional principle of equality unable to pierce the shield of a purported right of dissociation would have protected private racial discrimination.

Confronted with demands for affirmative or corrective measures requiring the state to address racial and economic inequalities, the Law Commission adopted a circumscribed and strategic view. It characterized affirmative action as usually linked to 'the recognition of socio-economic rights as fundamental rights'[118] and argued for the inclusion of a restricted form of affirmative action 'because idealism and enthusiasm for our new South Africa should not be dampened'.[119] The Commission's vision for constitutional provisions addressing apartheid's legacy was, however, limited to enabling the legislature voluntarily to adopt 'special programmes to guarantee that all members of society are afforded equal opportunities of realising their potential ... [and] involves the application of funds to give all citizens an equal position at the starting line as far as possible'.[120] The Commission's draft granted the highest legislative body the power, through the passage of

> legislation of general force and effect [to] introduce such programmes of affirmative action and vote such funds therefor as may reasonably be necessary to ensure that through education and training, financing programmes and employment all citizens have equal opportunities of developing and realising their natural talents and potential to the full.[121]

Thus the Law Commission would have restricted affirmative action to the adoption and implementation of legislative programmes 'of upliftment'; it effectively collapsed two different concepts – affirmative action and governmental development programmes – into one. No distinction was made between a legislative programme to address issues of homelessness, educational reform, job creation, etc., which are the normal responsibilities of a democratic government, and the Commission's notion of affirmative action. This lack of distinction was based on the Commission's presumption that any government programme to aid the poor, or to improve social conditions in a particular area, would amount to an unequal distribution of benefits to one or other racial group, since poverty would remain racially segregated. For the Law Commission, such programmes would be a violation of equal treatment and therefore need to be validated by an affirmative action exception to the constitutional guarantee of equal treatment. As stated in its Interim Report, the 'Commission's view of affirmative action is therefore not one of reverse discrimination or retribution, but a vigorous programme of upliftment and guarantees of equal opportunities'.[122]

The ANC's proposed Bill of Rights, on the other hand, introduced a constitutional vision of collective action to overcome South Africa's legacy of racial domination and inequality. This vision assumed a wider interpretation of the notion of equality, and both created, and incorporated a strategy for realizing, a constitutional duty – originally proposed in the ANC Constitutional Guidelines – actively to eradicate 'the economic and social inequalities produced by racial discrimination'.[123] Central to this vision was the guarantee of formal equality, asserting – in contradiction to the essence of all prior South African constitutions – that 'all South Africans are born free and equal in dignity and rights'.[124] Article 1 guaranteed that 'no individual or group shall receive privileges or be subjected to discrimination, domination or abuse on the grounds of race'.[125] Herein lies the clue to the ANC's wider conception of equality. If this were to be interpreted in isolation from the draft's other provisions as guaranteeing simply equal treatment, the proposal would fail to confront apartheid's imposed inequalities. However, when read in the spirit of the entire draft, it becomes clear that the conception of equality in the draft envisaged a process aimed at achieving equal opportunity, to be attained by addressing past discrimination, and maintained through the guarantee of non-discrimination and 'equal protection under the law'.[126]

The ANC's Draft strategy for attaining equal opportunity rested on five prongs. First, the Draft Bill of Rights guaranteed formal equality. Taken together with the guarantee of political rights[127] – including the entrenchment of multi-party democracy to be ensured through 'regular, free and fair' elections[128] – the promise of formal equality made it clear that legislative power would rest in the hands of the country's majority – a majority which had thus far been excluded from political participation. And although this power would be bounded by individual and collective rights guaranteed in a justiciable bill of rights, a democratically elected government would clearly have the power to introduce legislation and pass laws to improve the lot of the now enfranchised victims of apartheid.

Second, the ANC Draft proposed an explicit, constitutionally-mandated and protected process of affirmative action. Based on the principle of redressing past discrimination, Article 14 would have facilitated the creation of programmes to 'procure the advancement and the opening up of opportunities',[129] by both public and private bodies. The second clause of this article revealed the drafters' textured understanding of the notion of equality. In stating that 'any action taken in terms of the above [Article 14] shall not be deemed to contradict the principle of equal rights for all South Africans as set out in Article 1',[130] the draft makes it clear that the notion of equal treatment guaranteed by Article 1(2) and reiterated in the anti-discrimination provision in the section protecting children's rights[131] incorporated the prerequisite of equal opportunity. In fact, Article 14(2) was completely rewritten after it was pointed out that the wording of the earlier version, which stated that 'no provision of the Bill of Rights shall be construed as derogating from or limiting in any way the general provisions of this article',[132] was vague and subject to broad interpretation.[133] As the note to the new clause acknowledged, it 'was interpreted to mean that the principle of affirmative action would be so powerful as to override all personal rights and freedoms'.[134] This clarification makes it clear that the function of the affirmative action clause 'is to supplement and strengthen the equality clause, not to override other provisions of the Bill of Rights'. Thus Article 14's protection of affirmative action was designed to guarantee a process which would over time have confronted accumulated and structured patterns of inequality, while making it clear that the formal equality guaranteed by Article 1 was not a barrier to energetic action to redress apartheid's legacy.

Third, there was the adoption of a type of enhanced affirmative action principle in Article 15's mandate of 'positive measures'.[135] This section of the ANC Draft moved from a general assertion of the state's duty to promote both racial and gender equality to the inclusion of very specific mandates to transform the racial composition of the public service – including the 'defence and police forces and the prison service'.[136] It also made explicit the legislature's powers to enact laws to require 'nongovernmental organisations and private bodies to conduct themselves in accordance with the [articles'] principles'.[137] Provision was thus made for a constitutional mandate of positive obligations or enhanced affirmative action to be applied to private non-state action. Moreover, the inclusion of a duty to work towards the achievement of social and economic rights, implicit in the adoption of mandatory provisions requiring the state to take action to guarantee a 'progressively expanding floor of enforceable minimum rights',[138] provided the fourth prong in the ANC Draft's confrontation with apartheid's enforced inequalities. Although the inclusion of these socio-economic rights was understood as essential in confronting South Africa's vast inequalities, this prong of the ANC's Draft also promised that the new constitutional order would continue to be responsive to the rights and needs of the disadvantaged and less powerful beyond the necessary period of affirmative action. However, their application by the courts would be limited to a negative power to restrain interference with existing rights and as a means both to interpret legislation and to review subordinate legislation and administrative action.[139] Finally, Article 11(4) of the ANC Draft provided an explicit power to divert resources from the richer to the poorer regions of the country. Although this power is obviously related to the extension of a minimum floor of socio-economic rights, it had a distinct impact of its own in that it provided for the distribution of resources away from the so-called 'first world' parts of South Africa to the underdeveloped 'bantustan' regions that were the stepchildren of apartheid.

Emerging in the context of the preliminary negotiations for the democratic transition, the different drafts reveal the underlying conceptions the two sides had of the role of a bill of rights and constitutionalism in a post-apartheid South Africa. On the one hand, the government-sponsored South African Law Commission conceived of a bill of rights as a means to protect existing interests and social relations from future state interference. Adopting a nineteenth-century liberal conception of the relationship between the state and civil society, the Law Commission strove to protect individual citizens by imposing significant restraints on state action, particularly through its guarantees of civil and political rights. This was a welcome development in a context where state lawlessness had been the hallmark of government domination of the disenfranchised black majority. However, the only concession the Commission made to demands for a post-apartheid state to be constitutionally committed to addressing the legacy of apartheid was its reluctant acceptance of the state's duty to provide for the education of its citizens. This understanding is confirmed by the Law Commission's characterization of all rights as fundamental while simultaneously limiting their application to legislative and executive acts, that is, existing statutory provisions and prospective legislation or executive acts. Under this approach the Bill of Rights could not be applied to challenge existing common-law or customary-law rules that discriminate or violate any of its other provisions. It was this restricted notion of constitutionalism that revealed the essence of the Law Commission's approach. Instead of an embodiment of people's rights, the Bill of Rights proposed by the Law Commission would have built a wall between public and private action and in so doing have restricted the role of constitutional rights largely to protecting individuals and private interests from state interference. The consequence of this approach would have been to preserve areas of private activity from the process of legal and social transformation: in effect, protecting a privatized system of racial discrimination.

Taking a diametrically opposite approach, the ANC Constitutional Committee understood constitutionalism as a way both to enshrine rights and to direct state activity towards the achievement of the popular aspirations that infused the struggle against apartheid. While protecting individual autonomy from state interference by building protections against state lawlessness, the ANC Draft proposed the creation of a constitutional framework dedicated to the eradication of apartheid by exposing both public and private discrimination to legal attack. In its most innovative sections, the ANC Draft reached beyond the mere assertion of social and economic rights and attempted to frame so-called second and third generation rights – such as the rights to shelter and a clean environment – in a 'negative' way so as to make them justiciable in the same way as so-called first generation, or civil and political rights. Embracing an innovative constitutionalism, the ANC Draft tried both to empower the state and to place duties on the legislature to confront the legacy of apartheid. However, in one important aspect there was a convergence in the approaches of both the Law Commission and the ANC Constitutional Committee. Only in the areas of property and economic rights in the Law Commission's draft and in the area of workers' rights in the ANC Draft was emphasis placed on the recognition of individual and collective entitlements. Whether it was to restrain, or empower, both drafts retained a fundamentally statist approach to constitutionalism. Even the commitment to open government reflected in the ANC Draft's inclusion of a right to information was framed in limiting language, entitling recipients of the right only to 'all the information necessary to enable them to effective use of their rights'.[140]

Finally, the incompatibility of these opposing approaches to constitutionalism reflected both the conscious and unconscious goals of their authors. The Law Commission was engaged in an attempt to prevent the future Constitution and Bill of Rights from mandating a fundamental restructuring of the South African political economy. By restricting the role of a bill of rights to the creation of a protective wall between the state and private activity the Law Commission's proposals would have protected existing entitlements and deflected the impact of the shift in political power which was the consequence of the transition to democracy. On the other hand, the ANC Draft proposed to empower a future state to confront the inequalities created by the apartheid system. By requiring all South Africans – in both their public and private activities – to confront the separation and inequalities imposed by apartheid, the ANC's proposed Bill of Rights aimed to provide the constitutional basis for nation-building – in which the task of addressing South Africa's vast inequalities would serve to build a future citizenry with a common sense of belonging.[141] In this view it is only by confronting the legacy of apartheid that South Africa would be able to move towards the creation of a single but diverse nation. It was with these alternative visions that the main parties entered negotiations and the constitution-making process.

Entering Negotiations
The apartheid government's decision to launch a political opening by unbanning the ANC and other banned organizations in February 1990 brought the two sides into public engagement for the first time. However, when Codesa collapsed in mid-1992, the escalating communal violence led many to fear that a peaceful transition and a stable constitutional order was beyond South Africa's reach.[142] Faced with the consequences – social upheaval, mass action and escalating violence – of a failed Codesa, the negotiating parties entered into a series of bilateral negotiations which resulted in the formation of a multiparty negotiating forum. It was to be this body that would thrash out the interim Constitution, which went into force on 27 April 1994, as South Africans were taking part in their first ever democratic elections.

CHAPTER 5

CONSTITUTIONALISM IN THE DEMOCRATIC TRANSITION

Understanding the impact of globalization or international processes on the 'internal' dynamics that led to South Africa's constitutionalist shift does not however explain how such dominant international or global models are locally incorporated. Amidst the ideological celebration of markets, electoral democracy and justiciable rights – which were the products of the democratic transitions which dominated the last decade of the twentieth century – an open question remained as to the impact and sustainability of this newly globalized constitutionalism. While globalists of all stripes alternately celebrate, acknowledge or deplore the impact of global forces and developments on local or national possibilities, there is little discussion of how global models and norms play out in the local context. Exploring the interaction between global and local within the context of political reconstruction in South Africa, however, provides a way to explore the impact and incorporation of international political culture in a local context. By focusing on the dynamics of the constitution-making process as a particular source of pressures mediating the local incorporation of transnational norms, this chapter identifies the special role that constitutionalism may play in enabling a democratic transition.

In exploring this question, this chapter briefly considers what constitution-making options were available to South Africans, or argued for by the contending parties in the transition. Second, the chapter considers the relationship between the substantive aims of the different parties and the constitution-making processes they each advocated, as well as the role of political mobilization in either shaping debates or placing issues on the agenda at the negotiations. Finally, the chapter focuses on both the sources and significance of specific constitutional strategies and mechanisms that provided the opportunity to drag this particular camel – a country slipping into civil war and economic chaos in which the political leaderships seemed to be steadily losing their authority over their supporters or combatants – through the eye of the needle.

SOVEREIGN POSSIBILITIES

The end of the cold war and the recognition by international agencies such as the World Bank that a country's economic success may be in part related to how it is governed[1] are important markers of the changing international environment in which South Africa's constitution-making proceeded. The prevailing international situation may not only have made the democratic transition possible, as F. W. de Klerk argued in 1990,[2] but the timing also reinforced particular political options, including options in the constitution-making process. The post–Second World War period has seen a variety of internationally recognized constitution-making processes. These ranged from General MacArthur's imposition of a draft constitution on the Japanese legislature[3] or the supervised post-war constitution-making bodies in Germany[4] and Italy, to the emergence of India's elected Constituent Assembly, which, despite its initially limited powers, emerged as a fully sovereign, unrestricted, constitution-making body.[5] But the vast majority of constitutions adopted since the Second World War, particularly in the context of decolonization, involved the negotiated transfer of political power from a foreign state to local bodies. Crucial to these constitution-making processes was the role of the colonial power in formally passing new post-colonial constitutions. For the respective political élites – both colonial and indigenous – the issue of constitution-making generally took second place to the transfer of political power, particularly where the post-colonial constitution granted sovereign powers to the new legislature. Even where the post-colonial constitution gave the judiciary the power of constitutional review, and a justiciable bill of rights, as in Kenya, the impact of constitutionalism was limited by both positivist traditions within the judiciary and the political dominance of the legislature in which the special majorities required for constitutional amendment could be easily attained.[6]

During most of the cold war era, the outgoing colonial power could actively frame the terms of the independence constitution before holding a national plebiscite in a country on the eve of independence. Indeed, in former British colonies, the Westminster Parliament formally enacted each post-independence constitution. Although the process of constitution-making in these cases often involved negotiations between the colonial power and representatives of the nationalist movement (and in the case of Zimbabwe, even with representatives of opposing political factions within the colony), the former colonial power retained the initiative of framing the first post-independence constitution.[7] While the Zimbabwean parties left the Lancaster House negotiations in London with an agreement that led to the country's first democratic elections and independence, the Constitution inherited from that process and enacted by the British Parliament was replete with compromises – such as the ten-year guarantee of white seats – which the majority parties considered a necessary but temporary imposition. As soon as the ten-year period had expired, the Constitution was amended to remove the offending sections – however, long before then the practice of constitutional amendment as a means to avoid inconvenient restrictions on the ruling party's power had become common practice.

If Zimbabwe's new Constitution reflected the legacy of decolonization, the Namibian and South African constitutional processes, by contrast, reflected a new international moment. This moment has seen a new wave of constitutionalism – reflected in the proliferation of new constitutional orders since the end of the cold war – and is marked, even in existing constitutional democracies by the increasing politicization of constitutional change, accompanied by demands for greater participation. In Africa, Namibia's process in 1990 marked the re-emergence of a democratically elected constituent assembly as the source of a legitimate constitution.

Even in established democracies, this new constitutionalism had its influence. Indeed, some might say it was born there. In Canada, for example, the First Ministers' Conference, which brings together the political leaders of the federal government and the ten provincial governments, assumed a right in the 1970s to negotiate constitutional change.[8] But increasing and diverse political mobilization shaped and changed the constitution-making process: women's groups, First Nations, and broader public participation in hearings; in the Quebec referendum; and as an audience to whom politicians turned for support, opened up the process. Demands emanating from different sources and the establishment of different arenas significantly affected the constitutional agenda and introduced new participants into the process.[9] This expansion of participation in the constitution-making processes of established democracies helped legitimate the demands of those in the midst of democratic transitions who were claiming the heritage of participation inherent in the promise of democratic constitutionalism.

PROCEDURE AND SUBSTANCE IN THE CONSTITUTION-MAKING PROCESS

While each of the three major parties negotiating South Africa's transition to democracy – the African National Congress (ANC), National

Party government and the Inkatha Freedom Party (IFP) – preferred a particular process of constitution-making, these preferences were intimately bound up with each party's substantive goals, goals that were premised on its particular conception of South Africa's future constitutional identity. For the ANC, a future South Africa was to be based on a common citizenship and identity, which could only be achieved through a collective effort to overcome apartheid's legacy.[10] The IFP retreated from a national vision and sought regionalized protections that would allow it to maintain its political advantage in KwaZulu-Natal. The National Party conceived of a future South Africa in which local communities would be empowered to choose their own living arrangements without interference from the state.[11]

To this end the National Party government entered the negotiations, promising its constituency that its bottom line would be a system of power-sharing designed to secure the interests of different communities. First expressed in racial terms, this notion of power sharing soon evolved into a more internationally acceptable call for the recognition of minority rights and the assertion that all ethnic groups in South Africa constitute distinct minorities requiring a permanent balancing of political power on the basis of minority representation.[12] Attempting at first to provide an acceptable version of the failed 'consociationalism' of the 1983 Constitution, the National Party proposed a revolving presidency and a bicameral legislature with the upper house – consisting of 'minority representatives' – having veto powers over all legislation. After its proposals were rejected for their reliance on a thinly disguised framework of racial vetoes, the National Party modified its approach, demanding an extended period of transition and advocating what it described as 'constitutional rule in a participatory democracy'.[13] This proposal promoted a combination of individual rights, communal vetoes and consociationalism. Together these elements produced a framework designed to insulate private interests and action from public power, with the foreseeable effect of allowing those with the resources and desire to pursue a system of privatized apartheid.

At the national level, the protection of individual rights would be restricted to positively enforceable political and civil rights, while legislative power would be dominated by the regionally constituted upper house of a bicameral legislature. Significantly, regional representation, while analogized to the system of equal state representation in the Senate of the United States of America, would in fact have involved an additional level of parity, which would have ensured 'minority' veto power. While in the National Party's vision the regions would have been represented by an equal number of representatives, each region's delegates would be made up of an *equal* number of representatives from every political party achieving more than five per cent of electoral support in the region. The effect of this scheme would have been to ensure that parties representing racial or ethnic minorities would receive enough seats in the Senate effectively to veto any legislation requiring a heightened majority, such as future constitutional amendments or legislation having regional impacts that might threaten their interests.

Relying on this particular construction of a bill of rights and federalism to protect individual and community interests at the national level, the National Party's focus shifted to the local level, where it advocated a system of local government conceived as a form of consociationalism based on property rights as a means of securing 'participatory democracy'. According to this proposal, votes for local government positions would be apportioned according to property ownership within each voting district. Thus, despite the fact that even in apartheid's exclusively 'white' suburbs resident African employees made up a large proportion of the residential population, voting rights for local government would under this scheme have been restricted to a disproportionately white group of property holders. Participation in this framework would have given rise to racially-based political access, because the geographic patterns of segregation enforced by apartheid could be expected to remain relatively stable given the likely slow movement in property ownership. Local government would consequentially reflect a consociational model, where the different racial groups consigned by apartheid to different geographic areas would each have controlled their local arrangements – providing local self-government based on the one hand on local property rights, and on the other on the erection of a constitutional firewall between public and private activity.[14]

While the National Party focused its concern on local control, the IFP early on committed itself to the consolidation of its interests in one region of the country, KwaZulu-Natal. Although at the beginning of the negotiations process the IFP asserted itself as a third major player demanding parity with the ANC and the National Party government, it retreated to the advocacy of regional autonomy in an attempt to perpetuate its existing advantage as a bantustan government into the post-apartheid era.[15] The IFP's proposal advocated complete regional autonomy, which it described as 'federalism', as a means to ensure the self-determination of particular communities. The IFP's federalism envisioned a national government of limited, enumerated powers, and a national constitution which would remain subject to the constitutions of the individual states of the federation.[16] The IFP's notion of federalism was that the different regions of South Africa would constitute autonomous states whose constitutions would dictate interpretation of the 'federal' constitution. Applications of the federal constitution to issues within a region or to conflicts between regions would have to be consistent with the constitutions of the relevant regions.

This conception of 'autonomous federalism' was explicated in the IFP's proposed constitution of KwaZulu-Natal. Declaring the sovereignty of KwaZulu-Natal to be 'indivisible, inalienable and untransferable',[17] the proposed constitution would have required South African armed forces to obtain permission before entering Natal;[18] required South Africa to obtain local consent before levying taxes;[19] created an 'autonomous' Central Bank;[20] and granted the KwaZulu-Natal Constitutional Court exclusive jurisdiction to decide whether South African laws were valid within the region.[21] At the federal level, the IFP proposed a government of limited powers, whose actions would be limited to defined areas, including: a common monetary system, national defence, nationality and immigration, foreign affairs, federal judicial organization, intellectual property rights and external commercial relations. The national legislature was to be further empowered to pass general principles of legislation in the areas of environmental regulation, banking, interstate commerce and economic development, as well as to provide a framework to facilitate interstate negotiation over policies in these areas. Finally, any federal legislation would have to be passed by both houses of Parliament giving the Senate – made up of four representatives of each state – a final veto over national legislation.

The federal government would have been further disempowered under the IFP's proposals by the establishment of a series of independent commissions created to control and regulate federal government activity. Apart from a number of internationally recognizable bodies such as a Judicial Service Commission, Civil Service Commission and Electoral Commission, the proposal introduced the notion of independent policy-making institutions into the heart of traditionally government controlled activities such as economic regulation. The proposal called for the establishment of a series of such commissions including a Privatization Commission, Regulatory Relief Commission – to repeal or amend burdensome, unnecessary or inadequate regulations – an Environmental Commission, Consumer Affairs Commission and finally an Economic Development Commission. A significant feature of these commissions was that their membership was to be appointed from a variety of sources, including the President, federal Parliament and private bodies, such as the national Chamber of Commerce, consumer groups and representatives of industry. This introduction of different factions into the heart of government was a unique aspect of the IFP proposal, which in the South African context would have worked to promote established interests whose racial character was defined largely by apartheid's allocation of economic and social resources.

The different substantive goals of the major players in the democratic transition shaped in large measure the practices and procedures for constitution-making that they advocated. Significantly, the extent and nature of the participation allowed or conceded by each party (to party members, allies or the general public) in the formulation of its own proposals was likewise related to the party's substantive goals and had a profound impact on its procedural preferences.

The ANC, under pressure from its membership and the democratic movement, campaigned for an open democratic process in which a constitution was ideally to be drawn up by an unfettered, democratically elected, constituent assembly. However, confronted with escalating violence, endless talks-about-talks and the National Party government's commitment to a lengthy transition – including some form of power-sharing in which the white minority would continue to have a veto over power exercised by the black majority – the democratic movement launched a mass campaign demanding an interim government and a democratically elected constituent assembly. Despite this preference for a democratically controlled constituent assembly, the ANC Constitutional Committee decided to launch a public debate on the ANC's constitutional proposals and proposed Bill of Rights in 1990. This process was important both in engaging the ANC's own constituency and in reaching out to a broader South African and international audience. To this end the ANC Constitutional Committee participated in a series of broadly inclusive conferences to formulate and discuss the detail of these proposals. These conferences focused on the following substantive areas: electoral systems;[22] constitutional courts;[23] bills of rights;[24] affirmative action;[25] structures of government;[26] and the composition of the judiciary.[27]

This series of about ten conferences between 1990 and 1993 focused on the elucidation of substantive constitutional issues. Their format, however, was as important as their focus. They exhibited a degree of participation, by both ANC-aligned and independent (including foreign) participants, unique in the South African process. This was achieved first by the linkages between the ANC Constitutional Committee and a number of university-based legal institutes, allowing the co-hosting of these events. Second, invitations to different ANC regions, political structures, and members of the tripartite alliance (the ANC, South African Communist Party and Congress of South African Trade Unions) ensured the participation of a range of activists from the trade unions, non-government organizations and community-based organizations. Third, international participants and local academics were involved in most of these conferences.[28]

The ANC Constitutional Committee was at times criticized by ANC membership for not bringing the constitutional debates down to the grass roots, since the distribution of documents and proposals was hap-hazard and unreliable at the branch level. Although many ANC branches in the cities held discussions or political education sessions around many of the Constitutional Committee's documents, there is little evidence that these processes were characteristic of ANC branches in either the rural areas or for that matter in the urban 'townships', where violence and basic organizing consumed the available resources. Nevertheless, the impact of the Constitutional Committee's work profoundly reshaped the ANC's constitutional posture. This change was reflected in the results of the ANC's first national conference after its unbanning held in Durban in July 1991. The conference declared:

> We reiterate our adherence to the principles of a united, non-racial, non-sexist and democratic South Africa as enshrined in the Freedom Charter. These include the guarantee of the fundamental human rights of all South Africans, reinforced by an entrenched Bill of Rights, a multi-party system of government, a representative and independent judiciary and regular elections ...[29]

Although the 1988 Constitutional Principles were ostensibly based on the ANC's political manifesto – the 1955 Freedom Charter – their eluci-dation by the Constitutional Committee went well beyond the Charter, and, in retrospect, involved a significant shift in the ultimate vision. This shift was made possible by the participation and engagement of activists, regional representatives and the ANC leadership itself in the discussions and debates initiated by the Constitutional Committee. This culture of participation asserted itself in the change from constitutional debate to negotiations within the ANC by the demand for participation by the membership in the negotiations process, where many felt the negotiators were becoming increasingly distanced from their democratic base. Again the ANC responded by attempting to establish internal party-based nego-tiations fora at a regional and local level so as to keep a link between the negotiations process and membership. These, too, stretched the limits of resources and the representative capacities of local leaderships.

In stark contrast, the National Party government at first resisted calls for a democratically-elected constituent assembly, envisaging instead a long transition period in which a future constitution would be negoti-ated between the parties. As the holder of state power, the National Party was determined not to relinquish power before securing effective safe-guards against the future exercise of state power by the black majority. This aim was, however, coupled with an understanding of political par-ticipation based on the relatively unrestrained exercise of executive power and the achievement of political change through the negotiation of élite interests.

While ANC analysts tended to view the National Party's insistence that all 'recognized' political entities – including the minuscule political parties of respective self-governing bantustan governments, and the governments of 'independent' bantustans – be equal participants in the negotiations, as an attempt to stack the table in the regime's favour, in fact this demand accurately reflected the National Party's notion of participation, based on a notion of how competing political élites form a compact to govern. This type of élite decision-making reflected the National Party's own internal policy-making processes – which historically involved secret caucuses based on Broederbond membership and negotiations between the provincial leaderships of the party – as well as the state-centred tradition of investigating constitutional options through appointed government commissions. The government's constitutional proposals were indeed substantially informed by two reports issued by the South African Law Commission in 1991.[30]

From the outset, the structure of formal participation in the negotiation process was premised on a notion of consensus building between contending élites. This was given clear, if realistic, expression in the notion of sufficient consensus – agreement between the National Party government and the ANC – which became the formal deadlock-breaking mechanism within the negotiations process. The Conference for a Democratic South Africa (Codesa),[31] formed by a joint agreement of the parties to negotiate the transition to a new constitutional order, thus reflected National Party demands for an élite pact-making process. Nevertheless the National Party government still refused to permit Codesa to exercise legal powers, insisting that legal continuity required the approval of any new constitution by the National Party–dominated tricameral Parliament.[32] This assertion of the need for legal continuity carried the additional advantage for the National Party of precluding a democratically-elected constitution-making body and requiring that any future constitution be negotiated between the parties. In fact the apartheid government argued that there could not even be a non-racial election until a new constitution allowed a legal basis for universal adult franchise. For the National Party government, any suggestion that there should be a legal break with the apartheid past before this was legitimated by a new constitution enacted in terms of the existing legal framework raised issues of the sovereignty of the South African state and the legitimacy of its position as a *de jure* government and was thus non-negotiable. As holder of state power for over forty years, the National Party was determined to project its power into the future, if not to control the outcome, at least to ensure certain basic property and social interests through the insulation of private from state power in the post-apartheid order.[33] This project was threatened by claims asserting the right to immediate participation regardless of the provisions of the existing 1983 tricameral Constitution.

The IFP adopted an even more non-participatory position, viewing the very notion of a democratically-elected constituent assembly *as inherently undemocratic*.[34] In an astounding exercise of formal logic, the IFP argued that, since the purpose of a justiciable constitution and a bill of rights is to protect minorities from the tyranny of the majority, the minorities to be protected must give their assent to the particular framework. This requires that all parties which are going to live under this framework give their prior consent. In other words, the IFP and every other minor party at the negotiating table – regardless of the extent of their support – must reach consensus on the final constitution. As the IFP stated, it had 'on numerous occasions made clear its objection to any majoritarian approach to the drafting of the fundamental law of the land. Therefore the IFP would insist that even in such interim parliament the rule of consensus should be applied instead of special majority, whether such special majority be two-thirds as proposed by the ANC or seventy-five per cent as proposed by the government.'[35] Any other result would, by the IFP's definition, be antidemocratic.[36] Significantly, the IFP reversed its position after 1994 at least with respect to the making of provincial constitutions, insisting that, as the majority party – with less than fifty per cent of the vote – in KwaZulu-Natal, they had the right as the majority to determine the contents of the provincial constitution despite the constitutional requirement of a two-thirds majority. Frustrated at their inability to get their own way in the KwaZulu-Natal legislature, the IFP threatened new elections, claiming that they would secure a two-thirds majority so that they could pass their own constitution – a far cry from the demand for consensus which they continued to maintain at the national level. Unhappy with the direction of the Constitutional Assembly at the national level, the IFP boycotted Constitutional Assembly proceedings from late 1994. While virtually all systems of constitutional rule-making require super-majorities or even unanimity among particular constitutionally-defined institutions – such as the provincial governments under Canadian federalism – the IFP's demand for universal consensus among political participants whose electoral support was completely untested and whose constitutional standing was equally unspecified was indeed unique.

Recognizing the difficulties of obtaining universal consensus, the IFP called for a depoliticized process of constitution-making, with a group of constitutional experts retained to produce a constitution to be adopted by parties and endorsed in a national plebiscite.[37] The assumption that a constitutional framework can be inherently neutral and that its neutrality can be ensured by the appointment of constitutional experts is itself questionable; but the IFP's proposal for a national referendum to confirm a negotiated 'consensus' constitution reflects a Machiavellian conception of democracy. If all the parties were to reach official agreement on a constitution, a national plebiscite to endorse the result would involve only the shadow of formal democracy. While it is true, as happened in Canada with the Charlottetown constitutional proposals – which were finally agreed to by all the official parties in Canada but rejected in a national plebiscite – that the people could always reject what the élites presented, it is a highly unlikely scenario in the post-colonial context. While the Canadian experience provides an interesting example of the weakness of political parties in the constitutional politics of some developed democracies, this situation may be easily distinguished from that prevailing in newly emerging post-colonial democracies such as South Africa. In these circumstances, the anti-colonial political movements usually carry a significant degree of legitimacy in the immediate post-colonial situation, such that the possibility of public rejection of a consensus including the major anti-colonial party or parties would be very remote. The IFP itself failed to invite any other significant political formations to participate in drafting its original KwaZulu-Natal Constitution. However, it was consistent in its commitment to an expert-led process. IFP constitutional proposals were produced by a group of experts – dominated by two American constitutional lawyers, Professor Albert Blaustein and Dr Mario Ambrosini – and, in the case of the first KwaZulu-Natal Constitution, endorsed without discussion by the IFP-dominated KwaZulu 'bantustan' legislature.

After nearly two-and-a-half years of slow progress, South Africa's democratic transition ground to a halt in mid-1992, when Codesa collapsed. The ANC refused to concede the National Party's demand – which would have given the National Party an effective veto over future constitution-making – that the adoption of final constitutional provisions on the 'bill of rights, principle of three-tier government, multiparty democracy and effective participation of political minorities would require a majority of seventy-five per cent'.[38] While this refusal marked the outer limits of the National Party government's ability to assert a purely élite constitution-making process, the gunning down of ANC protestors outside Bisho in the Ciskei bantustan emphasized the ANC's inability either to seize power through insurrection or to insist upon an unfettered constituent assembly.[39] Although overcoming this stalemate would require concessions from both sides, it was the post-cold war international consensus on the parameters of democratic transitions which enabled the ANC to overcome both the National Party's and IFP's determination to avoid an elected constituent assembly.

Constructing an Historic Compromise: Sunset Clauses and a Two-Stage Constitution-Making Process

ANC leader Joe Slovo's 'sunset clause' proposals, adopted by the ANC National Executive Committee in February 1993,[40] seemed to represent the epitome of an élite pact. The essential feature of the 'sunset' proposal was the acceptance of a constitutionally entrenched system of executive power-sharing for five years after the first democratic election. During this period, the democratically-elected Parliament would be empowered to write a new constitution which could exclude these entrenched provisions – whose sun would thus set. In accepting the National Party's continued participation in government and the establishment of bilateral agreements which each party would respect in a future constituent assembly, the proposals seemed to grant the National Party's key demands: a negotiated constitution and future power-sharing.[41] While initially criticized within the ANC[42] and rejected by other parties such as the Pan Africanist Congress,[43] these proposals provided the linchpin enabling the political transition to continue.

In fact, Slovo's notion of a government of national unity was clearly distinct from the National Party's or other consociational power-sharing models.[44] Most importantly, where the National Party had called for a compulsory coalition government with a Cabinet drawn equally from the three major parties and a rotating presidency,[45] Slovo proposed an election to determine the proportions of who would represent the different parties in executive government – a less static and more representative vision.[46]

By conceding a government of national unity in November 1992, the ANC was responding to a more fundamental set of concessions implied in the National Party government's acceptance of an elected constituent assembly to write a final constitution, in the wake of the Bisho killings in mid-1992.[47] In a Cabinet *bosberaad* on 23 and 24 July 1992, the National Party and government leadership found itself caught between the urgency of restarting the negotiation process and increasing international concern and criticism of the government.[48] International frustration over the breakdown of Codesa and the continuing violence began to be reflected in a growing irritation with the National Party's proposals for the transition. Reflecting the sea-change in international consensus on democracy, Herman Cohen, United States Assistant Secretary of State for the Bureau of African Affairs in the Bush administration, told the Africa subcommittee of the US House of Representatives Foreign Affairs Committee on 23 July 1992, that all sides must recognize the 'right of the majority to govern, while assuring that all South Africans have a stake in their government', and rejected the right of any party to insist on 'overly complex arrangements intended to guarantee a share of power to particular groups which will frustrate effective governance'. Laying out a set of principles acceptable to the Bush administration, he insisted that although '[m]inorities have the right to safeguards; they cannot expect a veto'.[49] This implicit rejection of the National Party's notion of power-sharing may have been a decisive element in the National Party cabinet's decision to accept an elected constituent assembly.

The National Party's concession of an elected constituent assembly and the ANC's acceptance of a government of national unity under a transitional constitution provided the key elements of agreement in South Africa's democratic transition. By accepting a democratic consti-tution-making process, the National Party made it possible for the ANC to agree to the adoption of a negotiated interim Constitution, which would entrench a government of national unity for five years and ensure the legal continuity the National Party government required. The archi-tecture of this agreement, reflecting continuity and change, negotiation and participation, allowed the multiparty negotiations to resume at the World Trade Centre outside Johannesburg.

A New Process, a New Constitution: Negotiating the Interim Constitution

If South Africa's democratic transition was able to go forward on the premise of a two-stage process of constitution-making, it was the promise that the first stage would have some lasting impact that held the key to this agreement. While the first round, buffeted by popular participation and strengthened by elements of internal participation within the ANC alliance, was ultimately under the negotiating parties' control, the next round would clearly be controlled by the democratic majority. Even as the Multi-Party Negotiating Process put the negotiations back on track with the understanding that a final constitution would be created by a democratically-elected body, the problem of constitution-making con-tinued to dog the process. The task of suggesting solutions to this prob-lem was given to the Technical Committee on Constitutional Issues (TCCI), one of a number of technical committees established by the Negotiating Council of the Negotiating Forum to facilitate discussion. Among its members,[50] Arthur Chaskalson played a central role in the work of the committee.

The first reports of the TCCI to the Negotiating Council, between May and July 1993, reveal the unfolding of a solution – the development of a set of constitutional principles that would bind a future elected consti-tution-making body. In its first report to the Negotiating Council, the TCCI argued that a 'multiparty agreement on constitutional principles would in the first place provide fundamental direction to the constitu-tional debate',[51] and, if adopted 'as a set of principles binding on future

105

constitution-making, they will give direction and security to all relevant issues'.[52] It then noted that the 'Declaration of Intent on the Negotiating Process adopted by the Negotiating Council on 30 April 1993 records a commitment by the Council to reach agreement on binding constitutional principles'.[53] Despite this seeming accord, the second report of the TCCI noted that the debate on the constitution-making process and regional powers and functions continued to reflect the tension between those concerned about the legitimacy of the constitution-making process and those concerned that 'their interests will not adequately be protected if decisions are taken by a majority in a democratically elected constitution-making body'.[54]

Attempting to bridge this gap, the TCCI noted that it was mandated to provide a report on constitutional principles. It then proceeded to outline what it entitled an emerging consensus: democracy in the form of universal adult suffrage at all levels of government; supremacy of a rigid constitution, justiciable by an independent judiciary; inclusion of a set of fundamental rights; the constitutional separation of executive, legislative and judicial powers; the constitutional distribution of government powers among democratically elected national, regional and local institutions; and finally, the constitutional recognition and accommodation of the variety of cultures and religions being practised and languages used by various segments of the population.[55] Significantly, the same Report addressed the concerns of those parties in the Negotiating Council who at this time were still insisting on a confederal solution, by requesting them to 'provide us with more clarity on their proposals and in particular the territory and population of the envisaged separate state, and how it will meet the international law requirements of secession and self-determination'. This division of the parties into those whose positions could be refined into an emerging consensus and those whose proposals required further clarification and would by implication have to 'meet the international law requirements of secession and self-determination', demonstrates the manner in which the TCCI worked both to build consensus and to question the viability of those options that could not be incorporated into the emerging consensus. It is also extremely telling that this division also marks the difference between those options that accorded most closely with the universal principles of the dominant international political culture of constitutionalism in this period, and those which were equally at odds with the positions of the Organization of African Unity (with respect to the secession or alteration of the boundaries of African States), or the United Nations (with respect to the question of national self-determination in the process of decolonization). Significantly, both these issues – secession and self-determination – would undergo, in a matter of a few years, important shifts in their application and legal status internationally, yet they remained important bulwarks against the demands of the IFP and its allies in the South African transition.

Finally, in its Fourth Supplementary Report on Constitutional Principles, the TCCI reported that, on 26 July 1993, the Negotiating Forum adopted a set of Constitutional Principles and 'agreed that the Constitutional Principles shall be binding on the constitution making body and that the justiciability thereof shall be ensured by a constitutional court or tribunal'.[56] By the time the Constitutional Principles were formally adopted in the Fourth Schedule[57] of the interim Constitution, they contained an amalgam of broad democratic principles consistent with the post-cold war consensus on constitutionalism and a host of detail specific to the needs of the negotiating parties. For, once it was realized that the elected constitution-making body would be the source of the final Constitution, limited only by the agreed provisions of the Constitutional Principles, the attention of the parties was on ensuring that the Constitutional Principles contained those provisions of greatest concern to themselves. Most dramatic of these specific provisions were those requiring the recognition of 'traditional leadership, according to indigenous law',[58] and 'collective rights of self-determination'.[59] In addition, recognition of the Zulu King and the provision of a Volkstaat Council were added by amendment to the main body of the Constitution just prior to the April 1994 elections as a way to include parts of the Freedom Alliance, particularly the IFP and the Afrikaner right-wing 'Freedom Front', led by ex-South African Defence Force (SADF) head General Constant Viljoen. Finally, the Constitutional Principles were amended to provide that provincial recognition of a traditional monarch would be protected in a final constitution[60] and that any territorial entity established through the assertion of a right to self-determination by 'any community sharing a common culture and language heritage'[61] shall be entrenched in the new constitution.[62]

This inclusion of a plethora of constitutional principles and provisions enabled the elections to go forward and the democratic transition to proceed, but they also served to defer a range of substantive issues into the next phase of constitution-making. Although the individual Constitutional Principles remained open to differing interpretations, the interaction of the different principles would revive many of the conflicts their inclusion was designed to lay to rest. A significant difference, however, was that these conflicts would henceforth be played out in a completely different arena – the democratically-elected Constitutional Assembly, made up of a joint sitting of the National Assembly and the Senate of South Africa's first democratic Parliament.[63]

With the adoption of the Constitutional Principles by the Negotiating Forum, the TCCI was instructed by the Negotiating Council to draft a constitution for the transition.[64] Even then, the parties could only agree that this interim Constitution would provide for limited subject matter to facilitate the transition.[65] Although the notion of 'developing a set of constitutional principles at the Negotiating Forum, which [would] be binding in the elected constitution-making body', provided a means to resolve the irreconcilable conflict between the demands for either a '*pouvoir constituant*' or a '*pouvoir constitué*'; in fact, at every step of the way, the ANC argued for a less detailed interim Constitution, while the National Party insisted that the interim Constitution be as detailed as possible. Although the National Party assumed, and the ANC was concerned, that a comprehensive negotiated constitution would gain a life of its own and prevent or at least confine the scope of the Constitutional Assembly's constitution-making activity, it soon became clear that, in order to ensure the transition, the interim Constitution would address all major constitutional issues. Thus, in addition to the Constitutional Principles included in Schedule 4, the interim Constitution provided for the governing of the country in the period between the first elections and the adoption of a final constitution. In a further concession to the National Party, the ANC then accepted the provisions constitutionalizing the Government of National Unity for the full five-year term of the first government – until the 1999 elections – beyond the creation and possible adoption of the final constitution.

The sections of the interim Constitution providing for the creation of a final constitution clearly influenced the distribution of power in the Constitutional Assembly. Requiring that a new Constitution be passed within two years from the first sitting of the National Assembly,[66] Chapter 5 of the interim Constitution provided that at least two-thirds of all the members of the Constitutional Assembly must vote for the new Constitution.[67] In addition, sections of a final Constitution dealing with the boundaries, powers and functions of the provinces had to be adopted by two-thirds of all the members of the regionally constituted Senate, giving the provinces established under the interim Constitution an important lever of influence in the Constitutional Assembly.[68]

Given the possibility that the Constitutional Assembly could fail to obtain the necessary two-thirds agreement on either a new constitution or on the provincial arrangements, the interim Constitution provided elaborate deadlock breaking mechanisms. First, a panel of constitutional experts[69] appointed by two-thirds of the Constitutional Assembly (or alternatively, by each party holding forty seats in the Constitutional Assembly)[70] was required to seek amendments to resolve deadlocks within thirty days.[71] Second, if the draft text unanimously agreed upon by the panel of experts was not adopted by a two-thirds majority then the Constitutional Assembly could approve any draft text by a simple majority of its members.[72] However, in this latter case, the new text would have to be first certified by the Constitutional Court, then submitted to a national referendum, requiring ratification by at least sixty per cent of all votes cast.[73] Failure to obtain a sixty per cent ratification would force the President to dissolve Parliament and call a general election for a new Constitutional Assembly.[74] The new Constitutional Assembly would then have one year to pass a new constitution;[75] however, the majority required for passage of the constitution would be reduced from two-thirds to sixty per cent.[76]

Although the interim Constitution allowed any of these requirements to be amended by a two-thirds majority of a joint sitting of the National Assembly and Senate,[77] section 74 prohibited the repeal or amendment of both the Constitutional Principles contained in Schedule 4 of the 1993 Constitution and the requirement that the Constitutional Court certify that the new constitutional text comply with those principles. The possibility of amending the constitution-making procedures thus effectively reduced the interim Constitution's framework for producing the new constitution to three key elements. First, any amendment of the constitution-making procedures required a two-thirds majority of all the members of the National Assembly and Senate, requiring agreement between at least the ANC and the National Party or IFP. Second, under all circumstances the Constitutional Assembly was bound by the Constitutional Principles agreed to by the parties at the multiparty talks and included in Schedule 4 of the interim Constitution. And third, the Constitutional Court had to declare that the new constitutional text complied with the Constitutional Principles.

The tension between adherence to Constitutional Principles and the unfettered powers of a democratic constitution-making body was explicitly addressed in the negotiations and was reflected in the 1993 Constitution. Invoking the need for legal continuity and minority guarantees, the National Party government always insisted on entrenching basic constitutional principles agreed upon through negotiations.[78] Although this stance was at odds with the ANC's demand for a democratic constituent assembly with unlimited freedom to draft the final constitution, the ANC nevertheless accepted the need to provide certain assurances as to the future constitutional framework. To this end the ANC had itself introduced the practice of constitutional principles by both publishing its own constitutional guidelines in 1988 and lobbying for their international endorsement as the minimum conditions for an internationally accepted solution to the South African conflict. Conversely, while the National Party government eventually accepted that a new constitution would fail to gain popular acceptance unless it was adopted by an elected constitution-making body, it attempted to ensure that the

Constitutional Assembly would be bound to produce a constitution within a framework acceptable to the National Party.

PARTICIPATING FROM THE OUTSIDE: MOBILIZATION AND POPULAR PRESSURES ON THE MAKERS OF THE INTERIM CONSTITUTION

If Slovo's sunset clauses appeared to provide an example of élite pacting, mass action, demonstrations and petitions provided simultaneous illustrations of popular participation. Mass action played an important part in the ANC-alliance's campaign to shape the transition, and various forms of public display of claims, outrage and strength continued to be employed by groups on all sides, trying to ensure that their concerns or demands be placed on the agenda at the multi-party talks. These claims for the recognition of different identities and social interests took on new urgency, both as a consequence of, and in the context of, the highly charged circumstances.[79] Although subject to continuing dispute,[80] many of these claims were ultimately accommodated in the interim Constitution.

For example, victims of apartheid-forced removals marched on the site of the talks protesting the proposed constitutional protection of existing property rights, while from a completely different perspective the IFP joined with two other bantustan governments and ultra-right-wing racists to demand a halt to the negotiations and the cancellation of the April 1994 elections in order that the 'self-determination' of different ethnic groups be recognized. Although many different interests worked to influence the negotiations on the interim Constitution – including the publication of a host of books, pamphlets and newspaper articles offering specific constitutional alternatives or contributions to the constitutional debates[81] – the three most important areas of mobilization and contest involved issues of gender, ethnicity and labour. The assertion and relative success of gender claims in the making of the interim Constitution, through the multiparty Women's National Coalition and within different political groups, provides an example of a successful multifaceted strategy.

The ANC's Women's League staged a sit-in at the negotiations and won the requirement that each delegation at the negotiations have a woman as one of its two negotiating council representatives. South Africa is the first case where a constitution-making body was formally constituted by an equal number of men and women.[82] At the same time the Women's League continued to press for greater participation within the ANC, winning a recommendation from the ANC's national working committee that one-third of all ANC candidates in the April 1994 elections be women.[83]

Gender equality was, as a consequence, formally recognized in the interim Bill of Rights, and the interim Constitution included specific provisions for the establishment of a Commission on Gender Equality 'to advise and to make recommendations to Parliament or any other legislature with regard to any laws or proposed legislation which affects gender equality and the status of women'.[84] In addition, as part of a general attempt to pre-empt negotiations, the de Klerk government ratified the International Convention on the Elimination of All Forms of Discrimination against Women in January 1993, binding the South African state to particular international obligations in this area. This successful inclusion of the principle of gender equality in the interim Constitution was the product of the interaction of local women's mobilization against gender discrimination and the increased recognition of gender equality as an internationally-accepted norm of human rights and constitutionalism.

These gains did not reflect universal consensus, nor were they simply accumulative. Despite these breakthroughs in an otherwise deeply sexist society, and despite the popular repetition of the democratic movement's vision of a 'non-racial and non-sexist' South Africa, women active in the negotiations process had to fend off a challenge resulting from the interim Constitution's recognition of indigenous law. Traditional leaders' claims for the recognition of indigenous culture led to an attempt to include provisions in the interim Bill of Rights recognizing 'customary law' and regulating the contradictions between indigenous law and other 'fundamental rights'. Although it was rejected, one proposed interim Bill of Rights granted 'any court applying a system of customary law' the power to determine the extent to which customary law undermines the equality provision and to decide when and to what extent these rules – even where they discriminated against women – should be brought into conformity with the constitutional requirement of equality.[85] In the end, the interim Constitution came down in favour of gender equality, making indigenous law 'subject to regulation by law', implying its subordination to the fundamental rights contained in the Constitution, and gender equality in particular.[86]

Claims for the recognition of ethnicity posed the greatest threat to the democratic transition. While all the parties at the negotiating table said they wished to respect South African cultural diversity, dispute over the nature of that diversity forced negotiators to confront claims made by the ruling party and its allies since the early 1970s that the policy of separate development was based on the protection of different cultures. Although this justification ignored the reality of ethnic and racial hierarchies and of racist domination of the black majority, it remained a significant source of separatist claims during the negotiations.

While ANC negotiators remained committed to building a non-racial South Africa, the power and fear generated by a history of ethnic identification could not be ignored. Through the past forty years at least, South

African ethnic diversity has been recreated through government spon-
sorship of separate ethnic administrations and separate language radio
and television stations which, although controlled by apartheid propa-
gandists, purported to serve the needs of cultural diversity. The reproduction of this 'diversity' in the creation of bantustan élites and the
preservation and promotion of ethnic 'tribalism' created an apartheid
legacy which will continue to affect debates and political struggles over
issues of national development and democracy. In contrast, the African
National Congress was premised at its founding in 1912 on the desire
among African leaders to create a single nation, unifying Africans against
colonial domination regardless of ethnic affiliation. Over the century,
the quest for national liberation witnessed numerous reformulations
aimed at extending the category of oppressed in ethnic and class terms
while simultaneously presenting an alternative vision of a single non-
racial South African nation free of ethnic domination.

Despite the nonracial project's success in creating a united front
against apartheid – most visibly in the Congress Alliance and later the
United Democratic Front – questions of cultural diversity and language
and education policies have continued to plague the democratic movement. This tension between a commitment to non-racialism and the
recognition of cultural and other group-based differences has mediated
the ANC's communitarian traditions and led to an embrace, in part, of
individualism, constitutionalism and preferential policies. These proposals have not, however, placated those whose political standing
remains tied to distinct group or ethnic identities and difference.

Although opinion polls revealed limited popular support for any
ethnic-based party, ethnic assertions began to resonate across the political spectrum both during the negotiations on the interim Constitution
and the election campaign. Addressing a 20 000-strong Inkatha rally on
5 April 1994, an Inkatha regional secretary threatened that 'if our
demands cannot be addressed, then there is no election on the 27th of
April ... We will do everything in our power to destroy any attempt by any
state organ used by the ANC to divide the Zulu nation.'[87] Like Buthelezi's
Inkatha, hardline white separatists continued to insist on ethnic diversity.
Faced with the conclusion of negotiations for the transition to a democratic order in October 1993, an odd assortment of parties, including
Inkatha and right-wing white segregationists, formed the 'Freedom
Alliance', demanding that the new Constitution enshrine ethnic identities. This trend led to the appearance of new and as yet unsupported
claims, the most flamboyant being made by a 'coloured separatist movement' demanding an independent state stretching across the Southern
and Western Cape with Cape Town as its capital.[88] The ANC was forced
to respond by challenging Buthelezi's claim to speak for South Africa's

eight million Zulu-speakers as it did when Nelson Mandela celebrated Zulu history as part of the struggle to build a nation, telling 60 000 ANC supporters at an ANC rally in Durban that 'it is impossible to separate the threads that make the weave of our South African nation'.[89] Although not overtly addressed in the interim Constitution, the impact of mobilized ethnic claims on this first round of constitution-making is reflected in a range of constitutional provisions – including the structuring of a government of national unity – designed to ensure minority participation in governance.[90]

The interim Constitution contained a variety of provisions designed to reflect and offer protection to South Africa's acknowledged cultural diversity, yet it also laid the foundation stones for continued ethnic claims and divisions. Claims of cultural diversity and difference have come to reflect a complex interaction between real cultural and ethnic identities on the one hand and the claims of political leaders on the other. These leaders' assertions of cultural and ethnic particularities are intertwined with their own attempts either to preserve existing power or to seek future political advantage. It is this continuing ambiguity which is reflected in the interim Constitution's recognition of cultural diversity and the special accommodations made to Zulu and Afrikaner nationalists in the weeks prior to the April 1994 elections.

Cultural diversity was constitutionally recognized in a number of ways – first, in the recognition of eleven official South African languages,[91] whose equal use and enjoyment should be promoted. A Pan South African Language Board has been created to promote the official languages as well as 'other languages used by communities in South Africa', of which a further eleven are recognized in the Constitution.[92] Second, an individual's right to 'use the language and to participate in the cultural life of his or her choice' was guaranteed as a fundamental right,[93] along with an individual right to instruction in the language of choice 'where this is reasonably practicable'.[94] Furthermore, the interim Constitution guaranteed the right to 'establish, where practicable, educational institutions based on a common culture, language or religion, provided that there shall be no discrimination on the ground of race'.[95]

Third, while language and cultural rights were expressed in individual terms, the interim Constitution's recognition of traditional authorities and indigenous law[96] and the establishment of a Volkstaat Council[97] were phrased in the terminology of collective rights. The recognition of 'the right to self-determination by any community sharing a common cultural and language heritage', introduced a notion of collective rights on the basis of cultural identity and even cultural self-determination[98] which strengthened the hand of those claiming power on the grounds of ethnic particularity.

A significant countervailing influence and source of identity for those who might otherwise have placed more weight on the social linkages of language, family, clan and eventually ethnicity, has been the proletarianization of South Africa's workforce and the impact of class politics. As a countervailing source of identity, the labour movement's mobilization of working-class support for a non-racial order was central to the ANC's success. However, the labour movement also launched an important claim for recognition beyond the formal management–worker relationship, asserting its right to represent workers as a class and arguing for the explicit recognition of socio-economic or class interests in the new constitutional order. Labour's claim received a significant degree of recognition in South Africa's democratic transition. Given apartheid's effective amalgamation of race and class, advocates and representatives of the working class, both in the South African Communist Party and the Congress of South African Trade Unions (Cosatu), are clearly influential in the democratic movement. Moreover, the trade union movement – as the most tightly organized segment of the democratic movement – won significant recognition in the constitution-making process. Although the unions were refused direct representation in the constitutional negotiations, the ANC included extensive constitutional protections for workers in its proposed Bill of Rights and supported Cosatu's call for a National Economic Forum for negotiating South Africa's economic and development priorities. Despite these gains, the interim Bill of Rights coupled workers' and employers' rights and tied the right to strike to an employer's right to lock workers out. The trade unions also complained that in the interim Constitution the right to strike,[99] which was protected for the 'purpose of collective bargaining', was unduly circumscribed as it appeared to exclude strikes on social and economic issues. Correspondingly, unionists argued that the inclusion of an employer's right to impose a lock-out fails to recognize the fundamental disparity between the power of individual workers and individual employers in the labour market. Thus labour argued that, while the right to strike is fundamental, 'the issue of lock-outs is at best a matter left to statutory regulation'.[100] The alliance between Cosatu and the ANC ensured that this issue was reopened in the Constitutional Assembly.

Constitutionalism, Self-Binding, Representation and the Limits of Participation

Ultimately the most important issue resolved in the first round of constitution-making was how South Africa would adopt a new constitution as the final marker of the democratic transition. The centrality of this decision must not however distract us from acknowledging that the interim Constitution marked a dramatic, substantive revolution in South African law.[101] This revolution was represented by the triumph of constitutionalism over parliamentary sovereignty and, while its impact was yet to work its way fully through the labyrinth of South African law, its basic premise – a justiciable constitution – was fully guaranteed in the Constitutional Principles which guided the democratically elected Constitutional Assembly.

The context of constitution-making in South Africa was thus fundamentally changed. Unlike the drafting of the interim Constitution the next phase of constitution-making was controlled by a democratically elected Constitutional Assembly. This shift, from a non-elected negotiations forum to an elected body, had at least two major consequences for participation. First, it shifted the emphasis of participation away from mass action or public demonstrations towards a more individualistic, yet equally active, form of participation in the attendance of discussion-meetings and the making of formal submissions to the Constitutional Assembly. The only visible protest action in late 1995 was by groups who felt that they were not adequately represented, including: traditional leaders from both the IFP and the ANC who joined in protest outside the Union buildings in Pretoria; anti-abortion activists who were holding a vigil outside Parliament in Cape Town; and residents of the small KwaZulu-Natal hamlet of Hillcrest who displayed placards demanding the reimposition of the death penalty following the brutal murder of an elderly woman in a day-time car hijacking in the centre of the village. Second, with the failure of ethnically-based parties to make a significant impact in the national elections, there was less attention given to ethnically-framed demands and instead claims focusing on issues of material and individual equality, class and gender, received greater attention from the constitution-makers. This included a refocusing of attention on to questions of how to introduce social and economic rights[102] and away from the recognition of cultural and ethnic demands. As a result, the 1996 Constitution includes new clauses in the Bill of Rights creating new rights to 'reasonable and progressive legislative measures' for the provision of housing, land, health, food, water and social assistance, but reduced the status of traditional leaders from that granted in the interim Constitution. Instead of being guaranteed a national and provincial role in the legislative process, traditional leadership and law are now subject to both the Constitution and legislation. While local, pre-existing, traditional authorities were recognized and the courts required to apply indigenous law – subject to the Constitution – when that law is applicable, the constitutional status of the councils of traditional authorities provided for in the interim Constitution was down-graded to an enabling clause allowing national or provincial legislatures to provide for such councils.

Finally, the Constitutional Court rejected attempts to use the Constitutional Principles to frustrate the will of the majority. When, for example, the National Party (whose relative influence in the constitution-making process diminished as a result of the electoral process) in the Western Cape asserted that any national interference in the province's restructuring of local government was a violation of the principle of provincial autonomy, the Constitutional Court argued that the principles were only relevant as a guide to the Constitutional Assembly and could not be used to interpret the interim Constitution. Thus, while some members of the Constitutional Assembly may have been tempted to question South Africa's newly adopted constitutionalism as the product of an undemocratic negotiating process, the second round of constitution-making entrenched an essential feeling of belonging. Despite their origins, constitutional rights and their protection under a system of constitutionalism were remade in the process of constitution-making as a product of South African participation.

EMBRACING CONSTITUTIONALISM, ENABLING DEMOCRACY

By examining the visions of the major domestic or local political actors in the previous chapter, and by understanding their interaction with global perspectives and forces before and during the political transition, we are able to see how the local visions of political possibilities were first formed and later mediated by both global imperatives and local demands. While the global often worked to create boundaries around particular options and possibilities, local constraints framed the spaces within which alternative possibilities were successively claimed and contested. South Africa's new-found constitutionalism was not just the product of an élite pact, but was in many ways also a precondition to an internationally acceptable democratic transition. It also flowed directly from the claim to equal rights, which characterized the anti-apartheid struggle and which motivated popular participation in the constitution-making process. While a democratically-elected Constitutional Assembly could revolt against attempts to frustrate land reform or to exclude other socio-economic programmes in the first round of negotiated constitution-making, the question of whether the Constitutional Assembly could have rejected constitutionalism must be understood in a wider international context. Although the Constitutional Principles contained in the 1993 Constitution represent a compact of internal precommitments between the parties designed to facilitate the democratic transition, they also represent local acceptance of a broader international consensus on democratic governance.[103] The emergence of this supranational commitment to democratic constitutionalism seems, in turn, to impose a prior obligation – to adopt democratic forms of governance – on national constitution-making processes. It is this realm of hybridity,[104] created by the interaction of local participation, context and history with international influences and conditionalities, that shaped the conditions within which the Constitutional Assembly began its work.

CHAPTER 6

GLOBAL IMPACT: INTERNATIONAL IMPERATIVES AND THEIR HYBRIDIZATION

Despite the particularities of South Africa's history and democratic transition, the basic features of the new constitutional order – including a Bill of Rights, Constitutional Court, and a plethora of independent institutions – conform to the basic elements of the post–cold war international political culture as expressed in the processes of state reconstruction characterizing the last decade of the twentieth century. However, the constitutional outcomes – the 1993 'interim' and 1996 'final' Constitutions – of South Africa's democratic transition also reflect the post–cold war international political culture in a particular hybridity, reflecting the specific political struggles and historical legacies which shaped and gave legitimacy to each particular constitutional option. It is this interaction, between the authority of particular alternatives[1] and the conflicting demands of local politics, that is revealed through the debates, negotiations and compromises which surrounded the adoption or exclusion of particular constitutional options.

Understanding the constitutive role of law in processes of state reconstruction, and in the South African case in particular, requires a brief exploration of the origins and conflicts surrounding the inclusion of different elements of South Africa's new constitutional order. While it is possible to identify those elements which clearly reflect South Africa's embrace of the dominant international norms on the one hand, and also those elements that reflect the particularities of South African culture and history on the other, the clearest way to explore the interaction between these different elements will be to focus on those elements whose fate – inclusion, exclusion or hybridization – was the product of intense political conflict during the constitution-making process. First, however, it is instructive to consider the fate of those elements of the dominant international political culture that were embraced by all the major political players in the South African transition – a bill of rights, constitutional supremacy and a series of independent institutions seeking to guarantee democracy and human rights.

Despite very different agendas and interpretations, the parties came to accept the inclusion of a constitutional court and bill of rights at a very early stage in the transition. In fact, the African National Congress (ANC) had issued a list of constitutional principles as early as 1988, which committed the organization to the adoption of a bill of rights, while the National Party regime had requested the South African Law Commission – a government-sponsored law reform body – to investigate group and individual rights as part of its own preparations for the reform of apartheid. Thus, despite an initial ambivalence the central legal development in implementing the 'transitional' 1993 interim Constitution was the embrace of constitutional supremacy, institutionalized through the establishment of a Constitutional Court to give effect to the supremacy of the Constitution and the new human rights culture introduced by the commitment to constitutionalism.

The inclusion in the 1993 interim Constitution of a plethora of institutional checks and balances, however, reflects the attempt to fragment state power so common in post–cold war constitution-making. At one level, these were rooted locally in the difficulties of the political transition. First, in the need for an independent body to oversee the first democratic elections and, second, in the creation of a range of institutions designed to secure a level political playing field and accommodate the *de facto* exercise of dual power during the period leading up to the first elections. At another level, these institutions were inspired by the existence and practice of Independent Electoral Commissions in a number of foreign jurisdictions, including Guatemala. The idea of an Independent Electoral Commission was, in fact, introduced at an ANC Constitutional Committee–organized conference on electoral systems after the ANC was invited by the National Democratic Institute to send a delegate to join their election observer mission – headed by Bruce Babbitt – to Guatemala in October 1990.

While the dangers of governmental abuse of power were well recognized by the different parties, agreement to include mechanisms designed to disperse and control the exercise of power in the 1993 interim Constitution was facilitated by the emphasis on accountable and transparent government, reflected in the international debate on governance during this period. On the one hand mechanisms were introduced designed to distance certain decisions from party political or purely government control and to ensure transparent and clean government, while on the other hand there were various institutions designed to further human rights and to prevent the abuse of government power. The first category included the Independent Electoral Commission, the Judicial Service Commission, the Public Service Commission and the Financial and Fiscal Commission, which served to insulate the electoral system, judicial and public service appointments, as well as the distribution of financial allocations and resources between the regions, from purely party political dynamics. Provision was also made for the appointment of an ombudsman called the Public Protector,[2] an Auditor-General[3] and a parliamentary standing committee with powers of parliamentary supervision over the National Defence Force.[4] The procurement of goods and services by government was also to be insulated from political interference by the creation of independent tender boards at every level of government.[5]

The second category of mechanisms established to check abuses of power and to promote human rights includes the Human Rights Commission,[6] with a mandate to develop an awareness of fundamental rights and to investigate any alleged violation of human rights, and the Commission on Gender Equality[7] which was constitutionally charged with the duty to promote gender equality. Apart from an advisory function with respect to proposed legislation and the power to educate and investigate, the Human Rights Commission was empowered to receive complaints and to assist, even financially, those adversely affected by a violation of their fundamental rights to seek redress before a competent court.

Significantly, it was the embrace of independent institutions within the new state structure that permitted the emergence of a new form of independent institution designed to address certain particularities of the South African situation. Given the fact that democratization would most likely preclude the old political élite from political power, institutions were developed to ensure the participation of all formal political factions in particular decision-making processes. The Financial and Fiscal Commission, for example, was appointed by the President but was required to include representatives from each provincial executive council.[8] Although designed to render advice and to make recommendations to the relevant legislative authorities on the distribution of financial resources between the different levels of government, the constitutional requirement that the Commission be consulted prior to the allocation of revenue and that its recommendations be taken into account will give significant weight to the Commission's advice. The Parliamentary standing committee to monitor the National Defence Force also provided for the participation of all political parties in the control of a vital state institution.

This transmutation of the global form was taken a step further with the Constitution's recognition of traditional authorities – tribal chiefs or *amakhosi*. While the establishment of provincial Houses of Traditional

Leaders, which elect a national Council of Traditional Leaders, went a long way towards recognizing South Africa's heritage of legal pluralism, it also served to ensure the representation of social forces which would otherwise be excluded by the democratic process. Although they had only limited consultation functions, these bodies were empowered to delay legislation related to their own status and indigenous law. However, the ex officio governmental status accorded to traditional leaders – who were entitled to be members of local governments within whose jurisdictions they may reside – created a form of local autonomy based on ethnic status and provided access to governmental representation reminiscent of the consociational demands formally rejected in the negotiating process. Significantly, these provisions were downgraded in the final 1996 Constitution. Instead of the mandatory recognition of traditional leaders provided for in the interim Constitution, the Constitutional Assembly, from which the Inkatha Freedom Party (IFP) excluded itself, only granted constitutional recognition to the 'institution, status and role of traditional leadership', while simultaneously providing that the role of traditional leaders in local government institutions and the regional and national houses and council of traditional leaders may be provided for by legislation. In effect this removed the constitutional mandate and threw the question of the role of traditional leaders back into the political arena. While customary law is still recognized in the final Constitution, it is clearly subjugated to both the Constitution and statutory law.

The constitutional introduction of specific institutional mechanisms for the incorporation of particular interests – traditional leaders and Volkstaat adherents – reintroduced a degree of corporatism otherwise precluded by the central individualism of post–cold war constitutionalism. This in turn enabled the new South African legislature to take a further step back (or forward in social democratic terms) towards social corporatism by creating a statutory body to institutionalize negotiations between capital, labour, organized communities and the state.[9] Although this latter form of corporatism had many international precedents, the constitutional introduction of bodies designed to ensure the participation of traditional leaders and those 'who support the establishment of a Volkstaat for those who want it'[10] was a unique 'local' feature of the 1993 interim Constitution. Not consociational in form, nor corporatist in effect, these semi-corporatist institutions provided a unique attempt to recognize specific cultural identities within a formally democratic constitutional structure that recognized only one category of citizenship – South Africans. Both the *Council of Traditional Leaders Act* 31 of 1994 and the *Volkstaat Council Act* 30 of 1994 reflected this tension in their failure adequately to define the identity of persons competent to participate in these institutions. Unlike the *National Economic, Development and Labour*

Council Act 35 of 1994, which established the identity of participants as representatives of particular interest groups and defined in detail the manner in which participants would be elected, the *Volkstaat Council Act* and the *Council of Traditional Leaders Act* were deliberately vague as to the source of identity of their participants. The *Volkstaat Council Act* defined its participants purely in negative terms – for example a person could not be a member of the Council if they were not a South African citizen,[11] or if they were an unrehabilitated insolvent[12] or of unsound mind[13] – and relied, for a positive criterion, on s 184A(2) of the Constitution's definition of participants as those '20 members elected by members of Parliament who support the establishment of a Volkstaat'. This vagueness, born out of a conflict over the definition of the Afrikaner nation, must be unique in the history of struggles for the expression and protection of cultural identity. Similarly, the *Council of Traditional Leaders Act* referred to the participants as those who 'shall be elected by an electoral college constituted by the members of the Houses'.[14] It relied on the notion of traditional authorities contained in sections 181–184 of the Constitution to give specificity to the notion of a traditional authority. While the Act relied on the establishment of a House of Traditional Leaders in each province, as provided for in s 183(1)(a) of the Constitution, in effect the definition of a traditional leader was left unspecified. This opened the door to increased contestation and conflict over the identity of traditional leaders, particularly in a context where the removal and replacement of chiefs was an active component of 'native policy' under the colonial and later apartheid state. It is ironic that a post-apartheid Department of Constitutional Affairs is so actively engaged in the negotiation of an increasing number of claims to traditional leadership and also succession disputes, so reminiscent of the apartheid regime's encouragement and perpetuation of ethnicity and tribalism.

Most of these independent institutions embraced as part of the transitional agreement became permanent features of the post-apartheid state through their inclusion in the 'final' 1996 Constitution – including the Public Protector, Auditor-General, Electoral Commission, the Human Rights Commission, and the Commission for Gender Equality. They also achieved a significant consolidation of their status through their collective characterization as state institutions supporting constitutional democracy.[15] Significantly, however, both the Council of Traditional Leaders and the Volkstaat Council lost their constitutional standing in the 'final' 1996 Constitution. Instead, these interests were given a more general recognition, recognizing traditional leadership[16] on the one hand, and granting recognition on the other, to 'the notion of self-determination of any community sharing a common cultural and language heritage, within a territorial entity within the Republic or in any other way, determined by national legislation'.[17] These institutions were replaced, however, with a general Commission for the Promotion and Protection of the Rights of Cultural, Religious and Linguistic Communities, included among the State Institutions Supporting Constitutional Democracy.[18]

Another central feature of the post–cold war process of political reconstruction has been the de-linking of the control of currency values and fiscal policy from the government of the day through the creation of constitutionally independent central banks. Even the United Kingdom, which does not have a written constitution, saw the newly elected Labour Party government in 1997, in one of its first official acts, grant independence to the Bank of England. Similarly, both the 1993 'interim' Constitution and the 1996 Constitution provide for an independent central bank along with a number of other mechanisms designed to 'stabilize' the financial structure of the state by removing political discretion as to the distribution of revenue between different spheres of government – national, provincial and local – as well as an independent commission for determining the remuneration of public officials.

Despite this clear adherence to the dominant post–cold war paradigm of fragmented power and the insulation of financial powers from the 'instability' of democratic politics, the attempt to constitutionalize a particular economic orientation as well as to constitutionalize the relationship between capital and labour – through the inclusion of a right to engage freely in economic activity and a labour relations clause in the 1993 Constitution's Bill of Rights – proscribed the limits of the post-cold war paradigm in the context of South Africa's constitutional politics. First, the broadly crafted right to economic activity clause of the 1993 Constitution – interpreted by its proponents as guaranteeing a free market economy – was replaced by a more limited clause guaranteeing the right of individuals freely to choose their trade, occupation or profession. Second, due to the labour movement's central place within the ANC alliance[19] and through its repeated protests and threats of strike action, Cosatu succeeded in its demand that the interim Constitution's compromise giving equal rights to capital and labour[20] be rewritten. As a consequence, the right to strike remained enshrined in the final Constitution, but the provision guaranteeing the employer's recourse to lockout was removed.

Despite the emphasis in the post–cold war paradigm on limiting state power and leaving redistributive issues to the market, the South African process of reconstruction also brought forth particular mechanisms designed to address the legacy of apartheid. Significantly, the attempt to follow the dominant post–cold war paradigm by constitutionalizing economic priorities and existing property relations created political space for the inclusion of a counter-hegemonic trend which was further

123

consolidated in the 'final' 1996 Constitution. Thus, the 'final' Constitution includes various mechanisms designed to address the legacy of apartheid, including: constitutional protections for state policies of affirmative action; provisions for the restitution of land as well as specific protections for land reform; and also the introduction of socio-economic rights as justiciable rights within the Bill of Rights.

AT THE CORE IS PROPERTY

The conflicts, debates and final compromise on the inclusion of a property rights clause in the South African Constitution provide a window through which this particular interaction between global and local imperatives may be viewed. While the internationally endorsed process for the transition away from apartheid included a commitment to the rule of law and the inclusion of a justiciable bill of rights, there was no clarity on the contents of this commitment. As a result, the different political parties and interest groups entered into a process in which they sought to shape the meaning of these commitments so as to achieve their particular goals. While this 'debate' over the content of particular commitments or rights reflected the political goals and assumptions of the different parties, it was also substantially framed by the available intellectual resources. These included primarily the historical 'text' of local experience as well as the 'text' of international and foreign jurisdictions, which served simultaneously as exemplary resources in the pursuit of particular goals and as the bounded universe constraining the choices and options of the parties.

My own introduction to the debate over property coincided with de Klerk's February 1990 public announcement of the political opening that would set the stage for South Africa's democratic transition. At that moment I was at the headquarters of the ANC in Lusaka, Zambia, helping to organize a workshop on the 'Land Question', which had been initiated by fellow-ANC activists Bongiwe Njobe and Helena Dolny. While the workshop focused on analysing the state of rural South Africa, all the participants – ANC members who ranged from scholars and traditional leaders to peasant activists – seemed to assume that nationalization of existing land holdings, given a history of dispossession and the vast inequalities in land holdings between black and white,[21] would be high on the agenda of an ANC government. This shared assumption was based in no small part on our commitment to the 1955 Freedom Charter – recognized by the ANC as expressing the will of the South African people – which declared in part that the 'national wealth of our country … shall be restored to the people', and 'all the land redivided amongst those who work it, to banish famine and land hunger'.[22]

Despite our assumptions and the liberation movement's general rhetoric on the 'Land Question', activists at the workshop had a realistic view of the low priority rural issues had on the mainly urban-based ANC's political agenda in the late 1980s. We were, however, encouraged by the 'Economy and Land' sections of the ANC's constitutional guidelines, which had been issued in 1988 as part of the ANC's preparations for negotiations with the apartheid regime. Here, the ANC signalled its future intentions to both the international community and the apartheid regime, by announcing its intention constitutionally to protect property. While this promise went further than what might have been expected, given the rhetoric of socialization, nationalization and redistribution so dominant in the ANC at the time, the limited focus on property for 'personal use and consumption', allowed these conflicting visions of redistribution and property rights to coexist. This coexistence was aided by the document's commitment to 'devise and implement a land reform programme ... in conformity with the principle of affirmative action, taking into account the status of victims of forced removals'.[23] With the exact modes of implementation still open to debate, the Lusaka workshop opted to institutionalize the issue within the ANC by calling for the formation of an ANC Land Commission to address the lack of specific policies within the organization.

It was as a member of the ANC Land Commission's secretariat (first alone and joined later by two others)[24] that I returned to South Africa in June 1990. In setting up the Land Commission, we soon began to work with the already well-established community of lawyers, NGOs and activists who had long struggled against forced removals in the courts and on the land.[25] This informal coalition provided both the organizational basis, knowledge and experience which sustained the struggle for the recognition of dispossessed land rights during the political transition and constitution-making process. While the ANC Land Commission had access to the ANC's internal policy-making processes and could evoke strong public reaction as a voice of the ANC – as we experienced in the public furors over a suggested wealth tax to pay for compensation to landowners whose land would be expropriated for redistribution, or when suggestions were made about claims on land within the national parks – it was the return to land campaigns of land claimants, and their lawyers' continued engagement with the de Klerk government, that frustrated the apartheid regime's attempts to pre-empt future claims. This the apartheid government attempted to do by repealing the Land Acts in 1991[26] and establishing an Advisory Commission on Land Allocation[27] with the purpose of settling all claims before the political transition to democratic rule could be completed.

It was from this perspective then, that I was able both to participate in[28] and to view the debate over property rights and how the rules of the game were framed for the new South Africa. At first, discussion centred on the ANC's Draft Bill of Rights, which was published in 1990 and which contained a single Article addressing the 'economy, land and property'.[29] Within the ANC, the Land Commission began hearing from its constituency and opening debates on land reform, nationalization and restitution. This process began with newly formed branches and communities locked in land conflicts around the country, but increasingly focused on a series of internal discussions, joined at times by activists and lawyers of the land movement, with members of the Constitutional Committee[30] as well as in engagements with other activists and sectors in a series of conferences initiated by the Constitutional Committee – at which special sessions or subgroups focused on the issue of land and property. Outside the ANC, the Land Commission built links and worked closely with lawyers and activists of the return to land movement and became engaged in wider public debates over land claims and land redistribution. Central to these debates was the status that property rights would have in a future constitution.

Although the ANC's Draft Bill of Rights only protected, in our view, limited rights to personal property, it became clear at the May 1991 conference convened by the ANC Constitutional Committee, that the ANC was under a great deal of pressure to grant greater recognition to property rights. In fact, attempts at that conference to question whether there should be any constitutionally protected property rights at all elicited a highly charged response from one member of the Constitutional Committee, who warned that the rejection of property rights would directly endanger the democratic transition. In response, the participants at the conference called for a reworking of the draft in which land would be recognized as a specific form of property and treated separately from property in general. As such, concern was expressed about the recognition of property rights before the implementation of the necessary process of redistribution. Furthermore, participants made a commitment to include positive rights to land for the landless.[31]

While this internal debate sought simultaneously to limit the reach of existing property rights and to secure a more equitable distribution of property in the future, the response of the regime and the existing economic interests was expressed most clearly by the South African Law Commission – a nominally independent statutory body. In its August 1991 'Interim Report on Group and Human Rights', the Law Commission launched a sustained attack against the ANC draft, charging that the 'ANC's bill ... provides, in a manner which hardly disguises the aim, for nationalization of private property without objectively testable norms for compensation', and that what the ANC intended was 'in fact nothing but nationalization under the cloak of expropriation ... designed to secure state control over property'.[32]

Instead, the Law Commission called for the protection of private property and for the payment of just compensation in the event of expropriation in the public interest. Likewise, the Democratic Party, traditionally the party of big capital and white liberals, proposed a comprehensive right to property, which could only be derogated by lawful expropriation in the public interest, and only then, when subject to the 'proper payment of equitable compensation, which in the event of dispute, shall be determined by an ordinary court of law'.[33] Neither of these proposals provided for the restitution of property taken under apartheid and as such failed to comprehend the threat to property rights, and even the very notion of constitutional rights, that the legal entrenchment of apartheid's spoils entails.

While attention was focused on the question of property rights, the ANC Land Commission continued to hold meetings around the country to discuss land issues. Furthermore, activists working in or identified by the ANC Land Commission were being exposed to international experiences of land reform, including a Ford Foundation–funded, six-week, mini-course organized by the Land Tenure Center at the University of Wisconsin, Madison. These activities aimed both to increase awareness within the ANC, as well as to begin the formulation of a land policy for adoption by the movement. The first target of this campaign was to commit the organization to a set of principles upon which a policy could be built. With this as its goal, the ANC Land Commission held a national conference in June 1991 at which we produced a set of guidelines for the development of land policy. These guidelines were then presented and adopted at the ANC's National Conference in July 1991. The most important features of the Land Manifesto were: its simultaneous commitment to both land restitution and land redistribution; its recognition of a diversity of land tenure forms; and the advancement of a policy of affirmative action as the main device to achieve specific policy goals.[34] With these guidelines the ANC effectively endorsed a strategy against the simple constitutional recognition of private property as recognized by the apartheid state. First, by demanding both restitution and land reform, it questioned and threatened the legitimacy of existing property rights. Second, the recognition of different forms of tenure de-centred private land ownership and provided a basis for the recognition of communal and other forms of land tenure. Finally, the manifesto recognized that affirmative action–type policies would provide a structure in which the multitude of specific policy goals and claims of different constituencies within the ANC could be accommodated and targeted to address land issues and the interests of the rural poor.

At the October 1991 National Conference on Affirmative Action, convened by the ANC Constitutional Committee, a report back to the plenary session from the subgroup on land concluded that a 'wealth tax' would be necessary to fund land redistribution. Given the demand that any expropriation be compensated, we concluded that the only way to achieve the redistribution of land necessary to overcome the legacy of the 1913 Land Acts was to create a specific compensation account. In order to achieve the equitable redistribution required, this dedicated account would need to be funded by those who benefited from the limited land market created by the Land Acts, which had reserved eighty-seven per cent of land for white ownership and control. This could be achieved, it was argued, by the imposition of a 'wealth tax' similar to the equalization tax adopted in the Federal Republic of Germany in the aftermath of the Second World War. While the idea of special taxes to overcome the vast disparities created by apartheid has continued to raise interest, in 1991 the reaction was immediate – the major white-controlled newspapers went ballistic and within hours I was once again receiving death threats from those who had attempted to silence opposition during the height of apartheid. Although senior ANC leaders supported our right to conduct a debate on the 'wealth tax', it also became clear that any attempt to conduct an effective redistribution of land rights would meet extremely stiff opposition from the *ancien régime* as well as conflict with alternative demands for resources among the ANC's own constituencies.

Despite this fierce public exposure, when formal negotiations began at the Convention for a Democratic South Africa (Codesa) in December 1991, it seemed as if the land issue would, once again, be pushed into the background as the parties clashed over the very nature of the political transition. As far as property issues were concerned, they were subsumed in the larger debate over whether the purpose of Codesa was to produce a detailed interim constitution or broad constitutional principles, which would guide, but not frustrate, the work of a future democratically elected constitution-making body. Despite this marginalization of substantive issues in the negotiations, for land claimants and those active in support of their demands, the struggle over land and property rights continued simultaneously on two planes: first, in actual land occupations and attempts to return to land, from which communities had been forcibly removed – whether by occupation or legal and administrative negotiations with the Advisory Commission on Land Allocations[35] and the de Klerk government; second, at the level of ideas, with debates over different policy options continuing at a series of conferences and meetings, either organized by the ANC Constitutional Committee together with various university-based institutes or directly by the academy. One of the most important of these was organized by long-time land activist

Aninka Claassens through the Centre for Applied Legal Studies (CALS), to discuss 'the effect that a constitutionally entrenched right to property might have on future land reform legislation and programmes'.[36]

The opening of a discussion on particular options for the recognition of land rights and the consequences a property clause might have on land claims was, at this stage, a vital intervention, making it clear that the issue of land rights could not be divorced from the wider question of property. Furthermore, when this conference is placed in the context of the series of conferences, meetings and workshops held in this period,[37] its significance, as one in a series of intellectual loci of the South African transition, may be recognized. At these events, new substantive ideas were introduced into the public debate while simultaneously being framed through their presentation in the context of different international histories and examples. Among the important substantive interventions made at the CALS conference was the public floating of the suggestion for a land claims court – in the form of a report to the conference from a group of lawyers and activists from the 'land claims movement' who were working on this option at the behest of the ANC Land Commission.[38] Other important substantive interventions at this conference included Geoff Budlender's construction of a legal right to land for the landless,[39] as well as the work of Catherine Cross, who demonstrated the continued vitality and existence of an alternative understanding of land rights in opposition to the prevailing legal notions of individual private property rights.[40] Presentation of the Canadian decision to preclude the explicit recognition of property rights from their 1982 Charter of Rights[41] and the history of constitutional conflict over land reform in India in the post-independence years[42] introduced both substantive examples of alternative approaches and provided grist for debate over the dangers of, and alternatives to, the constitutional enshrinement of property rights.

It was these interventions that forced the ANC to re-evaluate its own proposed 'Draft Bill of Rights'. After several meetings with land activists and members of the Land Commission, Albie Sachs proposed new sections on Land and the Environment as well as a separate Property clause for the revised text of the ANC Draft Bill of Rights.[43] These new sections essentially expanded the ANC's proposals, making it clear that land rights would remain a central claim of the anti-apartheid movement and that the protection of property would remain subject to these claims. While property rights were given separate recognition for the first time in the new text, the text also suggested that these references to property, along with all other 'principles governing economic life' might be better placed outside the Bill of Rights in non-justiciable or interpretive sections of the constitution defined, as is the case in India, as 'Directive Principles of State Policy'.[44]

By the time this revised text was first published in May 1992, negotiations with the de Klerk government had formally broken down – collapsing Codesa into a morass of mutual recriminations.[45] At the same time the government's land claims forum was being rejected by communities[46] who were threatening physically to reoccupy their lands[47] and the ANC Land Commission was being thrust into an engagement with new actors – both national and international – who had recognized the centrality of land to the struggle over property rights. The first engagement, which culminated in a meeting in late 1992, was with the Urban Foundation, a policy institute funded by South African big business, who asked for a meeting with the ANC Land Commission to discuss land claims and the question of creating a land claims court. At this meeting, the ANC delegation, which included members of the Constitutional Committee as well as the Land Commission and its allies in the land movement, were presented with the argument that, while some form of limited land claims process might be necessary to legitimize future property relations, both the demand for land among the African majority and the reality of resource needs and allocations for future development required that this process be tightly circumscribed. While we recognized the problem of competition over resources under a future democratic government, we argued that any attempt to engage in an all but symbolic process of restitution would fail to build the legitimacy they seemed to recognize was needed to secure property relations in the new South Africa.

The second of these new engagements began in mid-1992, when the World Bank launched its own initiatives in South Africa. Our immediate response was to ask who had invited it to South Africa, and to reject the notion of engagement with this institution. Soon, however, we realized that the World Bank was developing its own strategy towards the 'new' South Africa[48] and would continue to do so whether or not we engaged. Refusal by definition meant lack of knowledge and influence. The Bank, at the same time, had been rebuffed by other sectors of the anti-apartheid movement – particularly the urban sector activists – and responded to our own hesitations by organizing an initial seminar outside South Africa, in Mbabane, Swaziland, in November 1992. To this event they invited representatives from different South African political groupings, government and non-government bodies to discuss a set of papers prepared by the World Bank and its consultants.[49]

These two engagements presented radically alternative possibilities and opportunities. While the Urban Foundation (UF) was convinced that the demand for land reform among Africans was being grossly exaggerated, Hans Binswanger, the senior World Bank adviser who dominated the Swaziland seminar, presented a vision of comparative development in which success depended upon the carrying out of a successful land reform.[50] While the UF suggested a limited process of restitution in order to legitimize property rights, Binswanger argued that land claims and even land invasions would drive a process of land reform and suggested that by facilitating land reform the government would be providing an essential catalyst for sustained economic development. Although the ANC Land Commission remained extremely sceptical of the equities of the World Bank's proposals – for a market-driven reform focused on small-scale producers – we realized immediately that the World Bank's position could be deployed as a way to keep the issue of land reform on the political agenda. With this aim we encouraged Binswanger to persuade the de Klerk government that land reform was and should remain an essential part of South Africa's political transition. At the same time we introduced Binswanger to members of the ANC's leadership, including the Constitutional Committee, facilitating ANC agreement to engage with the World Bank on these issues.

This engagement was pursued through the newly formed Land and Agricultural Policy Centre (LAPC) and was structured by the tension between the ANC's historic concerns about the role of the Bretton Woods institutions and by our concerns to retain some influence over the Bank's activities in the political transition. As we began to negotiate our working relationship with the Bank's representative, Robert Christiansen, I attended a meeting of NGOs in Johannesburg at which Martin Khor of the Malaysian-based Third-World Network and representatives of a World Bank monitoring group from Washington, DC, explained the structure and workings of the institution. Although we had already experienced the dramatic impact that interest by the Bank could have on an issue, the understanding we gained from these activists of the manner in which the Bank's missions operated convinced us of the need to engage the Bank closely and to retain some influence over the Bank's own information gathering and analytical process.

While the World Bank both wanted and needed our endorsement of its plan to prepare a Rural Restructuring Program (RRP) for South Africa, we demanded that the initial research work be conducted by and remain under the control of South Africans. This was made possible through the creation of terms of reference for the preparation of a series of background reports that would form the basis of the preparation of the RRP. The resulting 'aide memoire' was concluded on 15 June 1993, in which Christiansen committed the Bank to a process that would 'be fully transparent, consultative and collaborative at all stages'.[51] To this end, I was asked to head the legal research team, and to prepare the report on the constitutional requirements of a land restitution and reform process. Later, as a member of the World Bank's mission to South Africa in late 1993, I participated in the formulation of the Bank's proposal for an RRP for the country. While there were many parts of the report with which I was not in complete agreement, its importance from the perspective of the ANC Land Commission lay in its clear assertion that both land restitution and land reform were central to rural restructuring.[52] Furthermore, even though our argument that a constitutionalized property right would impede land redistribution was excised at the last moment, in favour of the Bank's ideal of a market-driven process, we were able to obtain a clear statement in the report to the effect that land restitution and even redistribution were so important that, in the event of market failure, government intervention would be both justified and necessary. When the World Bank's RRP was presented in South Africa at the LAPC-organized Land Redistribution Options Conference in October 1993, it had to compete with a range of suggestions and received serious academic and political criticism. As a result, the programme never gained a life of its own, but became yet another source of the smorgasbord of alternatives both enabling and constraining the options available to policy makers in the new South Africa. Its most enduring impacts may be its endorsement of land restitution and reform on the one hand and its emphasis upon the market in achieving these reforms on the other.

Prior to the beginning of substantive constitutional negotiations in early 1993, however, the ANC and government still held dramatically alternative notions of how property should be constitutionally protected. On the one hand, the ANC was willing to protect the undisturbed enjoyment of personal possessions, so long as property entitlements were to be determined by legislation and provision was to be made for the restoration of land to people dispossessed under apartheid.[53] The Government's proposals, on the other hand, aimed at protecting all property rights and would only allow expropriation for public purposes and subject to cash compensation determined by a court of law according to the market value of the property.[54] In response, the ANC suggested that no property clause was necessary.[55]

As negotiations with the de Klerk regime gained momentum in 1993, conflict over the property clause began to focus on specific issues. Although the ANC had initially insisted that an 'interim' constitution contain only those guarantees necessary to ensure an even political playing field, the momentum for entrenching rights could not be slowed, and before long we recognized that we were in the process of negotiating a complete bill of rights. It was in this context that the apartheid government insisted that property rights be included in the 'interim' Constitution and that the measure of compensation include specific reference to the market value of the property.[56] In response, the ANC insisted that the property clause not frustrate efforts to address land claims and that the state must have the power to regulate property without being obliged to pay compensation unless there was a clear expropriation of the property. Although the regime agreed that explicit provisions guaranteeing and providing for land restitution should be included, its negotiators insisted that such provisions should not be located within the property clause. Instead, it was proposed that if they were to be included, they should be incorporated into the corrective action provisions of the equality clause.

Fearing that their rights to land, long denied and actively destroyed by the apartheid regime, would be shut out by the constitutional recognition of existing property rights, communities active in the return to land movement joined those who brought their claims in the form of mass demonstrations, petitions, etc., directly to the World Trade Centre in Kempton Park – the site of the multiparty negotiations. A march on the World Trade Centre in June 1993, in which a land rights memorandum was delivered to the negotiators, was followed by a march in central Pretoria in September 1993, in which about 600 people from twenty-five rural communities threatened to reoccupy land from which they had been removed by the apartheid government as a way of highlighting their demands for the unconditional restitution of land, the establishment of a land claims court and guaranteed security of tenure for farm workers and labour tenants. The Transvaal Rural Action Committee, which organized the march, also called for the rejection of the proposed property clause in the Constitution.[57]

Answering these demands and conflicts, the interim 1993 Constitution provided a separate institutional basis for land restitution, which was guaranteed in the corrective action provisions of the equality clause,[58] and compromised on the question of compensation by including a range of factors the courts would have to consider in determining just and equitable compensation.[59] Significantly, as Matthew Chaskalson argues, the final outcome in terms of the specific wording adopted was as much a result of serendipity, legal ignorance and the particular quirks and concerns of the individual negotiators, as the logical product of an informed or even interest-based political debate and compromise.[60] This is demonstrated most aptly in the choice of the terminology of public purpose over public interest in the expropriation clause, despite agreement among the parties to give the state as much leeway as possible in this regard.

Even then, however, the substance of the outcome reflects both the general contours of the political conflict over the property clause and the bounded alternatives available to the parties – from the recognition of existing property rights on the one hand to the recognition of land claims on the other. Significantly, the factors to be considered in the determination of just compensation reflect this outcome. On the one hand, they were directed at the problem of land claims and included 'the use to which the property is being put, the history of its acquisition, the value of the investments in it by those affected and the interest of those affected',[61] while on the other hand, at the insistence of the *ancien régime* and making possible the inclusion of other factors, they enshrined 'market value'. It was under this constitutional regime that Mandela's government and South Africa's first democratic Parliament began to address land claims. Acting in terms of the specific clauses of the 1993 Constitution, which provided for the establishment of a land claims process, Parliament passed the *Restitution of Land Claims Act* in 1994, setting up regional Land Claims Commissions and the new Land Claims Court.[62]

Despite predictions that there would be very little change in the Constitution during the second phase of the constitution-making process, particularly on such sensitive issues as the property clause and the Bill of Rights, the property issue, in fact, once again became one of the unresolvable lightning rods in the Constitutional Assembly. Although the committee charged with reviewing the Bill of Rights was at first reluctant to change the formulation of the 1993 compromise, challenges centred on the question of land restitution and reform[63] once again forced open the process.[64] In this case the impetus came from a Workshop on Land Rights and the Constitution organized by the Constitutional Assembly's sub-committee, Theme Committee 6.3, whose task it was to resolve issues related to specialized structures of government such as the Land Claims Commission and Court provided for in the 1993 Constitution. Focusing on the land issue, this meeting once again raised the problem of property rights in the Constitution. While some participants again questioned whether there should be any property protection within the final Constitution, the major change from the period in which the 1993 Constitution was negotiated was that the participants in this workshop, even those representing long established interests like the National Party and the South African Agricultural Union, now agreed on the need 'to rectify past wrongs' and on land reform. Disagreement here was over the means. The South African Agricultural Union, for example, continued to assert that 'it should be done in a way without jeopardising the protection of private ownership', while the National Party now embraced the World Bank's proposals, arguing that land reform should 'be accomplished within the parameters of the market and should be demand-driven'.

The outcome of this workshop and the submissions made to Theme Committee 6.3 was a report to the Constitutional Assembly which both challenged the existing 1993 formulation of property rights and called for a specific land clause to provide a 'constitutional framework and protection for all land reform measures'.[65] While Theme Committee 4, which was responsible for the Bill of Rights, had thus far uncontroversially adopted a property clause which merely incorporated the 1993

Constitution's restitution provisions into the property clause itself, the report on Land Rights threw the proverbial cat among the pigeons. Some objected to Theme Committee 6.3's very discussion of property rights, while others sensed an opportunity to reopen the debate on property rights and to once again question their very inclusion in the Bill of Rights. As a result, the Draft Bill of Rights published by the Constitutional Assembly on 9 October 1995 included an option that there be 'no property clause at all'.

It was in this context that an alternative option, a property clause including within it specific land rights, as well as a subclause insulating land reform from constitutional attack, began to gain momentum. While a strategy to insulate land restitution and land reform from constitutional attack had been implicit from early on in the debate, it was a suggestion in a submission to Theme Committee 6.3 that the property clause include a specific subclause insulating state action aimed at redressing past discrimination in the ownership and distribution of land rights, that the negotiators were able to rely upon as a compromise between those demanding the removal of the property clause and those who, like the Democratic Party, remained opposed to even the social democratic formulation modelled on the German Constitution.[66] Still the debate raged on and the draft formulations of the property clause continued to evolve.[67] Political agreement on the property clause was only finally reached at midnight on 18 April 1996, when subsection 28(8), the 'affirmative action' or insulation subclause of the property clause, was modified so as to make it subject to s 36(1), the general limitations clause of the Constitution.[68]

The final property clause reflects the democratic origins of the Constitutional Assembly. It not only guarantees the restitution of land taken after 1913[69] and a right to legally secure tenure for those whose tenure is insecure as a result of racially discriminatory laws or practices,[70] but also includes an obligation on the state to enable citizens to gain access to land on an equitable basis.[71] Furthermore, the state is granted a limited exemption from the protective provisions of the property clause so as to empower it to take 'legislative and other measures to achieve land, water and related reform, in order to redress the results of past racial discrimination'.[72]

Despite agreement in the Constitutional Assembly, the property clause was presented to the Constitutional Court as violating the Constitutional Principles, this giving grounds for denying certification of the Constitution.[73] Two major objections were raised: first, that unlike the Interim Constitution, the new clause did not expressly protect the right to acquire, hold and dispose of property; second, that the provisions governing expropriation and the payment of compensation were inadequate.[74] The Constitutional Court rejected both of these arguments. First, the Court noted that the test to be applied was whether the formulation of the right met the standard of a 'universally accepted fundamental right' as required by Constitutional Principle II. Second the Court surveyed international and foreign sources and observed that '[i]f one looks to international conventions and foreign constitutions, one is immediately struck by the wide variety of formulations adopted to protect the right to property, as well as by the fact that significant conventions and constitutions contain no protection of property at all'.[75] In conclusion the Court argued that it could not 'uphold the argument that, because the formulation adopted is expressed in a negative and not a positive form and because it does not contain an express recognition of the right to acquire and dispose of property, it fails to meet the prescription of CPII'.[76] The second objection, against the standards for compensation, met the same fate, with the Court concluding that an 'examination of international conventions and foreign constitutions suggests that a wide range of criteria for expropriation and the payment of compensation exists', and thus the 'approach taken in NT 25 [new text s 25] cannot be said to flout any universally accepted approach to the question'.[77]

Although it may be argued that the property clause in the final Constitution is unique to South Africa and is the product of South Africa's particular history of dispossession, it is also important to note how resolution of the property question was framed by international options. While the Constitutional Court could argue that the particular formulation of the clause was compatible with global standards – given the variety of formulations in existence – it is also true that those who advocated that there should be no property clause in the Constitution were compelled by the politics of recognition of property rights to accept its inclusion.

The politics of constitution-making in this instance were thus bounded on both sides. Both the option of widespread nationalization initially advocated by the African National Congress, which may have been facilitated by the exclusion of a property clause, and the demands for a strict protection of property guaranteeing market-value compensation for any interference were silenced. Instead the parties were able to use the international and foreign lexicon of treaties, constitutions and case law to formulate a specifically South African compromise. This resolution both enabled the political transition and left open, for future fact-specific confrontations, the exact interpretation to be given to the new Constitution's property clauses.

SHAPING LOCAL OPTIONS: GLOBALISM AND HYBRIDIZATION

While I have tried to trace the contribution international forces, examples and legal sources had on the making of the property clause in South Africa's new Bill of Rights, as well as the impact of local histories, ideas and struggles on its ultimate form, I will conclude by trying to specify the conditions that made such hybridity possible and the often unintended consequences of these developments. First, it is important to recognize why 'the international' might have had such valence in South Africa's transition. While the specific examples drawn upon by the particular players had no individual significance – from the United States, German and Canadian constitutional formulations, to the histories of the Indian Claims Commission in the United States, land reforms in Taiwan and South Korea and the equalization tax in postwar Germany, to constitutional conflicts over land reform in post-colonial India and the affirmative land rights provisions in the Papua New Guinean Constitution – their role as part of an international text had a major impact on the shaping of the alternatives open to the South African participants. The power of 'international experience', I would suggest, came not only from a fundamental belief that international norms provide an external point of reference for conflicting parties, as well as the ANC's strategic commitment to international norms as a means of precluding some of the most cherished claims of the *ancien régime*, but also from a history in which the anti-apartheid movement had long looked to international norms to sustain its critique of apartheid. As Nelson Mandela argued in explaining the ANC's adoption of a 'human rights programme' at the opening of the ANC's workshop on a future Bill of Rights in May 1991:

> International human rights standards have provided the legal and moral inspiration for the struggle against the antithesis of civilised values: apartheid. By characterizing apartheid as a crime, by protecting our combatants, by describing certain aspects of apartheid as genocide, international rules have validated our struggle. As a result, the apartheid regime has treated such developments with disdain and contempt. We have been cut off from full membership of the international community through South Africa's refusal to adhere to the basic international texts governing human rights.[78]

Second, the process of negotiation and even serendipity – whether political or intellectual – in which the different interest groups and players posited alternative and often conflicting examples and formulations, created an unconscious process of hybridization. As some possibilities – such as nationalization or the total protection of all existing property rights – were precluded, other imaginable alternatives were produced from the remnants of past hopes and viable possibilities. These alternatives then became the building blocks of each successive formulation and reimagining.

Third, the two-stage constitution-making process adopted in the South African transition enabled the recognition of legitimate claims to restitution, even if narrowly defined, in the first phase, to become the basis for the explicit limitation of property rights in the final Constitution. Not only was it possible to bring the right of restitution into the property clause, where it logically belonged, but the shift in power enabled the Constitutional Assembly – despite desperate struggles to the contrary – to include positive rights to land and an explicit affirmative exception for future land and water reform to be included within the property clause of the final Constitution.

Finally, despite the obvious gains made by those who participated in the struggle for the restitution of land taken by the apartheid regime through acts of forced removal, which will always represent the darkest face of the crime of apartheid, it is also necessary to face up to the unintended consequence of our victory – the protection of the wealth of apartheid's beneficiaries. While it may be argued – and indeed was argued, at the ANC Conference on a Future Bill of Rights in 1991 – that a peaceful transition to democracy required important compromises including the recognition of existing property rights, it is also true that the focus on land left the country's real wealth – now in companies, mines, stocks and bonds as well as urban housing – completely unchallenged.

CHAPTER 7

THE CONSTITUTIONAL COURT AND THE INSTITUTIONAL DYNAMICS OF CONSTITUTIONALISM

Introducing a supreme Constitution has fundamentally changed the place of the judiciary in South Africa's constitutional and political order. Analysis of the judicial role, and the Constitutional Court in particular, has in consequence focused on developing an understanding of how the Court will go about its task of applying and interpreting the Constitution, and the Bill of Rights in particular. This approach relies, it has been argued, upon comparative constitutionalism to trace the history of 'ideological and jurisprudential struggle on the part of the judiciary to develop a coherent set of constitutional values which emanate clearly from a Bill of Rights and which can act as reliable signposts *en route* to a decision'.[1] While this approach may be central to understanding the practice of advocates before the courts and indeed for identifying the relevant issues to which the Court will look in formulating its opinions in particular cases, I will argue that this approach provides only a part of the answer to the 'mighty problem' of judicial review.[2]

Focusing on constitutional interpretation, and the explication of particular constitutional rights by courts in different parts of the world, fails to question how courts achieve the power, often in direct contradiction to a legislative majority or a popularly elected executive, to decide on issues of fundamental social importance. The doctrinal response is, of course, to point to the sections of the Constitution which explicitly grant the Court the power of judicial review, or failing which, to refer to case law in which the power was assumed. This response, however, fails in the face of a history in which courts, even when explicitly granted powers of judicial review, have either been 'executive-minded' in their deference to the executive or just failed to exercise this authority. This trajectory is evidenced even in the Supreme Court of the United States, which for long periods of its history failed to uphold the rights of citizens against government and private violation.[3]

In the late twentieth century there was a globalization of the notion that individual rights, inscribed in written constitutions, are an essential part of democratic governance. However, little attention was paid to the institutional requirements and consequences of placing greater reliance on the courts, in introducing a justiciable bill of rights or constitutional supremacy, even though in the United States, which provided the model for constitutional review, the issue of reliance on the courts has been much discussed. The capacity of the courts – and a constitutional court in particular – is an essential prerequisite to the judiciary's effective assertion of the power of constitutional review and thus becomes a central element in securing the future vibrancy of constitutional rights. I will argue that only an institutional analysis of how courts achieve, over time, the power to decide who decides, will enable us to develop a balanced understanding of the role the judiciary is now called upon to play in South Africa.

CREATING THE NEW CONSTITUTIONAL COURT

However, before turning to explore the role of the Constitutional Court, in both introducing constitutional review and managing the irreconcilable fissures of political conflict that continue to plague the new South Africa, it is necessary to look briefly at the creation of the Court itself. Once the parties in the Multi-Party Negotiating Process reached agreement requiring a future Constitutional Court to certify the consistency of the final Constitution with the Constitutional Principles,[4] thus enabling the democratic transition to proceed, the parties focused their attention on the content of the Constitutional Principles as a way of continuing their struggles for particular outcomes – especially over regional powers and racially or ethnically-defined governance. Similarly, the crucial role of the future Constitutional Court brought increased attention to bear on the process of appointment for the Constitutional Court. In fact, the conflict over this process brought the multiparty negotiations, once again, perilously close to deadlock.

Initially little political attention was paid to the Technical Committee's proposal that Constitutional Court judges be nominated by an all-party parliamentary committee and be appointed by a seventy-five per cent majority of both Houses of Parliament. However, as the significance of the Constitutional Court became increasingly clear, a major political conflict exploded.[5] Although Chief Justice Michael Corbett submitted two separate memoranda on behalf of the judiciary,[6] objecting to the proposals for a separate Constitutional Court contained in the Twelfth

Report of the Technical Committee on Constitutional Issues,[7] it was only after the National Party and African National Congress (ANC) reached a bilateral agreement[8] in the closing days of the multiparty talks that the issue exploded. The Democratic Party was particularly concerned because in its view the proposals gave the executive 'the decisive say in the process of appointment to the Constitutional Court'.[9]

The resolution involved an elaborate compromise, in which the executive appoints various members of the Constitutional Court for a non-renewable period of seven years,[10] following three distinct processes. First, the President appoints a President of the Constitutional Court in consultation with the Cabinet and Chief Justice.[11] Second, four members of the Court are appointed from among the existing judges of the Supreme Court after consultation between the President, Cabinet and the Chief Justice.[12] Finally, the President, in consultation with the Cabinet and the President of the Constitutional Court, appoints six members from a list submitted by the Judicial Service Commission,[13] which is dominated two-to-one by members of the legal fraternity.[14] While the process of appointment remained essentially unchanged in the 1996 Constitution, the period of appointment was extended to twelve years and provision made for the terms of the existing justices to be extended subject to the requirement that they retire at age seventy. The result is the creation of a process in which due to the ages of various justices — and now also due to the promotion of Justice Mahomed to Chief Justice and the untimely death of Justice Didcott — the composition of the Constitutional Court will evolve, ensuring continuity.

The appointment in October 1994 of the last six of the eleven Constitutional Court judges,[15] 'chosen after public hearings from a shortlist of 10 candidates compiled by the Judicial Services Commission',[16] completed the first public process of judicial appointments in South African history. Despite criticism by opposition political parties of President Mandela's selection of judges from the list provided by the Judicial Service Commission,[17] political commentator Steven Friedman argued that there was little public understanding of the Court's power. This he considered particularly worrying in a context where the political 'negotiators left parts of the constitution dealing with key political issues so vague that the court will have to use political judgment when it rules on them'.[18] Given the deliberate postponement of so many unresolvable political conflicts in this first stage of negotiated constitution-making, including the constitutionality of the death penalty, Friedman argued 'it is particularly crucial that [the Court] be as representative of society as possible: all the major political viewpoints should be represented on it'.[19] Although Friedman expressed concern that the public and the minority parties misunderstood the import of constitutionalism – believing that the Court would be a purely technical, legal, body – and were thus 'destined for an unpleasant surprise', the Constitutional Court has, after only four years, become a central institution in the new South Africa. Despite popular attacks on some of its decisions – including the outlawing of the death penalty – and a unique political attack calling on five justices to recuse themselves on the grounds that they were personal friends of and had been appointed by President Mandela,[20] the stream of election cases brought to the Court in the lead up to the 1999 elections demonstrated the institution's capacity to incorporate and thus diffuse issues of intense political conflict.

INTRODUCING CONSTITUTIONAL REVIEW

The German constitutional scholar Brun-Otto Bryde uses the histories of the German, Hungarian and South African Constitutional Courts to demonstrate the important institutional roles these courts have played in stabilizing democracy in the context of constitutional transitions.[21] His analysis describes the different courts' specific roles as educator,[22] protector of acquired rights[23] and past interests,[24] or as arbitrator[25] in the context of these particular democratic transitions. Bryde identifies 'institutional interests and preferences' as being of primary significance in explaining a court's strategic behaviour in protecting the constitution as 'the basic source of its own institutional power'. He remains skeptical, however, about the ability of courts to play a major political role, concluding that this is dependent upon the acceptance of the court's role by the wider legal culture and political system. It is, however, in my view, precisely the institutional dynamic of this 'acceptance' that is key to the institutionalization of judicial review.

To understand how a court achieves the institutional prerogative to decide who decides, it is necessary to focus on the judiciary's early exercise of the power of constitutional or judicial review, particularly, on those cases when the courts first strike down the actions of the highest democratically-elected bodies. While Marshall CJ in *Marbury v Madison* implies that the courts must have the final word, as it is the role of the court to declare the law and there is no one else to resolve the meaning of the Constitution, in fact constitutional interpretation is continually engaged in by other organs of government.[26] This section focuses on the question of how the courts achieve the institutional authority to decide who decides. It does not discuss the perhaps more fundamental issue of the differing capacities of competing institutions to make and implement particular decisions[27] – or the normative claims of competing institutions to make particular constitutional decisions. In this analysis, 'deciding who decides' has two distinct aspects. The first is when the courts must decide which institution – judicial, legislative or market – is best suited to resolve a particular social problem. The second involves the court's assumption of the role of the institution which is the ultimate and final source of constitutional understanding and decision-making, in which the court of last instance assumes the right to decide who decides on the correct understanding of the constitution and the constitution's allocation of decision-making powers. It is this latter aspect of the problem of institutional power that is the focus of my concern.

As a general proposition, I wish to begin by proposing that we should understand judicial or constitutional review as the historical consequence of two interacting elements. First, an objective element, produced by the interaction of two factors: (1) the traditional judicial role, as the determiner of rights; and (2) the emergence of systems of governance premised on the dispersion of governmental powers both horizontally among different branches of government and vertically among different levels of government – local, regional and national. On the one hand, judicial review is implicit in the judicial function and the adjudication of rights under the common law. Notions of natural rights and of the repugnancy of local laws to colonial statutes prefigure the assertion of the 'testing right'. Perhaps, as some have implied, these elements lead inevitably to the development of the wider power of judicial review.[28] On the other hand, the power of judicial review is implied in the creation of a supreme constitution and its allocation of governmental powers. The power to determine who decides is thus implicit, but remains largely unspecified, in a written constitution's claim of legal supremacy.

While written constitutions have increasingly based the structure of government on the separation of powers and the distribution of powers across jurisdictions or levels of government – local, regional or national – it is only recently that explicit provision has been made for the courts to resolve conflicts over these allocations of power.[29] For example, the question of jurisdiction over conflicts between branches of government became an issue of debate in the South African Constitutional Assembly and, while the power of constitutional review was extended to the Supreme Court of Appeal (former Appellate Division) and the High Courts (former Divisions of the Supreme Court), which have been given the power to declare an Act of Parliament invalid upon confirmation of the order by the Constitutional Court, the power to decide constitutional disputes between organs of state has been explicitly limited to the Constitutional Court.[30] Prior to this type of explicit constitutional assignment, however, the judicial assumption of power to decide on the allocation of governmental powers flowed from the court's common law role as determiner of rights in general and the law's claim, since Magna Carta, to limit the powers of government. The implementation of this right to decide who decides is one of the most important moments prefiguring the emergence of a vibrant constitutional democracy. It is the outcome of this moment, often repeated, in which the exercise of constitutional review by the judiciary is institutionally accepted, which secures the role of judicial review despite the oft-cited countermajoritarian dilemma.

A second, or subjective, element provides the space within which the court is able to develop increasing institutional legitimacy. It is interesting to note that in constitutional democracies as culturally and historically different as the Federal Republic of Germany and India, it is the Constitutional Court and the Supreme Court respectively that have consistently enjoyed, as institutions of governance, the highest degree of public approval and confidence. This second, or legitimating, element is premised, particularly in the early exercise of judicial power, on what may be termed – with no pun intended – judicious politics.[31] Particular histories and context – both international and local – play a significant part in setting the stage upon which judicial review is introduced. While its ability to build legitimacy through its formal judicial role is a source of strength, the comparative institutional weakness of the judicial branch, by its very nature, requires the judiciary to be circumspect in its exercise of authority over the more resourced and powerful arms of government.

Human Rights, Constitutional Values and the Assertion of Judicial Authority

In its first politically important and publicly controversial holding, the South African Constitutional Court struck down the death penalty.[32] Although there had been a moratorium placed on executions from the end of 1989, as part of the initial moves towards a negotiated transition, as many as 400 persons were awaiting execution at the time of the Court's ruling. In declaring capital punishment unconstitutional, the Court emphasized that the transitional Constitution established a new order in South Africa, in which human rights and democracy are entrenched, and in which the Constitution is supreme.

The unanimous opinion of the Court, authored by the President of the Constitutional Court Arthur Chaskalson, was, however, judiciously tailored. Finding that the death penalty amounted, under most circumstances, to cruel and unusual punishment, Chaskalson P's opinion declined to engage in a determinative interpretation of other sections of the Bill of Rights that may also have impacted upon the death penalty, such as the right to life, dignity and equality. The individual concurring opinions of the remaining ten justices were not as restrained. Despite their concurrence in Chaskalson P's opinion, the remaining ten members of the Court went far beyond the majority opinion in their interpretation of other rights and in their prescriptions on the future trajectory of the

Court's jurisprudence. However, all the judges did join Chaskalson P in giving explicit and great weight to the introduction of constitutional review. They emphasized that the Court 'must not shrink from its task' of review,[33] otherwise South Africa would return to parliamentary sovereignty and by implication to the unrestrained violation of rights so common under previous parliaments.[34] Even the recognition that public opinion seemed to favour the retention of the death penalty was met with a clear statement that the Court would not 'allow itself to be diverted from its duty to act as an independent arbiter of the Constitution',[35] and that public opinion in itself is 'no substitute for the duty vested in the Courts to interpret the Constitution and to uphold its provisions without fear or favour'.[36] If public opinion were to be decisive, Chaskalson P argues, 'there would be no need for constitutional adjudication'.[37]

The Court's blunt dismissal of public opinion is, however, mediated by a second line of argument which appears in a number of the concurring opinions. Here the Court grounds its approach to the death penalty in the recognition of a national will to transcend the past and to uphold the standards of a 'civilised democratic' society.[38] Society's will to break with its past and to establish a community built on values antithetical to capital punishment is evidenced, according to the Court, in the adoption of a new Constitution and Bill of Rights. As O'Regan J argues, the 'new Constitution stands as a monument to this society's commitment to a future in which all human beings will be accorded equal dignity and respect'.[39] In these arguments the justices seem to embrace the legal fiction of the 1993 Constitution's preamble, which, despite its negotiated status and formal adoption by the unrepresentative tricameral Parliament, announced that: 'We, the people of South Africa declare that … [and] therefore [adopt] the following provisions … as the Constitution of the Republic of South Africa.'[40]

Embracing the 'altruistic and humanitarian philosophy which animates the Constitution enjoyed by us nowadays', as the true aspirations of the South African people Didcott J simultaneously rejected the undue influence of public opinion. First, Didcott J repeats Chaskalson P's citation[41] of the statements by Powell and Jackson JJ of the United States Supreme Court, who argued respectively that the 'assessment of popular opinion is essentially a legislative, not a judicial, function',[42] and that 'the very purpose of a bill of rights is to withdraw certain subjects from the vicissitudes of political controversy, to place them beyond the reach of majorities'.[43] Didcott J then argues that the decision to abolish or retain capital punishment is a constitutional question, the determination of which is the duty of the Court and not of representative institutions.[44]

This concurrent rejection of public opinion and embracing of national values is repeated by Kentridge AJ. Arguing that public opinion, 'even if expressed in Acts of Parliament, cannot be decisive',[45] Kentridge

AJ suggests that, while clear public opinion 'could not be entirely ignored', the Court 'would be abdicating from [its] ... constitutional function' if it were 'simply to defer to public opinion'.[46] Kentridge AJ then proceeds to discount any evidence of public opinion on the grounds that there had been no referendum or recent legislation[47] and instead he suggests that the reduction in executions after 1990 and the official executive moratorium on the death penalty, 'while not evidence of general opinion, do cast serious doubt on the acceptability of capital punishment in South Africa'.[48] These countermajoritarian concerns over the 'appeal to public opinion',[49] are overshadowed, however, by a reliance on the 'evolving standards of civilization'[50] which the Court infers are incorporated into South African jurisprudence by the country's aspiration to be a free and democratic society.[51] It is this national ambition, contained in the constitutional commitment 'to promote the values which underlie an open and democratic society based on freedom and equality',[52] which the Court presents as the source of social mores underlying the new constitutional dispensation. It is in this context then that Kentridge AJ concludes that the 'deliberate execution of a human, however depraved and criminal his conduct, must degrade the new society which is coming into being'.[53] A similar reliance on the Constitution's inherent morality as a source of a public or national will which supersedes simple public opinion can be found in Langa J's argument that 'implicit in the provisions and tone of the Constitution are values of a more mature society, which relies on moral persuasion rather than force; on example rather than coercion'.[54]

The Court reached its unanimous conclusion despite evidence that capital punishment was subject to extensive debate in negotiations before and during the constitution-making process, which presented the Court with two interrelated problems. First, the Court had to position itself in relation to the constitution-making process, indicating what weight to give the views of the Constitution's framers in interpreting it. Adducing evidence of the intent of the framers – despite their presence in society and even among members of the Court – presented a second problem, requiring the Court to consider the role of legislative history in the interpretive process. While South African courts have traditionally limited the use of legislative history to evidence on the 'purpose and background of the legislation in question',[55] the Constitutional Court noted that courts in England, Australia and New Zealand had recently relaxed the exclusionary rule.[56] Furthermore, that in 'countries in which the constitution is similarly the supreme law, it is not unusual for the courts to have regard to the circumstances existing at the time the constitution was adopted, including the debates and writings which formed part of the process'.[57] Following these developments, the Court accepted the reports of the Technical Committees to the Multi-Party Negotiating Process as the 'equivalent of the *travaux préparatoires* relied upon by the international tribunals', to provide evidence of context for the interpretation of the Constitution.[58] The Court, however, limited the scope of its reliance on these materials to the specific context of this and similarly situated cases 'where the background material is clear, is not in dispute, and is relevant to showing why particular provisions were or were not included in the Constitution'.[59]

Although the founders are present, in society and in the Court, any attempt to ascertain their intent or to base interpretation of the Constitution on their original intent, is, according to the Court, confounded by the constitution-making process itself. While accepting the usefulness of background evidence provided by the record of the negotiations the Court cautions against reliance on the comments of individual participants in the constitution-making process 'no matter how prominent a role they might have played', as the Constitution is the 'product of a multiplicity of persons'.[60] The Court thus recognizes from its inception the problem of which most constitutional theories of original intent fail to take cognisance – the collective nature of the constitution-making exercise. While legislative history may provide a context in which to understand why various issues, such as the restitution clauses, were included or excluded as products of political compromises and exchanges between the negotiating partners, the rules of aggregation in fact provide a completely separate source of delegation to future generations of the need to decide on particular meanings or issues.[61] Thus the Court manages both to recognize the relevance of framers' intent and to free itself from claims to know that intent which many of the living framers might muster.

Having accepted the salience of legislative history, the Court argues that the 'clear failure to deal specifically in the Constitution with this issue [the death penalty] was not accidental'.[62] Support for this conclusion is found in the 'Solomonic solution' proposed by the South African Law Commission in its *Interim Report on Group and Human Rights* in 1991, under which 'a Constitutional Court would be required to decide whether a right to life expressed in unqualified terms could be circumscribed by a limitations clause contained in a bill of rights'.[63] Thus the Court concludes that the failure of the founders to resolve this issue left to the Constitutional Court the duty to decide whether the 'provisions of the pre-constitutional law making the death penalty a competent sentence for murder and other crimes', are consistent with the fundamental rights enshrined in the Constitution.[64]

In striking down the death penalty, the Constitutional Court, boldly and unanimously, asserted its constitutional authority despite concerns that its decision might have flown in the face of the democratic will.

However, it is important to remember here that despite what might have been general public support of the death penalty, here the Court was, as a new post-apartheid institution, striking down the practice of the old regime, a practice which had been laden with racial disparity and seen as a tool used against those who fought against apartheid – such as Solomon Mahlangu,[65] the young ANC guerilla after whom the exiled-ANC's Solomon Mahlangu Freedom College in Arusha, Tanzania, was named. In this context, then, it was possible for the Constitutional Court both to assert its authority as the new guardian of human rights and to assert its authority as interpreter of the Constitution.

Conflicting Powers and the Insinuation of Authority

The South African Court's bold assertion of its constitutional powers in the *Death Penalty Case* stands in marked contrast to the Court's dramatic shift in approach to the use of its power, just three months later, in a case involving the demarcation of local government boundaries and constituencies – the *Western Cape Case*[66] – in which the Court declared s 16A of the *Local Government Transition Act* 209 of 1993 (LGTA) an unconstitutional delegation of legislative power to the executive. Here the Court carefully crafted its assertion of constitutional authority so as to placate all the contending parties. In order to understand the Constitutional Court's response in *Western Cape*, it is necessary to provide some background. While South Africa's first democratic elections were held on 27 April 1994, the final demise of apartheid governance and the completion of the formal process of democratization would only be completed in 1999 with the full implementation of the 1996 Constitution. The second wave of democratization – the local government elections – took place in November 1995 and was to have extended democratic participation to local government. However, a number of areas including the whole of the province of KwaZulu-Natal and the important metropolitan area of Cape Town, were only able to hold local government elections in the first half of 1996.

Recognizing the difficulty of creating democratic local governments in a situation characterized by racial segregation and apartheid town planning, the negotiating parties established a special transitional regime for the restructuring of local government prior to the holding of local elections. Issues surrounding the restructuring of local government were, however, politicized by the determination of the National Party to protect a high degree of local autonomy, as a way to ensure local community control of resources. Furthermore, the ANC acknowledged that, given the system of proportional representation employed to elect national and regional government, it was important that there be some degree of direct representation at the local level so as to bring government closer to the people.

Tensions over the question of local government were resolved through a political compromise requiring that half the wards of any local government be assigned to formerly white, coloured and Indian race zones. This compromise was entrenched in the interim Constitution so as to ensure that within any local government area the 'minority' vote could prevent the African majority from obtaining the two-thirds majority needed to pass a local budget on its own. This consociational guarantee was negotiated by the apartheid regime as part of the transitional Constitution in order to prevent any dramatic transfer of local resources from the wealthy 'white' suburbs to the resource-starved African townships. The LGTA was negotiated under this constitutional framework as a mechanism to recreate local government before the holding of democratic local government elections.

It was within this contested political context and with the backdrop of the victory of the National Party in the provincial elections in the Western Cape that the demarcation case arose. The conflict erupted when President Mandela, acting in accordance with amending powers granted the executive in s16A of the LGTA, amended the Act: (1) transferring the power to appoint members of local demarcation committees away from provincial government – where it had been assigned when the administration of the LGTA had been assigned to provincial governments; and (2) limiting the wide powers of local administrators of the Act to make rules relating to the demarcation of local government structures and the division of such structures into wards. Mandela's actions were motivated by, and effectively reversed, an attempt by the National Party provincial government in the Western Cape to demarcate the Cape Town metropolitan area so as to concentrate all the resource-poor African areas into one local government area, thus excluding any of these areas from a neighbouring, extremely wealthy, white, Afrikaans-dominated area. Given the historic structure of the Western Cape, this would have excluded all Africans from voting in this particular area. While the ANC objected to this process of demarcation, the National Party in the Western Cape accused the national government of interfering in provincial matters. When the Provincial Government lost its first challenge to Mandela's directives, the National Party vowed to take the fight for Western Cape independence into the streets if the courts could not defend what they believed to be a constitutional right to provincial autonomy.

In rejecting the Western Cape claim, the Provincial Division of the Supreme Court said that the Parliament's amendment of the LGTA had effectively transferred Parliament's highest legislative powers to President

Mandela by 'allowing the President to make laws in its place'. On appeal, the Constitutional Court was faced with resolving a crisis that by early September 1995 was threatening to prevent the holding of nation-wide local government elections and to halt the very process of democratic transition away from apartheid. Deflecting the potentially explosive issue of provincial autonomy and avoiding the politically sensitive issue of local government demarcation, the Constitutional Court raised the constitutionality of the legislature's delegation of amending powers to the executive, calling into question the constitutionality of section 16A of the Act, which was the legal basis upon which President Mandela had acted.

In reversing the lower court and striking down Mandela's proclamations and Parliament's amendment of the LGTA, the Constitutional Court was hailed by opponents of the government as defenders of the Constitution, for standing up to the ANC-dominated executive and legislature, and for fulfilling the promise of judicial review. However, when President Mandela publicly praised the Constitutional Court's decision, stating that 'this judgment is not the first, nor will it be the last, in which the Constitutional Court assists both the government and society to ensure constitutionality and effective governance', it became clear that the Court had effectively traversed the 'fundamental questions of constitutional law' and 'matters of grave public concern' which Chaskalson J had raised in the opening paragraphs of the Court's decision.

The sting of the ruling against the legislature was removed, in part, by the remedy granted – giving the legislature a period of time to correct the defect in the Act – and executive concern was addressed by the Court's tacit support for the powers of central government over the provinces in controlling the restructuring and regulation of local government. To be sure, the Constitutional Court had, for the first time, struck down intensely politicized legislation passed by a democratically elected Parliament and a highly popular President, but closer examination of the Court's handling of the division of powers – particularly the transitional powers granted to the President by the Constitution for the purpose of moving the society beyond apartheid – reveals a judicious style of intervention reminiscent of *Marbury v Madison* in its satisfaction of the immediate interests of one side while asserting for itself, and in this case for the majority government, powers that were far more important over the long run.

The Western Cape provincial government's argument was based on three elements: first, on the constitutional protection of provincial autonomy in the constitutional requirement that the majority of Senators of a province must approve any legislation affecting the boundaries, powers or functions of the province; second, on similar protections of provincial autonomy in the amending sections of the interim Constitution;

and third, on the argument that the national government's action encroached upon the geographical, functional and institutional integrity of the province as guaranteed in Constitutional Principle XXII contained in Schedule 4 of the 1993 Constitution. Instead of finding for the Western Cape on issues of provincial autonomy, which would have played directly into the continuing and growing conflict between the ANC-dominated national government and the two provinces – Western Cape and KwaZulu-Natal, controlled by non-ANC governments – the Court determined that there was a larger, prior question that required it to declare the President's actions in the Western Cape unconstitutional. Simultaneously, however, the Court made it clear that control over local government is constitutionally assigned to the National Parliament. While the Western Cape won the case, it not only failed to achieve the degree of provincial autonomy it was seeking, but also established a precedent denying it that autonomy.

While the case focused on the constitutionality of s 16A of the LGTA and whether the President's proclamations could nevertheless be saved from constitutional attack by reliance upon the President's transitional powers, the case effectively introduced a constitutional scheme guiding the exercise of Presidential authority under the transitional sections of the Constitution and determining the allocation of powers between national and provincial government. Rejecting the President's argument that, despite the unconstitutionality of his amending powers, his actions were saved by the transitional powers granted to the executive in the Constitution, the Court carefully detailed the scope of Presidential power in terms of the transitional sections of the Constitution. Preserving the bulk of Presidential actions in the transition, the Court carefully crafted a clearer basis upon which the President could continue to act to facilitate the democratic transition.

The crafting of these powers illustrates the way in which the Court asserted its power to decide who decides while creating the opportunity for the dominant institutional powers to embrace its role. The Court's argument followed a number of steps. First, the Court argued that in order to ensure constitutional continuity, the interim Constitution contained specific mechanisms dealing with the continuation of laws and transitional arrangements for the allocation of executive authority. Second, the Court argued that the Constitution facilitates this process by empowering the President to assign the administration of particular categories of laws to 'competent authorities' and to amend or adapt such law to the extent that the President considers it necessary for the 'efficient carrying out of the assignment'.[67]

While the court easily agreed on the constitutional framework created to achieve these transitional goals, there was dissension over the definition of the President's powers to amend such laws in terms of s 235(8). While there seems to be agreement among the justices that the exercise of presidential authority under s 235(8) was limited to the degree an amendment was *necessary* for the *efficient carrying out of the assignment*, there were differing opinions as to the extent of amendment allowed once this jurisdictional fact entitling the President to amend or adapt had been satisfied. There were three distinct positions taken by the justices in this regard. The most expansive declaration of Presidential authority was articulated by Madala and Ngoepe JJ, who argued that the interim Constitution adopted 'a robust attitude towards the plethora of laws which were in force at the commencement of the Constitution',[68] and therefore the President is granted fairly extensive powers to deal with 'deficiencies which are already inherent in the law'. Although this analysis seemed to grant the President fairly extensive powers of amendment, it was in fact limited by the requirement that these powers address 'deficiencies which are already inherent in the law', which would raise doubts as to whether the President could amend in order to deal with deficiencies which arise in the post-constitutional period and which were not 'inherent in the law'. The most restrictive analysis of the President's power was that implicit in the judgments of Chaskalson and Kriegler JJ (joined by Langa and Didcott JJ), which limited the President's power to amendments that make the old laws '*fit* the new situation',[69] or which 'tailor existing laws to suit the new provincial structures'[70] in order to 'achieve efficiency in the functional administration of the assigned laws'.[71] The third analysis of the President's authority to amend in terms of s 235(8) is offered by Mahomed J, who argued that the amendment would not be subject to challenge so long as it 'is rationally capable of facilitating the efficient carrying out of the assignment and rationally capable of regulating the application or interpretation of the law'.[72]

While handing a public victory to the Western Cape provincial government, the Court achieved a number of important goals. First, the Court demonstrated its willingness to protect provincial governments from unconstitutional national interference, giving those who demand greater regional autonomy space in which to imagine the continued vitality of their own constitutional visions. Second, it clarified the President's powers to facilitate the political transition through executive amendment of pre-constitutional laws. Third, and most significant for the implementation of constitutional review, the Court asserted its own right to determine, through constitutional interpretation, to whom or to which institution the power to decide particular matters has been constitutionally assigned.

Differences between the *Death Penalty Case* and the *Western Cape* demarcation case are clear. The *Death Penalty Case* involved the interpretation of fundamental rights and the striking down of law and practice that was closely associated with the violations and inequalities of the apartheid era. The demarcation case involved the allocation of powers between levels of government under an Act negotiated by all parties as part of the transition to democracy. The salience of this difference lies in the distinction between a court's role in the adjudication of rights and in the allocation of powers. In deciding on the relative powers of the legislature and the executive and of the national and the provincial, the Court faces the threat that any of these sites of governmental power could ignore or publicly disregard the Court's decision.[73] As Chief Justice Warren Burger noted with respect to *Marbury*: 'the Court could stand hard blows but not ridicule, and the ale houses would [have rocked] with hilarious laughter' had Chief Justice Marshall issued a mandamus that the Jefferson administration ignored.[74]

Although the Constitutional Court could present itself in the *Death Penalty Case* as the guardian of human rights, declaring itself in contradistinction to the old judiciary to be a new and different court created specifically to overcome the legacy of apartheid, striking down the acts of both President Mandela and the new democratic Parliament posed greater dangers. Here was both the opportunity to consolidate the Court's role as guardian of a supreme Constitution and also the danger of being perceived to be upholding the anti-democratic designs of the former apartheid ruling party in the Western Cape. Ultimately, the Court's handling of this problem – despite initial uncertainty within the Court – was masterful. The Court took the opportunity to demonstrate the centrality of constitutional supremacy and its own authority as final interpreter of the allocation of constitutional power in the new constitutional order, but in a manner which drew acceptance if not unqualified support from all the parties.

Law's Majesty and Deference to Democratic Institutions

While the conclusion in the *Death Penalty Case*, that the issue of the death penalty was left for the Constitutional Court to resolve, was logically drawn from the history of the death penalty discussion in the negotiations, it simultaneously revealed how the Court's constitutional jurisdiction is viewed by both the participants in the constitution-making process and the members of the Court. While the justices of the Court understand their jurisdiction 'as the court of final instance over all matters relating to the interpretation, protection and enforcement of the provisions of this Constitution',[75] the assumption that the framers of the Constitution, in the name of 'We the people' would simply delegate such an important decision to the Court, is extraordinary. This extraordinary degree of delegation was, however, repeated and magnified in the role the Constitutional Court was given to determine whether a new 'final' Constitution, once sanctioned by at least two-thirds of the members of the democratically-elected Constitutional Assembly,[76] was substantively in accordance with the Principles contained in Schedule 4 of the interim Constitution. While these delegations of constitutional authority reflected both a postponement of conflicts among the framers of the interim Constitution as well as their faith in judicial processes, it also reflected a failure to understand the delicate institutional role the Court would find itself in. Poised as the lightning rod for claims of right and struggles to transform the country, the repeated concern of the Constitutional Court to address its countermajoritarian dilemma is understandable.

While the exercise of constitutional review in *Western Cape* may be viewed as an example of the Court mediating a conflict between different levels of government, its significance lies in the Court's exercise of its role as final arbiter in a conflict over the Constitution's allocation of the power to decide highly politicized questions of democratic participation. The certification process, in which the Constitutional Court was required to certify that the constitutional text produced by the Constitutional Assembly met the parameters of the Constitutional Principles contained in the 1993 Constitution, provides a further, unique example, in the context of a democratic transition, in which a Constitutional Court is required to exercise its role as final arbiter on constitutional scope and meaning, and in so doing is required to skirt the outer reaches of its institutional capacity. While unique in its specifics, the certification process reflects issues of constitutional review which may in the future arise in the context of challenges to duly enacted constitutional amendments similar to those that have been reflected in the 'basic structure' jurisprudence of the Indian Supreme Court. Not only is the Court being asked to interpret a Constitution adopted by 'the people', but in the case of constitutional amendments the Court is called upon to evaluate the very constituent power of 'the people' upon whose will its legitimacy as guardian of entrenched rights is premised.

Declaring the new text of the final constitution 'unconstitutional', despite its adoption after last-minute political compromises by eighty-six per cent of the democratically elected Constitutional Assembly, was on its face a bold assertion of the power of judicial review. Yet, the Constitutional Court's denial of certification was far more measured and subtly crafted than this bold assertion of 'unconstitutionality' implies. In fact, the Constitutional Court was careful to point out in its unanimous, unattributed, opinion, that 'in general and in respect of the overwhelming majority of its provisions', the Constitutional Assembly had met the predetermined requirements of the Constitutional Principles. In effect then, this was a very limited and circumscribed ruling. This view was confirmed when the major political parties rejected any attempt to use the denial of certification as a tool to reopen debates; instead the Constitutional Assembly focused solely on the issues raised by the Constitutional Court.[77]

This outcome was implicit in the Court's handling of its own role in the certification process. Instead of trumpeting its constitutional duty to review the work of the Constitutional Assembly, the Court was careful to point out that the Constitutional Assembly had a large degree of latitude in its interpretation of the principles and that the role of the Constitutional Court was judicial and not political. While this may be dismissed as the posture of a Court merely hiding behind legalism, in fact this deference to the democratic constitution-making process shaped the Court's approach to its task. In defining its mode of review, the Court specifically identified two separate questions. First, the Court would examine whether the 'basic structures and premises of the NT [were in] … accordance with those contemplated in the CPs [i.e., Constitutional Principles]'. Conducting this inquiry, the Court established a minimum threshold which the Constitutional Assembly had to meet and found that in fact the New Text satisfied those standards. The significance of this approach is that, despite arguments that the certification judgments are unique, in fact the Court is granted jurisdiction and called upon in the final Constitution to determine the constitutionality of any future Constitutional Amendment.[78] Significantly, at least two justices of the Constitutional Court have made reference to the notion of the basic structure of the Constitution used by the Indian Supreme Court in its jurisprudence striking down validly enacted Constitutional Amendments. To this extent the Constitutional Assembly and the Court have left open the future of the Court's role in the formal constitution-making or amending process under the final Constitution.

Second, the Court's methodology held that only once the Court decided that the New Text accorded with the basic structure and premises would the Court turn to an analysis of whether the details of the New Text complied with the Constitutional Principles. In making this turn to a detailed analysis of the content of the New Text, the Court asserted both its power and its duty to ensure compliance by testing the text against the Constitutional Principles, but the Court was also very careful to limit the scope of this review. This limiting strategy was accomplished by asserting the formal legal distinction between politics and law.[79] The Court noted that it 'has a judicial and not a political mandate' and that this 'judicial function, a legal exercise' meant that the Court had 'no power, no mandate and no right to express any view on the political choices made by the CA [i.e., Constitutional Assembly] in drafting the NT [i.e., New Text]'.[80] While the Court asserted that its interpretation of the Constitutional Principles was consistent with its jurisprudential commitment to a purposive and teleological application that gives 'expression to the commitment to "create a new order" based on a "sovereign and democratic constitutional state" in which "all citizens" are "able to enjoy and exercise their fundamental rights and freedoms"',[81] it also asserted that the Court was not concerned with the merits of the choices made by the Constitutional Assembly. In fact, the Court emphasized the scope of the Constitutional Assembly's latitude by arguing that, while the new text 'may not transgress the fundamental discipline of the CPs ... within the space created by those CPs, interpreted purposively, the issue as to which of several permissible models should be adopted is not an issue for adjudication by this Court. That is a matter for the political judgment of the CA, and therefore properly falling within its discretion ...'[82]

In contrast, however, the Court took a robust view of its judicial role of establishing legal precedent. Faced with the dilemma of alternative constructions in which one interpretation could be held to be in violation of the Constitutional Principles, the Court adopted the traditional judicial strategy of upholding that interpretation which would avoid a declaration of unconstitutionality. This raised the spectre of a future Court revisiting the issue and adopting an interpretation which would have been in violation of the Constitutional Principles. In this 'judicial' context the Court claimed the power to bind the future, holding that a 'future court should approach the meaning of the relevant provision of the NT on the basis that the meaning assigned ... in the certification process ... should not be departed from save in the most compelling circumstances'.[83]

The Court took a similarly robust attitude to its judicial role in its second certification judgment, when it finally certified the final Constitution.[84] In this case the Court was faced with attempts by political parties and other interested groups to reopen issues which had not been identified as the basis for the Court's refusal to certify in the first round of the certification process. While accepting these challenges, the Court noted the 'sound jurisprudential basis for the policy that a Court should adhere to its previous decisions unless they are shown to be clearly wrong ... [and that] having regard to the need for finality in the certification process and in view of the virtual identical composition of the Court that considered the questions barely three months ago, that policy is all the more desirable here'.[85] As a result, the Court made it clear that a party wishing to extend the Court's review beyond those aspects identified in the first certification judgment would have a 'formidable task'. Through this reliance on a classic judicial strategy of deference to past decisions, the Court was able significantly to limit the scope of its role in the final certification judgment. It was this change in posture towards the certification process and the fact that the Constitutional Assembly fully addressed all but one of the Court's concerns that ensured a swift certification on the second round. Significantly, the Court now relied less on the specifics of the Constitutional Principles and instead emphasized the fundamental elements of constitutionalism contained in the text – 'founding values which include human dignity, the achievement of equality, the recognition and advancement of human rights and freedoms, the supremacy of the Constitution and the rule of law'.[86] While the Court still had to recognize that the powers and functions of the provinces – the most contentious issue in the whole constitution-making process – remained in dispute between the parties, the Court held in essence that the removal of the presumption of constitutional validity of bills passed by the National Council of Provinces (NCOP) had tipped the balance.[87] Thus, despite the recognition that provincial powers and functions in the Amended Text remained less than or inferior to those accorded to the provinces in terms of the interim Constitution, this was not substantially so,[88] and therefore no longer a basis for denying certification.

Thrust into this unique role of arbiter in the second and final phase of the constitution-making process, the Constitutional Court was faced with a number of distinct pressures. First, the democratically-elected Constitutional Assembly represented the pinnacle of the country's new democratic institutions empowered with the task of producing the country's final Constitution – the end product of the formal transition. Given a history of parliamentary sovereignty and the failure of the courts to check the anti-democratic actions of the executive in the dark days of apartheid and during the States of Emergency, how was a newly appointed Constitutional Court going to stand up against the first truly democratic constitution-making body in South African history?

Second, the credibility of the Constitutional Court was at stake. As the Court heard argument on the Certification of the Constitution, numerous sectors, including important elements within the established legal profession, openly speculated whether the Court had sufficient independence to stand up to the Constitutional Assembly, particularly over the key issue of the entrenchment of the Bill of Rights. Had the Court not refused certification on at least this ground, it would, in this view, have amounted to a failure of the certification function and proof that the Court lacked the necessary independence.

Third, the Constitutional Court's certification powers were not only unique but were to be exercised on the basis of a set of Constitutional Principles negotiated in the pre-election transition. The Principles had, in the dying days of the multiparty negotiations and in the context of the Concerned South Africans Group (Consag) rebellion, become the focus of unresolved demands leading to the incorporation of a number of contradictory principles designed more to keep the contending participants within the process than to establish a coherent set of constitutional principles by which a future draft Constitution could be judged. Significantly, however, the basic framework of Principles, tracing their heritage from the ANC's Constitutional Principles of 1988, the Harare Declaration, the United Nations General Assembly Resolution on Apartheid, the Conference for a Democratic Future and finally adopted by the major parties at the Convention for a Democratic South Africa (Codesa) remained at the core of the Constitutional Principles. It was this basic framework, guaranteeing broad democratic participation, a justiciable bill of rights and an independent judiciary, that provided the fundamental assumptions of the Constitutional Court's analysis of both the content of the text and the Court's role in the certification process.

Fourth, the Constitutional Court's review of the text was permeated with the Court's own unarticulated assumptions with respect to the institutional implications of the new constitutionalism. These assumptions are exposed in the Court's response to those elements of the text which held implications for its own institutional role. In fact, many of the grounds upon which the Court declined to certify the text had institutional implications for the Court. This may be seen, for example, in the Court's demands to strengthen the procedures and threshold for amendment of the Bill of Rights, its striking down of attempts to insulate the labour clause from judicial review, and the use of the presumption that a bill passed by the NCOP could indicate a national interest overriding separate regional interest to tip the balance against the adequacy of the basket of regional powers. Thus, without explicit acknowledgment, nor even necessary awareness, the Court's approach to the new text indicated a profound concern with guaranteeing the institutional prerogatives of the Court as the institutional repository of the power to decide who decides. It was the imperative to secure the role of the Court as guardian of a constitutional democracy based on the explicit foundations of constitutional supremacy that weighted the balance in the *First Certification Judgment.*

DEFENDING THE COURT'S LEGITIMACY

In asserting its constitutional powers the judiciary constantly recognizes its ultimate reliance on both the executive and legislative branches to enforce its holdings on the one hand and to protect its independence on the other. As a consequence of this weak institutional position, the Court carefully negotiates its way through conflicts which could elicit direct attacks on the independence of the judiciary or the tenure of individual judges, and even attempts to restructure the Court's jurisdiction so as to limit the institution's power. It is the Court's ability to embrace and control the power of institutional choice – to allocate the right to decide as between the different coexisting jurisdictions – without becoming the target of overwhelming political conflict, which creates the space in which the power of judicial review may be institutionally consolidated. Of course this is no guarantee that the Court will avoid becoming embroiled in political conflict, but in an effort to do so we see the kind of judicious decision-making identified by students of constitutions with *Marbury v Madison* and exemplified in South Africa by the Court's approach in deciding the *Death Penalty* and *Western Cape* cases. In each the Court managed to issue a decision that asserted its ultimate authority to decide without drawing the fire of other governmental institutions or appearing to shake things up so much that its own institutional legitimacy was questioned. When a challenge did come in an application for the recusal of justices, which if acceded to would have destroyed the Court's quorum, it had little if any impact on the Court's growing legitimacy.

In this sense the judiciary's source of institutional legitimacy and power lies as much in its ability to insinuate itself institutionally in conflicts over the separation and distribution of powers as it does in its defence of rights. According to this understanding, it is the Court's success in achieving a viable institutional role *vis-à-vis* the co-ordinate branches of government which enables it to insist upon its role as the interpreter of rights. Thus it escapes questions over its self-appointment as the institution of choice for deciding the meaning and scope of constitutional rights. In this way the judiciary draws upon its legacy as the determiner of rights between parties and creates a space, or node of power, from within which continually to assert its institutional right to be the final arbiter of the meaning of the Constitution.

The legitimacy of judicial review in South Africa, but elsewhere as well, is built instead on twin foundations. First, on a strategy of judicial deference, in wielding the power of institutional choice between the more powerful sites of governmental power. Second, in the judicial seizing of a supreme role in the interpretation of constitutional rights, which is both historically consistent with the judicial function and is premised upon the self-allocation of the interpretive power. It is only in times of heightened social conflict – whether based on a rights consciousness engendered by constitutionally endorsed yet frustrated aspirations,[89] or on social changes beyond the Court's responsive capacities – that the power of the Court to make these determinant institutional choices is politically exposed and brought into question, and when the co-ordinate branches of government will successfully assert a greater role in either deciding on the parameters of the Constitution or abandoning it altogether.

CHAPTER 8

CONSTITUTIONAL IMAGINATIONS AND THE POSSIBILITIES OF JUSTICE

The adoption locally of a globally bounded notion of democratic constitutionalism both enables political reconstruction in the democratic transition and tests the capacity of the incorporated framework to address the conflicts arising from often irreconcilable political demands. The realm of bounded possibilities created by the introduction of constitutionalism is constantly infused with the incompatible constitutional imaginations of local contestants. The challenge in this context is whether constitutionalism may provide an institutional mechanism that would in effect civilize the political conflicts which until now have tended to degenerate into violent confrontation.

The creation and legitimation of a constitutional court provides a unique institutional site within which the process of mediation between alternative constitutional imaginations may be sustained. It creates the possibility that the judiciary in its role as ultimate interpreter of the Constitution will be able to sustain and civilize the tensions inherent in the repeated referral and contestation of essentially irreconcilable political differences. This chapter will explore how the introduction of constitutionalism creates a political space in which alternative and often irreconcilable visions may be pursued and contested. Focusing on particular struggles over participation, equality and social resources, I will seek to show how the constitutional aspirations of contesting forces may be simultaneously bounded and incorporated. I will argue that the impact of constitutionalism is to allow these different political factions the opportunity to continue to imagine their own place within a common constitutional future by keeping alive alternative spaces or possibilities of justice.

THE PARAMETERS OF CONSTITUTIONAL IMAGINATION

Despite the institutional fragility of constitutional review, its successful insinuation into public life provides a unique institutional mechanism for the management of irreconcilable political conflicts. Unlike the executive and legislature, which are viewed as dominated by particular, even if frequently changing, political interests, an independent constitutional court may provide a forum in which to seek goals or protections that are at least temporarily otherwise politically unattainable. This process requires, however, the applicants to mould their positions so that their claims will resonate with the social and normative commitments enshrined in the Constitution. Furthermore, the incremental approach taken by courts – deciding only what is absolutely necessary to dispose of each case – and the increasing application of or reliance on 'universal' values, makes it a prime site for the moulding of local initiatives with international or global prerogatives. The effect is to allow the contestants to continue to imagine their own preferred social options as constitutionally sustainable, while simultaneously requiring them to reshape and mould their visions into a tapestry of internationally recognized rights and locally generated variations.

Although such a constitution – steeped in 'universal' values – and such a constitutional court – both independent and legitimate – may be presented as an ideal type in a world of varied constitutions and politically-charged constitutional courts, it is also true that the post–cold war wave of constitutionalism has seen an expansion of this model to many new contexts. While these new constitutions and institutions are performing different roles with varied success and limited possibilities, it is the potential of this one particular role that is most clearly highlighted in the South African context. To illustrate these processes – of sustainable imaginations and bounded visions – this chapter will focus on two different aspects of the South African Constitutional Court's work. First, by looking once again to the *Makwanyane* (*Death Penalty*) decision, I will explore how the Court went about the process of defining the source and scope of the fundamental rights protected in the Constitution. This enables us to view the relative impact of both local and international values in the Court's early rights jurisprudence. Second, by looking to specific areas of conflict that have been 'civilized' in the political transition despite their propensity to evoke high emotions and often dangerous confrontations. The latter may be identified as two particular sets of problems, each arising in relation to two different and specific political communities. On the one hand, there are language and educational conflicts that have been the focus of the cultural claims of white Afrikaners who remained opposed to the political transition. On the other hand, there are conflicts over traditional leadership and regional autonomy which have been waged alternatively in the name of indigenous culture, Zulu tradition, federalism and limited government and have been most intense in KwaZulu-Natal, where they have been the political source of violent conflict between the Inkatha Freedom Party (IFP) and the African National

Congress (ANC). The Court's engagement with these two sets of political conflicts, and the enforced dialogue of the judicial process, demonstrate the potential that democratic constitutionalism holds for the management and 'civilizing' of these irreconcilable differences.

The Scope and Source of Fundamental Rights

Despite their concurrence in the *Makwanyane* decision and their general acceptance of the Court's two-stage approach to the interpretation of fundamental rights, the justices of the Constitutional Court adopted significantly different reasons for striking down the death penalty. All eleven opinions accepted that the method of interpretation involves a broad interpretation of the right followed by an application of the limitations clause,[1] requiring the state to justify its interference in the right 'according to the criteria prescribed by s 33'.[2] Where they differed was in their reliance on different rights as the basis of their analysis[3] and in whether they treated each of the different rights as a separate basis for striking down capital punishment or as informing the content of a single right, the violation of which was the sole ground upon which the decision was based.[4]

This difference, while of little significance to the outcome in the case, reflected a distinction between a case-by-case extrapolation of individual rights and an approach which makes bold declarations as to the extent of all rights implicated in a case and then relies on the limitations analysis to confine the implications of such expansive rights. These alternative approaches hold different implications for the scope and application of the fundamental rights protected by the Constitution. In the first approach, adopted by Chaskalson P, the Court tailored its analysis of the right by first giving a 'generous' and 'purposive' meaning to the right chosen – the right prohibiting 'cruel, inhuman or degrading treatment or punishment' – and then giving further texture to the meaning of s 11(2) by interpreting those rights associated with s 11(2) in Chapter 3: the rights to life, dignity and equality.[5] This judicious strategy enables the Court to give a broad and contextualized definition to the right at issue without being overly concerned about the impact its decision may have on other areas of legal conflict far removed from the case at hand. While the extrapolation of these associated rights does indeed give clues as to the Court's views on the scope and form of those rights, it does not create legal expectations as to the specific content of those rights.

In the second approach, followed by most of the concurring judgments, different rights are applied to the problem of capital punishment as 'separate and independent standards with which all punishments must comply'.[6] While this approach has the advantage of issuing broad declaratory definitions of all rights implicated in a particular case, it poses the danger of creating a jurisprudence of exceptions – requiring the Court, when faced with a different set of facts and concerns, either to modify its own previous definition or to fall back on the limitations clause so as to preclude the implications of its own declaratory positions. In *Makwanyane* the repeated declarations of the centrality of the right to life to all other fundamental rights[7] and even the insistence that the Court's decision be based primarily on the right to life,[8] led to a narrowing of the definition of the right to life itself. Didcott J, for example, based his reasoning, first, on the right to life and, second, on the prohibition against cruel, inhuman or degrading punishment. The need to define each right as a separate and independent ground for declaring capital punishment unconstitutional required Didcott J to adopt a narrow definition of the constitutional right to life, arguing:

> It suffices for the purposes of this case to say that the proclamation of the right and the respect for it demanded from the State must surely entitle one, at the very least, not to be put to death by the State deliberately, systematically and as an act of policy that denies in principle the value of the victim's life.[9]

The value of this approach is its emphasis on the broad definition of fundamental rights. Its more traditional application of the right, however, to as specific a level of generality as possible – so as to avoid deciding any more than what needs to be decided by the case before the Court – holds the danger of creating a sense of dissonance between the expectations created by a generous and purposive interpretation on the one hand, and the narrow scope given the right in its application on the other. A similar concern led to a debate over the application of the requirement that any limitation on a right not negate the essential content of the right. Although it was suggested that the death penalty would seem to violate this standard, the Court declined to give meaning to this provision and signalled that this particular requirement could present an interpretive problem in the future.[10] Taking this cue, the Constitutional Assembly in fact removed this particular standard from the limitations clause of the final Constitution.[11]

Just as the constitutional provision of the 1993 Constitution mandating that the essential content of a right not be negated was recognized as having 'entered constitutional law through the provisions of the German Constitution',[12] the Court's discussion of the source of constitutional values recognizes that the Court has the ability to draw on a vast range of sources in interpreting the Constitution. The Court, however, emphasized that s 35(1) of the 1993 Constitution did not require,[13] but rather permitted, the courts to 'have regard to'[14] public international law, which, it argued, 'may provide guidance as to the correct interpretation

of particular provisions' of Chapter 3.[15] Significantly, the admonition in
s 35 of the 1993 Constitution, requiring the courts to 'have regard to
public international law applicable to the protection of the rights
entrenched' was strengthened in s 39 of the 1996 Constitution to read
that, when interpreting the Bill of Rights, the Court 'must consider international law', so that the Court is now required to address the interpretation of rights given in international documents and by international
fora. Caution is urged, however, in respect to the use of comparative bill
of rights jurisprudence and foreign case law. The Court notes that these
sources 'will no doubt be of importance, particularly in the early stages
of the transition when there is no developed indigenous jurisprudence
in this branch of the law', but 'will not necessarily offer a safe guide to the
interpretation of Chapter Three of our Constitution'.[16]

The extensive use of both international materials and comparative law
in the *Death Penalty Case* is revealing. Instead of relying on the international and foreign materials as legal precedent, the Court used these
materials primarily as a means to distinguish the South African case. The
only case quoted with unqualified approval as equivalent and possibly a
source of the Court's holding was a decision of the Hungarian Constitutional Court.[17] Instead, the Court used the international and comparative materials as a source for specific lines of argument and justification
and in a more general sense as a source for supporting the general role
of the Court and judicial review in particular.[18]

Apart from using international and comparable foreign case law, six
of the justices made specific reference to *ubuntu* – a Zulu word and social
concept translated as 'human nature, good nature'[19] or as 'human
nature, humaneness, one's real self'[20] – as a source of indigenous values
in the interpretation of the Constitution.[21] The importance of these
statements lies as much in the application of the concept of *ubuntu* to the
question of the death penalty as in pointing to indigenous values as a
source for the development of a particular South African constitutional
jurisprudence. Despite these clear indications that the concept of *ubuntu*
– the core of which is the notion that a person can only be a person
through others – has been recognized by the Court as an important
source of the values which are to be inculcated in the development of an
indigenous constitutional jurisprudence, there is little commonality on
either the specific content given by the Justices to *ubuntu* or the sources
to which the Court may look in building its jurisprudence around the
principles of *ubuntu*.

The concept of *ubuntu* is given its most direct application in the opinion of Madala J,[22] who argues that the concept 'carries in it the ideas of
humaneness, social justice and fairness',[23] and states in his conclusion that

the death penalty 'is clearly in conflict with the Constitution generally and runs counter to the concept of *ubuntu*'.[24] This notion of *ubuntu* as a general ethos giving an indigenous content to the humanitarian principles underlying the new Constitution is repeated by Mahomed J,[25] and by Mokgoro J, who describes *ubuntu* as translatable as 'humaneness',[26] a 'shared value and ideal which runs like a golden thread across cultural lines'.[27] In this way, there seems to be an attempt to define the spirit of *ubuntu* as providing a connection between indigenous value systems and universal human rights embodied in international law and comparative constitutional jurisprudence.[28]

This search for connection is tied, however, to a recognition that *ubuntu* may also provide the reverse, a unique connection between South Africa's new commitment to constitutionalism and the possibility of constructing a particularly South African constitutional jurisprudence, one that will resonate with the indigenous values of the majority of South Africans. This project requires that the Court not only make an analogy between *ubuntu* and humaneness, or human rights in general, but that the concept of *ubuntu* be more clearly elucidated. Langa J begins this process by noting that *ubuntu* is not defined in the Constitution and then proceeds to identify elements of *ubuntu* which together form a 'culture which places some emphasis on communality and on the interdependence of the members of the community'.[29] The three central elements of *ubuntu* are defined by Langa J as: (1) recognition of a 'person's status as a human being, entitled to unconditional respect, dignity, value and acceptance' from fellow community members; (2) a corresponding 'duty to give the same respect, dignity, value and acceptance to each member of that community'; and, (3) a regulation of the exercise of rights by laying emphasis 'on sharing and co-responsibility and the mutual enjoyment of rights by all'.[30]

Even though specific reference to *ubuntu* was removed from the 'final' Constitution by the Constitutional Assembly, the concern to link the meanings of the Constitution with indigenous ideas and understandings remains. Although the provisions relating to amnesty – within which the notion of *ubuntu* had been included – remain within the ambit of the Constitution by virtue of the incorporation by reference, through Schedule Six of the 1996 Constitution, to the commitment to national reconciliation contained in the post-amble of the interim Constitution,[31] the fact that *ubuntu* is no longer in the text of the Constitution itself means that it may no longer play such a central role in this project. In this regard, Pius Langa, Deputy President of the Constitutional Court, expresses the need to engage with and exchange material with judges in other parts of Africa, as he is concerned about the individual focus of 'western law' and is worried that the majority of South Africans, who understand being part of a community as producing both duties and rights, 'will become alienated from rights unless interpretation gives a collective, communal meaning to rights'.[32] Justice Langa's concern about the importance of indigenous law and questions about the sources that may be drawn upon are shared by Justice Sachs. In *Makwanyane*, Sachs J insisted that it is possible to incorporate indigenous principles resurrected from 'the relatively well-developed judicial processes of indigenous societies'.[33] Reconstructing the evidence of 'traditional African jurisprudence',[34] Sachs J consciously engaged in a 'search for core and enduring values consistent with the text and spirit of the Constitution'.[35] Consistent with the long overdue recognition of 'African law and legal thinking as a source of legal ideas, values and practice',[36] this is a creative response to the failure to give due recognition to 'traditional African jurisprudence'. There is, however, a need to develop a sound theory, for both the identification of the relevant sources of African jurisprudence and for the selection and incorporation of specific values, particularly when the evidence demonstrates different and contrasting traditions. Sachs J attempted this by first identifying three contrasting aspects of the history of the death penalty in traditional African jurisprudence and then by announcing

> In seeking the kind of values which should inform our broad approach to interpreting the Constitution, I have little doubt as to which of these three contrasted aspects of tradition we should follow and which we should reject. The rational and humane adjudicatory approach is entirely consistent with and re-enforcing of the fundamental rights enshrined in our Constitution; the exorcist and militarist concepts are not.[37]

Finally, in contrast to the boldness of the Court's commitment to creating a new culture of human rights in South Africa and to upholding the supremacy of the Constitution, the Court has continued to assert its judicial role as interpreter, not maker, of the Constitution. This is expressed in the Court's cautious and often hesitating recognition of the complexity of its relationship to the framers of the Constitution, public opinion and the newly democratized representative institutions as articulated by Sachs J who, taking a surprisingly 'positivist' attitude to constitutional interpretation, argued that 'the idealism that we uphold with this judgment is to be found not in the minds of the judges, but in both the explicit text of the Constitution itself, and the values it enshrines'.[38]

Language, Education and Minority Culture

Issues of language, education and minority cultures are neither new nor unique to South Africa;[39] they have long been a source of conflict and nationalist mobilization in the South African context. Attempts by the British colonial administration to anglicize the Afrikaners after the Anglo-Boer War and the Apartheid regime's attempt to impose Afrikaans as a medium of instruction on black schools which sparked the student uprising in Soweto in 1976, have engraved these issues on to the soul of South African politics.

While it was impossible fully to resolve these issues in the Constitutional negotiations, the interim Constitution and the Constitutional Principles provided a framework within which constitutional challenges soon arose. The first was heard on 5 February 1996, within weeks of threatening confrontations between black and white participants in a struggle over admissions to the Laerskool Potgietersrus – a State-aided public school in a small Northern Province town, which had yet to admit a black student nearly two years after South Africa's democratic elections.

Laerskool Potgietersrus was officially an Afrikaans-medium school; however, it had developed a second, English-medium, 'stream', in which classes were taught in English. The case was brought by the parents of black children who were denied entrance into the school by blockading whites. The black applicants denied that the school was fully enrolled and argued that the refusal to admit their children as pupils into the English-medium stream at the school was a racially based violation of the equality clause of the interim Constitution. In response, the school's governing body – consisting of parents and teachers – argued that the school was 'entitled to refuse admission of pupils on grounds of culture'[40] in order to protect the school's exclusive Christian Afrikaans culture and ethos. This was justified in their submissions to the Court in terms of both the interim Constitution's protection of language, education and cultural rights as well as international law, which they argued grants 'the Afrikaner people, as a minority … an unquestionable and inalienable right to self-determination'.[41]

Finding *prima facie* discrimination, the Court identified four reasons that justified its finding and silenced the school's cultural protection argument. First, the Court pointed out that not one black pupil had been admitted to the school despite numerous applications over a two-year period. In fact, black parents had formed an *ad hoc* committee from 1994, when it became clear to them that the historically white schools in Potgietersrus were refusing to admit black students despite the formal end of apartheid. Second, the Court noted that the school was in fact a dual medium school in which English was the medium of instruction in three classes. Furthermore it was pointed out that, while the Afrikaans classes had twenty-eight students per class, the English classes only had twenty-two students per class, and therefore it could not be said that the English classes were full. Since it was the English-medium classes to which the black pupils had applied for admission, this negated the school's argument that it was full, despite having a long waiting list of students for the Afrikaans-medium classes. The Court noted in this regard that the school was actively bussing white students from a previously white primary school to the Laerskool Potgietersrus so that the Zebediela school now had only black children. While the school admitted that it was bussing white children, it argued that the primary school at Zebediela was now 'swamped by English-speaking pupils to the extent that the school has lost its erstwhile character' and that 'children now attend the respondent school because the character and ethos of this school still corresponds with that of the Zebediela school in earlier times'. Third, the Court attacked the very notion that the Afrikaans character and ethos of the school would be changed by the admission of black students. The Court argued that, even if all the available spaces in the English-medium classrooms were to be given to black applicants, there would still be a 6:1 ratio between Afrikaans and English-speaking students in the school and therefore the fear of being 'swamped by English-speaking pupils, whereby the Afrikaans character and ethos would be destroyed, is so far-fetched as to border on the ridiculous'.[42] Furthermore, the Court noted that the English-speaking children would represent a number of different cultures, including 'Tsonga, Pedi, Sotho and probably more', and that in the event that the numbers of English-speaking pupils should escalate dramatically, a case could be made for the establishment of separate English and Afrikaans schools. Finally, the Court noted that the school's waiting list contained only names of 'what appear to be white Afrikaans-speaking children', and that none of the names of the black pupils who applied were on the waiting list, leading the Court to 'infer that their names were intentionally omitted because they had not been seriously considered for acceptance into the bosom of the school'.[43]

While these facts led the Court to reject the school's governing body's arguments and to hold that the school had failed to demonstrate that its actions were not based on unfair discrimination, the Court also offered hope of plausible alternatives to the Afrikaans-speaking respondents. First, the Court explicitly noted that: 'Section 32(c) of the Constitution confers on such a minority people a right to establish their own educational institution based on the values the respondent [school] wishes to preserve.'[44] Second, the Court held out the possibility that, if sufficient numbers of English-speaking pupils were admitted into the school, there might be grounds for the establishment of separate English and Afrikaans speaking schools.[45] In this way, the Court's interpretation of the interim Constitution both silenced the option of applying racial distinctions in the name of cultural preservation in a State-aided school and explicitly pointed to the Constitutional protection of a right to establish private institutions through which the possibility of cultural preservation in the restricted form imagined by the governing board of Laerskool Potgietersrus could be sustained. The Court, presided over by an Afrikaans-speaking judge, also implied a new imagined alternative – the establishment of separate English and Afrikaans schools which would not be based on racial segregation, but rather on the mere escalation in demand for English-speaking places requiring the establishment of separate English- and Afrikaans-medium schools.

Within a month of this case being heard before the Transvaal Provincial Division of the Supreme Court, the same issues arose in related circumstances before the Constitutional Court. In *Ex Parte Gauteng Provincial Legislature: In Re Dispute Concerning the Constitutionality of Certain Provisions of the Gauteng School Education Bill of 1995*,[46] heard on 29 February 1996, one third of the members of the Gauteng legislature petitioned the Speaker of the provincial legislature to refer the Gauteng School Education Bill to the Constitutional Court for abstract review. They argued, among other issues, that the Bill was unconstitutional to the extent that it prohibited public schools from using language competence testing as an admission requirement. Here the Constitutional Court took the same basic direction as the Transvaal Provincial Division of the Supreme Court, both silencing attempts to perpetuate racial segregation and privilege and pointing to alternatives that could in part address the demands of those claiming cultural protection. Upholding the power of the provincial legislature to prohibit language testing as a basis for admission, the Court argued that the prohibition did not infringe 'two clear constitutional rights: the right to instruction at a public school in the language of their choice and the right to establish schools of their own based on a common culture, language or religion'.[47]

Writing his concurring opinion in Afrikaans, Kriegler J forcefully argued that the Constitution protects diversity but not racial discrimination. He argued that

> the Constitution keeps the door open for those for whom the State's educational institutions are considered inadequate as far as communal culture, language or religion are concerned. They are at liberty to preserve harmoniously the heritage of their fathers for their children. But there is a price, namely, that such a population group will have to stick its hand into its own pocket.[48]

Thus the Court simultaneously silenced claims that would have perpetuated indirect racial discrimination, while guaranteeing, for those who feel the state schools no longer meet their needs, the right to create their own alternatives. On the one hand, this recognized the power of the state to prohibit parent-controlled state institutions from effectively discriminating against black students attempting to gain access to formerly 'whites only' institutions through the administration of strict language tests. On the other hand, this approach prevented the state from constraining those not satisfied from leaving the system and establishing their own self-funded institutions outside of direct state control. The Court notes that this approach recognizes that the Constitutional guarantee of a right 'to establish, where practicable, educational institutions based on common culture, language or religion'[49] is a freedom entrenched in response to South Africa's particular history, in which the state perpetrated racial discrimination through education and 'actively discouraged and effectively prohibited private educational institutions from establishing or continuing private schools and insisted that such schools had to be established and administered subject to the control of the State'.[50]

This reliance on local historical circumstance as a source for this particular constitutional value is then bolstered through the explicit acknowledgment of international legal standards for the protection of minorities. Sachs J, in his concurring opinion, relies on international law in order to address the argument that the Constitution failed to guarantee the minority rights of the applicants. To test their proposition, Sachs J applies 'internationally accepted principles of minority rights protection', and comes to the conclusion that the interim Constitution is entirely consistent with the principles of human rights law because it:

- prevented the State from embarking on programmes intended or calculated to destroy the physical existence or to eliminate the cultural existence of, particular groups;
- required the State to uphold the principles of non-discrimination and equal rights in respect of members of minority groups;
- permitted and possibly required the State to take special remedial or preferential action to assist disadvantaged groups to achieve real equality;
- permitted but did not require the State to establish communal schools, or to support such schools already established; [and]
- permitted members of minority groups to establish their own schools.[51]

The effect of the Court's judgment is to deploy both local history and international norms effectively to circumscribe the outer boundaries of claims justifying exclusive access to a state resource – formerly white, English- and Afrikaans-medium state schools. But the Court's judgment also declines to foreclose on the aspirations of those seeking protection for their vision of maintaining a particular cultural community based on language and religion. Instead, the Court explicitly guarantees the rights of those seeking to secure their own vision of community so long as they pay their own way and do not discriminate on the basis of race. It is this second aspect of the judgment which allows the proponents of cultural exclusivity the scope to continue to imagine the achievement of their own particular aims but within the limits of both locally and internationally endorsed values and principles. In October 1996, the Northern Province government agreed to register a private 'volk' school established and financed by those parents wishing to maintain the cultural purity they felt was threatened by changes at Potgietersrus Laerskool.

Regionalism, Local Autonomy and Traditional Authority
In the process of negotiating the 1993 Constitution there were significant changes in the positions of the three major players as well as important continuities which became cobbled together in the interim Constitution. Most fundamentally, the ANC's initial demand for a unitary state came to be interpreted in the sense of national sovereignty over the 1910 boundaries of South Africa rather than in its initial meaning of a central government with pre-emptive power over regional authorities. With this new emphasis, the issue of regionalism, rejected initially by the ANC because of its historic association in South Africa with the white opposition Democratic Party and the emasculation of governmental powers, became a central feature of the constitutional debate.

The adoption of the language of 'strong regionalism' by both the ANC and the National Party government also reflected the National Party's acceptance that the absolute veto powers of the upper house of the legislature would be limited to regional matters and its notion of political party based consociationalism would be formally restricted to local government structures. Although the National Party government accepted the demise of its proposals for a rotating presidency and equal representation in the Senate, many of the provisions of the 1993 Constitution, and in particular its guarantee of a five-year Government of National Unity, satisfied many of the goals implicit in the apartheid government's earlier proposals.

Unlike the ANC and the National Party, however, the IFP refused to concede its central claim to regional autonomy and in its alliance with white pro-apartheid parties continued to threaten to disrupt the transitional process. Although factions of the IFP seemed ready to contest the elections for the KwaZulu-Natal regional government, the party's leader Chief Gatsha Buthelezi interpreted his party's poor showing in pre-election polls as cause to promote an even more autonomous position encouraging and supporting King Goodwill Zwelethini in his demand for the restoration of the nineteenth-century Zulu monarchy with territorial claims beyond even the borders of present-day KwaZulu-Natal.

Although the proponents of a federal solution for South Africa advocated a national government of limited powers, the 1993 Constitution reversed the traditional federal division of legislative powers by allocating enumerated powers to the provinces. This allocation of regional powers – according to a set of criteria incorporated into the Constitutional Guidelines and in those sections of the Constitution dealing with the legislative powers of the provinces – was, however, rejected by the IFP on the grounds that the Constitution failed to guarantee the autonomy of the provinces.

Despite the ANC's protestations that the provincial powers guaranteed by the Constitution could not be withdrawn, the IFP pointed to the fact that the allocated powers were only concurrent powers and that the national legislature could supersede local legislation through the establishment of a national legislative framework covering any subject matter. This tension between provincial autonomy and the ANC's assertion of the need to establish national frameworks guaranteeing minimum standards and certain basic equalities led to an amendment to the 1993 Constitution before it even came into force. According to the amendment, the provinces were granted exclusive powers in those enumerated areas of legislative authority. Areas deemed of exclusive jurisdiction to provincial legislatures included: agriculture; gambling; cultural affairs; education at all levels except tertiary; environment; health; housing; language policy; local government; nature conservation; police; state media; public transport; regional planning and development; road traffic regulation; roads; tourism; trade and industrial promotion; traditional authorities; urban and rural development; and welfare services. Difficulty arose in distinguishing the exact limits of a region's exclusive powers and the extent to which the national legislature was able to pass general laws effecting rather broad areas of governance.

Although the provinces have the power to assign executive control over these matters to the national government if they lack administrative resources to implement particular laws, the Constitution provided that the provinces had executive authority over all matters over which they had legislative authority as well as matters assigned to the provinces in terms of the transitional clauses of the constitution or delegated to the provinces by national legislation. The net effect of these provisions was continued tension between non-ANC provincial governments and the national government over the extent of regional autonomy and the exact definition of their relative powers.

It is in this context that three particular cases arose before the Constitutional Court in 1996 in which we may trace the role of the Court in both silencing and enabling the constitutional imaginations of the contending parties. All three cases involved, among other issues, claims of autonomy or accusations of national infringement of autonomy by the province of KwaZulu-Natal. As such they represent three moments in which the Court was called upon to help shape the boundary between contending claims of constitutional authority to govern, unresolved by the negotiated settlement. While two of the cases directly implicated actions of the KwaZulu-Natal legislature and its attempts to assert authority within the province – in one case over traditional leaders and in the other the constitution-making powers of the province – the first case involved a dispute over the National Education Policy Bill,[52] which was then before the National Assembly.

Objections to the National Education Policy Bill focused on the claim that the 'Bill imposed national education policy on the provinces' and thereby 'encroached upon the autonomy of the provinces and their executive authority'. The IFP made the further claim that the 'Bill could have no application in KwaZulu-Natal because it [the province] was in a position to formulate and regulate its own policies'.[53] While all parties accepted that education was defined as a concurrent legislative function under the interim Constitution, the contending parties imagined that different consequences should flow from the determination that a subject matter is concurrently assigned to both provincial and national government.

KwaZulu-Natal and the IFP in particular assumed a form of pre-emption doctrine in which the National Assembly and national government would be precluded from acting in an area of concurrent jurisdiction so long as the province was capable of formulating and regulating its own policies. In rejecting this argument, the Constitutional Court avoided the notion of pre-emption altogether and instead argued that the 'legislative competences of the provinces and Parliament to make laws in respect of schedule 6 [concurrent] matters do not depend upon section 126(3)', which the Court argued only comes into operation if it is necessary to resolve a conflict between inconsistent national and provincial laws.[54] The Court's rejection of any notion of pre-emption is an interpretation of the Constitution which enables both national and provincial legislators to continue to promote and even legislate on their own imagined solutions to issues within their concurrent jurisdiction without foreclosing on their particular options until there is an irreconcilable conflict.

Having avoided siding categorically with either national or provincial authority, the Court took a further step arguing that even if a 'conflict is resolved in favour of either the provincial or national law, the other is not invalidated' it is merely 'subordinated, and to the extent of the conflict, rendered inoperative'.[55] Supported by the comparative jurisprudence of Canada[56] and Australia,[57] the Court was able to make a distinction between 'laws that are inconsistent with each other and laws that are inconsistent with the Constitution',[58] and thereby argue that 'even if the

National Education Policy Bill deals with matters in respect of which provincial laws would have paramountcy, it could not for that reason alone be declared to be unconstitutional'.[59]

While the Constitutional Court's approach clearly aimed to reduce the tensions inherent in the continuing conflict between provincial and national governments, particularly in relation to the continuing violent tensions in KwaZulu-Natal, it also took the opportunity explicitly to preclude an alternative interpretation. Focusing on argument before the Court which relied upon the United States Supreme Court's decision in *New York v United States*,[60] the Court made the point that '[u]nlike their counterparts in the United States of America, the provinces in South Africa are not sovereign states'.[61] Furthermore, the Court warned that '[d]ecisions of the courts of the United States dealing with state rights are not a safe guide as to how our courts should address problems that may arise in relation to the rights of provinces under our Constitution'.[62] In effect the Court's approach was to begin to draw a boundary around the outer limits of provincial autonomy while simultaneously allowing concurrent jurisdiction to provide a space in which different legislatures can continue to imagine and assert their own, at times contradictory, solutions to legislative problems within their jurisdiction.

The scope of such a definition of concurrent jurisdiction was immediately tested in a case challenging two bills before the KwaZulu-Natal provincial legislature, which purported in part to preclude national action effecting the payment of salaries to traditional authorities in KwaZulu-Natal.[63] In this case, brought by ANC members of the KwaZulu-Natal legislature, the objectors argued that the bills were unconstitutional as they amounted to an attempt to 'frustrate the implementation of the [national] Remuneration of Traditional Leaders Act', by preventing the Ingonyama (Zulu King) and traditional leaders 'from accepting remuneration and allowances which might become payable to them in terms of the national legislation'.[64] Furthermore, the object of this provincial legislation 'was to create a relationship of subservience between them [traditional leaders] and the provincial government', an object outside the scope of the province's concurrent powers with respect to traditional authorities.[65]

The Court's response was first to lament that the political conflict concerning KwaZulu-Natal had degenerated to a state in which the right to pay traditional authorities, as a means to secure influence over them, should have become an issue. Recalling that traditional leaders 'occupy positions in the community in which they can best serve the interests of their people if they are not dependent or perceived to be dependent on political parties or on the national or provincial governments', the Court noted that its role is limited to deciding 'whether the proposed provincial legislation is inconsistent with the Constitution'.[66]

Faced with intractable political conflicts between the IFP and ANC in KwaZulu-Natal, the Court reasserted its duty to interpret legislation narrowly so as to avoid constitutional conflicts and upheld the legislative competence of the KwaZulu-Natal legislature and the constitutionality of the two bills. In effect the Court allowed the KwaZulu-Natal legislature to continue to imagine its own authority in this area, merely postponing clear questions of conflict between the national and provincial legislation to a later date.

The outer limits of the Court's tolerance for alternative constitutional visions was, however, reached in the third case in which the Court was asked to certify the Constitution of the Province of KwaZulu-Natal.[67] Although the KwaZulu-Natal draft Constitution had been unanimously adopted by the provincial legislature the Constitutional Court held that there are 'fundamental respects in which the provincial Constitution is fatally flawed',[68] and therefore declined to certify it. The Court considered these flaws under three headings. Two sets of problems were essentially procedural in nature and involved attempts by the KwaZulu-Natal legislature: (1) to avoid the Court's determination of the text's inconsistency with the interim Constitution;[69] or (2) to suspend the certification process itself until particular sections could be tested against the final Constitution.[70] While the Court rejected these devices as being in conflict with the certification process and attempting to circumvent the process respectively, the most significant problem with the text was the KwaZulu-Natal legislature's usurpation of national powers.

Referring to the Court's decision in the *National Education Policy Bill* case, in which it made a 'distinction between the history, structure and language of the United States Constitution which brought together several sovereign states … and that of our interim Constitution',[71] the Court held that parts of the proposed KwaZulu-Natal ('KZN') Constitution appeared to have 'been passed by the KZN Legislature under a misapprehension that it enjoyed a relationship of co-supremacy with the national Legislature and even the Constitutional Assembly'.[72] Drawing a clear boundary around the permissible constitutional aspirations of the IFP in KwaZulu-Natal, the Court rejected the draft text's attempt both to 'confer' legislative and executive authority upon the province[73] and to 'recognize' the authority of the government and 'competence' of the national Parliament in other respects.[74] While recognizing the right of the IFP-dominated KwaZulu-Natal legislature to exercise its powers to draft a provincial constitution, even possibly including its own bill of rights, the Court clearly rejected the attempt by the IFP to assert its vision of regional autonomy beyond the core meaning of the negotiated compromise represented by the 1993 Constitution. Furthermore, the Court clearly silenced the extreme option of provincial sovereignty, stating that the assertions of recognition were 'inconsistent with the interim

Constitution because KZN is not a sovereign state and it simply has no power or authority to grant constitutional "recognition" to what the national Government may or may not do'.[75]

Although the IFP had walked out of the negotiations in which the interim Constitution was drafted and refused to participate in the Constitutional Assembly during the making of the 1996 Constitution, it nevertheless proceeded to produce its own provincial Constitution and submitted it to the Constitutional Court in terms of the 1993 Constitution. Even as its vision of regional autonomy became increasingly isolated, the IFP still imagined that it could be achieved within the parameters of the 1993 Constitution. Its rejection by the Constitutional Court silenced this particular attempt, but did not foreclose on the IFP's vision of greater regional autonomy.

Instead of suffering defeat, the IFP was able to take solace from the Court's refusal, on the same day, to certify the draft of the final Constitution, and in particular the Court's decision that the draft of the final Constitution had failed to grant provinces the degree of autonomy they were guaranteed in the Constitutional Principles.[76] However, when the 1996 Constitution was finally certified by the Constitutional Court,[77] the IFP remained dissatisfied over the limited degree of provincial autonomy recognized in the Constitution. But by that time the IFP, as the governing party in KwaZulu-Natal, was not about to exit the system; instead it joined the other opposition parties in saying that it would take the opportunity in the following year's legislative session to review the Constitution,[78] thus keeping its visions alive.

BOUNDED ALTERNATIVES, BOUNDED CONFLICTS

While South Africa's 'final' 1996 Constitution has been profoundly shaped by the struggles – political, social and intellectual – which continue to be waged over political participation, constitutional rights to property and equality, and the allocation of goernment power between different levels of government, the adoption of a common constitutional framework has begun to trace the boundaries of these at times irreconcilable differences.

This harnessing of political conflict is, it seems, achieved in two primary ways. First, through the inherently open form of the Constitution, which despite all attempts to the contrary, is interpreted by opposing factions as supporting, at least in part, their particular vision of what is either possible or mandated. Second, by incorporating external formulations of constitutional rights and structures, as well as explicitly providing for the use of international and foreign legal sources, the constitutional framework implicitly silences options that cannot be justified in terms of the Constitution read in a global context.

While the new constitutional framework has enabled the political transition by allowing opposing forces to imagine the possibility of achieving, at least in part, their particular vision within the terms of the Constitution, it has also worked to shape these imaginings through the creation of external reference points which delegitimize incompatible alternatives or visions. There remain, however, fairly large and incompatible differences between the alternative yet viable interpretations advocated in the context of these different political and social struggles. Constitutionalism here provides the institutional space for repeated attempts to advance any particular vision that may conceivably be presented as a compatible interpretation of the Constitution. The courts and in particular the new Constitutional Court could thus perform an essential institutional role in both keeping alive these alternative possibilities and seeking justice in each particular case that presents itself within their jurisdiction.

CONCLUSION

The Constitutional Court's decision, in September 1996, to deny certi-fication of the first text of South Africa's final Constitution, epitomized South Africa's surprising post-colonial turn. Instead of following in the tradition of African decolonization and granting government nearly untrammeled legislative authority – whether in the form of Westmin-ster democracies, Leninist-party states, military dictatorships or African socialisms – South Africa has embraced judicial review. The embrace of a constitutional form which limits government and aims to circum-scribe pure majoritarian democracy is a particularly surprising out-come given more than 300 years of racial domination and the struggle for popular democracy which have engraved the landscape of South Africa's recent history.

The Constitutional Court's certification judgments represented the crest of the wave of a legal revolution which flowed out of South Africa's remarkable democratic transition. The judgments provided a window through which it was possible to view the emerging shape of a post-apartheid constitutionalism. This new constitutionalism – reflected also in other judgments of the Constitutional Court and the Court's engage-ment with other political institutions – is the product of, and bears the indelible mark of, South Africa's particular democratic transition. At the same time, the success of this new constitutionalist project has been rein-forced by the Constitutional Court's own judicious politics. The Court has repeatedly asserted its right to decide central questions of gover-nance, while simultaneously limiting its role to a clearly specified judicial function which pays open respect and deference to the new democratic institutions and processes.

The essence of this new South African constitutionalism has been its ability to absorb and civilize seemingly irreconcilable political conflicts. This capacity relies for its existence on two distinct elements. First, it is facil-itated by the refusal, through the political process or the Courts, to pre-clude future alternative interpretations of the open-textured formulations which characterize Constitutional texts. Through both legal methods of interpretation and the political decisions of the parties, the constitutional formulations adopted at each stage of the transition allowed all significant participants in these struggles to imagine the possibility of sustaining their own visions of outcomes that they viewed as essential to their future well-being as political players, communities or rights claimants.

Second, this imagining and reimagining of acceptable outcomes and the shaping and reshaping of political coalitions around these different scenarios reflect the interaction of local conditions and global options. While South Africa's state sovereignty secures a space for the assertion of particular local visions and alternatives, global discourses of democracy, rights and markets shape the boundaries of these internal options. This constraint on local autonomy is most explicitly revealed in the genealogy of the Constitutional Principles themselves. Although it may be argued that South Africans had long talked in terms of rights and even the need for a bill of rights, it was the evolution of the notion of a specific set of Constitutional Principles that would guide future constitutional negotiations – such as the 1988 ANC Constitutional Guidelines – that provided the vehicle for building trust and security between the parties in the political transition. This process was strengthened by the international endorsement of these principles in the Harare Declaration and United Nations Declaration on Apartheid as the minimum basis for internationally acceptable post-apartheid options in South Africa.

While these principles were endorsed by all the South African parties at the Convention for a Democratic South Africa (Codesa) in December 1991 and reflected the post–cold war thrust of justiciable rights, they also effectively silenced normative arguments for majoritarian democracy in the form of parliamentary sovereignty or people's democracy in the form of a one-party state. The adoption of this broad international framework did not, however, define the precise content of the range of acceptable alternatives. Instead, the specifics of this framework have been constantly reshaped by the processes of its local adoption. From the adoption of the Constitutional Principles in Schedule 4 of the interim Constitution of 1993 to the Constitutional Court's decision to refuse to certify that the new text met the requirements of the Principles in September 1996, the Constitutional Principles remained the repository of the hopes and conflicts of the opposing parties in the transition.

This reliance on the Constitutional Principles implied a role for the judiciary in mediating the construction of a post-apartheid political order. On its face it indicated a shared faith in the ability of the judicial branch of government to resolve conflicts often too difficult to negotiate between opposing political players. This faith in the judiciary to uphold the new democratic order is particularly striking given the past failure of the judiciary to uphold basic principles of justice in the face of apartheid policies and laws. It may, however, be argued that the problem of apartheid judges has been addressed institutionally through the establishment of a new Constitutional Court. While it is true that the majority of justices appointed to the new Court are lawyers with impeccable anti-apartheid credentials who will have the ultimate authority to interpret the Constitution, this does not explain the new faith in judicial decision-making as a source of legitimacy in the governance of a post-apartheid South Africa.

An analysis of the local dimension leads to the conclusion that the new faith in judicial decision-making seems to be based on the real and imagined political space created by the introduction of democratic constitutionalism. While it has been argued that war was the continuation of politics by other means, I wish to postulate the converse, that the turn to judicial review involves a move towards the civilization of potentially unnegotiable political conflicts. The resolution of extreme political differences often involves mutual compromise, but always seems to foreclose on alternative visions. Judicial decision-making – and by implication democratic constitutionalism, which relies on the ongoing process of constitutional interpretation – does not foreclose on alternative options, but rather provides a mechanism through which space for alternative approaches and visions, within a set of bounded alternatives, is continually retained. In this sense, then, it is not a matter of a new or renewed faith in the judiciary, but rather a reliance on the opportunities for continuing conflict implicit in judicial decision-making.

Instead of seeking the source of this new faith in the legal and political developments within South Africa alone, I have argued that it is equally important to explore the global context within which the democratic transition unfolded. While international constitutional experts offered different visions of how South Africa should reconstruct its constitution, it is striking how they all assumed that South Africa would replace its tradition of parliamentary sovereignty with a justiciable constitution and a bill of rights.[1] This assumption reflects a global pattern: by the late twentieth century, an American-style bill of rights had come to be seen as a crucial component of liberal democratic governance, the adoption of which was apparently a prerequisite to full participation in a globalized international political economy.

Like many other countries which went through decolonization or democratic transitions in the post–Second World War era, it may be argued that South Africa has merely adopted an imported constitutional framework that will bring fundamental change to its local institutions of governance. But discussions of democratic transitions that focus entirely on the adoption of an internationally acceptable liberal democratic model overlook the ways in which local histories give content to legal forms; conversely, approaches that stress only local negotiations and élite pacting overlook the way imported forms shape future possibilities. As Stephen Krasner argues, although 'current institutional structures may

be a product of some peculiar historical conjuncture ... once an historical choice is made, it both precludes and facilitates alternative future
choices'.[2] The globalization of constitutionalism in the post-war era
builds on and reshapes local struggles. The interaction between the
international forum and local histories circumscribes the options for
political reconstruction by drawing and sustaining the boundaries of
acceptable governance; on the other hand, this interaction infuses
imported international forms with local content in the shaping and
implementation of particular constitutional institutions and issues.

In exploring South Africa's new faith in judicial decision-making and
constitutionalism, it is inadequate to adopt either a purely local perspective or a global gaze. Instead I have demonstrated that the source of this
new faith is a product of the particular dynamics of constitutionalism
adopted as a product of the interaction between global and local developments. Faith in the judiciary is, I have argued, based less on the past,
or the perceived legitimacy of the South African legal system, than on the
space democratic constitutionalism allows for the maintenance of contending perceptions and concerns amongst political factions. For the victims of apartheid, the new reliance on constitutionalism, even with the
establishment of a genuinely democratic government, is based on the
expectation that constitutional rights will protect individuals and society
from the return of injustice and oppression. This understanding assumes
that the Constitution will enable the newly enfranchised majority to
achieve a significant democratic shift in the balances of both public and
private power, while promoting a long-denied equality among South
Africans. The old ruling élite, however, see the shift to constitutionalism
as a protection against the redistributive demands of the new democratic
majority and view judicial review as the last bastion protecting their property and freedom against threats they perceive to be implicit in the
notion of an unrestrained democratic will with access to the levers of
public power.

In the first year of its existence, the Constitutional Court was called
upon by both sides. Proponents of human rights successfully challenged
the constitutionality of the death penalty, while minority parties in the
provincial and national legislatures frustrated speedy social change by
delaying new legislation – for example in education – through repeated
threats or actual constitutional challenges. However, with the partial and
incomplete victories and defeats that have characterized the outcomes of
these cases and which are implicit in judicial decision-making, faith in
the judiciary and the new constitutionalism, at least among political participants, has been repeatedly tested and reinvigorated.

Finally, it is possible to sketch a number of general conclusions
relevant to the broader, global question of renewed faith in judicial

decision-making. First, I have argued that the construction of democratic constitutional orders in the post-1945 era takes place in the context of particular elements: the transmission and globalization of political traditions; the emergence and development of an international human rights movement containing both hegemonic and counter-hegemonic aspects; and the particular national context, including both the pre-existing institutions and legal culture as well as the political struggles or circumstances leading to the creation of a new constitutional order. Second, that the reproduction of a constitutional order involves both the continuing influences of those factors determining its creation as well as the dynamic impact of the consequences of its own existence – the impact of social movements and social change generated within the constitutional order affecting the future interpretation, amendment or revision of the new constitutional framework. Third, that the making and implementation of a constitutional order constitutes new relations of power between the different institutional sites of social integration – the state, economic society and civil society. Fourth, that the emergence of democratic constitutionalism as a particular form of constitutionalism in the post–Second World War era has produced a unique opportunity for the flowering of the public sphere or public spaces representing diverse interests and discourses. Fifth, that this understanding of democratic constitutionalism has important implications for debates over judicial legitimacy as the importance of this legitimacy seems to be confined to the politically active classes in society and is not dependent on a broader social acknowledgement. Finally, that the triumph of diversity in public discourse is the consequence of constitutional democracies reordering the relations of power between property, equality and governance as the background conditions of democratic constitutionalism.

NOTES

INTRODUCTION

1 See Anthony Lewis, 'Revolution by Law', *New York Times*, 13 January 1994, p. A15.

2 See generally Adam Przeworski, *Democracy and the Market: Political and economic reforms in Eastern Europe and Latin America* (New York: Cambridge University Press, 1991).

3 Albie Sachs, *Protecting Human Rights in a New South Africa* (Cape Town: Oxford University Press, 1990), 9–10.

4 *Republic of South Africa Constitution Act* 200 of 1993 (SAfr).

5 *Republic of South Africa Constitution Act* 108 of 1996 (SAfr).

6 World Bank, press release, Washington, DC, 18 October 1994, 1.

7 David Beatty, 'Human Rights and the Rules of Law', in David Beatty (ed.), *Human Rights and Judicial Review: A Comparative Perspective* (Dordrecht; Boston: M. Nijhoff; Norwell, MA: Kluwer Academic, 1994), 1.

8 Bruce Ackerman, 'The Rise of World Constitutionalism' (1997) 83 *Virginia Law Review* 771.

9 Douglas Greenberg et al., 'Introduction' to Douglas Greenberg et al. (eds.), *Constitutionalism and Democracy: Transitions in the Contemporary World* (New York: Oxford University Press, 1993), xxi.

10 See Carol V. Rose, 'The "New" Law and Development Movement in the Post–Cold War Era: A Vietnam Case Study' (1998) 32 *Law & Society Review* 93.

11 J. A. Gardner, *Legal Imperialism: American Lawyers and Foreign Aid in Latin America* (Madison: University of Wisconsin Press, 1980), 9.

12 Ibid. 283.

13 See David M. Trubek & Marc Galanter, 'Scholars in Self-Estrangement: Some reflections on the crisis in law and development studies in the United States' [1974] *Wisconsin Law Review* 1062.

14 Gardner, *Legal Imperialism*, 7.

15 Brian Z. Tamanaha, 'The Lessons of Law-and-Development Studies' (1995) 89 *The American Journal of International Law* 470, 486.

16 Arthur Taylor von Mehren & James Russell Gordley, *The Civil Law System* (2nd edn., Boston: Little, Brown, 1977), 7.

17 R. B. Schlesinger, H. W. Baade, M. R. Damaska & P. E. Herzog, *Comparative Law: Cases, Text, Materials* (5th edn., Mineola, NY: Foundation Press, 1988), 231.

18 F. H. Lawson, *A Common Lawyer Looks at the Civil Law* (Ann Arbor: University of Michigan Law School, 1955), 48–51.

19 See Susan S. Silbey, ' "Let Them Eat Cake": Globalization, Postmodern Colonialism, and the Possibilities of Justice' (1997) 31 *Law & Society Review* 207.

20 P. *Rathinam/Nagbhusan Patnaik, Petitioners v. Union of India and another, Respondents* [1994] AIR (Supreme Court) 1844, 1868.

21 Cf. Yves Dezalay & Bryant Garth, 'Merchants of Law as Moral Entrepreneurs: Constructing International Justice from the Competition for Transnational Business Disputes' (1995) 29 *Law & Society Review* 27; and Yves Dezalay & Bryant Garth, *Dealing in Virtue: International Commercial Arbitration and the Construction of a Transnational Legal Order* (Chicago: University of Chicago Press, 1996).

22 See generally T. O. Elias, 'The Evolution of Law and Government in Modern Africa', in Hilda & Leo Kuper (eds.), *African Law: Adaptation and Development* (Berkeley: University of California Press, 1965); Robert B. Seidman, 'Law and Economic Development in Independent, English-Speaking, Sub-Saharan Africa', in T. W. Hutchison (ed.), *Africa and Law: Developing Legal Systems in African Commonwealth Nations* (Madison: University of Wisconsin Press, 1968); Cliff F. Thompson, 'The Sources of Law in the New Nations of Africa: A Case Study from the Republic of the Sudan', in T. W. Hutchison (ed.), *Africa and Law: Developing Legal Systems in African Commonwealth Nations*.

23 See Boaventura de Sousa Santos, *Toward a New Common Sense: Law, Science, and Politics in the Paradigmatic Transition* (New York: Routledge, 1995), 250–377.

24 See Paul DiMaggio & Walter Powell, 'The Iron Cage Revisited: Institutional Isomorphism and Collective Rationality in Organizational Fields' (1983) 48 *American Sociological Review* 147.

25 See, e.g., Guillermo O'Donnell, Philippe C. Schmitter & Laurence Whitehead (eds.), *Transitions from Authoritarian Rule: Tentative Conclusions about Uncertain Democracies* (Baltimore: Johns Hopkins University Press, 1986).

26 See Ackerman, 'The Rise of World Constitutionalism'.

27 See Cass R. Sunstein, 'On Property and Constitutionalism' (1993) 14 *Cardozo Law Review* 907.

28 Bruce Ackerman, *The Rise of World Constitutionalism*, Yale Law School Occasional Papers, Second Series, Number 3 (1997), 9–10.

29 S. P. Huntington, *The Third Wave: Democratization in the Late Twentieth Century* (Norman: University of Oklahoma Press, 1991), 228–31.

30 Sara Schatz, 'A Neo-Weberian Approach to Constitutional Courts in the Transition from Authoritarian Rule: The Mexican Case (1994–1997)' (1998) 26 *International Journal of the Sociology of Law* 217.

31 Ruti Teitel, 'Transitional Jurisprudence: The Role of Law in Political Transformation' (1997) 106 *Yale Law Journal* 2009, 2012.

32 Ibid. 2014.

33 See, for example, Arend Lijphart, *Democracies: Patterns of Majoritarian and Consensus Government in Twenty-One Countries* (New Haven: Yale University Press, 1984); and Courtney Jung & Ian Shapiro, 'South Africa's Negotiated Transition: Democracy, Opposition and the New Constitutional Order' (1995) 23 *Politics and Society* 269, 71.

34 See Hannah Arendt, *On Revolution* (1963), 142–3 and 232–4; and Bruce Ackerman, *The Future of Liberal Revolution* (New Haven: Yale University Press, 1992), 61.

35 Teitel, 'Transitional Jurisprudence', 2054.

36 Ibid. 2011.

37 Ibid. 2016.

38 See Dezalay & Garth, 'Merchants of Law as Moral Entrepreneurs'.

39 Teitel, 'Transitional Jurisprudence', 2014.

40 See Philip Thomas, 'Ambiguity: The Management of Dissent', in Andre-Jean Arnand (ed.), *Sociology of Law: Splashes and Sparks, Onati Proceedings-2* (Onati, Spain: International Institute for the Sociology of Law, 1990).

41 See A. E. Dick Howard, 'The Indeterminacy of Constitutions' (1996) 31 *Wake Forest Law Review* 383.

42 See, Lawrence W. Beer, 'Introduction: Constitutionalism in Asia and the United States', in Lawrence W. Beer (ed.), *Constitutional Systems in Late Twentieth Century Asia* (Seattle: University of Washington Press, 1992), 4 and 40, Figure 1.

43 Ibid. Figure 1.

44 Ibid. 15.

45 Said A. Arjomand, 'Constitutions and the Struggle for Political Order: A Study in the Modernization of Political Traditions' (1992) 33 *Archives of European Society* 39.

46 Arjomand, 'Constitutions and the Struggle for Political Order', 41–5. Cf. K. Pennington, *The Prince And The Law 1200–1600: Sovereignty and Rights in the Western Legal Tradition* (Berkeley: University of California Press, 1993).

47 Robert Allen Dahl, *Democracy and its Critics* (New Haven: Yale University Press, 1989), 30–3.

48 Beer, 'Introduction', 1.

49 Richard Tur & William Twining (eds.), *Essays on Kelsen* (Oxford: Oxford University Press, 1986), 1. See generally David Dyzenhaus, *Legality and Legitimacy: Carl Schmitt, Hans Kelsen and Hermann Heller in Weimar* (Oxford: Oxford University Press, 1997).

50 All figures used were calculated from a survey of constitutions using A. P. Blaustein & G. H. Flanz (eds.), *Constitutions of the Countries of the World* (Dobbs Ferry, NY: Oceana Publications, 1971–) and the web site http://www.uni-wuerzburg.de/law/index.html.

51 Ahmed Ibrahim & M. P. Jain, 'The Constitution of Malaysia and The American Constitutional Influence', in Lawrence W. Beer (ed.), *Constitutional Systems in Late Twentieth Century Asia* (Seattle: University of Washington Press, 1992), 528.

52 See C. Neal Tate & Torbjorn Vallinder (eds.), *The Global Expansion of Judicial Power* (New York: NYU Press, 1995).

53 See Herbert Jacob et al., *Courts, Law and Politics in Comparative Perspective* (New Haven, CT: Yale University Press, 1996).

54 Boaventura de Sousa Santos, 'The Gatt of Law and Democracy: (Mis)Trusting the Global Reform of Courts, Globalization and Legal Cultures', in Johannes Feest (ed.), *Onati Summer Course 1997* (Onati, Spain: International Institute for the Sociology of Law, 1999).

55 See Ackerman, 'The Rise of World Constitutionalism' (1997) 83 *Virginia Law Review* 771.

1 POST–TWENTIETH-CENTURY CONSTITUTIONALISM?

1 Douglas Greenberg et al., Introduction to Douglas Greenberg et al. (eds.), *Constitutionalism and Democracy: Transitions in the Contemporary World: The American Council of Learned Societies Comparative Constitutionalism Papers* (New York: Oxford University Press, 1993), xxi.

2 Robert Allen Dahl, *Democracy and its Critics* (New Haven: Yale University Press, 1989), 188.

3 See generally, Lawrence H. Tribe, *American Constitutional Law* (2nd edn., New York: Foundation Press, 1988), 10–12; Dennis Davis, Matthew Chaskalson & Johann de Waal, 'Democracy and Constitutionalism: The Role of Constitutional Interpretation', in D. van Wyk et al. (eds.), *Rights and Constitutionalism: The New South African Legal Order* (Kenwyn: Juta, 1994).

4 Alexander Bickel, *The Least Dangerous Branch* (2nd edn., New Haven, CT: Yale University Press, 1986), 16–17.

5 See generally Charles L. Black, Jr., *The People and the Court: Judicial Review in a Democracy* (Westport, CT: Greenwood Press, 1960); Bickel, *The Least Dangerous Branch*; Jesse H. Choper, *Judicial Review and the National Political Process* (Chicago: Chicago University Press, 1980); John Hart Ely, *Democracy and Distrust* (Cambridge, MA: Harvard University Press, 1980); and M. Perry, *The Constitution, the Courts and Human Rights: An Inquiry into the Legitimacy of Constitutional Policymaking by the Judiciary* (New Haven: Yale University Press, 1982).

6 Stephen Holmes, 'Precommitment and the Paradox of Democracy', in Jon Elster & Rune Slagstad (eds.), *Constitutionalism and Democracy* (Cambridge; New York: Cambridge University Press; Paris: Maison des sciences de l'homme, 1988), 198.

7 See Hugh Corder, 'Lessons from (North) America (Beware the "Legalization of Politics" and the "Political Seduction of the Law")' (1992) 109 *South African Law Journal* 204.

8 Holmes, 'Precommitment', 231.

9 J. Elster, Introduction to *Constitutionalism and Democracy*, 9.

10 Holmes, 'Precommitment', 235.

11 Lawrence H. Tribe & Thomas K. Landry, 'Reflections on Constitution-Making' (1993) 8 *American University Journal of International Law & Policy* 627, 630.

12 Holmes, 'Precommitment', 209.

13 Ibid.

14 See Holmes, 'Precommitment'.

15 See generally Elster, Introduction to *Constitutionalism and Democracy*, 1–17.

16 See generally, Stephen Holmes, 'Gag Rules or the Politics of Omission', in Jon Elster & Rune Slagstad (eds.), *Constitutionalism and Democracy*, 19–58.

17 See generally Holmes, 'Precommitment', 195–240.

18 See Cass R. Sunstein, 'Constitutions and Democracies: An Epilogue', in Jon Elster & Rune Slagstad (eds.), *Constitutionalism and Democracy*, 348–52.

19 See S. D. Krasner, 'Approaches to the State: Alternative Conceptions and Historical Dynamics' (1984) 16 *Comparative Politics* 223, 234.

20 Alan Hunt, *Explorations in Law and Society: Towards a Constitutive Theory of Law* (New York: Routledge, 1993), 325.

21 See, J. Nedelsky, 'American Constitutionalism and the Paradox of Private Property', in Jon Elster & Rune Slagstad (eds.), *Constitutionalism and Democracy*, 241–73.

22 1 Cranch (5 US) 137, 2 L Ed 60 (1803).

23 Morton Halperin, 'Limited Constitutional Democracy: Lessons from the American Experience' (1993) 8 *American University Journal of International Law & Policy* 523, 528.

24 See Roger Pilon, 'On the First Principle of Constitutionalism: Liberty, Then Democracy' (1993) 8 *American University Journal of International Law & Policy* 531.

25 Jean Cohen & Andrew Arato, 'Politics and the Reconstruction of the Concept of Civil Society', in Axel Honneth et al. (eds.), *Cultural-Political Interventions in the Unfinished Project of Enlightenment*, trans. Barbara Fultner (Cambridge, MA: MIT Press, 1992), 137–9.

26 See Nancy Fraser, 'Rethinking the Public Sphere: A Contribution to the Critique of Actually Existing Democracy', in Craig Calhoun (ed.), *Habermas and the Public Sphere* (Cambridge, MA: MIT Press, 1992), 109–42.

27 Hunt, *Explorations in Law and Society*, 324.

28 See Ely, *Democracy and Distrust*.

29 See, Jürgen Habermas, *Between Facts and Norms: Contributions to a Discourse Theory of Law and Democracy*, trans. William Rehg (Cambridge, MA: MIT Press, 1996).

30 See, Hendrik Hartog, 'The Constitution of Aspiration and "The Rights That Belong to Us All" ', (1987) 74 *The Journal of American History* 1013.

31 See, Claude Lefort, *The Political Forms of Modern Society: Bureaucracy, Democracy, Totalitarianism*, ed. John Thompson (Cambridge, MA: MIT Press, 1986), 266 and 260.

32 See, W. E. Scheuerman, *Between the Norm and the Exception: The Frankfurt School and the Rule of Law* (Cambridge, MA: MIT Press, 1994), 228.

33 See Jon Elster, 'Forces and Mechanisms in the Constitution-Making Process' (1995) 45 *Duke Law Journal* 364.

34 Charles Simkins, 'Must Contemporary South African Liberals be Thatcherites?' in R. W. Johnson & David Welsh (eds.), *Ironic Victory: Liberalism in Post-Liberation South Africa* (Oxford: Oxford University Press, 1998), 56. See generally F. A. Hayek, *The Constitution of Liberty* (London: Routledge and Kegan Paul, 1960).

35 Professor Fink Haysom, quoted in *The Making of the Constitution: The Story of South Africa's Constitutional Assembly, May 1994 to December 1996* (Cape Town: Churchill Murray, for the Constitutional Assembly, 1997), 72.

36 Ibid.

37 See, Gunther Teubner (ed.), *Global Law Without a State* (Aldershot: Dartmouth, 1997).
38 The European Court of Justice and the European Court on Human Rights. See, Anne-Marie Slaughter, Alec Sweet & Joseph Weiler (eds.), *The European Courts and National Courts: Doctrine and Jurisprudence* (Oxford: Hart, 1997).
39 See Basic Law of the Federal Republic of Germany, 1949.
40 See The Constitution of India, 1950.
41 See the Namibian Constitution, 1990.
42 See, for example, the South African and Colombian constitutions
43 See A. Appadurai, 'Disjuncture and Difference in the Global Cultural Economy', (1990) 2(2) *Public Culture* 1.
44 Ibid. 21.
45 Ibid. 5.
46 Appadurai argues that the 'imagination is now central to all forms of agency, is itself a social fact, and is the key component of the new global order'. Ibid. 5.
47 Said A. Arjomand, 'Constitutions and the Struggle for Political Order: A Study in the Modernization of Political Traditions' (1992) 33 *Archives of European Society* 39, 75.
48 See, C. Neal Tate & Torbjorn Vallinder (eds.), *The Global Expansion of Judicial Power* (New York: NYU Press, 1995).
49 See D. Beatty, 'Human Rights and the Rules of Law', in *Human Rights and Judicial Review: A Comparative Perspective* (Dordrecht; Boston: M. Nijhoff; Norwell, MA: Kluwer Academic, 1994), 1–56. See also David Held, 'Democracy, the Nation-State and the Global System', in David Held (ed.), *Political Theory Today* (Oxford: Polity; Stanford: Stanford University Press, 1991), 197–235.

2 LEGAL LEGACIES AND CONSTITUTIONAL PATHS

1 See generally: M. Benson, *The African Patriots: The story of the African National Congress of South Africa* (London: Faber & Faber, 1963); S. M. Davis, *Apartheid's Rebels: Inside South Africa's Hidden War* (New Haven: Yale University Press, 1987); G. M. Gerhart, *Black Power in South Africa: The Evolution of an Ideology* (Berkeley: University of California Press, 1978); T. Lodge, *Black politics in South Africa since 1945* (Johannesburg: Ravan Press, 1983); E. Roux, *Time Longer Than Rope: A History of the Black Man's Struggle for Freedom in South Africa* (Madison: University of Wisconsin Press, 1964); Jack & Ray Simons, *Class & Colour in South Africa, 1850–1950* (Harmondsworth: Penguin African Library, 1969, rpt London: International Defence and Aid Fund, 1983); P. Walshe, *The Rise of African Nationalism in South Africa: The African National Congress, 1912–1952* (Berkeley: University of California Press, 1971).
2 Mary Benson, *Nelson Mandela: The Man and the Movement* (London; New York: Norton, 1986); L. Foreman & E. S. Sachs, *The South African Treason Trial* (New York: Monthly Review Press, 1958); Nelson Mandela, *No Easy Walk to Freedom: Speeches and Documents*, ed. Ruth First (London: Heinemann, 1965).
3 Richard L. Abel, *Politics by Other Means: Law in the Struggle Against Apartheid, 1980–1994* (New York: Routledge, 1995).

4 Although most histories of South African law emphasize the reception of European law – some tracing it back to Roman times – the history of South African law needs to be placed in the context of South Africa's colonial experience; see Martin Chanock, *Fear, Favour and Prejudice: The Making of South African Legal Culture* (forthcoming).

5 Douglas C. North, *Institutions, Institutional Change and Economic Performance* (New York: Cambridge University Press, 1990), 100.

6 John Dugard, *Human Rights and the South African Legal Order* (Princeton: Princeton University Press, 1978), 37–49.

7 *South Africa Act* 1909, 9 Edw 7, c 9 (Imp).

8 Leonard Thompson, 'The Compromise of Union', in Monica Wilson & Leonard Thompson (eds.), *The Oxford History of South Africa*, vol. 2 (New York: Oxford University Press, 1975).

9 Mahmood Mamdani, *Citizen and Subject: Contemporary Africa and the Legacy of Late Colonialism* (Princeton: Princeton University Press, 1996), 16–23.

10 Adam Ashforth, *The Politics of Official Discourse in Twentieth-Century South Africa* (Oxford: Clarendon Press, 1990), 34.

11 T. R. H. Davenport, *South Africa: A Modern History* (2nd edn., Toronto; Buffalo: University of Toronto Press, 1978), 147–69.

12 T. R. H. Davenport & K. S. Hunt (eds.), *The Right to the Land* (Cape Town: David Philip, 1974), 1–30.

13 South African Customs Union Conference, Minutes of Proceedings, Bloemfontein, March 1903, British Parliamentary Papers, Cd 1640, 9.

14 Walshe, *Rise of African Nationalism*, 17.

15 The source of this idea is a paper by Cape liberal R. W. Rose-Innes discussing the *Glen Grey Act* and supplied to the Commission in 1903. See Marian Lacey, *Working for Boroko: The Origins of a Coercive Labour System in South Africa* (Johannesburg: Ravan Press, 1981).

16 Davenport, *South Africa: A Modern History*, 152.

17 Leonard Thompson, 'Co-operation and Conflict: The Zulu Kingdom and Natal', in Monica Wilson & Leonard Thompson (eds.), *The Oxford History of South Africa*, vol. 1 (New York: Oxford University Press, 1969), 376.

18 Ashforth, *Politics of Official Discourse*, 41.

19 Ibid.

20 See *South Africa Act* 1909, 9 Edw 7, c 9 (Imp), s 34(i), in which the quota of representatives from each province is to be 'obtained by dividing the total number of European male adults in the Union ... by the total number of members'.

21 Roux, *Time Longer Than Rope*, 87–100.

22 Lord Milner, 'A Review of the Present Mutual Relations of the British South Africa Colonies', 1907, Cd 3564; Thompson, 'The Compromise of Union', 347.

23 Davenport, *South Africa: A Modern History*, 120–46.

24 Dugard, *Human Rights and the South African Legal Order*, 26.

25 *South Africa Act* 1909, 9 Edw 7, c 9 (Imp), s 35. Although the first proposal would have required a two-thirds majority of each house of parliament, the final compromise was weaker – two-thirds vote of both houses sitting

together. H. R. Hahlo & Ellison Kahn, *South Africa: The Development of its Laws and Constitution* (London: Stevens, 1960), 122.

26 William Blackstone, *Commentaries on the Laws of England* (first published 1765, 4th edn., Boston: Beacon Press, 1876), 129.

27 See, e.g., the decision of Sir Edward Coke in *Dr Bonham's Case* (1610) 8 Co Rep 113b; 77 ER 646 (CP 1610); R. Pound, *The Development of Constitutional Guarantees of Liberty* (New Haven: Yale University Press, 1957).

28 Dugard, *Human Rights and the South African Legal Order*, 14–18.

29 Hahlo & Kahn, *South Africa: The Development of its Laws and Constitution*, 72–83; Dugard, *Human Rights and the South African Legal Order*, 18–19.

30 Dugard, *Human Rights and the South African Legal Order*, 19.

31 (1892) 9 Cape L J 58.

32 Hahlo & Kahn, *South Africa: The Development of its Laws and Constitution*, 78.

33 Dugard, *Human Rights and the South African Legal Order*, 19.

34 Ibid. 21. See *Brown v Leyds NO* (1897) 4 Off Rep 17.

35 Hahlo & Kahn, *South Africa: The Development of its Laws and Constitution*, 91.

36 Ibid. 108–9.

37 Dugard, *Human Rights and the South African Legal Order*, 24.

38 Ibid. 23. See also, Hahlo & Kahn, *South Africa: The Development of its Laws and Constitution*, 107–10.

39 *Colonial Laws Validity Act* 1865, 28 & 29 Vict c 63 (Imp).

40 *Representation of Natives Act* 12 of 1936 (SAfr).

41 *Republic of South Africa Constitution Act* 32 of 1961 (SAfr).

42 *South Africa Act Amendment Act* 9 of 1956 (SAfr), s 2.

43 Ellison Kahn, *The New Constitution: With Comparative Tables of the Republic of South Africa Constitution Act, 1961, and the South Africa Act and Earlier Provisions, and the Text of the Republic of South Africa Constitution Act, No. 32 of 1961*: Supplement to H. R. Hahlo & Ellison Kahn, *South Africa: The Development of its Laws and Constitution* (London: Stevens, 1962), 2.

44 *Sachs v Minister of Justice* 1934 AD 11, 36–7.

45 Dugard, *Human Rights and the South African Legal Order*, 36.

46 Abel, *Politics By Other Means.*

47 1906 TS 135.

48 See, Heinz Klug, 'Defining the Property Rights of Others: Political Power, Indigenous Tenure and the Construction of Customary Land Law', (1995) 35 *Journal of Legal Pluralism* 1.

49 The South African Native Affairs Commission 1903–1905 was appointed in 1903 with the 'object of arriving at a common understanding of native policy'; South African Customs Union Conference, 'The Native Question', Minutes, Bloemfontein, March 1903, British Parliamentary Papers, Cd 1640 [10].

50 South African Native Affairs Commission, *Report of the South African Native Affairs Commission*, 5 vols. (Cape Town: Government Printer, 1905), 214.

51 68 of 1951 (SAfr).

52 T. R. H. Davenport, 'Some Reflections on the History of Land Tenure in South Africa, Seen in the Light of Attempts by the State to Impose Political and Economic Control' [1985] *Acta Juridica* 53, 69.

53 Ashforth, *Politics of Official Discourse*, 35.
54 Ibid. 37.
55 See generally Mamdani, *Citizen and Subject.*
56 See Hahlo & Kahn, *South Africa: The Development of its Laws and Constitution,* 54.
57 Dugard, *Human Rights and the South African Legal Order,* 20.
58 Leonard Thompson, 'Great Britain and the Afrikaner Republics', in *The Oxford History of South Africa* vol. 2 (New York: Oxford University Press, 1971), 309.
59 Dugard, *Human Rights and the South African Legal Order,* 18.
60 Interestingly, the definition of European in Natal at this time was constructed more around the threefold distinction between indigenous Africans, indentured Indians and other members of colonial society. For example, 'prison regulations classified prisoners into three groups, Africans, Indians and Europeans, but the definition of Europeans was unusual in that it included "all persons of European descent, Eurasians ... American Negroes, French Creoles and West Indians"'. A. Sachs, *Justice in South Africa* (Berkeley: University of California Press, 1973), 89.
61 See Dugard, *Human Rights and the South African Legal Order,* 18.
62 Hahlo & Kahn, *South Africa: The Development of its Laws and Constitution,* 67.
63 Peter Warwick, *Black People and the South African War, 1899–1902* (Cambridge: Cambridge University Press, 1983), 181.
64 Davenport, *South Africa: A Modern History,* 152.
65 South African National Convention 1908–1909, *Minutes of Proceedings with Annexures (selected)* (Cape Town: Government Printers, 1911), 23.
66 Ibid. 66. See also Hahlo & Kahn, *South Africa: The Development of its Laws and Constitution,* 54.
67 *Women's Enfranchisement Act* 18 of 1930 (SAfr).
68 *Franchise Laws Amendment Act* 41 of 1931 (SAfr).
69 *Report of the South African Native Affairs Commission, 1903–1905* (1905), 442.
70 Act 38 of 1927 (SAfr).
71 1930 AD 484.
72 Ibid. 494.
73 Ibid. 496.
74 Ibid. 492–3.
75 12 of 1936 (SAfr).
76 1937 AD 229.
77 Ibid. 238.
78 Hahlo & Kahn, *South Africa: The Development of its Laws and Constitution,* 165.
79 28 of 1946 (SAfr).
80 Hahlo & Kahn, *South Africa: The Development of its Laws and Constitution,* 165–6.
81 1937 AD 229.
82 1952 (2) SA 428 (AD). See Joshua Davidson, 'The History of Judicial Oversight of Legislative and Executive Action in South Africa' (1985) 8 *Harvard Journal of Law and Public Policy* 687, 710; Dugard, *Human Rights and the South African Legal Order,* 29; and Hahlo & Kahn, *South Africa: The Development of its Laws and Constitution,* 154–9.
83 35 of 1952 (SAfr).
84 Dugard, *Human Rights and the South African Legal Order,* 30–1.

85 Ibid. 31.
86 27 of 1955 (SAfr).
87 53 of 1955 (SAfr).
88 Davidson, 'The History of Judicial Oversight', 718–19; and Dugard, *Human Rights and the South African Legal Order*, 31.
89 46 of 1950 (SAfr).
90 Dion Basson & Henning Viljoen, *South African Constitutional Law* (1988, 2nd Impression, Cape Town: Juta, 1991), 307–18. See also, Henry J. Richardson III, 'Self-Determination, International Law and the South African Bantu-stan Policy' (1985) 17 *Columbia Journal Transnational Law* 185.
91 For an early critique of the policy of separate development and the idea of Bantustan development, see Govan Mbeki, *South Africa: The Peasants' Revolt* (2nd edn., London: International Defence and Aid Fund for Southern Africa, 1984), 73–94.
92 48 of 1963 (SAfr). See W. J. Hosten, A. B. Edwards, C. Nathan & F. Bosman, *Introduction to South African Law and Legal Theory* (Durban: Butterworths, 1983), 665–78.
93 21 of 1971 (SAfr).
94 *See*, M. P. Vorster et al., *The Constitutions of Transkei, Bophuthatswana, Venda and Ciskei* (Durban: Butterworths, 1985), 15.
95 Heinz Klug, 'Self-Determination and the Struggle Against Apartheid' (1990) 8 *Wisconsin International Law Journal* 251, 294–5.
96 Laurine Platzky & Cherryl Walker, *The Surplus People: Forced Removals in South Africa* (Johannesburg: Raven Press, 1985), 11.
97 T. R. H. Davenport, 'Some Reflections on the History of Land Tenure in South Africa', 61. See also Native Land Commission (Beaumont Commission), *Minutes of Evidence*, Union Government 26-1916, 271, 276–7, 333, 351, 327–8, quoted in T. R. H. Davenport & K. S. Hunt (eds.), *The Right to Land* (Cape Town: David Philip, 1974), Document 65.
98 *Black Land Act* 27 of 1913 (SAfr).
99 1911 AD 635.
100 Ibid. 643–4.
101 Ibid.
102 Ibid.
103 1934 AD 167.
104 David Dyzenhaus, *Hard Cases in Wicked Legal Systems: South African Law in the Perspective of Legal Philosophy* (Oxford: Clarendon Press, 1991), 55 (citation omitted).
105 *Minister of Posts and Telegraphs v Rasool* 1934 AD 167, 190–1.
106 Significantly this case arose as an appeal against the conviction of Abdurahman, who, as a member of a 'Train Apartheid Resistance Committee', was inciting blacks to enter railway coaches reserved for the exclusive use of 'Europeans'; Dyzenhaus, *Hard Cases*, 64.
107 1950 (3) SA 136 (A).
108 [1898] 2 QB 91.
109 *R v Abdurahman* 1950 (3) SA 136 (A) 145.
110 49 of 1953.
111 Platzky & Walker, *The Surplus People*, 35.

112 Ibid. See also A. Dodson, 'The Group Areas Act: Changing Patterns of Enforcement', in Christina Murray & Catherine O'Regan (eds.), *No Place to Rest: Forced Removals and the Law in South Africa* (Cape Town: Oxford University Press in association with the Labour Law Unit, University of Cape Town, 1990).

113 41 of 1950 (SAfr), later amended and consolidated in Act 36 of 1966.

114 Michael Robertson, 'Dividing the Land: An Introduction to Apartheid Land Law', in Murray & O'Regan (eds.), *No Place to Rest*, 125.

115 Ibid. 126.

116 1959 (3) SA 651 (A).

117 Dyzenhaus, *Hard Cases*, 71.

118 1958 (2) SA 67 (E).

119 Dyzenhaus, *Hard Cases*, 73–4.

120 *Cassem*, 633, Dyzenhaus, *Hard Cases*, 73, relying on Edwin Cameron's translation of the passage in 'Legal Chauvinism, Executive-Mindedness and Justice: L. C. Steyn's Impact on South Africa Law', (1982) 99 *South African Law Journal* 56.

121 Dyzenhaus, *Hard Cases*, 73.

122 Ibid. 75.

123 Innes CJ in *Dadoo Ltd v Kruger(s)dorp Municipal Council* 1920 AD 530, 552.

124 *Minister of the Interior v Lockhat and Others* 1961 (2) SA 587 (AD).

125 Dyzenhaus, *Hard Cases*, 81.

126 *Minister of the Interior v Lockhat and Others* 1961 (2) SA 587 (AD) 602.

127 Stephen Ellmann, 'Law and Legitimacy in South Africa' (1995) 20 *Law and Social Inquiry* 407, 425, concluded that public opinion surveys in South Africa find that 'Blacks expressed a substantial level of confidence in the legal system in 1981 and an even greater level in 1990'.

128 Ibid. 409.

129 Ibid. 427–8. In my view the problems of polling in South Africa during the 1980s and early 1990s cannot be rationalized away. Ellmann, 'Law and Legitimacy in South Africa', for example, argues that the decrease in confidence expressed in the 1993 poll merely indicates disappointment following the elation experienced at the beginning of the democratic transition in 1990. Yet, another explanation may be that in 1993 those polled felt more inclined to offer their true feelings in a context where it had become clear that the democratic transition had become irreversible. Neither explanation is self-evident.

130 Nicholas Haysom & Steven Kahnovitz, 'Courts and the State of Emergency', in Glenn Moss & Ingrid Obrey (eds.), *South African Review 4* (Johannesburg: Ravan Press, 1987), 192.

131 Ibid. See also Dion Basson, 'Judicial Activism in a State of Emergency: An Examination of Recent Decisions of the South African Courts', (1987) 3 *South African Journal on Human Rights* 28; and C. Rickard, 'This Year's Message to Despondent Civil Rights Lawyers: Pack Your Bags', *Weekly Mail* (Johannesburg), 24 Dec. 1987–14 Jan. 1988, p. 8, col. 3.

132 George Bizos, *No One to Blame? In Pursuit of Justice in South Africa* (Cape Town: David Philip/Mayibuye, 1998), 6–7.

133 Haysom & Kahanovitz, 'Courts and the State of Emergency', 191.

134 Muriel Crewe, 'Punishment by Process', *SASH*, May 1987, 19–20.

135 Ibid.
136 Ibid. 20.
137 Ibid.
138 P. Sidley, 'World Jurists Slam SA Courts', *Weekly Mail* (Johannesburg), 14–20 Nov. 1986, p. 2, col. 1.
139 M. M. Corbett, 'Presentation to the Truth and Reconciliation Commission' (1998) 115 *South African Law Journal* 17, 18.
140 Truth and Reconciliation Commission, Final Report, 5 vols., October 29 1998, Vol. 4, Chapter 4 [18] [TRC Final Report].
141 Ibid.
142 Ibid. There is a wealth of scholarship addressing the question of the judiciary under apartheid in addition to the material already cited above, including: Geoffrey Bindman (ed.), *South Africa: Human Rights and the Rule of Law* (International Commission of Jurists, London: Pinter, 1988); Hugh Corder, 'The record of the judiciary (2)', in Hugh Corder (ed.), *Democracy and the Judiciary* (Cape Town: Idasa, 1989); John Dugard, 'Should Judges Resign? (And Lawyers Participate)', in *Democracy and the Judiciary*; Stephen Ellmann, *In a Time of Trouble: Law and Liberty in South Africa's State of Emergency* (Oxford: Clarendon Press, 1992); International Commission of Jurists, *South Africa and the Rule of Law* (1960); International Commission of Jurists, *Erosion of the Rule of Law in South Africa* (1968); Michael Lobban, *White Man's Justice: South African Political Trials in the Black Consciousness Era*, (Oxford: Clarendon Press, 1996); Anthony Matthews, *Freedom, State Security and the Rule of Law: Dilemmas of Apartheid Society* (Cape Town: Juta, 1986); Etienne Mureinik, 'Dworkin and Apartheid', in Hugh Corder (ed.), *Essays on Law and Social Practice in South Africa* (Cape Town: Juta, 1988); Adrienne van Blerk, 'The record of the judiciary (1)', in *Democracy and the Judiciary*.
143 For an excellent account of the hearings and critique of the role of the judiciary under apartheid, see David Dyzenhaus, *Truth, Reconciliation and the Apartheid Legal Order* (Cape Town: Juta, 1998).
144 TRC Final Report, Vol. 4, Ch. 4 [32].
145 Ibid. [33].
146 Ibid. [36].
147 Ibid. [40].

3 CONSTITUTIONALISM IN GLOBAL PERSPECTIVE

1 I draw here on the new institutionalist tradition in social science. See John W. Meyer, John Boli & George M. Thomas, 'Ontology and Rationalization in the Western Cultural Account', in G. M. Thomas, J. W. Meyer, F. O. Ramirez & J. Boli (eds.), *Institutional Structure: Constituting State, Society, and the Individual* (Newbury Park, CA: Sage, 1987), 36–7, in which they argue that by 'institution, we mean a set of cultural rules that give generalized meaning to social activity and regulate it in a patterned way. Institutionalization, then, involves processes that make such sets of rules seem natural and taken for granted while eliminating alternative interpretations and regulations. In the Western

tradition, rules become more institutionalized as they are linked more closely to universal moral authority and lawful order in nature.'

2 The metaphor of a passport, which I owe to a suggestion by Sol Picciotto, is used here to invoke a social constructivist understanding of the 'international'. See John Gerard Ruggie, *Constructing the World Polity: Essays on International Institutionalization* (London; New York: Routledge, 1998).

3 See Jan Nederveen Pieterse, *Globalization As Hybridization*, Working Paper Series No. 152 (The Hague: Institute of Social Studies, 1993). Cf. Robert J. C. Young, *Colonial Desire: Hybridity in Theory, Culture, and Race* (London; New York: Routledge, 1995).

4 Gay W. Seidman, 'Adjusting the Lens: What Do Globalization, Transnationalism and the Anti-Apartheid Movement Mean for Social Movement Theory?' forthcoming Guidry John, Michael Kennedy & Mayer Zald (eds.), in *Globalization in the Public Sphere* (Ann Arbor: University of Michigan Press).

5 See, e.g., Paul Hirst & Grahame Thompson, 'The Problem of "Globalization": International Economic Relations, National Economic Management and the Formation of Trading Blocs' (1992) 21(4) *Economy & Society* 357; William Robinson, 'Beyond Nation-State Paradigms: Globalization, Sociology, and the Challenge of Transnational Studies', (1998) 13(4) *Sociological Forum* 561; and Roger Burbach and William Robinson, 'The Fin de Siècle Debate: Globalization as Epochal Shift' (1999) 63(1) *Science and Society* 10.

6 This means that 'human society must now more than ever before be understood and treated as an interconnected whole'; S. Picciotto, 'The Regulatory Criss-Cross: Interaction Between Jurisdictions and The Construction of Global Regulatory Networks', in William Bratton et al. (eds.), *International Regulatory Competition and Coordination: Perspectives on Economic Regulation in Europe and the United States* (Oxford: Clarendon Press, 1996), 94.

7 See, Seidman, 'Adjusting the Lens'; see also Boadventura de Sousa Santos, *Toward a New Common Sense: Law, Science and Politics in the Paradigmatic Transition* (New York: Routledge, 1995), 250–377.

8 Anthony Giddens, *Consequences of Modernity* (Stanford: Stanford University Press, 1990), 64.

9 See, e.g., Jean-Marie Guehenno, *The End of the Nation-State* (Minneapolis: University of Minnesota Press, 1995).

10 See, e.g., Kenichi Ohmae, *The Borderless World: Power and Strategy in the Interlinked Economy* (New York: Harper Business, 1990); Kenichi Ohmae, *The End of the Nation State: The Rise of Regional Economies* (New York: Free Press, 1995); Benjamin R. Barber, *Jihad v McWorld: How the Planet is Both Falling Apart and Coming Together and What this Means for Democracy* (New York: Times Books, 1995); William Greider, *One World, Ready or Not: The Manic Logic of Global Capitalism* (New York: Simon & Schuster, 1997); Walter LaFeber, *Michael Jordan and the New Global Capitalism* (New York: W. W. Norton & Co., 1999); Kevin Danaher (ed.), *Corporations are gonna to get your mama: Globalization and the Downsizing of the American Dream* (Monroe: ME, Common Courage Press, 1996).

11 See, Mickey Davis, 'Where the Working Class Lives: International Law and the Global Division of Labor' (draft, February 1995).

12 David Held, 'Democracy, the Nation-State and the Global System', in David Held (ed.), *Political Theory Today* (Oxford: Polity; Stanford: Stanford University Press, 1991), 197.

13 Paul Hirst & Grahame Thompson, *Globalization in Question: The International Economy and the Possibilities of Governance* (Cambridge: Polity Press, 1996), 183.

14 E. Helleiner, 'Democratic Governance in an Era of Global Finance', forthcoming in M. Molot and F. O. Hampson (eds.), *Canada Among Nations*.

15 Hirst & Thompson, *Globalization in Question*, 184.

16 Ibid. 184.

17 Ibid. 185.

18 Picciotto, 'Regulatory Criss-Cross', 98.

19 See David Held, 'Democracy: From City-States to a Cosmopolitan Order?' in David Held (ed.), *Prospects for Democracy: North, South, East, West* (Cambridge: Polity Press, 1993), 32–7.

20 Hirst & Thompson, *Globalization in Question*, 171–2.

21 David Kennedy, 'Receiving the International' (1994) 10 *Connecticut Journal of International Law* 1, 9.

22 As David Held, *Democracy and the Global Order: From the Modern State to Cosmopolitan Governance* (Stanford: Stanford University Press), 46, argues, the discourse of sovereignty set in motion a debate about the claim of powers by rulers and about the 'standing of the state in relation to other corporate bodies and collectivities'.

23 See, Benedict Andersen, *Imagined Communities: Reflections on the Origin and Spread of Nationalism* (2nd edn., London; New York: Verso, 1991).

24 Picciotto, 'The Regulatory Criss-Cross', 99. This is reflected, too, in the jurisdictional competence of states under international law, including in the case of criminal jurisdiction: the territorial, nationality, protective and universality principles. See Ian Brownlie, *Principles of Public International Law*, 3rd edn. (Oxford: Clarendon Press, 1979), 298–305.

25 Picciotto, 'The Regulatory Criss-Cross', 99.

26 Ibid.

27 Ibid.

28 See Held, 'Democracy: From City-States to a Cosmopolitan Order?', 39.

29 Ibid.

30 The centrality of the apartheid issue to this process at the United Nations is confirmed by Eric Stein, who, as an adviser to the United States Delegation to the UN, recalls the 'great debates of the 1950s on whether the UN General Assembly had the authority to include in its agenda the item on the treatment of people of Indian origin in the Union of South Africa, and whether such action would amount to the prohibited intervention in the domestic jurisdiction of the "sovereign" Union'; Eric Stein, 'Sovereignty and Human Rights' (1999) 42(3) *Law Quadrangle Notes* 5, 5–6.

31 John Dugard, *International Law: A South African Perspective* (Cape Town: Juta, 1994), 18 and 200–3.

32 In June 1946 the South African Indian Congresses launched a passive resistance campaign against the enactment of the *Asiatic Land Tenure and Indian Representation Act* 28 of 1946, which both prohibited people of Indian descent from acquiring land and excluded them from the political process.

196

33 Field-Marshal Smuts, quoted in Louis B. Sohn, *Rights in Conflict: The United Nations & South Africa* (Irvington, NY: Transnational Publishers, 1994), 49.
34 Sohn, *Rights in Conflict*, 49–50.
35 Ibid. 52.
36 Treatment of Indians in the Union of South Africa, GA Res 44, 1 UN GAOR, Article 2, UN Doc A/Res/44 (8 December 1946), Article 2.
37 PCIJ Rep, Series B, No. 4 (1923).
38 Ibid. 24.
39 Sohn, *Rights in Conflict*, 51.
40 Ibid. 55.
41 Ibid. 54.
42 Ibid. 55.
43 Ibid. 57.
44 See Letter dated 12 September 1952, addressed to the Secretary-General by the permanent representatives of Afghanistan, Burma, Egypt, India, Indonesia, Iran, Iraq, Lebanon, Pakistan, the Philippines, Saudi Arabia, Syria, and Yemen, UN Doc A/2183 (1952); rpt in *The United Nations and Apartheid 1948–1994*, The United Nations Blue Book Series, Volume I, (New York: Department of Public Information, United Nations, 1994), Sales No. E.95.I.7 (Soft), 233.
45 Sohn, *Rights in Conflict*, 64.
46 See, F. W. de Klerk, Second Submission of the National Party to the Truth and Reconciliation Commission, 23 March 1997, http://www.truth.org.za/submit/np2.htm.
47 Ibid. 17–18.
48 GA Res 616B, 7 UN GAOR, Supp No 21, UN Doc A/2361 (1952), 8–9.
49 UN Commission on the Racial Situation in the Union of South Africa established in terms of GA Res 616B, 7 UN GAOR, Supp No 21, UN Doc A/2361 (1952), 8–9.
50 Report of the United Nations Commission on the Racial Situation in the Union of South Africa, GA Res 2505, 8 UN GAOR, Supp No 16, UN A/2505 & A/2505/Add1 (1953), [893(i)]; rpt in *The UN and Apartheid*, 228.
51 Report of the United Nations Commission on the Racial Situation in the Union of South Africa, GA Res 2505, 8 UN GAOR, Supp No 16, UN A/2505 & A/2505/Add1 (1953), 16–22 and 114–19.
52 The Policies of Apartheid of the Government of the Republic of South Africa, GA Res 1761, 17 UN GAOR, UN Doc A/RES/1761 (6 November 1962).
53 Credentials of Representatives to the Twenty-Ninth Session of the General Assembly, GA Res 3206, 29 UN GAOR, UN Doc A/RES/3206 (30 September 1974); and Relationship between the United Nations and South Africa, GA Res 3207, 29 UN GAOR, UN Doc A/RES/3207 (30 September 1974). See also, Ruling by the President of the General Assembly, Mr Abdelaziz Bouteflika (Algeria), Concerning the Credentials of the Delegation of South Africa A/PV 2281, 12 November 1974; rpt in *The UN and Apartheid*, 333 (Doc. 75).
54 Policies of Apartheid of the Government of South Africa – Special Responsibility of the United Nations and the International Community Towards the Oppressed People of South Africa, GA Res 3411 C 30 UN GAOR, UN Doc A/RES/3411C (28 November 1975); rpt in *The UN and Apartheid*, 336.

55 The Question of South Africa, SC Res 418, 32 UN SCOR (2046th mtg), UN Doc S/RES/418 (4 November 1977). See also, Statement by Secretary-General Kurt Waldheim in the Security Council after the Adoption of Resolution 418 (1977) Concerning Mandatory Arms Embargo against South Africa, UN Doc S/PV2046, 2046th mtg (4 November 1977), stating: 'The adoption of this resolution marks the first time in the 32-year history of the Organization that action has been taken under Chapter VII of the Charter against a Member State'; rpt in *The UN and Apartheid*, 348 (Doc. 90).

56 The Question of South Africa, SC Res 554, 39 UN SCOR (2551st mtg), UN Doc S/RES/554 (17 August 1984), rpt in *The UN and Apartheid*, 390.

57 On the Report of the Ad Hoc Committee of the Whole of the Sixteenth Special Session. Declaration on Apartheid and its Destructive Consequences in Southern Africa, GA Res S-16/1, S-16 UN GAOR (6th plen mtg), UN Doc A/RES/S-16/1 (14 December 1989); rpt in *The UN and Apartheid*, 419.

58 Picciotto, 'Regulatory Criss-Cross', 98.

59 Thomas M. Franck, 'The Emerging Right to Democratic Governance' (1992) 86 *The American Journal of International Law* 46, 50.

60 Picciotto, 'Regulatory Criss-Cross', 98–9.

61 Ibid. 99.

62 Yves Dezalay & Bryant Garth, *Dealing in Virtue: International Commercial Arbitration and the Construction of a Transnational Legal Order* (Chicago: University of Chicago Press, 1996), 312–17.

63 See Claudio Grossman & Daniel D. Bradlow, 'Are We Being Propelled Towards a People-Centered Transnational Legal Order?' (1993) 9 *American University Journal of International Law and Policy* 1.

64 See James Crawford, *Democracy in International Law: Inaugural Lecture Delivered 5 March 1993*, (Cambridge: Cambridge University Press, 1994).

65 Franck, 'The Emerging Right to Democratic Governance', 46.

66 Thomas M. Franck, *Fairness in International Law and Institutions* (Oxford: Clarendon Press, 1995), 83–137.

67 Franck, 'The Emerging Right to Democratic Governance', 55.

68 Ibid. 58–9.

69 International Covenant on Civil and Political Rights, opened for signature 19 December 1966, 999 UNTS 171, 6 ILM 368 (entered into force 23 March 1976).

70 See T. Risse-Kappen, 'Ideas do not Float Freely: Transnational Coalitions, Domestic Structures, and the End of the Cold War' (1994) 48 *International Organization* 185.

71 See Thomas Buergenthal, 'The CSCE Rights System' (1991) 25 *George Washington Journal of International Law & Economics* 333.

72 Enhancing the Effectiveness of the Principle of Periodic and Genuine Elections, GA Res 150, 45 UN GAOR (69th plen mtg), UN Doc A/RES/45/150 (1990).

73 Enhancing the Effectiveness of the Principle of Periodic and Genuine Elections, GA Res 137, 46 UN GAOR (75th plen mtg), UN Doc A/RES/46/137 (17 December 1991).

74 Malvina Halberstam, 'The Copenhagen Document: Intervention in Support of Democracy' (1993) 34 *Harvard International Law Journal* 163.
75 Conference on Security and Co-operation in Europe, *Document of the Copenhagen Meeting of the Conference on the Human Dimension of the CSCE*, 29 June 1990, rpt in (1990) 29 ILM 1305, 1309 [6].
76 Conference on Security and Co-operation in Europe, *Charter of Paris for a New Europe*, 21 Nov. 1990, rpt in 30 ILM 193 (1991).
77 See 'Guidelines on the Recognition of New States in Eastern Europe and in the Soviet Union' (1991) 24(12) *Bulletin of the European Communities* 119. These European Community Guidelines require, among other things: '(i) respect for the provisions of the Charter of the United Nations and the commitments subscribed to in the Final Act of Helsinki and in the Charter of Paris, especially with regard to the rule of law, democracy and human rights; (ii) guarantees for the rights of ethnic and national groups and minorities in accordance with the commitments subscribed to in the framework of the CSCE'; quoted in K. Knop, 'The "Righting" of Recognition: Recognition of States in Eastern Europe and the Soviet Union' [1992] *Canadian Council on International Law Proceedings* 36, 44.
78 Knop, 'The "Righting" of Recognition'.
79 Universal Declaration of Human Rights, GA Res 217A, 3 UN GAOR (183rd plen mtg), UN Doc A/Res/217A (1948).
80 European Convention for the Protection of Human Rights and Fundamental Freedoms, done at Rome, 4 Nov. 1950 (entered into force 3 Sept. 1953), EuropTS No. 5.
81 American Convention on Human Rights, done at San Jose, 22 Nov., 1969, entered into force, July 18, 1978, OAS TS No. 36, 1, OAS Off Rec OEA/Ser L/V/II.23 doc 21 rev 6 (1979); rpt in (1970) 9 ILM 673.
82 African Charter on Human and Peoples' Rights, adopted June 26, 1981, OAU Doc. CAB/LEG/67/3 Rev 5, tpy in 21 ILM 58.
83 Art. 2(7), Charter of the United Nations, done at San Francisco, 26 June 1945, entered into force for the United States, Oct. 24, 1945, 59 Stat 1031, TS No. 993, 3 Bevans 1153, 1976 YBUN 1043.
84 Cf., David Rieff, 'The Precarious Triumph of Human Rights', *NYT Magazine*, 8 Aug. 1999, pp. 36–41.
85 See Grossman & Bradlow, 'Are We Being Propelled Towards A People-Centered Transnational Legal Order?' 17.
86 See The Report of the NGO Forum, UN Doc A/Conf 157/7.
87 See Kathryn Sikkink, 'Human Rights, Principled Issue-Networks, and Sovereignty in Latin America' (1993) 47 *International Organization* 411; see also Margaret E. Keck & Kathryn Sikkink, *Activists Beyond Borders: Advocacy Networks in International Politics* (Ithaca, NY: Cornell University Press, 1998).
88 Keck & Sikkink, *Activists Beyond Borders*, 2.
89 Sikkink, 'Human Rights, Principled Issue-Networks', 414.
90 See R. D. Lipschutz, 'Reconstructing World Politics: The Emergence of Global Civil Society' (1992) 21(3) *Millennium: Journal of International Studies* 389.

91 Richard Falk, 'The Making of Global Citizenship', in Jeremy Brecher et al. (eds.), *Global Visions: Beyond the New World Order* (Boston: South End Press, 1993), 40.

92 Michel Rosenfeld, 'Modern Constitutionalism as Interplay between Identity and Diversity: An Introduction' (1993) 14 *Cardozo Law Review* 497, 497.

93 Benjamin Obi Nwabueze, *Judicialism in Commonwealth Africa: The Role of the Courts in Government* (London: Hurst, 1977), 309.

94 Ibid. 308.

95 See Bruce Ackerman, *The Rise of World Constitutionalism* (Yale Law School Occasional Papers, Second Series, Number 3, 1997).

96 See Rosenfeld, 'Modern Constitutionalism'; see generally David Beatty (ed.), *Human Rights and Judicial Review: A Comparative Perspective* (Dordrecht; Boston: M. Nijoff; Norwell, MA: Kluwer Academic, 1994).

97 Knop, 'The "Righting" of Recognition', 37.

98 Mauro Cappelletti (ed.), with the collaboration of Paul Kollmer & Joanne Olson, *The Judicial Process in Comparative Perspectives* (Oxford: Clarendon Press, 1989), 185–7.

99 Universal Declaration of Human Rights, GA Res 217A, 3 UN GAOR (183rd plen mtg), UN Doc A/Res/217A (1948).

100 European Economic Community Treaty 1957, UKTS 1979 No. 15 Cmnd 7480; 298 UNTS 11.

101 Cappelletti, *Judicial Process*, 173.

102 *Internationale Handelsgesellschaft mbH v Einfuhr- und Vorratsstelle für Getreide und Futtermittel* [1974] 37 BVerfGE 271, 14 Comm Mkt LR 540.

103 Joint Declaration on Fundamental Rights, issued at Luxembourg on 5 April 1977, 1977 O J Eur Comm (no. C103/1).

104 See Letter Dated 12 June 1982 From the Representatives of Canada, France, Germany, Federal Republic of, the United Kingdom of Great Britain and Northern Ireland and the United States of America Addressed to the Secretary-General Annex. Principles Concerning the Constituent Assembly and the Constitution for an Independent Namibia, UN Doc S/15287 (1982), transmitted to the Secretary-General of the United Nations on 12 July 1982.

105 See Peter H. Merkl, *The Origin of the West German Republic* (Oxford: Oxford University Press, 1963).

106 See Tetsuka Kataoka, *The Price of a Constitution: The Origin of Japan's Postwar Politics* (New York: Crane Russak, 1991).

107 See, Thomas D. Grant, 'Internationally Guaranteed Constitutive Order: Cyprus and Bosnia as Predicates for a New Nontraditional Actor in the Society of States' (1998) 8(1) *Journal of Transnational Law and Policy* 1.

108 M. Wiechers, 'Namibia: The 1982 Constitutional Principles and Their Legal Significance', in D. van Wyk et al. (eds.), *Namibia: Constitutional and International Law Issues*, Pretoria: VerLoren van Themaat Centre for Public Law Studies, University of South Africa, 1991), 17.

109 Security Council Res. 632 of Feb. 16, 1989, see, S/20412 of 23 Jan. 1989, para 35.

110 Wiechers, 'Namibia', 20.

111 Francois Venter, 'Requirements For A New Constitutional Text: The Imperatives of the Constitutional Principles' (1995) 112 *South African Law Journal* 32.

112 See Andrew Henderson, 'Cry, the Beloved Constitution? Constitutional Amendment, the Vanished Imperative of the Constitutional Principles and the Controlling Values of Section 1' (1997) 114 *South African Law Journal* 542.

113 See Buergenthal, 'The CSCE Rights System'.

114 Ibid. 370.

115 Conference on Security and Co-operation in Europe, *Document of the Copenhagen Meeting of the Conference on the Human Dimension of the CSCE,* 29 June 1990, rpt in (1990) 29 ILM 1305. See Halberstam, 'The Copenhagen Document'.

116 See Ibrahim J. Wani, 'The Rule of Law and Economic Development in Africa, 1' (1993) *East African Journal of Peace & Human Rights* 52.

117 David M. Trubek, 'Social Justice in a Borderless World: Multiple Utopias, Local Struggles, and Complex Architectures (draft, April 1995), 2.

118 Rule of Law Consortium, ARD/Checci Joint Venture, Program Circular (18 Nov. 1994), 1.

119 World Bank, press release, Washington, DC, 18 October 1994, 1.

120 Remarks of the Hon. Mark L. Schneider, Assistant Administrator for Latin America and the Caribbean, to the First Global Rule of Law Conference, Washington, DC, 13 July 1994, 1.

121 Ibid.

122 D. M. Trubek, 'The Rule of Law' (draft, 1994) p. 3.

123 D. Held, 'Democracy: From City-States to a Cosmopolitan Order?', 25.

124 Louis Henkin, 'A New Birth of Constitutionalism: Genetic Influences and Genetic Defects' (1993) 14 *Cardozo Law Review* 533, 535–6.

125 Keith Banting & Richard Simeon, 'Introduction: The Politics of Constitutional Change', in Keith Banting & Richard Simeon (eds.), *Redesigning the State: The Politics of Constitutional Change* (Toronto; Buffalo: University of Toronto Press, 1985), 1.

126 Said A. Arjomand, 'Constitutions and the Struggle for Political Order: A Study in the Modernization of Political Traditions' (1992) 33 *Archives of European Society* 39, 73.

127 See A. W. O. Okoth-Ogendo, 'Constitutions without Constitutionalism: Reflections on an African Political Paradox', in Douglas Greenburg et al. (eds.), *Constitutionalism and Democracy: Transition in the Contemporary World: The American Council of Learned Societies Comparative Constitutionalism Papers* (New York: Oxford University Press, 1993), 65–82; Yash Ghai, 'The Theory of the State in the Third World and the Problematics of Constitutionalism', in Douglas Greenburg et al. (eds.), *Constitutionalism and Democracy: Transitions in the Contemporary World: The American Council of Learned Societies Comparative Constitutionalism Papers* (New York: Oxford University Press, 1993), 186–96; Robert B. Seidman, 'Perspectives on Constitution Making: Independence Constitutions for Namibia and South Africa' (1987) 3 *Lesotho Law Journal* 45; R. H. Green, 'Participatory Pluralism and Persuasive Poverty: Some Reflections' [1989] *Third World Legal Studies* 21; and Adrien Katherine Wing, 'Communitarianism vs. Individualism: Constitutionalism in Namibia and South Africa' (1993) 11 *Wisconsin International Law Journal* 295, 316–20. For the debate on Constitutionalism in Africa see generally Issa G. Shivji, 'State and Constitutionalism: A New Democratic Perspective', in Issa G.

Shivji (ed.), *State and Constitutionalism: An African Debate on Democracy* (Harare: SAPES Trust, 1991), 27–54; B. Barry, 'The One-Party System, Multiple Parties and Constitutionalism in African', in Shivji (ed.), *State and Constitutionalism*, 151–68; and Ziyad Motala, *Constitutional Options for a Democratic South Africa: A Comparative Perspective* (Washington, DC: Howard University Press, 1994), 96–101.

128 Arjomand, 'Constitutions and the Struggle for Political Order', 40.

129 See World Bank, *Sub-Saharan Africa: From Crisis to Sustainable Growth: A Long-Term Perspective Study* (Washington, DC: World Bank, 1989).

130 State President F. W. de Klerk argued in his speech announcing South Africa's political opening on 2 February 1990 that the removal of the threat of communism, following its collapse in eastern Europe, allowed the government the opportunity to open up the political process in South Africa; rpt as Document 16, pp. 466–82, in Hassan Ebrahim, *The Soul of a Nation: Constitution-making in South Africa* (Cape Town: Oxford University Press, 1998). See also F. W. de Klerk, Submission to the Truth and Reconciliation Commission by Mr F. W. de Klerk, Leader of the National Party, August 1996, at http://www.truth.org.za/submit/np-truth.htm.

131 Declaration of the OAU Ad-hoc Committee on Southern Africa on the Question of South Africa, Harare, Zimbabwe, 21 Aug. 1989; rpt in ANC Department of Political Education, *The Road to Peace: Resource Material on Negotiations* (Johannesburg: ANC Department of Political Education June 1990), 34.

132 On the Report of the Ad Hoc Committee of the Whole of the Sixteenth Special Session. Declaration on *Apartheid* and its Destructive Consequences in Southern Africa, GA Res S-16/1, S-16 UN GAOR (6th plen mtg), UN Doc A/RES/S-16/1 (1989).

4 CONSTITUTIONAL STRATEGIES

1 Kader Asmal, 'The Making of a Constitution' [March/April 1995] *Southern African Review of Books* 11.

2 Allister Sparks, *Tomorrow is Another Country: The Inside Story of South Africa's Negotiated Revolution* (Sandton: Struik Publishers, 1994); and Patti Waldmeir, *Anatomy of a Miracle* (Harmondsworth: Penguin, 1997).

3 Hassen Ebrahim, *The Soul of a Nation: Constitution-Making in South Africa* (Cape Town: Oxford University Press, 1998), 30.

4 See generally Gerry Simpson, 'The Diffusion of Sovereignty: Self-Determination in the Post-Colonial Age' (1996) 32 *Stanford Journal of International Law* 255; and Harold Hongju Koh, 'Why Do Nations Obey International Law?' (1997) 106 *Yale Law Journal* 2599.

5 See 'Buthelezi's Divisive Advisor', *Weekly Mail & Guardian* (Johannesburg), 2 June 1995.

6 Discussion with Christina Murray, Madison, October 1999.

7 See above, pp. 30–5.

8 See above, pp. 35–47.

9 Asmal, 'The Making of a Constitution', 14.

10 Nelson Mandela, *Long Walk to Freedom: The Autobiography of Nelson Mandela* (Boston: Little, Brown & Co., 1994), 452–86.

11 See Richard Rosenthal, *Mission Improbable: A Piece of the South African Story* (Cape Town: David Philip, 1998).

12 See, The Groote Schuur Minute, Cape Town, 4 May 1990; rpt in South African History Archive, *History in the Making: Documents Reflecting a Changing South Africa*, Vol. 1, No. 2 (November 1990), 17; The Pretoria Minute Pretoria, 6 August 1990; rpt in *History in the Making* Vol. 1, No. 2, 21–2.

13 See The D. F. Malan Accord, Cape Town, 12 February 1991, rpt in Ebrahim, *Soul of a Nation*, Document 19, 493–7; and the National Peace Accord, Johannesburg, September 14, 1991, rpt in *History in the Making* Vol. 2. No. 1, 50–80.

14 Record of Understanding, 26 September 1992, reprinted in Ebrahim, *Soul of a Nation*, Document 27, 588–94.

15 *The Republic of South Africa Constitution Act* 200 of 1993 (SAfr) and *The Republic of South Africa Constitution Act* 108 of 1996 (SAfr).

16 See Heribert Adam & Kogila Moodley, *The Negotiated Revolution: Society and Politics in Post-Apartheid South Africa* (Johannesburg: Jonathan Ball, 1993).

17 See Gay W. Seidman, *Manufacturing Militance: Workers' Movements in Brazil and South Africa, 1970–1985* (Berkeley: University of California Press, 1994). I am grateful to Fink Haysom for emphasizing this point to me.

18 ANC, 'Mass Action for People's Power: Statement of the National Executive Committee of the ANC, January 8, 1989' [February 1989] *Sechaba* 2, 4. See also Molao wa Batho, 'The Myth of Independence of the South African Judiciary' [November 1987] *Sechaba* 7; and Kader Asmal, 'Judges and Justice in South Africa' [March 1989] *Sechaba* 19.

19 Oliver Tambo, 'Make South Africa Ungovernable' (Extract from the Political Report of the National Executive Committee to the second National Consultative Conference, Lusaka, 16–23 June 1985), in *Preparing for Power: Oliver Tambo Speaks* (New York: George Braziller, 1988), 151.

20 African National Congress, 'Communique of the Second National Consultative Conference of the African National Congress', presented by President Oliver Tambo at a press conference, Lusaka, Zambia, 25 June 1985', rpt in *Documents of the Second National Consultative Conference of the African National Congress, Zambia, 16–23 June, 1985* (Lusaka: Zambia, ANC, 1985), 39.

21 Ibid.

22 See Dan O'Meara, *Forty Lost Years: The Apartheid State and the Politics of the National Party, 1948–1994* (Johannesburg: Ravan Press, 1996), 320–81.

23 Ibid. 337.

24 See Scott Thomas, *The Diplomacy of Liberation: The Foreign Relations of the African National Congress since 1960* (New York: I. B. Tauris, 1996), 62.

25 See Oliver Tambo, 'South Africa at the Crossroads' (Cannon Collins Annual Memorial Lecture, 28 May 1987), in *Preparing for Power*, 255.

26 See Oliver Tambo, 'Strategic Options for International Companies' (Address to the Business International Conference, London, 27 May 1987), in *Preparing for Power*, 254.

27 The Commonwealth Group of Eminent Persons, *Mission to South Africa: The Commonwealth Report*, (Harmondsworth: Penguin Books, 1986), 132–3.

28 *Republic of South Africa Constitution Act* 110 of 1983 (SAfr).

29 F. W. de Klerk, Opening of Parliament Speech, 2 February 1990, rpt in Ebrahim, *The Soul of a Nation*, Document 16, 466–82.

30   O'Meara, *Forty Lost Years*, 405.
31   See generally ibid.
32   John Dugard, 'Changing Attitudes towards a Bill of Rights in South Africa', in J. V. van der Westhuizen & H. P. Viljoen (eds.), *A Bill of Rights for South Africa (Menseregtehandves vir Suid-Afrika)* (Durban, Butterworths, 1988), 30.
33   African National Congress, The Freedom Charter, 26 June 1955, rpt in Ebrahim, *The Soul of a Nation*, Document 7, 415–19.
34   M. Benson, *The African Patriots: The Story of the African National Congress of South Africa* (London: Faber and Faber, 1963), 117.
35   See Raymond Suttner & Jeremy Cronin, *30 Years of the Freedom Charter* (Johannesburg: Ravan Press, 1986).
36   Raymond Suttner, *The Freedom Charter: The People's Charter in the Nineteen-Eighties* (Cape Town: University of Cape Town Press, 1984), 1.
37   Chief Gatsha Buthelezi, Progressive Party Conference, Durban, September 4, 1973, cited in Barend van Niekerk, 'The Dream of Liberty – Bills of Rights for the Bantustans' [1973] *South African Law Journal* 403, 403.
38   Ibid.
39   See *S v Marwane* 1982 (3) SA 717 (A).
40   See *Nyamakazi v President of Bophuthatswana* 1992 (4) SA 540 (B) and University of Witwatersrand Faculty of Law, *Annual Survey of South African Law 1992*, Cape Town: Juta (1949–1995), 719–24.
41   See generally Hendrik Hartog, 'The Constitution of Aspiration and "The Rights That Belong to Us All" ' (1987) 74 *The Journal of American History* 1013.
42   See, South African Law Commission, Project 58, *Interim Report on Group and Human Rights* (August 1991), 6–7.
43   Jeremy Sarkin, 'The Drafting of South Africa's Final Constitution From a Human-Rights Perspective' (1999) 47 *American Journal of Comparative Law* 67.
44   Albie Sachs, 'South Africa's Unconstitutional Constitution: The Transition from Power to Lawful Power' (1997) 41 *Saint Louis University Law Journal* 1249.
45   Dugard, 'Changing Attitudes towards a Bill of Rights', 34.
46   Justice A. C. Kriegler, 'Closing Address', in J. V. Van der Westhuizen & H. P. Viljoen (eds.), *A Bill of Rights for South Africa; N' Menseregtehandves vir Suid-Afrika* (Durban: Butterworths, 1988) 165.
47   Sachs, 'South Africa's Unconstitutional Constitution', 1251.
48   This was recognized by the ANC even before it initiated the process of negotiations in 1987; see African National Congress, Statement of the National Executive Committee of the African National Congress on the Question of Negotiations, Lusaka, 9 October 1987.
49   African National Congress, Communique of the Second National Consultative Conference, June 25, 1985, *Documents of the Second National Consultative Conference*, 39.
50   Telephone interview with Albie Sachs, Judge of the Constitutional Court, Cape Town, 1 August 1998.
51   Interview with Kader Asmal, Minister of Water Affairs and Forestry, Johannesburg International Airport, 2 August 1998.
52   Telephone interview with Albie Sachs, Judge of the Constitutional Court, Cape Town, 1 August 1998. Interview with Kader Asmal, Minister of Water Affairs and Forestry, Johannesburg International Airport, 3 August 1998.

53 Commonwealth Eminent Persons Group, *Mission to South Africa*, 20.

54 Vladimir Shubin, *ANC: A View From Moscow* (Western Cape: Mayibuye Books, 1999), 98–100.

55 Ibid. 248–63.

56 See Michael McFaul, 'The Demise of the World Revolutionary Process: Soviet–Angolan Relations Under Gorbachev', (1990) 16(1) *Journal of Southern African Studies* 165.

57 Shubin, *ANC: A View from Moscow*, 318.

58 African National Congress, 'Advance to People's Power, 8 January 1987'; rpt [February 1987] *Sechaba* 6.

59 Ibid.

60 Ibid. 5.

61 African National Congress, 'Statement on Negotiations, 9 October 1987', rpt [December 1987] *Sechaba.*

62 Ibid. 4.

63 Provision for the Council was made in the *Promotion of Constitutional Development Act* 86 of 1988; Johan van der Vyver, 'Constitutional Options for Post-Apartheid South Africa' (1991) 40 *Emory Law Journal* 745, 758–9.

64 Zola Skweyiya, 'Constitutional Guidelines of the ANC: A Vital Contribution to the Struggle Against Apartheid', paper delivered at the meeting between the ANC and Afrikaner Lawyers and Academics in Harare in January 1989, rpt [June 1989] *Sechaba* 6.

65 *The Citizen* (Johannesburg), 20 April 1985.

66 See South African Institute of Race Relations, *Race Relations Survey 1985* (1986), 62. See generally Samuel P. Huntington, 'Reform and Stability in a Modernizing, Multi-Ethnic Society' (1981) 8(2) *Politikon* 8, 8–26.

67 African National Congress, 'Constitutional Guidelines for a Democratic South Africa' (1988), rpt in *The Road to Peace* (ANC Department of Political Education, June 1990), 29 [henceforth ANC Constitutional Guidelines].

68 African National Congress, 'Mass Action for People's Power: Statement of the National Executive Committee of the ANC, January 8, 1989' [February 1989] *Sechaba* 2, 6.

69 Zola Skweyiya, 'Constitutional Guidelines of the ANC', 6.

70 See Declaration of the Organization of African Unity Ad-hoc Committee on Southern Africa on the Question of South Africa, Harare, Zimbabwe, 21 Aug. 1989; rpt in *The Road to Peace*, 34.

71 Ian Phillips, 'The Political Role of The Freedom Charter', in Nico Steytler (ed.), *The Freedom Charter and Beyond: Founding Principles for a Democratic South African Legal Order* (Cape Town: Wyvern, 1991), 78.

72 Declaration on the Question of South Africa by the Ad Hoc Committee on Southern Africa of the Organization of African Unity, Harare, 21 August 1989, United Nations Centre Against Apartheid, *Notes and Documents* 7/89 (New York, October 1989).

73 For a critical discussion of the introduction of a constitutionalist discourse into the National Liberation Movements perspective, see Firoz Cachalia, 'Constitutionalism and the Transition to Democracy' (draft, December 1992).

74 See Report of the Politico-Military Strategy Commission (the 'Green Book') to the ANC National Executive Committee, Parts One and Two with two

annexures, August 1979, rpt in Thomas Karis & Gail Gerhart (eds.), *From Protest to Challenge: A Documentary History of African Politics in South Africa, 1882–1990*, Vol. 5: Nadir and Resurgence, 1964–1979 (Pretoria: Unisa Press, 1997) Document 114, 720–34.

75 See, Oliver Tambo, 'The Dream of Total Liberation of Africa is in Sight: President's Message for 1984', 8 January 1984, rpt [March 1984] *Sechaba* 3, 4

76 Interview with Neil Morrison, one of the organizers of the Conference for a Democratic Future, Johannesburg, 27 July 1998 – reporting first to Valli Moosa before his detention and then to Cyril Ramaphosa, then still Secretary-General of the National Union of Mineworkers (NUM).

77 Ibid.

78 Ibid.

79 Ibid.

80 ANC Constitutional Guidelines. See also Albie Sachs, *Protecting Human Rights in a New South Africa* (Cape Town: Oxford University Press, 1990).

81 Albie Sachs, 'Towards a Bill of Rights for a Democratic South Africa' 12(2) *Hastings International and Comparative Law Journal* 289 (1989) 307.

82 Ibid.

83 Ibid. 308.

84 Ibid.

85 Ibid.

86 Ibid. 308–9.

87 Zola Skweyiya, 'Constitutional Guidelines of the ANC', 8.

88 Ibid.

89 David van Wyk, 'Introduction to the South African Constitution', in David van Wyk et al. (eds.), *Rights and Constitutionalism: The New South African Legal Order* (Kenwyn: Juta, 1994), 135–6.

90 Interview with Pius Langa, Deputy-President, Constitutional Court, Johannesburg, 27 July 1998.

91 Discussion with John Dugard, Johannesburg, 24 July 1998.

92 Interview with Pius Langa, Deputy-President, Constitutional Court, Johannesburg, 27 July 1998.

93 Ibid. Also interview with Arthur Chaskalson, President, Constitutional Court, Johannesburg, 30 July 1998.

94 Interview with Arthur Chaskalson, President, Constitutional Court, Johannesburg, 30 July 1998.

95 Ibid.

96 African National Congress Constitutional Committee, *What Is A Constitution? A Discussion Document Prepared by the Constitutional Committee of the African National Congress of South Africa to Encourage and Promote Discussion on the Structure and Content of a New, Non-Racial Non-Sexist and Democratic Constitution for South Africa* (1990), 7–8.

97 Article 16(1), African National Congress Constitutional Committee, *A Bill of Rights for a New South Africa* (Belleville: University of the Western Cape, Centre for Development Studies), 34.

98 Ibid. Article 16(2).

99 Zola Skweyiya, 'Introductory Note', in ANC Constitutional Committee, *A Bill of Rights for a New South Africa*, iii–iv.

100 South African Law Commission, *Interim Report on Group and Human Rights* (August, 1991), [1.5].

101 See, Report of the Conference on Security and Co-operation in Europe Meeting of Experts on National Minorities, Geneva 1991 (1991) 30 ILM 1692.

102 See, South African Law Commission, Project 58, *Interim Report on Group and Human Rights* (August 1991), [1.109].

103 See, South African Law Commission, *Working Paper 25 on Group and Human Rights* (11 March 1989).

104 See, South African Law Commission, Project 58, *Interim Report on Group and Human Rights* (August 1991), [1.30 and 1.31].

105 National Party, 'Manifesto for the New South Africa' (1 February 1991); rpt in *History in the Making*, Vol. 1, No. 4 (March 1991), 65–6.

106 Ibid. 65.

107 Convention for a Democratic South Africa (Codesa) I, Declaration of Intent, 21 December 1991, rpt in Ebrahim, *Soul of a Nation*, Document 22, 529–31.

108 See Francis Wilson & Mamphela Ramphele, *Uprooting Poverty in South Africa* (New York: Hunger Project, 1989).

109 See National Party, 'Grontwetplan/Constitutional Plan' (1991) 9(11) *The Nationalist* 9, 12.

110 See ANC Constitutional Guidelines.

111 African National Congress Constitutional Committee, *ANC Draft Bill of Rights: Preliminary Version 1.1* (May 1992) [hereinafter ANC Draft]; see also African National Congress, *A Bill of Rights for a New South Africa* (Belleville: University of the Western Cape, Centre for Development Studies, 1990) [hereinafter ANC 1990 Draft].

112 South African Law Commission, Project 58, *Group and Human Rights: Interim Report* (August 1991) [hereinafter Law Commission Draft]. Although formally an independent body, the Law Commission is essentially a government think tank and its proposals reflected the most advanced of the government's thinking on these issues at that time. However, the government's proposals on a 'Charter of Fundamental Rights' published on 2 February 1993 differed substantially from the Commission's proposals.

113 Law Commission Draft, Art. 1.

114 See generally John H. Garvey & T. Alexander Aleinikoff, 'Methods of Constitutional Interpretation', in John H. Garvey & T. Alexander Aleinikoff (eds.), *Modern Constitutional Theory: A Reader* (2nd edn., St Paul: West Publishing Co., 1991), 26–113.

115 Art. 3(a) does precede this explanation of the right to equality before the law with the statement that the right 'means, *inter alia* ...', which leaves scope for other meanings.

116 South African Law Commission, *Summary of Interim Report, Group and Human Rights* (August 1991) 23 [k] [hereinafter Law Commission Summary]. See also, Law Commission Draft, Art. 17(c).

117 Law Commission Draft, Art. 17(b).

118 Law Commission Summary, 15, [1.51].

119 Ibid. 15, [1.54].

120 Law Commission Draft, 303, [7.97].

121 Ibid. p. 303, [7.98]. See, Article 3(b) of the draft.
122 Law Commission Draft, 303, [7.97].
123 ANC Constitutional Guidelines, [I].
124 ANC Draft, at Art.1(1).
125 Ibid. Art. 1(2).
126 Ibid. Art. 1(3).
127 ANC Draft, Art. 3.
128 Ibid. Art. 3(4).
129 Ibid. Art. 14(1).
130 Ibid. Art. 13(2).
131 Ibid. Art. 10(3).
132 ANC 1990 Draft, Art. 13(2).
133 Ibid.
134 ANC Draft, Note to Art.14(2), p. 15.
135 ANC Draft, Art. 15.
136 Ibid. Art. 15(6).
137 Ibid. Art. 15(9).
138 Ibid. Art. 11(2).
139 See African National Congress, ' "ANC Draft Bill of Rights: A Preliminary Revised Text" May 1992', in Albie Sachs, *Advancing Human Rights in South Africa*, Cape Town: Oxford University Press, 1992, Appendix 1, 25, Art. 17(11) and (12).
140 ANC Draft, Art. 4(3).
141 See generally, Kenneth Karst, *Belonging to America: Equal Citizenship and the Constitution* (New Haven: Yale University Press, 1989).
142 See Steven Friedman, *The Long Journey: South Africa's Quest for a Negotiated Settlement* (Johannesburg: Ravan Press, 1993).

5 CONSTITUTIONALISM IN THE DEMOCRATIC TRANSITION

1 See World Bank, *Sub-Saharan Africa: From Crisis to Sustainable Growth* (Washington, DC: World Bank, 1989).
2 State President F. W. de Klerk argued in his speech announcing South Africa's political opening on 2 February 1990 that the removal of the threat of communism, following its collapse in eastern Europe, gave the government the opportunity to open up the political process in South Africa.
3 Tetsuya Kataoka, *The Price of a Constitution: The Origin of Japan's Postwar Politics* (New York: Crane Russak, 1991), 7.
4 See Peter Merkl, *The Origin of the West German Republic* (New York: Oxford University Press, 1963).
5 R. N. Aggarawala, *National Movement & Constitutional Development of India* (8th edn., Delhi: Metropolitan Book Co., 1973), 271–4.
6 See J. B. Ojwang, *Constitutional Development in Kenya: Institutional Adaptation and Social Change* (Nairobi: ACTS Press, 1990).
7 Cf. Vivien Hart, 'The Contagion of Rights: Constitutions as Carriers', in Patrick Hanafin & Melissa Williams (eds.), *Identity, Rights and Constitutional*

Transformation (Aldershot: Ashgate, 1999), who argues that it was the nationalist movements who demanded the inclusion of rights.

8 See Andrew Cohen, *A Deal Undone: The Making and Breaking of the Meech Lake Accord* (Vancouver: Douglas & McIntyre, 1990).

9 See Alan C. Cairns, 'The Politics of Constitutional Renewal in Canada', in Keith Banting & Richard Simeon (eds.), *Redesigning the State: The Politics of Constitutional Change* (Toronto; Buffalo: University of Toronto Press, 1985).

10 African National Congress, *The Reconstruction and Development Programme: A Policy Framework* (Johannesburg: Umanyano Publications, 1994), 1–3.

11 National Party, Constitutional Rule in a Participatory Democracy: The National Party's Framework for a New Democratic South Africa (1991); and National Party, 'Grontwetplan/Constitutional Plan' (1991) 9(11) *The Nationalist* 9, 12.

12 See UN Center for Human Rights: Commission on Human Rights, Draft Declaration on the Rights of Persons Belonging to National or Ethnic, Religious and Linguistic Minorities, ESC Res 1992/16, UN ESCOR, UN Doc E/Res/1992/16 (1992).

13 See National Party, *Constitutional Rule in a Participatory Democracy.*

14 Ibid. 15–18.

15 See Marina Ottaway, *South Africa: The Struggle for a New Order* (Washington DC: Brookings Institution, 1993), 64–72.

16 Inkatha Freedom Party, 'The Constitution of the Federal Republic of South Africa' (draft), 18 June 1993; rpt in A. P. Blaustein, South Africa Supplement 93–6 (October 1993), to A. P. Blaustein & G. H. Flanz (eds.), *Constitutions of the Countries of the World* (Dobbs Ferry, NY: Oceana Publications, 1971), 1.

17 *The Constitution of the State of KwaZulu-Natal,* 1 December 1992, Art 3; rpt in A. P. Blaustein, South Africa Supplement 93–2 (April 1993) 19.

18 Ibid. Art. 67(b).

19 Ibid. Art. 67(d).

20 Ibid. Art. 81.

21 Ibid. Art. 67(c) and Art. 77.

22 Centre for Development Studies & ANC Constitutional Department, *Seminar on Electoral Systems,* Stellenbosch, 2–4 November 1990.

23 African National Congress, Centre for Applied Legal Studies & Lawyers for Human Rights, *Conference on a Constitutional Court for a Future South Africa,* Magaliesberg, 1–3 February 1991.

24 Constitutional Committee of the ANC & The Centre for Socio-Legal Studies, University of Natal, Durban, *Conference on a Bill of Rights for a Democratic South Africa,* Salt Rock, Natal, 10–12 May 1992.

25 Constitutional Committee of the ANC & The Community Law Center, *National Conference on Affirmative Action.* University of the Western Cape, Port Elizabeth, 10–12 October 1991.

26 Community Law Centre, Constitutional Committee of the ANC & Centre for Development Studies, *Conference on the Structures of Government for a United Democratic South Africa,* University of Western Cape, Cape Town, 26–28 March 1992.

27 Constitutional Committee of the ANC and the Community Law Centre, *Towards a Non-Racial, Non-Sexist Judiciary in South Africa*, Conference held at the University of the Western Cape, Cape Town, 26–28 March 1993.

28 The proceedings of a number of these conferences were subsequently published including: Centre for Development Studies, Community Law Centre & Constitutional Department of the ANC, *Electoral Systems – A Discussion Document* (Belleville: University of the Western Cape, Centre for Development Studies, 1990); Centre for Development Studies (ed.), *A Bill of Rights for a Democratic South Africa: Papers and Report of a Conference Convened by the ANC Constitutional Committee* (Belleville: University of the Western Cape, Centre for Development Studies, 1991); and Centre for Development Studies (ed.), *Affirmative Action in a New South Africa: The Apartheid Legacy and Comparative International Experiences and Mechanisms of Enforcement* (Belleville: University of the Western Cape, Centre for Development Studies, 1992).

29 Section 10, Declaration of the 48th National Conference of the African National Congress, 6 July 1991; rpt in South African History Archive, *History in the Making: Documents Reflecting a Changing South Africa*, Vol. 1, No. 6 (July 1991), 41.

30 See South African Law Commission, Project 58, *Interim Report on Group and Human Rights* (August 1991); and South African Law Commission, Project 77, *Constitutional Models* (3 vols., October 1991).

31 See Steven Friedman (ed.), *The Long Journey: South Africa's Quest for a Negotiated Settlement* (Braamfontein: Ravan Press, 1993), 21–128.

32 Established in terms of the *Republic of South Africa Constitution Act* 110 of 1983 (SAfr).

33 Friedman, *The Long Journey*, 26–7.

34 Inkatha Freedom Party, 'Why the Inkatha Freedom Party Objects to the Idea of the New Constitution Being Written by a Popularly Elected Assembly (whether called "Constituent Assembly" or called by any other name)', undated submission to Codesa Working Group 2 (1992).

35 See Inkatha Freedom Party, 'Comments of IFP on document of Working Group 2 [Codesa] Steering Committee proposal on CMB [Constitution-making Body]' 27 April 1992.

36 Friedman, *The Long Journey*, 71.

37 Inkatha Freedom Party, 'Position Paper of the Inkatha Freedom Party for Submission to the Codesa Meeting of February 6, 1992'; rpt in Blaustein, South Africa Supplement 92–2 (March 1992), 173.

38 Friedman, *The Long Journey*, 78.

39 Johannes Rantete, *The African National Congress and the Negotiated Settlement in South Africa* (Pretoria: J. L. van Schaik, 1998), 183–204.

40 Bill Keller, 'Mandela's Group Accepts 5 Years of Power Sharing' *New York Times*, 19 February 1993, p. A1, Col. 1. Slovo's article proposing the compromise first appeared in the *African Communist*.

41 For an example of this misunderstanding of the proposals, see Stanley Uys, 'Four Rites of Passage', *The Star* (Johannesburg), 16 January 1993, p. 9, col. 1.

42 See Charlene Smith, 'Top ANC Man in Scathing Attack on "Sunset" Joe Slovo', *Sunday Times*, 8 November 1992, p. 11, col. 1; Paul Stober, 'Daggers Drawn in the Slovo Sunset', *The Weekly Mail* (Johannesburg), 13–19 Novem-

ber 1992, p. 8, col. 1.; Paul Stober, 'Slovo's "Sunset" Debate is Red Hot', *The Weekly Mail* (Johannesburg), 30 October–5 November 1992, p. 16, col. 1; and Firoz Cachalia, 'Case Against Power Sharing', *The Star* (Johannesburg), 2 February 1993, p. 10, col. 2.

43 Barney Desai, 'Proposed Agreement Can Lead Only to Conflict', *The Star* (Johannesburg), 13 October 1992, p. 12, col. 1.

44 See Stephen Ellmann, 'The New South African Constitution and Ethnic Division' (1994) 26 *Columbia Human Rights Law Review* 5, 16. Ellmann notes that in 'Lijphart's terms, the new South African Constitution provides for a measure of 'executive power-sharing', but does not, in general, offer a binding 'minority veto', even on important issues (fn. 38).

45 Allister Sparks, 'Clever Footwork as FW Redefines "Power-Sharing" ', *The Star* (Johannesburg), 10 February 1993, p. 12, col. 2.

46 Shaun Johnson & Ester Waugh, '"Sunset Clause" Offer as Slovo Seeks Harmony', *The Star* (Johannesburg), 1 October 1992, p. 1, col. 7.

47 On 26 September 26 1992, Mandela and de Klerk signed the Record of Understanding, in which the government first accepted the notion of a democratically-elected constitution-making body. Friedman, *The Long Journey*, 160.

48 Ibid. 156–60.

49 Herman J. Cohen, Assistant Secretary of State for African Affairs, Testimony before the House Foreign Affairs Subcommittee of Africa, *Violence in South Africa and its Effect on the Convention for Democratic South Africa (Codesa): Hearing and Markup before the Subcommittee on Africa of the Committee on Foreign Affairs*, HRes 497 H., 102nd Cong., 2d Sess., 23 July 1992. Assistant Secretary Cohen laid down the following points he considered (pp. 49–50) 'basic to a genuine democratic solution: that solution should include all relevant parties and promote tolerance in a country of great diversity; it should acknowledge the right of the majority to govern while assuring that all South Africans have a stake in their government; it should ensure that government functions within an agreed framework which includes protection of the fundamental rights of all citizens, but it should avoid overly complex arrangements intended to guarantee a share of power to particular groups which will frustrate effective governance. Minorities have the right to safeguards; they cannot expect a veto.'

50 Membership of the Committee included, A. Chaskalson, B. Ngoepa, M. Olivier, W. Olivier, F. Venter, G. E. Devenish, D. E. Moseneke and M. Wiechers.

51 Technical Committee on Constitutional Issues, *1st Report of the Technical Committee on Constitutional Issues to the Negotiating Council*, 13 May 1993, 6, [5].

52 Ibid.

53 Ibid. 7, [6.3].

54 Technical Committee on Constitutional Issues, *2nd Report of the Technical Committee on Constitutional Issues to the Negotiating Council*, 19 May 1983, 1, [1.2].

55 Ibid. [2.2(a)]–[2.2(f)].

56 Technical Committee on Constitutional Issues, *Fourth Supplementary Report on Constitutional Principles of the Technical Committee on Constitutional Issues to the Negotiating Council*, 26 July 1993, 1, [1].

57 *Republic of South Africa Constitution Act* 200 of 1993 (SAfr), Fourth Schedule.

58 Ibid. Fourth Schedule, Principle XIII.
59 Ibid. Fourth Schedule, Principle XII.
60 Ibid. Fourth Schedule, Principle XIII (2).
61 Ibid. Fourth Schedule, Principle XXXIV (1).
62 Ibid. Fourth Schedule, Principle XXXIV (3).
63 Ibid. s 68.
64 Technical Committee on Constitutional Issues, *Eighth Report of the Technical Committee on Constitutional Issues to the Negotiating Council*, 26 July 1993, 1, [1.1].
65 Ibid. 1, [1.1.1]–[1.1.5].
66 *Republic of South Africa Constitution Act* 200 of 1993 (SAfr), s 73(1).
67 Ibid. s 73(2). The acceptance of a two-thirds threshold involved an important shift in position for the National Party, which had attempted to require a seventy-five per cent majority to pass a new Constitution within the constitution-making body. This demand led to the collapse of negotiations within the Codesa framework; Friedman, *The Long Journey*, 31.
68 Ibid.
69 *Republic of South Africa Constitution Act* 200 of 1993 (SAfr), s 72(2).
70 Ibid. s 72(3).
71 Ibid. s 73(3) and (4).
72 Ibid. s 73(5).
73 Ibid. ss 73(6)–(8).
74 Ibid. s 73(9).
75 Ibid. s 73(10).
76 Ibid. s 73(11).
77 Ibid. s 62(1).
78 Friedman, *The Long Journey*, 62.
79 See Yash Ghai, 'Legal Responses to Ethnicity in South and South East Asia', Ford Foundation (mimeo), 6, who argues that, 'when the survival of a group and the stability of the state may appear as alternatives ... [the] choices (and the scope of compromise) are limited by the pressures on the negotiators'.
80 For example, traditional leaders were continuing to demand that their recognition and powers be increased under the interim constitution; 'Power to the Chiefs', *Weekly Mail & Guardian* (Johannesburg), 15–22 December 1994, p. 2, col. 5.
81 Examples of non-party political interventions include: Bobby Godsell, *Shaping the Future South Africa: A Citizens' Guide to Constitution-Making* (Cape Town: Tafelberg & Human & Rousseau, 1990), the copyright of which was held by the Anglo American Corporation of South Africa Limited, South Africa's single largest corporate enterprise; Hugh Corder et al., *A Charter for Social Justice: A Contribution to the South African Bill of Rights Debate* (December 1992), produced by a prominent group of progressive lawyers and law teachers; I. Semenya & M. Motimele, *Constitution for a Democratic South Africa: A Draft* (Johannesburg: Skotaville, 1993), produced by two South African Advocates who had taken part in drafting the South West African People's Organization's (SWAPO) draft constitution, which was placed before the constituent assembly in Namibia; and 'Constitution for a New South Africa ... Cribbed from the United States Constitution', *Sunday Times*, 22 August 1993, p. 23, a

Sunday Times editorial presentation modelling its proposal for South Africa on the United States Constitution.

82 Lourens du Plessis & Hugh Corder, *Understanding South Africa's Transitional Bill of Rights* (Kenwyn: Juta, 1994), 8.

83 *Saturday Star* (Johannesburg), 16 October 1993, p. 6, col. 1.

84 *Republic of South Africa Constitution Act* 200 of 1993 (SAfr), s 119(3).

85 See s 32(2) of the proposed chapter on fundamental rights; Technical Committee on Fundamental Rights During the Transition, *Tenth Progress Report*, 1 October 1993.

86 *Republic of South Africa Constitution Act* 200 of 1993 (SAfr), s 181(2).

87 Donatella Lorch, 'Arms Ban is Defied at Rally by Zulu Party', *New York Times*, 6 April 1993, p. A13.

88 *The Weekly Mail & Guardian* (Johannesburg), 1–7 October 1993, p. 9, col. 4.

89 *New York Times*, 25 October 1993, p. 1, col. 3.

90 See Stephen Ellmann, 'The New South African Constitution and Ethnic Division' (1994) 26 *Columbia Human Rights Law Review* 5.

91 Republic of South Africa Constitution Act 200 of 1993 (SAfr), s 3(1).

92 Ibid. s 3(10)(c).

93 Ibid. s 31.

94 Ibid. s 32(b).

95 Ibid. s 32(c).

96 Ibid. ss 181–184.

97 Ibid. s 184A-B.

98 Ibid. Schedule 4, Constitutional Principle XXXIV.

99 Ibid. s 27(4).

100 Ebrahim Patel, 'Ditch the Lock-Out Clause!' (1994) 95 *Work in Progress* 18.

101 See Anthony Lewis, 'Revolution by Law', *New York Times*, 13 January 1994, p. A15.

102 See Kader Asmal & Ronald Roberts, 'South Africa Needs Economic Rights', *International Herald Tribune* (New York), 31 October 1994.

103 See Thomas M. Franck, 'The Emerging Right to Democratic Governance' (1992) 86 *The American Journal of International Law* 46.

104 See H. K. Bhabha, 'The Commitment to Theory' (1988) 5 *New Formations* 5.

6 GLOBAL IMPACT: INTERNATIONAL IMPERATIVES AND THEIR HYBRIDIZATION

1 See, Kim Lane Scheppelle and Karol Edward Soltan, 'The Authority of Alternatives', in J. Roland Pennock & John W. Chapman (eds.), *Authority Revisited: Nomos XXIX* (New York: New York University Press, 1987).

2 *Republic of South Africa Constitution Act* 200 of 1993 (SAfr), s 110.

3 Ibid. s 191.

4 Ibid. s 228(3).

5 Ibid. s 187.

6 The *Human Rights Commission Act* 54 of 1994 (SAfr) established an independent and impartial Human Rights Commission, as mandated in ss 115–118 of the 1993 Constitution.

7 *Republic of South Africa Constitution Act* 200 of 1993 (SAfr), s 119.

8 Ibid. s 200.

9 See *National Economic, Development and Labour Council Act* 35 of 1994 (SAfr).

10 The Volkstaat is a proposal by right-wing Afrikaners that a territorial area or areas be created within which Afrikaners will be able to exercise self-determination as a nation or at least as a community. See, section 184A(2) of the 1993 interim Constitution.

11 *Volkstaat Council Act* 30 of 1994 (SAfr), s 2(1)(a).

12 Ibid. s 2(1)(d).

13 Ibid. s 2(1)(e).

14 *Council of Traditional Leaders Act* 31 of 1994 (SAfr), s 4(1).

15 This increased status has not, however, precluded a constant tension with the new government over financial resources and questions of independence as well as arguments over the role of these institutions in a democratic South Africa.

16 *Republic of South Africa Constitution Act* 108 of 1996 (SAfr), Chapter 12, Traditional Leaders, ss 211 and 212.

17 Ibid. Chapter 14, Other Matters, Self-determination, s 235.

18 Ibid. ss 185 and 186.

19 See above, p. 114.

20 Ibid.

21 See Aninka Claassens, 'For Whites Only: Land Ownership in South Africa', in M. de Klerk (ed.), *A Harvest of Discontent: The Land Question in South Africa* (Cape Town: Idasa, 1991); see also Michael Robertson, 'Dividing the Land: An Introduction to Apartheid Land Law', in Christina Murray & Catherine O'Regan (eds.), *No Place to Rest: Forced Removals and the Law in South Africa* (Cape Town: Oxford University Press, 1990).

22 African National Congress, The Freedom Charter (26 June 1955); rpt in Hassen Ebrahim, *The Soul of a Nation: Constitution-Making in South Africa*, Cape Town: Oxford University Press, 1998, Document 7, 415–19; see also (1989) 12 *Hastings International and Comparative Law Review* 318, 319.

23 African National Congress, 'Constitutional Guidelines for a Democratic South Africa' (1988); rpt (1989) 12 *Hastings International & Comparative Law Review* 323–4.

24 Bongiwe Njobe, now Director-General (the most senior civil servant) in the Department of Agriculture, and Derek Hanekom, Minister of Land Affairs and Agriculture in Mandela's cabinet.

25 For an excellent account of this activity see, Richard Abel, *Politics by Other Means: Law in the Struggle Against Apartheid, 1980–1994* (New York: Routledge, 1995).

26 See, *Abolition of Racially Based Land Measures Act* 108 of 1991 (SAfr).

27 Ibid. ss 89–96.

28 For an example of an early contribution to the land reform debate from the perspective of the ANC Land Commission, see H. Dolny & H. Klug, 'Land Reform: Legal Support and Economic Regulation', in G. Moss & I. Obrey (eds.), *South African Review 6: From 'Red Friday' to Codesa* (Johannesburg: Ravan Press, 1992).

29 African National Congress Constitutional Committee, *A Bill of Rights for a New South Africa* (Belleville: University of the Western Cape, Centre for Development Studies, 1990), Art. 11.

30 The Constitutional Committee was chaired by Zola Skweyiya, head of the ANC's legal department, under whose authority the land commission initially fell. Skweyiya's interest in and commitment to these issues are reflected in: Zola Skweyiya, 'Towards a Solution to the Land Question in Post-Apartheid South Africa: Problems and Models' (1990) 6 *South African Journal on Human Rights* 195.

31 See, Centre for Development Studies (ed.), *A Bill of Rights for a Democratic South Africa: Papers and Report of a Conference Convened by the ANC Constitutional Committee* (Belleville: University of the Western Cape, Centre for Development Studies, 1991), 129–32.

32 South African Law Commission, Project 58, *Interim Report on Group and Human Rights* (August 1991), 359–65.

33 Democratic Party, *Freedom Under the Rule of Law: Advancing Liberty in the New South Africa, Draft Bill of Rights* (May 1993), Art. 9.

34 ANC Land Commission, *Land Manifesto for ANC National Conference* (July 1991).

35 For one critique of the government's Advisory Committee on Land Allocation (ACLA), see H. Klug, 'Bedeviling Agrarian Reform: The Impact of Past, Present and Future Legal Frameworks', in J. Van Zyl, J. Kirsten & H. P. Binswanger (eds.), *Agricultural Land Reform in South Africa: Policies, Markets and Mechanisms* (Cape Town: Oxford University Press, 1996), 166–71.

36 Aninka Claassens, 'Editorial' (1992) 8 *South African Journal on Human Rights* v.

37 See above, p. 99.

38 E. Swanson, 'A Land Claims Court for South Africa: Report on Work in Progress' (1992) 8 *South African Journal on Human Rights* 332. This group also discussed the experience of the Indian Claims Commission (ICC) in the United States as both an example of a land claims process and as a warning against limiting the claimants' remedies to monetary compensation instead of the return of land, which was the basic demand of claimants. In the debates that followed we were able to use the experience of the ICC to argue that cash settlements could never satisfy demands for the return of land, pointing to the fact that despite thirty years and millions of dollars, Native American claims remained unsatisfied.

39 Geoff Budlender, 'The Right to Equitable Access to Land' (1992) 8 *South African Journal on Human Rights* 295. Budlender served as Director-General of the Department of Land Affairs, the highest ranking civil servant in the department from 1995 to 1999.

40 C. Cross, 'An Alternative Legality: The Property Rights Question in Relation to South African Land Reform' (1992) 8 *South African Journal on Human Rights* 305.

41 R. W. Bauman, 'Property Rights in the Canadian Constitutional Context' (1992) 8 *South African Journal on Human Rights* 344.

42 John Murphy, 'Insulating Land Reform from Constitutional Impugnment: An Indian Case Study' (1992) 8 *South African Journal on Human Rights* 362.

43 African National Congress, ' "ANC Draft Bill of Rights: A Preliminary Revised Text" May 1992', in Albie Sachs, *Advancing Human Rights in South Africa* (Cape Town: Oxford University Press, 1992), Appendix 1, 224. See also, Albie Sachs, *Protecting Human Rights in a New South Africa* (Cape Town: Oxford University Press, 1990), 104–38.

44 Constitution of India 1950, Part IV Directive Principles of State Policy, Arts. 36–51. See also: Constitution of Ireland 1937, Directive Principles of Social Policy, Art. 45,; Constitution of the Republic of Namibia 1990, Chapter 11, Principles of State Policy, Art. 101.

45 See, Steven Friedman (ed.), *The Long Journey: South Africa's Quest for a Negotiated Settlement* (Braamfontein: Ravan Press, 1993).

46 Statement from 19 Communities on the Government's Advisory Commission on Land Allocation (15 September 1991).

47 Letter dated 31 July 1991, from J. De Villiers, Minister of Public Works and Land Affairs, responding to a letter from lawyers representing a claimant community and stating in part: 'I do appeal to you to advise your clients not to take the law into their own hands because that would unnecessarily complicate consideration of possible claims. It would only serve to increase the temperature of the debate rather than to arrive at a solution.'

48 See, World Bank Southern Africa Department, *South African Agriculture: Structure, Performance and Options for the Future* (Washington, DC: World Bank, 1994) as an example of one in the World Bank's series of 'Informal Discussion Papers on Aspects of the Economy of South Africa', published between 1992 and 1994.

49 World Bank, *Experience with Agricultural Policy: Lessons for South Africa* (Washington, DC: World Bank, 1992).

50 This paper was eventually published as Hans Binswanger and Klaus Deininger, 'South Africa Land Policy: The Legacy of History and Current Options' (1993) 21(9) *World Development* 1451.

51 Robert Christiansen, 'Aide Memoire: Preparation of a Rural Restructuring Program' (June 15, 1993).

52 See, World Bank, 'Summary: Options for Land Reform and Rural Restructuring', in *Land Redistribution Options Conference 12–15 October 1993: Proceedings* (Land and Agricultural Policy Centre, June 1994).

53 ANC Draft Bill of Rights: Preliminary Revised Version (February 1993), Art. 13.

54 See Republic of South Africa, *Government's Proposals on a Charter of Fundamental Rights* (2 February 1993).

55 As late as October 1995 the Draft Bill of Rights being considered by the Constitutional Assembly's Theme Committee 4, included as Option 2, 'No property clause at all'; Constitutional Assembly, Theme Committee 4, *Draft Bill of Rights* (9 October 1995). See also, Constitutional Assembly, Constitutional Committee Sub-Committee: *Draft Bill of Rights, Volume One, Explanatory Memoranda* (9 October 1995), 126–40, which includes a discussion of the nature of the right to property in international law.

56 Lourens du Plessis & Hugh Corder, *Understanding South Africa's Transitional Bill of Rights* (Kenwyn: Juta, 1994), 182–4.

57 Adrian Hadland, 'Demonstrators Hand Govt Land Ultimatum', *Business Day* (Johannesburg), 2 September 1993.

58 *Republic of South Africa Constitution Act* 200 of 1993 (SAfr), s 8(3)(b).

59 Ibid. s 28(3).

60 Matthew Chaskalson, 'Stumbling Towards Section 28: Negotiations over Property Rights at the Multiparty Talks' (1995) 11 *South African Journal on Human Rights* 222.

61 *Republic of South Africa Constitution Act* 200 of 1993 (SAfr), s 28(3).

62 See Heinz Klug, 'Historical Claims and the Right to Restitution', in Johan Van Zyl, Johann Kirsten & Hans P. Binswanger (eds.), *Agricultural Land Reform in South Africa: Policies, Markets and Mechanisms* (Cape Town: Oxford University Press, 1996).

63 See Constitutional Assembly, Constitutional Committee Subcommittee, *Documentation: Land Rights* (Monday, 9 October 1995); Theme Committee 6.3: *Specialised Structures of Government: Land Rights, Documentation* (11 September 1995); and, Constitutional Assembly, Theme Committee 6.3: *Specialised Structures of Government: Documentation Volume 2A: Land Rights* (15 September 1995).

64 See Hassen Ebrahim, *The Soul of a Nation: Constitution-Making in South Africa* (Cape Town: Oxford University Press, 1998), 189–221.

65 See Constitutional Assembly, Constitutional Committee Subcommittee, *Documentation: Land Rights*.

66 Constitutional Assembly, Constitutional Committee, *Documentation: Volume 2A Land Rights*, 13–41.

67 New versions were published in the 30 October 1995 Refined Working Draft (2nd edn.) of the Constitution; another ANC proposal was published in the 9–16 February 1996 edition of *Constitutional Talk* – the official newsletter of the Constitutional Assembly; and yet another was published in the 22 April – 18 May 1996 edition of *Constitutional Talk*.

68 See Paul Bell (ed.), *The Making of the Constitution: The Story of South Africa's Constitutional Assembly, May 1994 to December 1996* (Cape Town: Churchill Murray Publications, 1997); see also, Dene Smuts, 'Etienne Mureinik's Contribution to Property Rights' (1998) 14 *South African Journal on Human Rights* 197.

69 *Republic of South Africa Constitution Act* 108 of 1996 (SAfr), s 25(7).

70 Ibid. s 25(6).

71 Ibid. s 25(5).

72 Ibid. s 25(8).

73 Under the original political compromise, the Constitutional Assembly was to be constrained by the Constitutional Principles negotiated between the parties and appended to the 1993 interim Constitution. The Constitutional Court was empowered to certify whether a draft Constitution prepared by the Constitutional Assembly met the requirements of the Constitutional Principles. In 1996 the Constitutional Court first declined to certify the draft and then certified the new text adopted in response to the Court's first certification judgment.

74 *Ex parte Chairperson of the Constitutional Assembly: In re Certification of the Constitution of the Republic of South Africa, 1996* 1996 (4) SA 744 (CC) (*First Certification Case*) [70].

75 Ibid. [71].

76 Ibid. [72].

77 Ibid. [73].

78 Nelson Mandela, 'Address: On the occasion of the ANC's Bill of Rights Conference', in *Papers and Report of a Conference convened by the ANC Constitutional Committee* (Centre for Development Studies, University of the Western Cape, May 1991).

7 THE CONSTITUTIONAL COURT AND THE INSTITUTIONAL DYNAMICS OF CONSTITUTIONALISM

1 'Democracy and Constitutionalism: The Role of Constitutional Interpretation', in David van Wyk et al. (eds.), *Rights and Constitutionalism: The New South African Legal Order* (Kenwyn: Juta, 1994), 4.

2 See Mauro Cappelletti, with the collaboration of Paul Kollmer & Joanne Olson, *The Judicial Process in Comparative Perspectives* (Oxford: Clarendon Press, 1989), 150.

3 See Gerald N. Rosenberg, *The Hollow Hope: Can Courts Bring About Social Change?* (Chicago: University of Chicago Press, 1993).

4 *Republic of South Africa Constitution Act* 200 of 1993 (SAfr), s 71(2).

5 See Etienne Mureinik, 'Rescued from Illegitimacy?', *Weekly Mail & Guardian* (Johannesburg), Review/Law, Supplement, Vol. 1, No. 5, December 1993, p. 1; and Nicholas Haysom, 'An expedient Package Deal?' *Weekly Mail & Guardian* (Johannesburg), Review/Law, Supplement, Vol. 1, No. 5, December 1993, p. 1.

6 See M. M. Corbett, 'Memorandum Submitted on Behalf of the Judiciary of South Africa on the Chapter on the Administration of Justice in the Draft Interim Constitution' (3 September 1993); and 'Memorandum Submitted on Behalf of the Judiciary of South Africa on the 12th Report of the Technical Committee on Constitutional Issues' (3 September 1993).

7 Technical Committee on Constitutional Issues, *Twelfth Report of the Technical Committee on Constitutional Issues to the Negotiating Council* (2 September 1993).

8 See Technical Committee on Constitutional Issues, *Preliminary Draft to the Technical Committee on Constitutional Issues arising from Bilateral Discussions between the SA Government and the ANC* (12 November 1993).

9 Tony Leon, 'Etienne Mureinik's Role in Securing and Constitutionalising the Independence of the Universities and Judicial Selection' (1998) 14 *South African Journal on Human Rights* 190, 194.

10 *Republic of South Africa Constitution Act* 200 of 1993 (SAfr), s 99(1).

11 Ibid. s 97(2)(a).

12 Ibid. s 99(3).

13 Ibid. s 99(3).

14 Ibid. s 105(1).

15 See Kierin O'Malley, 'The Constitutional Court', in Murray Faure & Jan-Erik Lane (eds.), *South Africa: Designing New Political Institutions* (London: Sage Publications, 1996).

16 Steven Friedman, 'Constitutional Court: Puzzling Silence on Appointments' (1994) 1 (2) *TransAct* 5.

17 The Judicial Service Commission was created by Act 9 of 1994, which implemented the mandate contained in s 105 of the Constitution.

18 Friedman, 'Constitutional Court', 5.

19 Ibid.

20 See *The President of the Republic of South Africa and Ors v South African Rugby Union and Ors* 1999 (7) BCLR 725 (CC).

21 Brun-Otto Bryde, 'Constitutional Courts in Constitutional Transition', presented at Conference on Constitutional Transitions, Hong Kong, June, 1997 (draft, March 1997).

22 The German Constitutional Court in the post-Second World War period of democratic construction. See also Brun-Otto Bryde, 'The Role of Constitutional Jurisprudence in German Democracy', in Gunter Weick (ed.), *Competition or Convergence: The Future of European Legal Culture* (Frankfurt: Peter Lang, 1999).

23 The Hungarian Constitutional Court's protection of social welfare benefits under the property clause of the post-socialist constitution.

24 The role of the German Constitutional Court in protecting the reunification agreements made with a now disappeared German Democratic Republic.

25 Describing the role of the South African Constitutional Court and particular the first Constitutional Certification judgment.

26 See L. Fisher & N. Devins, *Political Dynamics of Constitutional Law* (St Paul, MO: West Publishing, 1992).

27 See Neil K. Komesar, *Imperfect Alternatives: Choosing Institutions in Law, Economics, and Public Policy* (Chicago: University of Chicago Press, 1994).

28 M. Capelletti, *The Judicial Process in Comparative Perspective*, 126–31.

29 *Republic of South Africa Constitution Act* 200 of 1993 (SAfr), s 98(2)(e).

30 *Republic of South Africa Constitution Act* 108 of 1996 (SAfr), s 167(4)(a).

31 This ties in with Alexander Bickel's notion of judicial restraint as a deferential strategy; *The Least Dangerous Branch: The Supreme Court at the Bar of Politics* (2nd edn., New Haven, CT: Yale University Press, 1962).

32 *S v Makwanyane and Another* 1995 (3) SA 391 (CC); 1995 (6) BCLR 665 (CC) (*Death Penalty Case*).

33 Ibid. [22], quoting the South African Law Commission, Project 58, *Interim Report on Group and Human Rights* (August 1991) [7.33].

34 *S v Makwanyane* 1995 (3) SA 391; 1995 (6) BCLR 665 [88].

35 Ibid. [89].

36 Ibid. [88].

37 Ibid.

38 Ibid. [199].

39 Ibid. [344].

40 *Republic of South Africa Constitution Act* 200 of 1993 (SAfr), Preamble.

41 *S v Makwanyane* 1995 (3) SA 391; 1995 (6) BCLR 665 [89].
42 *Furman v State of Georgia* 408 US 238, 443 (1972).
43 *West Virginia State Board of Education v Barnette and Others* 319 US 624, 638 (1942).
44 *S v Makwanyane* 1995 (3) SA 391; 1995 (6) BCLR 665 [188].
45 Ibid. [200].
46 Ibid.
47 Ibid. [201].
48 Ibid.
49 Ibid.
50 Ibid. [199].
51 Ibid. [198] and [199].
52 *Republic of South Africa Constitution* Act 200 of 1993 (SAfr), s 35.
53 *S v Makwanyane* 1995 (3) SA 391; 1995 (6) BCLR 665 [199].
54 Ibid. [222].
55 Ibid. [13].
56 Ibid. [14]–[15].
57 Ibid. [16].
58 Ibid. [17].
59 Ibid. [19].
60 Ibid. [18].
61 See Neil K. Komesar, 'Back to the Future – An Institutional View of Making and Interpreting Constitutions' (1987) 81(2) *Northwestern University Law Review* 191, 203–10.
62 *S v Makwanyane* 1995 (3) SA 391; 1995 (6) BCLR 665 [20].
63 Ibid. [22].
64 Ibid. [25].
65 Michael Lobban, *White Man's Justice: South African Political Trials in the Black Consciousness Era* (Oxford: Clarendon Press, 1996), 155–9.
66 *Executive Council of the Western Cape Legislature v President of the Republic of South Africa* 1995 (4) SA 877 (CC) (*Western Cape Case*).
67 Ibid. [9].
68 Ibid. [228].
69 Ibid. [97].
70 Ibid. [169].
71 Ibid. [97].
72 Ibid. [145].
73 L. Fisher, 'One of the Guardians Some of the Time', Robert A. Licht (ed.), in *Is the Supreme Court the Guardian of the Constitution?* (Washington, DC: The AEI Press, 1993).
74 Warren E. Burger, 'The Doctrine of Judicial Review: Mr Marshall, Mr Jefferson, and Mr Marbury', in Mark Cannon and David O'Brien (eds.), *Views from the Bench* (Chatham, NJ: Chatham House Publishers, 1985), 14.
75 *Republic of South Africa Constitution Act* 200 of 1993 (SAfr), s 98(2).
76 Ibid. s 73(2).
77 C. Madlala, 'Final fitting for the cloth of nationhood', *Sunday Times*, 13 October 1996, p. 4. col. 2.

78 *Republic of South Africa Constitution Act* 108 of 1996 (SAfr), s 167(4)(d).
79 This strategy of judicial deference is interesting in a context where the Constitutional Assembly had, in its drafting of the new text, gone so far as to incorporate the precise language of Constitutional Court opinions where the Court had expressly addressed a constitutional question – for example, in the Constitutional Assembly's reformulation of the limitations clause so as to exclude the notion of the essential content of the right. Furthermore, despite popular political pressure to rescind the Court's holding against the death penalty, the Constitutional Assembly merely retained the previous formulation of the rights relied upon by the Court in that case.
80 *Ex parte Chairperson of the Constitutional Assembly: In re Certification of the Constitution of the Republic of South Africa, 1996* 1996 (4) SA 744 (CC) [27] (*First Certification Judgment*).
81 Ibid. [34].
82 Ibid. [39].
83 Ibid. [43].
84 *Ex parte Chairperson of the Constitutional Assembly: In re Certification of the Amended Text of the Constitution of the Republic of South Africa, 1996,* 1997 (2) SA 97 (CC) (*Second Certification Judgment*).
85 Ibid. [8].
86 Ibid. [25].
87 Ibid. [153]–[157].
88 Ibid. [204(e)].
89 See for example, the history of struggles over civil rights or conflicts over abortion in the United States.

8 CONSTITUTIONAL IMAGINATIONS AND THE POSSIBILITIES OF JUSTICE

1 *S v Makwanyane and Another* 1995 (3) SA 391 (CC); 1995 (6) BCLR 665 (CC) (*Death Penalty Case*) [100].
2 Ibid. [102].
3 E.g., ibid. [273]: Mahomed J's application of the right to equality.
4 Ibid. [10].
5 Ibid. [8]–[10].
6 Ibid. [10].
7 Ibid. [214].
8 Ibid. [346].
9 Ibid. [176].
10 Ibid. [132], [167] and [193]–[195].
11 *Republic of South Africa Constitution Act* 108 of 1996 (SAfr), s 36.
12 *S v Makwanyane* 1995 (3) SA 391; 1995 (6) BCLR 665 [132].
13 Ibid. [39]; cf *Republic of South Africa Constitution Act* 108 of 1996 (SAfr), s 39(1)(b), which states that the courts 'must consider international law'.
14 *S v Makwanyane* 1995 (3) SA 391; 1995 (6) BCLR 665 [37].
15 Ibid. [35].
16 Ibid. [37].

17 Ibid. [38].
18 E.g., ibid. [14], [15], [17], [18] and [89].
19 G. R. Dent & C. L. S. Nyembezi, *Scholar's Zulu Dictionary* (Pietermaritzburg: Shuter & Shooter, 1969).
20 C. M. Doke, D. McK. Malcolm & J. M. A. Sikakana, *English and Zulu Dictionary* (Johannesburg: Witwatersrand University Press, 1982).
21 *S v Makwanyane* 1995 (3) SA 391; 1995 (6) BCLR 665 [130], [131], [223]–[227], [237], [241]–[245], [250], [260], [263], [307]–[313] and [374].
22 Ibid. [241]–[243].
23 Ibid. [237].
24 Ibid. [260].
25 Ibid. [263].
26 Ibid. [308].
27 Ibid. [307].
28 Ibid. [308], [309], [311] and [313].
29 Ibid. [224].
30 Ibid. [224].
31 *Republic of South Africa Constitution Act* 108 of 1996 (SAfr), s 22, Schedule 6.
32 Interview with Pius Langa, Deputy President of the Constitutional Court, Johannesburg, 27 July 1998.
33 *S v Makwanyane* 1995 (3) SA 391; 1995 (6) BCLR 665 [381].
34 Ibid. [373].
35 Ibid. [374].
36 Ibid. [365].
37 Ibid. [382].
38 Ibid. [392].
39 See *Minority Schools in Albania Case* 1935 PCIJ (ser A/B) No, 64, 20.
40 *Matukane and Others v Laerskool Potgietersrus* 1996 (3) SA 223 [231(F)].
41 Ibid. 233 (B–G).
42 Ibid. 232 (E–F).
43 Ibid. 232 (G–H).
44 Ibid. 233 (I).
45 Ibid. 232 (G).
46 1996 (3) SA 165 (*Gauteng Education Bill Case*).
47 Ibid. [17] (Mahomed DP).
48 Ibid. [42] (my translation): 'hou die Grondwet daarmee die deur oop vir diegene vir wie die Staat se onderwysinstellings ontoereikend geag word wat betref gemeenskaplike kultuur, taal of godsdiens. Dit staan hul vry om eendragtig die erwe van hul vaders vir hul kinders to behou. Daar is egter 'n prys, naamlik dat so 'n bevolkingsgroep daarvoor die hand in eie sak moet steek'.
49 *Republic of South Africa Constitution* Act 200 of 1993 (SAfr), s 32(c).
50 *Ex Parte Gauteng Provincial Legislature* 1996 (3) SA 165 [8].
51 Ibid. [90].
52 *Ex Parte Speaker of the National Assembly: In Re Dispute Concerning the Constitutionality of Certain Provisions of the National Education Policy Bill 83 of 1995* 1996 (3) SA 289 (CC) (*National Education Bill Case*).

53 Ibid. [8].
54 Ibid. [16].
55 Ibid.
56 Ibid. [17].
57 Ibid. [18].
58 Ibid. [16].
59 Ibid. [20].
60 505 US 144 (1992).
61 *Ex parte Speaker of the National Assembly* 1996 (3) SA 289 [23].
62 Ibid. [23].
63 *Ex parte Speaker of the KwaZulu-Natal Provincial Legislature: In re KwaZulu-Natal Amakhosi and Iziphakanyiswa Amendment Bill of 1995; Ex parte Speaker of the KwaZulu-Natal Provincial Legislature: In re Payment of Salaries, Allowances and Other Privileges to the Ingonyama Bill of 1995,* 1996 (4) SA 653 (CC) (*KwaZulu Amakosi and Ingonyama Bill Cases*).
64 Ibid. [16].
65 Ibid.
66 Ibid. [18].
67 *Ex Parte Speaker of the KwaZulu-Natal Provincial Legislature: In re Certification of the Constitution of the Province of KwaZulu-Natal, 1996,* 1996 (4) SA 1098 (CC) (*KwaZulu-Natal Constitution Case*).
68 Ibid. [13].
69 Ibid. [36]–[38].
70 Ibid. [39]–[46].
71 Ibid. [14].
72 Ibid. [15].
73 Ibid. [32].
74 Ibid. [34].
75 Ibid.
76 *Ex parte Chairperson of the Constitutional Assembly: In re Certification of the Constitution of the Republic of South Africa, 1996* 1996 (4) SA 744 (CC) (*First Certification Judgment*), heard on 1–5 and 8–11 July 1996, and decided on 6 September 1996.
77 *Ex parte Chairperson of the Constitutional Assembly: In re Certification of the Amended Text of the Constitution of the Republic of South Africa, 1996* 1997 (2) SA 97 (CC) (*Second Certification Judgment*), heard on 18, 19 and 20 November 1996 and decided on 4 December 1996.
78 *Mail & Guardian* (Johannesburg), 11 November 1996.

CONCLUSION

1 See Cass R. Sunstein, 'Federalism in South Africa? Notes from the American Experience' (1993) 8 *American University Journal of International Law & Policy* 421.
2 S. D. Krasner, 'Approaches to the State: Alternative Conceptions and Historical Dynamics' (1984) 16 *Comparative Politics* 223, 225.

BIBLIOGRAPHY

CASES

Canada
Action Travail des Femmes v Canadian National Railways Co (1987) 40 DLR
4th 193; (1987) 5 ACWS 3d 37 [Canadian National Railways Case].

Germany
Internationale Handelsgesellschaft mbH v Einfuhr- und Vorratsstelle für Getreide
und Futtermittel [1974] 37 BVerfGE 271, 14 Comm Mkt LR 540.

India
P. Rathinam/Nagbhusan Patnaik, Petitioners v Union of India and another,
Respondents [1994] AIR (Supreme Court) 1844.

South Africa (Post-Union)
Cassem v Oos-Kaapse Kommittee va die Groepsgebieddraad 1959 (3) SA 651
(AD).
Dadoo Ltd v Kruger(s)dorp Municipal Council [1920] AD 530.
Executive Council of the Western Cape Legislature v President of the Republic of
South Africa 1995 (4) SA 877 (CC) (Western Cape Case).
Ex parte Chairperson of the Constitutional Assembly: In re Certification of the
Constitution of the Republic of South Africa, 1996 1996 (4) SA 744 (CC)
(First Certification Judgment).
Ex parte Chairperson of the Constitutional Assembly: In re Certification of the
Amended Text of the Constitution of the Republic of South Africa, 1996,
1997 (2) SA 97 (CC) (Second Certification Judgment).
Ex parte Speaker of the National Assembly: In re Dispute Concerning the Consti-
tutionality of Certain Provisions of the National Education Policy Bill 83
of 1995 1996 (3) SA 289 (CC) (National Education Bill Case).
Ex parte Speaker of the Gauteng Provincial Legislature: In re Dispute Concerning
the Constitutionality of Certain Provisions of the Gauteng School Education
Bill of 1995 1996 (3) SA 165 (CC) (Gauteng Education Bill Case).

Ex parte Speaker of the KwaZulu-Natal Provincial Legislature: In re Certification of the Constitution of the Province of KwaZulu-Natal, 1996 1996 (4) SA 1098 (CC) (*KwaZulu-Natal Constitution Case*).

Ex parte Speaker of the KwaZulu-Natal Provincial Legislature: In re KwaZulu-Natal Amakhosi and Iziphakanyiswa Amendment Bill of 1995; Ex parte Speaker of the KwaZulu-Natal Provincial Legislature: In re Payment of Salaries, Allowances and Other Privileges to the Ingonyama Bill of 1995 1996 (4) SA 653 (CC) (*KwaZulu Amakosi* and *Ingonyama Bill Cases*).

Harris v Minister of the Interior 1952 (2) SA 428 (AD)

Matukane and Others v *Laerskool Potgietersrus* 1996 (3) SA 223 (T).

Minister of Posts and Telegraphs v Rasool 1934 AD 167.

Minister of the Interior v Lockhat and Others 1961 (2) SA 587 (AD).

Moller v Keimoes School Committee 1911 AD 635.

Ndlwana v Hofmeyr NO and Others 1937 AD 229.

Nyamakazi v President of Bophuthatswana 1992 (4) SA 540 (B).

The President of the Republic of South Africa and Ors v South African Rugby Union and Ors 1999 (7) BCLR 725 (CC).

R v Abdurahman 1950 (3) SA 136 (AD).

Ramjee v Eastern Cape Committee, Group Areas Board 1958 (2) SA 67 (E).

Rex v Ndobe 1930 AD 484.

S. v Makwanyane and Another 1995 (3) SA 391 (CC); 1995 BCLR 665 (CC) (*Death Penalty Case*).

Sachs v Minister of Justice; Diamond v Minister of Justice 1934 AD 11.

South Africa (Pre-Union)

Orange Free State

Cassim and Solomon v The State (1892) 9 Cape LJ 58.

Transvaal

Hermansberg Mission Society v Commissioner of Native Affairs and Darius Mogale 1906 TS 135.

South African Republic (ZAR)

Brown v Leyds NO (1897) 4 Off Rep 17.

England

Dr Bonham's Case (1610) 8 Co Rep 113b; 77 ER 646 (Sir Edward Coke).

Kruse v Johnson [1898] 2 QB 91.

United States

Furman v State of Georgia 408 US 238 (1972).

Marbury v Madison 1 Cranch (5 US) 137, 2 L Ed 60 (1803).

New York v United States 505 US 144 (1992).

West Virginia State Board of Education v Barnette and Others 319 US 624 (1942)

International
Nationality Decrees Issues in Tunis and Morocco 1923 PCIJ Rep, Series B, No. 4.
Minority Schools in Albania Case 1935 PCIJ (ser A/B) No. 64.

STATUTES

Imperial
Colonial Laws Validity Act 1865, 28 & 29 Vict, c 63.
South Africa Act 1909, 9 Edw 7, c 9.

India
The Constitution of India, 26 January 1950

Ireland
Constitution of Ireland 1937

Namibia
Constitution of the Republic of Namibia 1990.

South Africa (Post-Union)
Abolition of Racially Based Land Measures Act 108 of 1991
Appellate Division Quorum Act 27 of 1955.
Asiatic Land Tenure and Indian Representation Act 28 of 1946.
Bantu Authorities Act 68 of 1951.
Black Land Act 27 of 1913.
Black States Constitution Act 21 of 1971.
Council of Traditional Leaders Act 31 of 1994
Franchise Laws Amendment Act 41 of 1931.
Group Areas Act 41 of 1950 (amended and consolidated in Act 36 of 1966).
High Court of Parliament Act 35 of 1952.
Judicial Service Commission Act 9 of 1994.
Local Government Transition Act 209 of 1993.
National Economic, Development and Labour Council Act 35 of 1994.
Native Administration Act 38 of 1927.
Promotion of Bantu Self-Government Act 46 of 1959
Promotion of Constitutional Development Act 86 of 1988.
Representation of Natives Act 12 of 1936.
Republic of South Africa Constitution Act 108 of 1996.

Republic of South Africa Constitution Act 200 of 1993.
Republic of South Africa Constitution Act 110 of 1983.
Republic of South Africa Constitution Act 32 of 1961.
Reservation of Separate Amenities Act 49 of 1953.
Restitution of Land Rights Act 22 of 1994.
Senate Act 53 of 1955.
Separate Representation of Voters Act 46 of 1951
South Africa Act Amendment Act 9 of 1956.
Transkei Constitution Act 48 of 1963.
Volkstaat Council Act 30 of 1994
Women's Enfranchisement Act 18 of 1930.

KWAZULU LEGISLATURE

The Constitution of the State of KwaZulu-Natal December 1992 (Proposal presented to the KwaZulu Legislative Assembly).

South Africa (pre-Union)

Cape
Glen Grey Act 1894.
Cape School Board Act 1905.

Natal
Parliament Law No. 11 (1865).

INTERNATIONAL TREATIES AND DOCUMENTS

African Charter on Human and Peoples' Rights, adopted 26 June, 1981, OAU Doc. CAB/LEG/67/3 Rev 5, rpt in 21 ILM 58.
American Convention on Human Rights, done at San José, 22 November 1969, entered into force, July 18, 1978, OAS TS No. 36, 1, OAS Off Rec OEA/Ser L/V/II.23 doc 21 rev 6 (1979); rpt in (1970) 9 ILM 673.
Charter of the United Nations, done at San Francisco, 26 June 1945, entered into force for the United States, 24 October, 1945, 59 Stat 1031, TS No. 993, 3 Bevans 1153, 1976 YBUN 1043.
Conference on Security and Co-operation in Europe, *Document of the Copenhagen Meeting of the Conference on the Human Dimension of the CSCE*, 29 June 1990, rpt in (1990) 29 ILM 1305.
Conference on Security and Co-operation in Europe, *Charter of Paris for a New Europe*, 21 November 1990, rpt in 30 ILM 193 (1991).
Declaration of the Organization of African Unity Ad-hoc Committee on Southern Africa on the Question of South Africa, Harare,

Zimbabwe, 21 August 1989; rpt in ANC Department of Political Education, *The Road to Peace: Resource Material on Negotiations*, Johannesburg: ANC Dept. of Political Education, June 1990.

Declaration on the Question of South Africa by the Ad Hoc Committee on Southern Africa of the Organization of African Unity, Harare, 21 August 1989, United Nations Centre Against Apartheid, *Notes and Documents* 7/89 (New York, October 1989).

European Economic Community Treaty 1957, UKTS 1979 No. 15 Cmnd 7480; 298 UNTS 11 ('Treaty of Rome').

European Community, Joint Declaration on Fundamental Rights, issued at Luxembourg on 5 April 1977, 1977 O J Eur Comm (no. C103/1).

European Convention for the Protection of Human Rights and Fundamental Freedoms, done at Rome, 4 November 1950 (entered into force 3 September 1953), EuropTS No. 5.

'Guidelines on the Recognition of New States in Eastern Europe and the Soviet Union' (1991) 24(12) *Bulletin of the European Communities* 119.

International Covenant on Civil and Political Rights, opened for signature 19 December 1966, 999 UNTS 171, 6 ILM 368 (entered into force 23 March 1976).

International Covenant on Economic, Social and Cultural Rights, adopted by the General Assembly of the UN on 16 December 1966, 993 UNTS 3, 6 ILM 360 (entered into force 3 January 1976).

Report of the Conference on Security and Co-operation in Europe Meeting of Experts on National Minorities, Geneva 1991 (1991) 30 ILM 1692.

UNITED NATIONS DOCUMENTS

General Assembly

Comprehensive Review of the Whole Question of Peace-Keeping Operations in All Their Aspects, GA Res 49, 44 UN GAOR (78th plen mtg), Supp No 49, UN Doc A/Res/44/49 (1990).

Credentials of Representatives to the Twenty-Ninth Session of the General Assembly, GA Res 3206, 29 UN GAOR, UN Doc A/RES/3206 (1974).

Enhancing the Effectiveness of the Principle of Periodic and Genuine Elections, GA Res 137, 46 UN GAOR (75th plen mtg), UN Doc A/RES/46/137 (1991).

Enhancing the Effectiveness of the Principle of Periodic and Genuine Elections, GA Res 150, 45 UN GAOR (69th plen mtg), UN Doc A/RES/45/150 (1990).

GA Res 616B, 7 UN GAOR, Supp No 21, UN Doc A/2361 (1952). On the Report of the Ad Hoc Committee of the Whole of the Sixteenth Special Session. Declaration on *Apartheid* and its Destructive Consequences in Southern Africa, GA Res S-16/1, S-16 UN GAOR (6th plen mtg), UN Doc A/RES/S-16/1 (1989).

Policies of Apartheid of the Government of South Africa – Special Responsibility of the United Nations and the International Community Towards the Oppressed People of South Africa, GA Res 3411 C 30 UN GAOR, UN Doc A/RES/3411C (1975).

Policies of Apartheid of the Government of South Africa – International Solidarity with the Liberation Struggle in South Africa, GA Res 27A, 44 UN GAOR (63rd plen mtg), UN Doc A/RES/44/27 A (1989).

Policies of Apartheid of the Government of South Africa – International Support for the Eradication of Apartheid in South Africa through Genuine Negotiations, GA Res 27B, 44 UN GAOR (63rd plen mtg), UN Doc A/RES/44/27B (1989).

Policies of Apartheid of the Government of South Africa – Concerted International Action for the Elimination of Apartheid, GA Res 27K, 44 UN GAOR (63rd plen mtg), UN Doc A/RES/44/27K (1989).

Relationship between the United Nations and South Africa, GA Res 3207, 29 UN GAOR, UN Doc A/RES/3207 (1974).

Report of the United Nations Commission on the Racial Situation in the Union of South Africa, GA Res 2505, 8 UN GAOR, Supp No 16, UN A/2505 & A/2505/Add1 (1953).

The Policies of Apartheid of the Government of the Republic of South Africa, GA Res 1761, 17 UN GAOR, UN Doc A/RES/1761 (1962).

The Question of Race Conflict in South Africa Resulting from the Policies of the Government of the Union of South Africa, GA Res 616B, 7 UN GAOR, UN Doc A/Res/616B (1952).

Treatment of Indians in the Union of South Africa, GA Res 44, 1 UN GAOR, Article 2, UN Doc A/Res/44 (1946).

Universal Declaration of Human Rights, GA Res 217A, 3 UN GAOR (183rd plen mtg), UN Doc A/Res/217A (1948).

Security Council

Further Report of the Secretary-General Concerning the Implementation of Security Council Resolution 435 (1978) and 439 (1978) Concerning the Question of Namibia Annex: Principles for a Peaceful Settlement in South-Western Africa, SC Res 20412, 44 UN SCOR, UN Doc S/20412 (1989).

Resolution 632 (1989), adopted by the Security Council at its 2848th Meeting on 16 February 1989, SC Res 632, 44 UN SCOR (2848th mtg), UN Doc S/Res/632 (1989).

The Question of South Africa, SC Res 418, 32 UN SCOR (2046th mtg), UN Doc S/RES/418 (1977).
The Question of South Africa, SC Res 554, 39 UN SCOR (2551st mtg), UN Doc S/RES/554 (1984).

Other United Nations Documents
Letter Dated 12 September 1952, Addressed To The Secretary-General By The Permanent Representatives of Afghanistan, Burma, Egypt, India, Indonesia, Iran, Iraq, Lebanon, Pakistan, the Philippines, Saudi Arabia, Syria, and Yemen, UN Doc A/2183 (1952).
Letter Dated 12 June 1982 From the Representatives of Canada, France, Germany, Federal Republic of, the United Kingdom of Great Britain and Northern Ireland and the United States of America Addressed to the Secretary-General Annex. Principles Concerning the Constituent Assembly and the Constitution for an Independent Namibia, UN Doc S/15287 (1982), transmitted to the Secretary-General of the United Nations on 12 July 1982.
Ruling by the President of the General Assembly, Mr Abdelaziz Bouteflika (Algeria), Concerning the Credentials of the Delegation of South Africa, A/PV 2281, 12 November 1974.
Statement by Secretary-General Kurt Waldheim in the Security Council after the Adoption of Resolution 418 (1977) Concerning Mandatory Arms Embargo against South Africa, UN Doc S/PV2046, 2046th mtg (1977).
The Report of the NGO Forum, UN Doc A/Conf 157/7.
UN Center for Human Rights: Commission on Human Rights, Draft Declaration on the Rights of Persons Belonging to National or Ethnic, Religious and Linguistic Minorities, ESC Res 1992/16, UN ESCOR, UN Doc E/Res/1992/16 (1992).

INTERVIEWS

[Asmal], Interview with Kader Asmal, Minister of Water Affairs and Forestry, Johannesburg International Airport, 2 August 1998.
[Chaskalson], Interview with Arthur Chaskalson, President, Constitutional Court, Johannesburg, 30 July 1998.
[Dugard], Discussion with John Dugard, Johannesburg, 24 July 1998.
[Langa], Interview with Pius Langa, Deputy-President, Constitutional Court, Johannesburg, 27 July 1998.
[Morrison], Interview with Neil Morrison, one of the organizers of the Conference for a Democratic Future, Johannesburg, 27 July 1998.
[Murray], Discussion with Christina Murray, Madison, October 1999.

[Sachs], Telephone interview with Albie Sachs, Judge of the Constitutional Court, Cape Town, 1 August 1998.

BOOKS, ARTICLES AND CONFERENCE PROCEEDINGS

Abel, Richard, *Politics by Other Means: Law in the Struggle Against Apartheid, 1980–1994*, New York: Routledge, 1995.

Abraham, David, 'Liberty without Equality: The Property–Rights Connection in a "Negative Citizenship" Regime' (1996) 21 *Law & Social Inquiry* 1.

Ackerman, Bruce, *The Future of Liberal Revolution*, New Haven: Yale University Press, 1992.

—— 'The Rise of World Constitutionalism' (1997) 83 *Virginia Law Review* 771.

—— *The Rise of World Constitutionalism*, Yale Law School Occasional Papers, Second Series, Number 3, 1997.

—— *We the People*, Cambridge, MA: Belknap Press of Harvard University Press, 1991.

Adam, Heribert, & Kogila Moodley, *The Negotiated Revolution: Society and Politics in Post-Apartheid South Africa*, Johannesburg: Jonathan Ball, 1993.

African National Congress, 'Advance to People's Power, 8 January 1987', rpt [February 1987] *Sechaba* 6.

—— ' "ANC Draft Bill of Rights: A Preliminary Revised Text" May 1992', in Albie Sachs, *Advancing Human Rights in South Africa*, Cape Town: Oxford University Press, 1992, Appendix 1, 224.

—— ANC Draft Bill of Rights: Preliminary Revised Version, February 1993.

—— 'Communique of the Second National Consultative Conference of the African National Congress, presented by President Oliver Tambo at a press conference, Lusaka, Zambia, 25 June 1985', rpt in *Documents of the Second National Consultative Conference of the African National Congress, Zambia, 16–23 June, 1985*, Lusaka: Zambia, ANC, 1985, 39.

—— 'Constitutional Guidelines for a Democratic South Africa', 1988; rpt (1989) 12 *Hastings International & Comparative Law Review* 322, also rpt in *The Road to Peace*, ANC Dept. of Political Education, June 1990.

—— Declaration of the 48th National Conference of the African National Congress, 6 July 1991; rpt in South African History Archive, *History in the Making: Documents Reflecting a Changing South Africa*, vol. 1, No. 6 (July 1991).

—— 'Mass Action for People's Power: Statement of the National Executive Committee of the ANC, January 8, 1989' [February 1989] *Sechaba* 2.

—— Report of the Politico-Military Strategy Commission (the 'Green Book') to the ANC National Executive Committee, Parts One and Two with two annexures, August 1979, rpt in Thomas Karis & Gail Gerhart (eds.), *From Protest to Challenge: A Documentary History of African Politics in South Africa, 1882–1990*, Vol. 5: Nadir and Resurgence, 1964–1979, Pretoria: Unisa Press, 1997, Document 114, 720–34.

—— Statement of the National Executive Committee of the African National Congress on the Question of Negotiations, Lusaka, 9 October 1987.

—— 'Statement on Negotiations, 9 October 1987', rpt [December 1987] *Sechaba.*

—— 'Strategy and Tactics of the South African Revolution', in Alex La Guma (ed.), *Apartheid: A Collection of Writings on South African Racism by South Africans*, Berlin: Seven Seas Publisher, 1972.

—— The Freedom Charter, 26 June 1955; rpt in Hassen Ebrahim, *The Soul of a Nation: Constitution-Making in South Africa*, Cape Town: Oxford University Press, 1998, Document 7, 415–19.

—— *The Reconstruction and Development Programme: A Policy Framework*, Johannesburg: Umanyano Publications, 1994.

— Centre for Applied Legal Studies & Lawyers for Human Rights, *Conference on a Constitutional Court for a Future South Africa*, Magaliesberg, 1–3 February, 1991

African National Congress Constitutional Committee, *A Bill of Rights for a New South Africa*, Belleville: University of the Western Cape, Centre for Development Studies, 1990.

—— *ANC Draft Bill of Rights: Preliminary Version 1.1*, May 1992.

—— *What Is A Constitution? A Discussion Document Prepared by the Constitutional Committee of the African National Congress of South Africa to Encourage and Promote Discussion on the Structure and Content of a New, Non-Racial Non-Sexist and Democratic Constitution for South Africa*, 1990.

Aggarawala, R. N., *National Movement & Constitutional Development of India*, 8th edn., Delhi: Metropolitan Book Co., 1973.

ANC Land Commission, *Land Manifesto for ANC National Conference*, July 1991.

Andersen, Benedict, *Imagined Communities: Reflections on the Origin and Spread of Nationalism*, 2nd edn., London; New York: Verso, 1991.

Anglo-American Corporation, 'Shaping the Future: A Citizens Guide to Constitution-Making and Democratic Politics in South Africa' (4th draft), January 1990 (on file with author).

Appadurai, A., 'Disjuncture and Difference in the Global Cultural Economy' (1990) 2(2) *Public Culture* 1; see also (1990) 7 *Theory, Culture & Society* 295.

Arendt, Hannah, *On Revolution*, New York: Viking Press, 1963.

Arjomand, Said A., 'Constitutions and the Struggle for Political Order: A Study in the Modernization of Political Traditions' (1992) 33 *Archives of European Society* 39.

Ashforth, Adam, *The Politics of Official Discourse in Twentieth-Century South Africa*, Oxford: Clarendon Press, 1990.

Ashley, R. K., & R. B. J. Walker, 'Reading Dissidence/Writing the Discipline: Crisis and the Question of Sovereignty in International Studies' (1990) 34 *International Studies Quarterly* 367.

Asmal, Kader, 'Judges and Justice in South Africa' (March 1989) *Sechaba* 19.

—— 'The Making of a Constitution' [March/April 1995] *Southern African Review of Books* 11.

— & Ronald Roberts, 'South Africa Needs Economic Rights', *International Herald Tribune* (New York), 31 October 1994.

Atkinson, D., 'Brokering a Miracle? The multiparty negotiating forum', in S. Friedman & D. Atkinson (eds.), *South African Review 7: The Small Miracle*, Randburg: Ravan Press, 1994.

Banting, Keith, & Richard Simeon, 'Introduction: The Politics of Constitutional Change', in Keith Banting & Richard Simeon (eds.), *Redesigning the State: The Politics of Constitutional Change*, Toronto; Buffalo: University of Toronto Press, 1985.

Barber, Benjamin R., *Jihad v McWorld: How the Planet is Both Falling Apart and Coming Together and What this Means for Democracy*, New York: Times Books, 1995.

Barry, B., 'The One-Party System, Multiple Parties and Constitutionalism in Africa', in Issa G. Shivji (ed.), *State and Constitutionalism: An African Debate on Democracy*, Harare: SAPES Trust, 1991.

Basson Dion, 'Judicial Activism in a State of Emergency: An Examination of Recent Decisions of the South African Courts' (1987) 3 *South African Journal on Human Rights* 28.

— & Henning Viljoen, *South African Constitutional Law*, 1988, 2nd Impression, Cape Town: Juta, 1991.

Bauman, R. W., 'Property Rights in the Canadian Constitutional Context' (1992) 8 *South African Journal on Human Rights* 344.

Beatty, David (ed.), *Human Rights and Judicial Review: A Comparative Perspective*, Dordrecht; Boston: Martinus Nijhoff; Norwell, MA: Kluwer Academic, 1994.

—— 'Human Rights and the Rules of Law', David Beatty (ed.), *Human Rights and Judicial Review: A Comparative Perspective*, Dordrecht; Boston: Martinus Nijhoff; Norwell, MA: Kluwer Academic, 1994.

Beer, Lawrence W., 'Introduction: Constitutionalism in Asia and the United States', in Lawrence W. Beer (ed.), *Constitutional Systems in Late Twentieth Century Asia*, Seattle: University of Washington Press, 1992.

Beitz, Charles R., 'Sovereignty and Morality in International Affairs', in David Held (ed.), *Political Theory Today*, Oxford: Polity; Stanford: Stanford University Press, 1991.

Bell, Paul (ed.), *The Making of the Constitution: The Story of South Africa's Constitutional Assembly, May 1994 to December 1996*, Cape Town: Churchill Murray, for the Constitutional Assembly, 1997.

Benson, Mary, *Nelson Mandela: The Man and the Movement*, London; New York: Norton, 1986.

—— *The African Patriots: The Story of the African National Congress of South Africa*, London: Faber and Faber, 1963.

Benyon, John (ed.), *Constitutional Change in South Africa*, Pietermaritzburg: University of Natal Press, 1978.

Bhabha, H. K., 'The Commitment to Theory', in (1988) 5 *New Formations* 5.

Bickel, Alexander, *The Least Dangerous Branch: The Supreme Court at the Bar of Politics*, 2nd edn., New Haven, CT: Yale University Press, 1986.

Bindman, Geoffrey (ed.), *South Africa: Human Rights and the Rule of Law*, International Commission of Jurists, London: Pinter, 1988.

Binswanger, Hans, & Klaus Deininger, 'South Africa Land Policy: The Legacy of History and Current Options' (1993) 21(9) *World Development* 1451.

Bizos, George, *No One to Blame? In Pursuit of Justice in South Africa*, Cape Town: D. Philip/Mayibuye, 1998.

Black, Charles L., Jr., *The People and the Court: Judicial Review in a Democracy*, Westport, CT: Greenwood Press, 1960.

Black, Henry Campbell, *Black's Law Dictionary: Definitions of the Terms of American and English Jurisprudence, Ancient and Modern*, 5th edn., by Joseph R. Nolan, St Paul: West Publishing Co.,1979.

Blackstone, William, *Commentaries on the Laws of England*, vol. 1, first published 1765, 4th edn., Boston: Beacon Press, 1876.

Blaustein, A. P., & G. H. Flanz (eds.), *Constitutions of the Countries of the World*, Dobbs Ferry, NY: Oceana Publications, 1971–.

Boulle, Laurence J., *South Africa and the Constitutional Option: A Constitutional Analysis*, Cape Town: Juta, 1984.

Brownlie, Ian, *Principles of Public International Law*, 3rd edn., Oxford: Clarendon Press, 1979.

Bryde, Brun-Otto, 'Constitutional Courts in Constitutional Transition', presented at Conference on Constitutional Transitions, Hong Kong, June 1997 (draft), March 1997.

—— 'The Role of Constitutional Jurisprudence in German Democracy', in Gunter Weick (ed.), *Competition or Convergence: The Future of European Legal Culture*, Frankfurt: Peter Lang, 1999.

Budlender, Geoff, 'The Right to Equitable Access to Land' (1992) 8 *South African Journal on Human Rights* 295.

—— 'Towards a Right to Housing', in A. J. van der Walt (ed.), *Land Reform and the Future of Landownership in South Africa: Papers Read at a Seminar Presented by the Department of Private Law of the University of South Africa on 2 November 1990*, Cape Town: Juta, 1991.

Buergenthal, Thomas, 'The CSCE Rights System' (1991) 25 *George Washington Journal of International Law & Economics* 333.

Burbach, Roger, & William Robinson, 'The Fin De Siecle Debate: Globalization as Epochal Shift' (1999) 63(1) *Science and Society* 10.

Burger, Warren E., 'The Doctrine of Judicial Review: Mr Marshall, Mr Jefferson, and Mr Marbury', in Mark Cannon and David O'Brien (eds.), *Views from the Bench*, Chatham, NJ: Chatham House Publishers, 1985.

'Buthelezi's Divisive Advisor', *Weekly Mail & Guardian* (Johannesburg), 2 June 1995.

Cachalia, Firoz, 'A Progress Report on Codesa' (1992) 8(2) *South African Journal on Human Rights* 249.

—— 'Case Against Power Sharing', *The Star* (Johannesburg), 2 February 1993, p. 10, col. 2.

—— 'Constitutionalism and the Transition to Democracy' (draft), December 1992 (on file with author).

Cairns, Alan C., 'The Politics of Constitutional Renewal in Canada', in Keith Banting & Richard Simeon (eds.), *Redesigning the State: The Politics of Constitutional Change*, Toronto; Buffalo: University of Toronto Press, 1985.

Cameron, Edwin, 'Legal Chauvinism, Executive-Mindedness and Justice: L. C. Steyn's Impact on South African Law' (1982) 99 *South African Law Journal* 56.

Cappelletti, Mauro (ed.), with the collaboration of Paul Kollmer & Joanne Olson, *The Judicial Process in Comparative Perspectives*, Oxford: Clarendon Press, 1989.

Cassese, Antonio, 'Violence, War and the Rule of Law in the International Community', in David Held (ed.), *Political Theory Today*, Oxford: Polity; Stanford: Stanford University Press, 1991.

Centre for Development Studies (ed.), *A Bill of Rights for a Democratic South Africa: Papers and Report of a Conference Convened by the ANC Constitutional Committee*, Belleville: University of the Western Cape, Centre for Development Studies, 1991.

—— (ed.), *Affirmative Action in a New South Africa: The Apartheid Legacy and Comparative International Experience and Mechanisms of*

Enforcement, Belleville: University of the Western Cape, Centre for Development Studies, 1992.

— & Constitutional Committee of the ANC, *Seminar on Electoral Systems*, Stellenbosch, 2–4 November 1990.

— Community Law Centre & Constitutional Department of the ANC, *Electoral Systems – A Discussion Document*, Belleville: University of the Western Cape, Centre for Development Studies, 1990.

Chanock, Martin, *Fear, Favour and Prejudice: The Making of South African Legal Culture*, forthcoming.

Chaskalson, Matthew, 'Stumbling Towards Section 28: Negotiations over Property Rights at the Multiparty Talks' (1995) 11 *South African Journal on Human Rights* 222.

Choper, Jesse H., *Judicial Review and the National Political Process*, Chicago: Chicago University Press, 1980.

Christiansen, Robert, 'Aide Memoire: Preparation of a Rural Restructuring Program', 15 June 1993 (on file with author).

Citizen, The (Johannesburg), 20 April 1985.

Claassens, Aninka, 'Editorial' (1992) 8 *South African Journal on Human Rights* v.

—— 'For Whites Only: Land Ownership in South Africa', in M. de Klerk (ed.), *A Harvest of Discontent: The Land Question in South Africa*, Cape Town: Idasa, 1991.

Cohen, Andrew, *A Deal Undone: The Making and Breaking of the Meech Lake Accord*, Vancouver: Douglas & McIntyre, 1990.

Cohen, Herman J., Assistant Secretary of State for African Affairs, Testimony before the House Foreign Affairs Subcommittee of Africa, *Violence in South Africa and its Effect on the Convention for Democratic South Africa (Codesa): Hearing and Markup before the Subcommittee on Africa of the Committee on Foreign Affairs*, HRes 497 H., 102nd Cong., 2d Sess., 23 July 1992.

Cohen, Jean, & Andrew Arato, 'Politics and the Reconstruction of the Concept of Civil Society', in Axel Honneth et al. (eds.), *Cultural-Political Interventions in the Unfinished Project of Enlightenment*, trans. Barbara Fultner, Cambridge, MA: MIT Press, 1992.

Commonwealth Group of Eminent Persons, The, *Mission to South Africa: The Commonwealth Report*, Harmondsworth: Penguin Books, 1986.

Community Law Center, ANC Constitutional Committee & Center for Development Studies, *Conference on the Structures of Government for a United Democratic South Africa*, University of Western Cape, Cape Town, 26–28 March 1992.

Conference on the Constitutional Models and Constitutional Change in South Africa, *Constitutional Change in South Africa: Proceedings of a Conference on Constitutional Models and Constitutional Change in South*

Africa, held in the University of Natal, Pietermaritzburg 14–16 February 1978, ed. John A. Benyon, Pietermaritzburg: University of Natal Press, 1978.

'Constitution for a New South Africa ... Cribbed from the United States Constitution', *Sunday Times,* 22 August 1993, p. 23.

Constitutional Assembly, Constitutional Committee, *Documentation: Volume 2A Land Rights,* Friday, 15 September 1995.

Constitutional Assembly, Constitutional Committee Subcommittee, *Documentation: Land Rights,* Monday, 9 October 1995.

—— *Draft Bill of Rights, Volume One, Explanatory Memoranda,* 9 October 1995.

Constitutional Assembly, Theme Committee 4, *Draft Bill of Rights,* 9 October 1995.

Constitutional Assembly, Theme Committee 6.3, *Specialised Structures of Government: Documentation Volume 2A: Land Rights,* 15 September 1995.

—— *Specialised Structures of Government: Land Rights, Documentation,* 11 September 1995.

Constitutional Committee of the ANC, *A Bill of Rights for a New South Africa,* Belleville: University of the Western Cape, Centre for Development Studies, 1990.

—— & The Center for Socio-Legal Studies, University of Natal, Durban, *Conference on a Bill of Rights for a Democratic South Africa,* Salt Rock, Natal, 10–12 May 1992.

—— & The Community Law Center, *National Conference on Affirmative Action. University of the Western Cape,* Port Elizabeth, 10–12 October 1991.

—— *Towards a Non-Racial, Non-Sexist Judiciary in South Africa,* Conference held at the University of the Western Cape, Cape Town, 26–28 March 1993.

Convention for a Democratic South Africa (Codesa) I, Declaration of Intent, 21 December 1991, rpt in Hassen Ebrahim, *The Soul of a Nation: Constitution-Making in South Africa,* Cape Town: Oxford University Press, 1998, Document 22, 529–31.

Copelyn, J., 'Collective Bargaining: A Base for Transforming Industry' (March 1991) 15(6) *South African Labour Bulletin* 26.

Corbett, M. M., 'Memorandum Submitted on Behalf of the Judiciary of South Africa on the Chapter on the Administration of Justice in the Draft Interim Constitution', 3 September 1993.

—— 'Memorandum Submitted on Behalf of the Judiciary of South Africa on the 12th Report of the Technical Committee on Constitutional Issues', 13 September 1993.

—— 'Presentation to the Truth and Reconciliation Commission' (1998) 115 *South African Law Journal* 17.

Corder, Hugh, *Judges at Work: The Role and Attitudes of the South African Appellate Judiciary, 1910–50*, Cape Town: Juta, 1984.

—— 'Lessons from (North) America (Beware the "Legalization of Politics" and the "Political Seduction of the Law")' (1992) 109 *South African Law Journal* 204.

—— 'The record of the judiciary (2)', in Hugh Corder (ed.), *Democracy and the Judiciary*, Cape Town: Idasa, 1989.

—— et al., *A Charter for Social Justice: A Contribution to the South African Bill of Rights Debate*, December 1992.

Crawford, James, *Democracy in International Law: Inaugural Lecture Delivered 5 March 1993*, Cambridge: Cambridge University Press, 1994.

Crewe, Muriel, 'Punishment by Process', *SASH*, May 1987.

Cross, C., 'An Alternative Legality: The Property Rights Question in Relation to South African Land Reform' (1992) 8 *South African Journal on Human Rights* 305.

Cullinan, Kerry, 'Union–Community Clash Avoided' (August 1993) 12 *Reconstruct: A Work in Progress Supplement* 16.

D. F. Malan Accord, The, Cape Town, 12 February 1991; rpt in Hassen Ebrahim, *The Soul of a Nation: Constitution-Making in South Africa*, Cape Town: Oxford University Press, 1998, Document 19, 493–7.

Dahl, Robert Allen, *Democracy and its Critics*, New Haven: Yale University Press, 1989.

Danaher, Kevin (ed.), *Corporations are Gonna Get your Mama: Globalization and the Downsizing of the American Dream*, Monroe: ME, Common Courage Press, 1996.

Daniels, Glenda, 'Beyond Protest Politics' (July/August 1991) 76 *Work In Progress* 13.

—— 'The Great VAT Strike' (December 1991) 79 *Work In Progress* 18.

Davenport, T. R. H., 'Some Reflections on the History of Land Tenure in South Africa, Seen in the Light of Attempts by the State to Impose Political and Economic Control' [1985] *Acta Juridica* 53.

—— *South Africa: A Modern History*, 2nd edn., Toronto; Buffalo: University of Toronto Press, 1978.

—— & K. S. Hunt (eds.), *The Right to Land*, Cape Town: David Philip, 1974.

Davidson, Joshua, 'The History of Judicial Oversight of Legislative and Executive Action in South Africa' (1985) 8 *Harvard Journal of Law and Public Policy* 687.

Davis, Dennis, *South Africa and Transition: From Autocracy to What? A Preliminary Analysis about a Tentative Process*, Center for Applied Legal Studies, Working Paper 18, June 1992.

— Matthew Chaskalson & Johann de Waal, 'Democracy and Constitutionalism: The Role of Constitutional Interpretation', in David van Wyk et al. (eds.), *Rights and Constitutionalism: The New South African Legal Order*, Kenwyn: Juta, 1994.

Davis, Mickey, 'Where the Working Class Lives: International Law and the Global Division of Labor' (draft) February 1995 (on file with author).

Davis, S. M., *Apartheid's Rebels: Inside South Africa's Hidden War*, New Haven: Yale University Press, 1987.

de Klerk, F. W., Opening of Parliament Speech, 2 February 1990, rpt in Hassen Ebrahim, *The Soul of a Nation: Constitution-Making in South Africa*, Cape Town: Oxford University Press, 1998, Document 16.

—— Second Submission of the National Party to the Truth and Reconciliation Commission, 23 March 1997, http://www.truth.org.za/submit/np2.htm.

—— Submission to the Truth and Reconciliation Commission by Mr F. W. de Klerk, Leader of the National Party, August 1996, http://www.truth.org.za/submit/np-truth.htm.

Democratic Party, *Freedom Under the Rule of Law: Advancing Liberty in the New South Africa, Draft Bill of Rights*, May, 1993.

Dent, G. R. & C. L. S. Nyembezi, *Scholar's Zulu Dictionary*, Pietermaritzburg: Shuter & Shooter, 1969.

Desai, Barney, 'Proposed Agreement Can Lead Only to Conflict', *The Star* (Johannesburg), 13 October 13 1992, p. 12, col. 1.

Dexter, Philip, 'Make the RDP Make the Left' (February/March 1994) 95 *Work in Progress* 30.

Dezalay, Yves, & Bryant Garth, *Dealing in Virtue: International Commercial Arbitration and the Construction of a Transnational Legal Order*, Chicago: University of Chicago Press, 1996.

—— 'Merchants of Law as Moral Entrepreneurs: Constructing International Justice from the Competition for Transnational Business Disputes' (1995) 29 *Law & Society Review* 27.

Dicken, Peter, *Global Shift: The Internationalization of Economic Activity*, 2nd edn., New York: Guilford Press, 1992.

DiMaggio, Paul, & Walter Powell, 'The Iron Cage Revisited: Institutional Isomorphism and Collective Rationality in Organizational Fields' (1983) 48 *American Sociological Review* 147.

Dodson, A., 'The Group Areas Act: Changing Patterns of Enforcement', in Christina Murray & Catherine O'Regan (eds.), *No Place to Rest: Forced Removals and the Law in South Africa*. Cape Town: Oxford University Press in association with the Labour Law Unit, University of Cape Town, 1990.

Doke C. M., D. McK. Malcolm & J. M. A. Sikakana, *English and Zulu Dictionary*, Johannesburg: Witwatersrand University Press, 1982.

Dolny, H., & H. Klug, 'Land Reform: Legal Support and Economic Regulation', in G. Moss & I. Obrey (eds.), *South African Review 6: From 'Red Friday' to Codesa*, (Johannesburg: Ravan Press, 1992).

Du Plessis, Lourens, & Hugh Corder, *Understanding South Africa's Transitional Bill of Rights*, Kenwyn: Juta, 1994.

Dugard, John, 'Changing Attitudes towards a Bill of Rights in South Africa', in J. V. van der Westhuizen & H. P. Viljoen (eds.), *A Bill of Rights for South Africa (Menseregtehandves vir Suid-Afrika)*, Durban, Butterworths, 1988, 30.

—— *Human Rights and the South African Legal Order*, Princeton, NJ: Princeton University Press, 1978.

—— *International Law: A South African Perspective*, Cape Town: Juta, 1994.

—— *Recognition and the United Nations*, Cambridge: Grotius Press, 1987.

—— 'Should Judges Resign? (And Lawyers Participate)', in Hugh Corder (ed.), *Democracy and the Judiciary*, Cape Town: Idasa, 1989.

Dworkin, Ronald M., *Taking Rights Seriously*, Cambridge, MA: Harvard University Press, 1977.

Dyzenhaus, David, *Hard Cases in Wicked Legal Systems: South African Law in the Perspective of Legal Philosophy*, Oxford: Clarendon Press, 1991.

—— *Legality and Legitimacy: Carl Schmitt, Hans Kelsen and Hermann Heller in Weimar*, Oxford: Oxford University Press, 1997.

—— *Truth, Reconciliation and the Apartheid Legal Order*, Cape Town: Juta, 1998.

Ebrahim, Hassen, *The Soul of a Nation: Constitution-Making in South Africa*, Cape Town: Oxford University Press, 1998.

Elazar, Danuel J., 'Constitution-Making: The Pre-eminently Political Act', in Keith Banting and Richard Simeon (eds.), *Redesigning the State: The Politics of Constitutional Change*, Toronto; Buffalo: University of Toronto Press, 1985.

Elias, T. O., 'The Evolution of Law and Government in Modern Africa', in Hilda & Leo Kuper (eds.), *African Law: Adaptation and Development*, Berkeley: University of California Press, 1965.

Elkin, Stephen L., 'Constitutionalism's Successor', in Stephen L. Elkin & Karol E. Soltan (eds.), *A New Constitutionalism: Designing Political Institutions for a Good Society*, Chicago: University of Chicago Press, 1993.

Ellmann, Stephen, *In a Time of Trouble: Law and Liberty in South Africa's State of Emergency*, Oxford: Clarendon Press, 1992.

—— 'Law and Legitimacy in South Africa' (1995) 20 *Law and Social Inquiry* 407.

—— 'The New South African Constitution and Ethnic Division' (1994) 26 *Columbia Human Rights Law Review* 5.

Elster, Jon, 'Forces and Mechanisms in the Constitution-Making Process' (1995) 45 *Duke Law Journal* 364.

—— Introduction to Jon Elster & Rune Slagstad (eds.), *Constitutionalism and Democracy*, Cambridge: Cambridge University Press; Paris: Maison des sciences de l'homme, 1988.

Ely, James W., Jr., *The Guardian of Every Other Right: A Constitutional History of Property Rights*, New York: Oxford University Press, 1992.

Ely, John Hart, *Democracy and Distrust: A Theory of Judicial Review*, Cambridge, MA: Harvard University Press, 1980.

Epstein, Richard A., 'All Quiet on the Eastern Front' (1991) 58 *University of Chicago Law Review* 555.

Falk, R., 'The Making of Global Citizenship', in Jeremy Brecher et al. (eds.), *Global Visions: Beyond the New World Order*, Boston: South End Press, 1993.

First Global Rule of Law Conference, Washington, DC, 13 July 1994.

Fisher, L., 'One of the Guardians Some of the Time', in Robert A. Licht (ed.), *Is the Supreme Court the Guardian of the Constitution?* Washington, DC: The AEI Press, 1993.

—— & N. Devins, *Political Dynamics of Constitutional Law*, St Paul, MO: West Publishing, 1992.

Fisher, William W., III., 'Making Sense of Madison: Nedelsky on Private Property' (1993) 18 *Law and Social Inquiry* 547.

Foreman, L., & E. S. Sachs, *The South African Treason Trial*, New York: Monthly Review Press, 1958.

Forsyth, C. F., *In Danger for Their Talents: A Study of the Appellate Division of the Supreme Court of South Africa 1950–1980*, Cape Town: Juta, 1985.

Foucault, Michel, 'What is Enlightenment?' in Paul Rabinow (ed.), *The Foucault Reader*, New York: Pantheon Books, 1984.

Franck, Thomas M., *Fairness in International Law and Institutions*, Oxford: Clarendon Press, 1995

—— 'The Emerging Right to Democratic Governance' (1992) 86 *The American Journal of International Law* 46.

Franklin, D. P., & M. J. Baun (eds.), *Political Culture and Constitutionalism: A Comparative Approach*, Armonk, NY: M. E. Sharpe, 1995.

Fraser, Nancy, 'Rethinking the Public Sphere: A Contribution to the Critique of Actually Existing Democracy', in Craig Calhoun (ed.), *Habermas and the Public Sphere*, Cambridge, MA: MIT Press, 1992.

Freeman, Alan, 'Legitimizing Racial Discrimination through Antidiscrimination Law: A Critical Review of Supreme Court Doctrine', in Piers Beirne & Richard Quinney (eds.), *Marxism and Law*, New York: Wiley, 1982.

Friedman, Steven, 'Constitutional Court: Puzzling Silence on Appointments' (1994) 1(2) *TransAct* 5.

—— (ed.), *The Long Journey: South Africa's Quest for a Negotiated Settlement,* Braamfontein: Ravan Press, 1993.

Gardner, J. A., *Legal Imperialism: American Lawyers and Foreign Aid in Latin America,* Madison: University of Wisconsin Press, 1980.

Garvey, John H., & T. Alexander Aleinikoff, 'Methods of Constitutional Interpretation', in John H. Garvey & T. Alexander Aleinikoff (eds.), *Modern Constitutional Theory: A Reader,* 2nd edn., St Paul: West Publishing Co., 1991.

Gerhart, G. M., *Black Power in South Africa: The Evolution of an Ideology,* Berkeley: University of California Press, 1978.

Ghai, Yash, 'Legal Responses to Ethnicity in South Africa and South East Asia', Ford Foundation (mimeo; on file with author).

—— 'The Theory of the State in the Third World and the Problematics of Constitutionalism', in Douglas Greenberg et al. (eds.), *Constitutionalism and Democracy: Transitions in the Contemporary World: The American Council of Learned Societies Comparative Constitutionalism Papers,* New York: Oxford University Press, 1993.

Giddens, Anthony, *Beyond Left and Right: The Future of Radical Politics,* Stanford: Stanford University Press, 1994.

—— *Consequences of Modernity,* Stanford: Stanford University Press, 1990.

Godsell, Bobby (ed.), *Shaping the Future South Africa: A Citizens' Guide to Constitution-Making,* Cape Town: Tafelberg & Human & Rousseau, 1990.

Goldmand A. H., 'Affirmative Action', in Marshall Cohen et al. (eds.), *Equality and Preferential Treatment,* Princeton: New Jersey, 1977.

Grant, Thomas D., 'Internationally Guaranteed Constitutive Order: Cyprus and Bosnia as Predicates for a New Nontraditional Actor in the Society of States' (1998) 8(1) *Journal of Transnational Law & Policy* 1.

Green, R. H., 'Participatory Pluralism and Persuasive Poverty: Some Reflections' [1989] *Third World Legal Studies* 21.

Greenberg, Douglas, et al., Introduction to Douglas Greenberg et al. (eds.), *Constitutionalism and Democracy: Transitions in the Contemporary World: The American Council of Learned Societies Comparative Constitutionalism Papers,* New York: Oxford University Press, 1993.

Greider, William, *One World, Ready or Not: The Manic Logic of Global Capitalism,* New York: Simon & Schuster, 1997.

Groote Schuur Minute, The, Cape Town, 4 May 1990; rpt in South African History Archive, *History in the Making: Documents Reflecting a Changing South Africa,* Vol. 1, No. 2 (November 1990), 17.

Grossman, Claudio, & Daniel D. Bradlow, 'Are We Being Propelled Towards a People-Centered Transnational Legal Order?' (1993) 9 *American University Journal of International Law and Policy* 1.

Guehenno, Jean-Marie, *The End of the Nation-State,* trans. Victoria Elliot, Minneapolis: University of Minnesota Press, 1995.

Gunther, Gerald, *Cases and Materials on Constitutional Law*, 10th edn., Mineola, NY: Foundation Press, 1980.

Habermas, Jürgen, *Between Facts and Norms: Contributions to a Discourse Theory of Law and Democracy*, trans. William Rehg, Cambridge, MA: MIT Press, 1996.

Hadland, Adrian, 'Demonstrators Hand Govt Land Ultimatum', *Business Day* (Johannesburg), 2 September 1993.

Hahlo, H. R., & Ellison Kahn, *South Africa: The Development of its Laws and Constitution*, London: Stevens, 1960.

Halberstam, Malvina, 'The Copenhagen Document: Intervention in Support of Democracy' (1993) 34 *Harvard International Law Journal* 163.

Halperin, Morton, 'Limited Constitutional Democracy: Lessons from the American Experience' (1993) 8 *American University Journal of International Law & Policy* 523.

Hamilton, P., 'The Enlightenment and the Birth of the Social Science', in Stuart Hall & Bram Gieben (eds.), *Formations of Modernity*, Cambridge: Polity Press, 1992.

Hannum, Hurst, *Autonomy, Sovereignty and Self-Determination: The Accommodation of Conflicting Rights*, Philadelphia: University of Pennsylvania Press, 1990.

Hart, Vivien, 'The Contagion of Rights: Constitutions as Carriers', in Patrick Hanafin & Melissa Williams (eds.), *Identity, Rights and Constitutional Transformation*, Aldershot: Ashgate, 1999.

Hartog, Hendrik, 'The Constitution of Aspiration and "The Rights That Belong to Us All" ' (1987) 74 *The Journal of American History* 1013.

Hayek, F. A., *The Constitution of Liberty*, London: Routledge and Kegan Paul, 1960.

Haysom, N., 'An Expedient Package Deal?' *Weekly Mail & Guardian* (Johannesburg), Review/Law, Supplement, vol. 1, No. 5, December 1993.

— & S. Kahnovitz, 'Courts and the State of Emergency', in G. Moss & I. Obrey (eds.), *South African Review 4*, Johannesburg: Ravan Press, 1987.

Held, David, *Democracy and the Global Order: From Modern State to Cosmopolitan Governance*, Stanford: Stanford University Press, 1995.

—— 'Democracy: From City-States to a Cosmopolitan Order?' in *Prospects for Democracy: North, South, East, West*, David Held (ed.), Cambridge: Polity Press, 1993.

—— 'Democracy, the Nation-State and the Global Systems', in David Held (ed.), *Political Theory Today*, Oxford: Polity; Stanford: Stanford University Press, 1991.

Helleiner, E., 'Democratic Governance in an Era of Global Finance', forthcoming in M. Molot & F. O. Hampson (eds.), *Canada Among Nations*.

Henderson, Andrew, 'Cry, the Beloved Constitution? Constitutional Amendment, the Vanished Imperative of the Constitutional Principles and the Controlling Values of Section 1' (1997) 114 *South African Law Journal* 542.

Henkin, Louis, 'A New Birth of Constitutionalism: Genetic Influences and Genetic Defects' (1993) 14 *Cardozo Law Review* 533.

Hirst, Paul, & Grahame Thompson, *Globalization in Question: The International Economy and the Possibilities of Governance*, Cambridge: Polity Press, 1996.

—— 'The Problem of "Globalization": International Economic Relations, National Economic Management and the Formation of Trading Blocs' (1992) 21(4) *Economy & Society* 357.

Hlangeni, M., 'Implementing the RDP' (May/June 1994) 4(5) *Mayibuye* 23, col. 2.

Holmes, Stephen, 'Gag Rules or the Politics of Omission', in Jon Elster & Rune Slagstad (eds.), *Constitutionalism and Democracy*, Cambridge; New York: Cambridge University Press; Paris: Maison des sciences de l'homme, 1988.

—— 'Precommitment and the Paradox of Democracy', in Jon Elster & Rune Slagstad (eds.), *Constitutionalism and Democracy*, Cambridge; New York: Cambridge University Press; Paris: Maison des sciences de l'homme, 1988.

Horowitz, Donald L., *A Democratic South Africa? Constitutional Engineering in a Divided Society*, Berkeley: University of California Press, 1991.

Hosten, W. J., A. B. Edwards, C. Nathan & F. Bosman, *Introduction to South African Law and Legal Theory*, Durban: Butterworths, 1983.

Howard, A. E. Dick, 'The Indeterminacy of Constitutions' (1996) 31 *Wake Forest Law Review* 383.

Hugo, P., & L. Stack, 'Whites in South African Public Service: Angst and the Future', in P. Hugo (ed.), *Redistribution and Affirmative Action: Working on South Africa's Political Economy*, Halfway House: Southern Book Publishers, 1992.

Hunt, Alan, *Explorations in Law and Society: Towards a Constitutive Theory of Law*, New York: Routledge, 1993.

— & Gary Wickham, *Foucault and Law: Towards a Sociology of Law as Governance*, London; Boulder: Pluto, 1994.

Huntington, Samuel P., 'Reform and Stability in a Modernizing, Multi-Ethnic Society' (1981) 8(2) *Politikon* 8.

—— *The Third Wave: Democratization in the Late Twentieth Century*, Norman: University of Oklahoma Press, 1991.

Ibrahim, Ahmed, & M. P. Jain, 'The Constitution of Malaysia and The American Constitutional Influence', in Lawrence W. Beer (ed.),

Constitutional Systems in Late Twentieth Century Asia, Seattle: University of Washington Press, 1992.

Inkatha Freedom Party, 'Comments of IFP on document of Working Group 2 [Codesa] Steering Committee proposal on CMB [Constitution-making Body]' 27 April 1992.

—— 'Position Paper of the Inkatha Freedom Party for Submission to the Codesa Meeting of February 6, 1992'; rpt in A. P. Blaustein, South African Supplement 9202 (March 1992) to A. P. Blaustein & G. H. Flanz (eds.), *Constitutions of the Countries of the World*, Dobbs Ferry, NY: Oceana Publications, 1971–.

—— 'The Constitution of the Federal Republic of South Africa' (draft), 18 June 1993; rpt in A. P. Blaustein, South African Supplement 93–6 (October 1993), to A. P. Blaustein & G. H. Flanz (eds.), *Constitutions of the Countries of the World*, Dobbs Ferry, NY: Oceana Publications, 1971–.

—— 'Why the Inkatha Freedom Party Objects to the Idea of the New Constitution Being Written by a Popularly Elected Assembly (whether called "Constitutent Assembly" or called by any other name)', undated submission to Codesa Working Group 2 (1992).

International Commission of Jurists, *Erosion of the Rule of Law in South Africa*, 1968.

—— *South Africa and the Rule of Law*, 1960.

Jacob, Herbert, Erhard Blankenburg, Herbert M. Kritzer, Dorris Marie Provine & Joseph Sanders, *Courts, Law and Politics in Comparative Perspective*, New Haven, CT: Yale University Press, 1996.

Johnson, Shaun, & Ester Waugh, ' "Sunset Clause" Offer as Slovo Seeks Harmony', *The Star* (Johannesburg) 1 October 1992, p. 1, col. 7.

Jung, Courtney, & Ian Shapiro, 'South Africa's Negotiated Transition: Democracy, Opposition and the New Constitutional Order' (1995) 23 *Politics and Society* 269.

Kahn, Ellison, *The New Constitution: With Comparative Tables of the Republic of South Africa Constitution Act, 1961, and the South Africa Act and Earlier Provisions, and the Text of the Republic of South Africa Constitution Act, No. 32 of 1961*: Supplement to H. R. Hahlo & Ellison Kahn, *South Africa: The Development of its Laws and Constitution*, London: Stevens, 1962.

Karst, Kenneth L., *Belonging to America: Equal Citizenship and the Constitution*, New Haven: Yale University Press, 1989.

Kataoka, Tetsuya, *The Price of a Constitution: The Origin of Japan's Postwar Politics*, New York: Crane Russak, 1991.

Keck, Margaret E., & Kathryn Sikkink, *Activists Beyond Borders: Advocacy Networks in International Politics*, Ithaca, NY: Cornell University Press, 1998.

Keller, Bill, 'Mandela's Group Accepts 5 Years of Power Sharing' *New York Times*, 19 February 1993, p. A1, Col. 1.

Kennedy, David. 'Receiving the International' (1994) 10 *Connecticut Journal of International Law* 1.

Klug, Heinz, 'Bedeviling Agrarian Reform: The Impact of Past, Present and Future Legal Frameworks', in J. Van Zyl, J. Kirsten & H. P. Binswanger (eds.), *Agricultural Land Reform in South Africa: Policies, Markets and Mechanisms*, Cape Town: Oxford University Press, 1996.

—— 'Constitutional Law' [1992] *Annual Survey of South African Law* 719–24.

—— 'Defining the Property Rights of Others: Political Power, Indigenous Tenure and the Construction of Customary Land Law' (1995) 35 *Journal of Legal Pluralism* 119.

—— 'Guaranteeing Free and Fair Elections' (1992) 8(2) *South African Journal on Human Rights* 263.

—— 'Historical Claims and the Right to Restitution', in Johan Van Zyl, Johann Kirsten & Hans P. Binswanger (eds.), *Agricultural Land Reform in South Africa: Policies, Markets and Mechanisms*, Cape Town: Oxford University Press, 1996.

—— 'Rethinking Affirmative Action in a Non-Racial Democracy' (1991) 7 *South African Journal on Human Rights* 317.

—— 'Self-Determination and the Struggle Against Apartheid' (1990) 8 *Wisconsin International Law Journal* 251.

Knop, K., 'The "Righting" of Recognition: Recognition of States in Eastern Europe and the Soviet Union' [1992] *Canadian Council on International Law Proceedings* 36.

Koh, Harold Hongju, 'Why Do Nations Obey International Law?' (1997) 106 *Yale Law Journal* 2599.

Komesar, Neil K., 'Back to the Future – An Institutional View of Making and Interpreting Constitutions' (1987) 81 *Northwestern University Law Review* 191.

—— *Imperfect Alternatives: Chosing Institutions in Law, Economics and Public Policy*, Chicago: University of Chicago Press, 1994.

Krasner, S. D., 'Approaches to the State: Alternative Conceptions and Historical Dynamics' (1984) 16 *Comparative Politics* 223.

Lacey, Marian, *Working for Boroko: The Origins of a Coercive Labour System in South Africa*, Johannesburg: Ravan Press, 1981.

LaFeber, Walter, *Michael Jordan and the New Global Capitalism*, New York: W. W. Norton, 1999.

Lawson, F. H., *A Common Lawyer Looks at the Civil Law*, Ann Arbor: University of Michigan Law School, 1955.

Lefort, Claude, *The Political Forms of Modern Society: Bureaucracy, Democracy, Totalitarianism*, ed. John Thompson, Cambridge, MA: MIT Press, 1986.

Leon, Tony, 'Etienne Mureinik's Role in Securing and Constitutionalising the Independence of the Universities and Judicial Selection' (1998) 14 *South African Journal on Human Rights* 190.

Lewis, Anthony, 'Revolution by Law', *New York Times*, 13 January 1994, p. A15.

Licht, Robert A., & Bertus de Villiers (eds.), *South Africa's Crisis of Constitutional Democracy: Can the US Constitution Help?* Washington DC: The AEI Press, 1994.

Lijphart, Arend, *Democracies: Patterns of Majoritarian and Consensus Government in Twenty-One Countries*, New Haven: Yale University Press, 1984.

Lipschutz, R. D., 'Reconstructing World Politics: The Emergence of Global Civil Society' (1992) 21(3) *Millennium: Journal of International Studies* 389.

Lobban, Michael, *White Man's Justice: South African Political Trials in the Black Consciousness Era*, Oxford: Clarendon Press, 1996.

Lodge, T., *Black Politics in South Africa since 1945*, Johannesburg: Ravan Press, 1983.

Lorch, Donatella, 'Arms Ban is Defied at Rally by Zulu Party', *New York Times*, 6 April 1993, A13.

McFaul, Michael, 'The Demise of the World Revolutionary Process: Soviet–Angolan Relations Under Gorbachev', (1990) 16(1) *Journal of Southern African Studies* 165.

McMichael, P., 'Globalization: Myths and Realities' (1996) 61(1) *Rural Sociology* 25.

Madlala, C., 'Final Fitting for the Cloth of Nationhood,' *Sunday Times*, 13 October 1996, p. 4. col. 2.

Mail & Guardian (Johannesburg), 11 November 1996.

Mamdani, Mahmood, 'Citizen and Subject: Contemporary Africa and the Legacy of Late Colonialism' Princeton: Princeton University Press, 1996.

Mandela, Nelson, 'Address: On the occasion of the ANC's Bill of Rights Conference', in *Papers and Report of a Conference Convened by the ANC Constitutional Committee, Centre for Development Studies, University of the Western Cape, May 1991*.

—— *Long Walk to Freedom: The Autobiography of Nelson Mandela*, Boston: Little, Brown & Co., 1994.

—— *No Easy Walk to Freedom: Speeches and Documents*, ed. Ruth First, London: Heinemann, 1965.

Maphai, V. T., 'Affirmative Action in South Africa: A Genuine Option?' (1989) 15(2) *Social Dynamics* 1.

Marais, Etienne, & Janine Rauch, 'Policing the Accord' (October/November 1991) 78 *Work In Progress* 14.

Marais, Hein, 'Snatching Defeat from the Jaws of Victory' (February/March 1994) 95 *Work in Progress* 25.

Mare, Gerhard, & Georgina Hamilton, *An Appetite for Power: Buthelezi's Inkatha and South Africa,* Johannesburg: Ravan Press; Bloomington: Indiana University Press, 1987.

Marx, Karl, 'The Eighteenth Brumaire of Louis Bonaparte', in *Surveys from Exile: Political Writings,* Vol. 2, ed. David Fernbach, Harmondsworth: Penguin Books in association with New Left Review, 1973.

Matthews, Anthony, *Freedom, State Security and the Rule of Law: Dilemmas of Apartheid Society,* Cape Town: Juta, 1986.

Mbeki, Govan, *South Africa: The Peasants' Revolt,* 2nd edn., London: International Defence and Aid Fund for Southern Africa, 1984.

Meli, Francis, *A History of the ANC: South Africa Belongs to Us,* Harare: Zimbabwe Publishing House; Bloomington: Indiana University Press, 1988.

Merkl, Peter H., *The Origin of the West German Republic,* Oxford: Oxford University Press, 1963.

Meyer, John W., John Boli & George M. Thomas, 'Ontology and Rationalization in the Western Cultural Account', in G. M. Thomas, J. W. Meyer, F. O. Ramirez & J. Boli (eds.), *Institutional Structure: Constituting State, Society, and the Individual,* Newbury Park, CA: Sage, 1987.

Milner, Lord, 'A Review of the Present Mutual Relations of the British South African Colonies', 1907, Cd 3564.

Molao wa Batho, 'The Myth of Independence of the South African Judiciary' [November 1987] *Sechaba* 7.

Motala, Ziyad, *Constitutional Options for a Democratic South Africa: A Comparative Perspective,* Washington, DC: Howard University Press, 1994.

Mureinik, Etienne, 'Dworkin and Apartheid', in Hugh Corder (ed.), *Essays on Law and Social Practice in South Africa,* Cape Town: Juta, 1988.

—— 'Rescued from Illegitimacy?', *Weekly Mail & Guardian* [Johannesburg], Review / Law, Supplement, Vol. 1, No. 5, December 1993.

Murphy, John, 'Insulating Land Reform from Constitutional Impugnment: An Indian Case Study' (1992) 8 *South African Journal on Human Rights* 362.

Nagel, Robert F., *Constitutional Cultures: The Mentality and Consequences of Judicial Review,* Berkeley: University of California Press, 1989.

Nagel Thomas, 'Equal Treatment and Compensatory Discrimination', in Marshall Cohen et al. (eds.), *Equality and Preferential Treatment,* Princeton: Princeton University Press, 1977.

National Party, *Constitutional Rule in a Participatory Democracy: The National Party's Framework for a New Democratic South Africa*, 1991.

—— 'Grontwetplan / Constitutional Plan' (1991) 9(11) *The Nationalist* 9.

—— 'Manifesto for the New South Africa', 1 February 1991; rpt in South African History Archive, *History in the Making: Documents Reflecting a Changing South Africa*, Vol. 1, No. 4 (March 1991), 65–6.

National Peace Accord, Johannesburg, 14 September 1991, rpt in South African History Archive, *History in the Making: Documents reflecting a changing South Africa*, Vol. 2, No. 1 (October 1991), 50–80.

Native Land Commission (Beaumont Commission), *Minutes of Evidence*, Union Government 26-1916.

Nedelsky, Jennifer, 'American Constitutionalism and the Paradox of Private Property', in Jon Elster & Rune Slagstad (eds.), *Constitutionalism and Democracy*, Cambridge: Cambridge University Press; Paris: Maison des sciences de l'homme, 1988.

—— *Private Property and the Limits of American Constitutionalism: The Madisonian Framework and its Legacy*, Chicago: University of Chicago Press, 1990.

New York Times, 25 October 1993, p. 1, col. 3.

Nkosi, D., 'Building Civil Society for Reconstruction' (June/July 1993) 2(3) *The Shopsteward* 4.

North, Douglas C., *Institutions, Institutional Change and Economic Performance*, New York: Cambridge University Press, 1990.

Nwabueze, Benjamin Obi, *Judicialism in Commonwealth Africa: The Role of the Courts in Government*, London: Hurst, 1977.

O'Donnell, Guillermo, Philippe C. Schmitter & Laurence Whitehead (eds.), *Transitions from Authoritarian Rule: Tentative Conclusions about Uncertain Democracies*, Baltimore: Johns Hopkins University Press, 1986.

Ohmae, Kenichi, *The Borderless World: Power and Strategy in the Interlinked Economy*, New York: Harper Business, 1990.

—— *The End of the Nation State: The Rise of Regional Economies*, New York: Free Press. 1995.

Ojwang, J. B., *Constitutional Development in Kenya: Institutional Adaptation and Social Change*, Nairobi: ACTS Press, 1990.

Okoth-Ogendo, H. W. O., 'Constitutions without Constitutionalism: Reflections on an African Political Paradox', in Douglas Greenberg et al. (eds.), *Constitutionalism and Democracy: Transition in the Contemporary World: The American Council of Learned Societies Comparative Constitutionalism Papers*, New York: Oxford University Press, 1993.

O'Malley, Kierin, 'The Constitutional Court', in Murray Faure & Jan-Erik Lane (eds.), *South Africa: Designing New Political Institutions*, London: Sage Publications, 1996.

O'Meara, Dan, *Forty Lost Years: The Apartheid State and the Politics of the National Party, 1948–1994,* Johannesburg: Ravan Press, 1996.

Ottaway, Marina, *South Africa: The Struggle for a New Democratic Order,* Washington DC: Brookings Institution, 1993.

Patel, Ebrahim, 'Ditch the Lock-Out Clause!' (1994) 95 *Work in Progress* 18.

—— 'New Institutions of Decision-Making: The Case of the National Economic Forum', in Ebrahim Patel (ed.), *Engine of Development? South Africa's National Economic Forum,* Kenwyn: Juta, 1993.

Pennington, K., *The Prince and the Law, 1200–1600: Sovereignty and Rights in the Western Legal Tradition,* Berkeley: University of California Press, 1993.

Perry, M., *The Constitution, the Courts and Human Rights: An Inquiry into the Legitimacy of Constitutional Policymaking by the Judiciary,* New Haven: Yale University Press, 1982.

Phillips, Ian, 'The Political Role of The Freedom Charter', in Nico Steytler (ed.), *The Freedom Charter and Beyond: Founding Principles for a Democratic South African Legal Order,* Cape Town: Wyvern, 1991.

Picciotto, Sol, 'The Regulatory Criss-Cross: Interaction Between Jurisdictions and The Construction of Global Regulatory Networks', in William Bratton et al. (eds.), *International Regulatory Competition And Co-ordination: Perspectives on Economic Regulation in Europe and the United States,* Oxford: Clarendon Press, 1996.

Pieterse, Jan Nederveen, *Globalization As Hybridization,* Working Paper Series No. 152, The Hague: Institute of Social Studies, 1993.

Pilon, Roger, 'On the First Principle of Constitutionalism: Liberty, Then Democracy' (1993) 8 *American University Journal of International Law & Policy* 531.

Platzky, Laurine, & Cherryl Walker for the Surplus People Project, *The Surplus People: Forced Removals in South Africa,* Johannesburg: Raven Press, 1985.

Polley, J. A. (ed.), *The Freedom Charter and the Future,* Johannesburg: A. D. Donker, for the Institute for a Democratic Alternative for SA, 1988.

Pound, Roscoe, *The Development of Constitutional Guarantees of Liberty,* New Haven: Yale University Press, 1957.

'Power to the Chiefs', *Weekly Mail & Guardian* (Johannesburg), 15–22 December 1994, p. 2, col. 5.

Pretoria Minute, The, Pretoria, 6 August 1990; rpt in South African History Archive, *History in the Making: Documents Reflecting a Changing South Africa,* Vol. 1, No. 2 (November, 1990), 21–2.

Preuss, Ulrich Klauss, *Constitutional Revolution: The Link Between Constitutionalism and Progress,* trans. Deborah Lucas Schneider, Atlantic Highlands, NJ: Humanities Press, 1995.

Przeworski, Adam, *Democracy and the Market: Political and Economic Reforms in Eastern Europe and Latin America*, New York: Cambridge University Press, 1991.

Rantete, Johannes, *The African National Congress and the Negotiated Settlement in South Africa*, Pretoria: J. L. van Schaik, 1998.

Record of Understanding, 26 September 1992, rpt in Hassen Ebrahim, *The Soul of a Nation: Constitution-Making in South Africa*, Cape Town: Oxford University Press, 1998, Document 27, 588–94.

Republic of South Africa, *Government's Proposals on a Charter of Fundamental Rights*, 2 February 1993.

Richardson, Henry J., III, 'Self-Determination, International Law and the South African Bantustan Policy' (1978) 17 *Columbia Journal Transnational Law* 185.

Rickard, C., 'This Year's Message to Despondent Civil Rights Lawyers: Pack Your Bags', *Weekly Mail* (Johannesburg), 24 December 1987 – 14 January 1988.

Rieff, David, 'The Precarious Triumph of Human Rights', *NYT Magazine*, 8 August 1999, pp. 36–41.

Risse-Kappen, Thomas, 'Ideas do not Float Freely: Transnational Coalitions, Domestic Structures, and the End of the Cold War' (1994) 48 *International Organization* 185.

Robertson, Michael, 'Dividing the Land: An Introduction to Apartheid Land Law', in Christina Murray & Catherine O'Regan (eds.), *No Place to Rest: Forced Removals and the Law in South Africa*, Cape Town: Oxford University Press, 1990.

Robinson, William, 'Beyond Nation-State Paradigms: Globalization, Sociology, and the Challenge of Transnational Studies', (1998) 13(4) *Sociological Forum* 561.

Rose, Carol V., 'The "New" Law and Development Movement in the Post–Cold War Era: A Vietnam Case Study' (1998) 32 *Law & Society Review* 93.

Rosenberg, Gerald N., *The Hollow Hope: Can Courts Bring About Social Change?* Chicago: University of Chicago Press, 1993.

Rosenfeld, Michel, 'Affirmative Action, Justice, and Equalities: A Philosophical and Constitutional Appraisal' (1985) 46 *Ohio State University Law Journal* 845.

—— 'Habermas on Law and Democracy: Critical Exchange' (1996) 17 *Cardozo Law Review* 767.

—— 'Modern Constitutionalism as Interplay between Identity and Diversity: An Introduction' (1993) 14 *Cardozo Law Review* 497.

Rosenthal, Richard, *Mission Improbable: A Piece of the South African Story*, Cape Town: David Philip, 1998.

Roux, E., *Time Longer Than Rope: A History of the Black Man's Struggle for Free-dom in South Africa*, Madison: University of Wisconsin Press, 1964.

Ruggie, John G., *Constructing the World Polity: Essays in International Insti-tutionalization*, London, New York: Routledge, 1998.

Rule of Law Consortium, ARD/Checci Joint Venture, Program Circular, 18 November 1994 (on file with author).

Ryan, C., 'NEF: Likely Results' (1993) 11(11) *People Dynamics* 8.

Sachs, Albie, *Advancing Human Rights in South Africa*, Cape Town: Oxford University Press, 1992.

—— *Justice in South Africa*, Berkeley: University of California Press, 1973.

—— *Protecting Human Rights in a New South Africa*, Cape Town: Oxford University Press, 1990.

—— 'South Africa's Unconstitutional Constitution: The Transition from Power to Lawful Power' (1997) 41 *Saint Louis University Law Journal* 1249.

—— 'Towards a Bill of Rights for a Democratic South Africa' (1989) 12 *Hastings International & Comparative Law Review* 289.

Sachs, Jeffrey D., 'Consolidating Capitalism' (1995) 98 *Foreign Policy* 50.

Santos, Boaventura de Sousa, 'The Gatt of Law and Democracy: (Mis)Trusting the Global Reform of Courts, Globalization and Legal Cultures', in Johannes Feest (ed.), *Onati Summer Course 1997*, Onati, Spain: International Institute for the Sociology of Law, 1999.

—— *Toward a New Common Sense: Law, Science, and Politics in the Paradig-matic Transition*, New York: Routledge, 1995.

Sarkin, Jeremy, 'The Drafting of South Africa's Final Constitution From a Human-Rights Perspective' (1999) 47 *American Journal of Compar-ative Law* 67.

Sassen, Saskia, 'Economic Globalization: A New Geography, Composi-tion, and Institutional Framework', in Jeremy Brecher et al. (eds.), *Global Visions: Beyond the New World Order*. Boston: South End Press, 1993.

Saturday Star [Johannesburg], 16 October 1993, p. 6, col. 1.

Schatz, Sara, 'A Neo-Weberian Approach to Constitutional Courts in the Transition from Authoritarian Rule: The Mexican Case (1994–1997)' (1998) 26 *International Journal of the Sociology of Law* 217.

Scheppelle, Kim Lane, & Karol Edward Soltan, 'The Authority of Alter-natives', in J. Roland Pennock & John W. Chapman (eds.), *Author-ity Revisited: Nomos XXIX*, New York: New York University Press, 1987.

Scheuerman, William, *Between the Norm and the Exception: The Frankfurt School and the Rule of Law*, Cambridge, MA: MIT Press, 1994.

Schlesinger, R. B., Baade, H. W., Damaska, M. R. & Herzog, P. E., *Com-parative Law: Cases, Text, Materials*, 5th edn., Mineola, NY: Founda-tion Press, 1988.

Sedler, Robert A., 'Racial Preference and the Constitution: The Societal Interest in the Equal Participation Objective' (1980) 26 Wayne Law Review 1227.

Seidman, Gay W., 'Adjusting the Lens: What Do Globalization, Transnationalism and the Anti-Apartheid Movement Mean for Social Movement Theory?', forthcoming Guidry John, Michael Kennedy & Mayer Zald (eds.), in *Globalization in the Public Sphere*, Ann Arbor: University of Michigan Press.

—— *Manufacturing Militance: Workers' Movements in Brazil and South Africa, 1970–1985*, Berkeley: University of California Press, 1994.

Seidman, Robert B., 'Law and Economic Development in Independent, English-Speaking, Sub-Saharan Africa', in T. W. Hutchison (ed.), *Africa and Law: Developing Legal Systems in African Commonwealth Nations*, Madison: University of Wisconsin Press, 1968.

—— 'Perspectives on Constitution Making: Independence Constitutions for Namibia and South Africa' (1987) 3 *Lesotho Law Journal* 45.

Semenya, I., & M. Motimele, *Constitution for a Democratic South Africa: A Draft*, Johannesburg: Skotaville, 1993.

Sharma, Surya P., 'Co-Existence of the Old and New Models of the World Legal Order of Territoriality – Where Does the Primacy Lie?' (1991) 18 *Jurnal Undang-Undang* 1.

Shearing, Clifford, 'Police and Government: The Quest for Impartial Policing' (October/November 1991) 78 *Work In Progress* 17.

Shivji, Issa G., 'State and Constitutionalism: A New Democratic Perspective', in Issa G. Shivji (ed.), *State and Constitutionalism: An African Debate on Democracy*, Harare: SAPES Trust, 1991.

Shubin, Vladimir, *ANC: A View From Moscow*, Western Cape: Mayibuye Books, 1999.

Sidley, P., 'World Jurists Slam SA Courts', *Weekly Mail* (Johannesburg), 14–20 November 1986.

Sikkink, Kathryn, 'Human Rights, Principled Issue-Networks, and Sovereignty in Latin America' (1993) 47 *International Organisation* 411.

Silbey, Susan S., ' "Let Them Eat Cake": Globalization, Postmodern Colonialism, and the Possibilities of Justice' (1997) 31 *Law & Society Review* 207.

Simkins, Charles, 'Must Contemporary South African Liberals be Thatcherites?' in R. W. Johnson & David Welsh (eds.), *Ironic Victory: Liberalism in Post-Liberation South Africa*, Oxford: Oxford University Press, 1998.

Simons, J., & R. Simons, *Class and Colour in South Africa 1850–1950*, Harmondsworth: Penguin African Library, 1969, rpt London: International Defence and Aid Fund, 1983.

Simpson, Gerry, 'The Diffusion of Sovereignty: Self-Determination in the Post-Colonial Age' (1996) 32 *Stanford Journal of International Law* 255.

Skweyiya, Zola, 'Constitutional Guidelines of the ANC: A Vital Contribution to the Struggle Against Apartheid', paper delivered at the meeting between the ANC and Afrikaner Lawyers and Academics in Harare in January 1989, rpt [June 1989] *Sechaba* 6.

—— 'Introductory Note', in Constitutional Committee of the ANC, *A Bill of Rights for a New South Africa*, Belleville: University of the Western Cape, Centre for Development Studies, 1990.

—— 'Towards a Solution to the Land Question in Post-Apartheid South Africa: Problems and Models' (1990) 6 *South African Journal on Human Rights* 195.

Slaughter, Anne-Marie, Alec Sweet & Joseph Weiler (eds.), *The European Courts and National Courts: Doctrine and Jurisprudence*, Oxford: Hart, 1997.

Smith, Charlene, 'Top ANC Man in Scathing Attack on "Sunset" Joe Slovo', *Sunday Times*, 8 November 1992, p. 11, col. 1.

Smuts, Dene, 'Etienne Mureinik's Contribution to Property Rights' (1998) 14 *South African Journal on Human Rights* 197.

Sohn, Louis B., *Rights in Conflict: The United Nations & South Africa*, Irvington, NY: Transnational Publishers, 1994.

Soltan, Karol Edward, 'What is the New Constitutionalism?', in Stephen L. Elkin & Karol Edward Soltan (eds.), A New Constitutionalism: Designing Political Institutions for a Good Society, Chicago: University of Chicago Press, 1993.

South African Institute of Race Relations, *Race Relations Survey 1985*, 1986.

South African Inter-Colonial Customs Conference, 'The Native Question', Minutes, Bloemfontein, March 1903, British Parliamentary Papers, Cd 1640.

South African Labour Bulletin, Interview with J. Naidoo, National General Strike: 'It's More Than VAT, It's the Entire Economy' (1991) 16(2) *South African Labour Bulletin* 13.

—— 'Special Focus: The Reconstruction of South Africa' (1991) 15(6) *South African Labour Bulletin* 14.

South African Law Commission, Project 58, *Interim Report on Group and Human Rights*, August 1991.

South African Law Commission, Project 77, *Constitutional Models*, 3 vols., October 1991.

—— *Summary of Interim Report, Group and Human Rights*, August 1991.

—— *Working Paper 25 on Group and Human Rights* (11 March 1989).

South African National Convention 1908–1909, *Minutes of Proceedings and Annexures (selected)*, Cape Town: Government Printers, 1911.

South African Native Affairs Commission, *Report of the South African Native Affairs Commission*, 4 vols., Cape Town: Government Printer, 1905.

South African Native Affairs Commission, *Report of the South African Native Affairs Commission, 1903–1905*, Cape Town: Government Printers, 1905.

Sparks, Allister, 'Clever Footwork as FW Redefines "Power-Sharing"', *The Star* (Johannesburg) 10 February 1993, p. 12, col. 2.

—— *Tomorrow is Another Country: The Inside Story of South Africa's Negotiated Revolution*, Sandton: Struik Publishers, 1994.

Statement from 19 Communities on the Government's Advisory Commission on Land Allocation, 15 September 1991.

Stein, Eric, 'Sovereignty and human rights' (1999) 42(3) *Law Quadrangle Notes* 5.

Stober, Paul, 'Daggers Drawn in the Slovo Sunset', *The Weekly Mail* (Johannesburg), 13–19 November 1992, p. 8, col. 1.

—— 'Slovo's "Sunset" Debate is Red Hot', *The Weekly Mail* (Johannesburg), 30 October–5 November 1992, p. 16, col. 1.

Streeck, Wolfgang, 'Public Power Beyond the Nation-State? The Case of the European Community' (draft), June 1994, to be published in R. Boyer and D. Drache (eds.), *The Future of Nations and the Limits of Markets*, Toronto: McGill–Queen's University Press (on file with author).

Sunstein, Cass R., 'Constitutions and Democracies: An Epilogue', in Jon Elster & Rune Slagstad (eds.), *Constitutionalism and Democracy*, Cambridge: Cambridge University Press; Paris: Maison des sciences de l'homme, 1988.

—— 'Federalism in South Africa? Notes from the American Experience' (1993) 8 *American University Journal of International Law & Policy* 421.

—— 'On Property and Constitutionalism' (1993) 14 *Cardozo Law Review* 907.

—— 'Rights after Communism: Institutional and Psychological Perspectives on Postcommunist Rights' (1995) 4 *Eastern European Constitutional Reviews* 61.

—— *The Partial Constitution*, Cambridge, MA: Harvard University Press, 1993.

Suttner, Raymond, *The Freedom Charter: The People's Charter in the Nineteen-Eighties*, Cape Town: University of Cape Town Press, 1984.

— & Jeremy Cronin, *30 Years of the Freedom Charter*, Johannesburg: Ravan Press, 1986.

Swanson, E., 'A Land Claims Court for South Africa: Report on Work in Progress' (1992) 8 *South African Journal on Human Rights* 332.

Tamanaha, Brian Z., 'The Lessons of Law-and-Development Studies' (1995) 89 *The American Journal of International Law* 470.

Tambo, Oliver, 'Make South Africa Ungovernable' (Extract from the Political Report of the National Executive Committee to the second National Consultative Conference, Lusaka, 16–23 June 1985), in

Preparing for Power: Oliver Tambo Speaks, New York: George Braziller, 1988.

—— 'South Africa at the Crossroads' (Cannon Collins Annual Memorial Lecture, 28 May 1987), in *Preparing for Power: Oliver Tambo Speaks*, New York: George Braziller, 1988, 255.

—— 'Strategic Options for International Companies (Address to the Business International Conference, London, 27 May 1987)', in *Preparing for Power: Oliver Tambo Speaks*, New York: George Braziller, 1988.

—— 'The Dream of Total Liberation of Africa is in Sight: President's Message for 1984', 8 January 1984, rpt [March 1984] *Sechaba* 3.

Tate, C. Neal, & Torbjorn Vallinder (eds.), *The Global Expansion of Judicial Power*, New York: NYU Press, 1995.

Technical Committee on Constitutional Issues, *1st Report of the Technical Committee on Constitutional Issues to the Negotiating Council*, 13 May 1993.

—— *2nd Report of the Technical Committee on Constitutional Issues to the Negotiating Council*, 19 May 1983.

—— *Eighth Report of the Technical Committee on Constitutional Issues to the Negotiating Council*, 26 July, 1993.

—— *Fourth Supplementary Report on Constitutional Principles of the Technical Committee on Constitutional Issues to the Negotiating Council*, 26 July 1993.

—— *Preliminary Draft to the Technical Committee on Constitutional Issues Arising from Bilateral Discussions between the SA Government and the ANC*, 12 November 1993.

—— *Twelfth Report of the Technical Committee on Constitutional Issues to the Negotiating Council*, 2 September 1993.

Technical Committee on Fundamental Rights During the Transition, Tenth Progress Report, 1 October 1993.

Teitel, Ruti, 'Transitional Jurisprudence: The Role of Law in Political Transformation' (1997) 106 *Yale Law Journal* 2009.

Teubner, Gunther (ed.), *Global Law Without a State*, Aldershot: Dartmouth, 1997.

Thomas, Philip, 'Ambiguity: The Management of Dissent', in Andre-Jean Arnand (ed.), *Sociology of Law: Splashes and Sparks, Onati Proceedings–2*, Onati, Spain: International Institute for the Sociology of Law, 1990.

Thomas, Scott, *The Diplomacy of Liberation: The Foreign Relations of the African National Congress Since 1960*, New York: I. B. Tauris, 1996.

Thompson, Cliff F., 'The Sources of Law in the New Nations of Africa: A Case Study from the Republic of the Sudan', in T. W. Hutchison (ed.), *Africa and Law: Developing Legal Systems in African Commonwealth Nations* 1968.

Thompson, Leonard, 'Co-operation and Conflict: The Zulu Kingdom and Natal', in Monica Wilson & Leonard Thompson (eds.), *The Oxford History of South Africa*, vol. 1, New York: Oxford University Press, 1975.

—— 'Great Britain and the Afrikaner Republics', in Monica Wilson & Leonard Thompson (eds.), *The Oxford History of South Africa*, vol. 2, New York: Oxford University Press, 1975.

—— 'The Compromise of Union', in Monica Wilson & Leonard Thompson (eds.), *The Oxford History of South Africa*, vol. 2, New York: Oxford University Press, 1975.

Tribe, Lawrence H., *American Constitutional Law*, 2nd edn., New York: Foundation Press, 1988.

— & Thomas K. Landry, 'Reflections on Constitution-Making' (1993) 8 *American Universities Journal of International Law & Policy* 627.

Trubek, David M., 'Economic, Social and Cultural Rights in the Third World: Human Rights Law and Human Needs Programs', in Theodor Meron (ed.), *Human Rights in International Law: Legal and Policy Issues*, Oxford: Clarendon Press, 1984.

—— 'The Rule of Law' (draft), 1994 (on file with author).

—— 'Social Justice in a Borderless World: Multiple Utopias, Local Struggles, and Complex Architectures (draft), April 1995 (on file with author).

— & Marc Galanter, 'Scholars in Self-Estrangement: Some reflections on the crisis in law and development studies in the United States' [1974] *Wisconsin Law Review* 1062.

Truth and Reconciliation Commission, Final Report, 5 vols., October 29 1998 [TRC Final Report].

Tur, Richard, & William Twining (eds.), *Essays on Kelsen*, Oxford: Oxford University Press, 1986.

Tushnet, M., 'The Politics of Constitutional Law', in David Kairys (ed.), *The Politics of Law: A Progressive Critique*, rev. edn. New York: Pantheon Books, 1990.

United Nations and Apartheid 1948–1994, The, The United Nations Blue Book Series, Volume I, New York: Department of Public Information, United Nations, Sales No. E.95.I.7(Soft).

University of Witwatersrand Faculty of Law, *Annual Survey of South African Law 1992*, Cape Town: Juta (1949–1995).

Uys, Stanley, 'Four Rites of Passage', *The Star* (Johannesburg), 16 January 1993, p. 9, col. 1.

van Blerk, Adrienne, 'The record of the judiciary (1)', in Hugh Corder (ed.), *Democracy and the Judiciary*, Cape Town: Idasa, 1989.

van der Vyver, Johan D., 'Constitutional Options for Post-Apartheid South Africa' (1991) 40 *Emory Law Journal* 745.

van der Walt, A. J., 'The Future of Common Law Landownership', in A. J. van der Walt (ed.), *Land Reform and the Future of Landownership in South Africa: Papers Read at a Seminar Presented by the Department of Private Law of the University of South Africa on 2 November 1990*, Cape Town: Juta, 1991.

Van der Westhuizen, J. V., & H. P. Viljoen (eds.), *A Bill of Rights for South Africa; N' Menseregtehandves vir Suid-Afrika*, Durban: Butterworths. 1988.

van Holdt, K., 'From Resistance to Reconstruction: The Changing Role of Trade Unions' (March 1991) 15(6) *South African Labour Bulletin* 14.

—— 'Towards Transforming SA Industry: A 'Reconstruction Accord' Between Unions and the ANC?' (1991) 15(6) *South African Labour Bulletin* 17.

van Niekerk, Barend, 'The Dream of Liberty – Bills of Rights for the Bantustans' [1973] *South African Law Journal* 403.

van Wyk, David, 'Introduction to the South African Constitution', in David van Wyk et al. (eds.), *Rights and Constitutionalism: The New South African Legal Order*, Kenywn: Juta, 1994.

Venter, Francois, 'Requirements For A New Constitutional Text: The Imperatives of the Constitutional Principles' (1995) 112 *South African Law Journal* 32.

von Mehren, Arthur Taylor, & James Russell Gordley, *The Civil Law System*, 2nd edn., Boston: Little, Brown, 1977.

Vorster, M. P., et al., *The Constitutions of Transkei, Bophuthatswana, Venda and Ciskei*, Durban: Butterworths, 1985.

Wallerstein, Immanuel, *The Capitalist World-Economy: Essays*, Cambridge: Cambridge University Press, 1979.

Waldmeir, Patti, *Anatomy of a Miracle*, Harmondsworth: Penguin, 1997.

Walshe, P., *The Rise of African Nationalism in South Africa: The African National Congress, 1912–1952*, Berkeley: University of California Press, 1971.

Wani, Ibrahim J., 'The Rule of Law and Economic Development in Africa, 1' (1993) *East African Journal of Peace & Human Rights* 52.

Warwick, Peter, *Black People and the South African War, 1899–1902*, Cambridge: Cambridge University Press, 1983.

Weekly Mail & Guardian, The (Johannesburg), 1–7 October 1993, p. 9, col. 4.

Wiechers, M., 'Namibia: The 1982 Constitutional Principles and Their Legal Significance', in David van Wyk et al. (eds.), *Namibia: Constitutional and International Law Issues*, Pretoria: VerLoren van Themaat Centre for Public Law Studies, University of South Africa, 1991.

Wilson, Francis, & Mamphela Ramphele, *Uprooting Poverty in South Africa*, New York: Hunger Project, 1989.

Wing, Adrien Katherine, 'Communitarianism vs. Individualism: Constitutionalism in Namibia and South Africa' (1993) 11 *Wisconsin International Law Journal* 295.

World Bank, *Experience with Agricultural Policy: Lessons for South Africa*, Washington, DC: World Bank, 1992.

—— Press Release, Washington, DC, 18 October 1994.

—— *Sub-Saharan Africa: From Crisis to Sustainable Growth: A Long-Term Perspective Study*, Washington, DC: World Bank, 1989.

—— 'Summary: Options for Land Reform and Rural Restructuring', in *Land Redistribution Options Conference 12–15 October 1993: Proceedings* (Land and Agricultural Policy Centre), June 1994.

World Bank Southern Africa Department, *South African Agriculture: Structure, Performance and Options for the Future*, Washington, DC: World Bank, 1994.

'Writing for the Future, Special Focus on the Constitutional Assembly', A Supplement to the *Mail & Guardian* (Johannesburg), 30 June–6 July 1995.

Young, Robert J. C., *Colonial Desire: Hybridity in Theory, Culture, and Race*, London; New York: Routledge, 1995.

INDEX